Pamela Vandyke Price was born in Coventry, educated at
Somerville College, Oxford, and The Central School of Speech
Training and Dramatic Art. Having spent her working life in
feature journalism and public relations, she has specialized in
recent years entirely in wines and spirits. She was the first
person outside the wine and spirit trade to be allowed to take
the examinations of The Wine Trade Club Education
Committee (attaining honours for four years). After editing
Wine & Food for three years she became gastronomic
correspondent of the *Spectator*. For articles in this and in
Catering Times, she was awarded the first Glenfiddich Trophy
as Wine and Food Writer of the Year in 1971, and the
Glenfiddich Silver Medal for excellence in wine and food
writing in 1973. Since 1972 she has been wine correspondent
of *The Times*, and she contributes the regular wine talk to the
British Forces Broadcasting Service. She was the first
Englishwoman to become a member of the Commanderie du
Bontemps du Médoc et des Graves in 1962. In 1978 Pamela
Vandyke Price received the special Diplôme d'Honneur from
the Comité International du Vin de Champagne. Her other
books include *A Directory of Wines & Spirits*, *Wines & Spirits*,
The Taste of Wine, *Entertaining with Wine*, *Guide to the Wines
of Bordeaux* and *Guide to the Wines of Champagne*. She was also
English consultant to *The Great Wine Châteaux of Bordeaux*
and is editor of the Pitman series of wine guides.

The Penguin Book of

SPIRITS AND LIQUEURS

Pamela Vandyke Price

PENGUIN BOOKS

Penguin Books Ltd, Harmondsworth,
Middlesex, England
Penguin Books, 625 Madison Avenue,
New York, New York 10022, U.S.A.
Penguin Books Australia Ltd, Ringwood,
Victoria, Australia
Penguin Books Canada Ltd, 2801 John Street,
Markham, Ontario, Canada L3R 1B4
Penguin Books (N.Z.) Ltd, 182–190 Wairau Road,
Auckland 10, New Zealand

First published by Allen Lane 1979
Published in Penguin Books 1980

Copyright © Pamela Vandyke Price, 1979
All rights reserved

Set, printed and bound in Great Britain by
Cox & Wyman Ltd, Reading
Set in Monotype Ehrhardt

This book is dedicated to
Martin Bamford, M.W., Château Loudenne
John Davies, M.W., Château Lascombes
John Salvi, M.W., Maison Sichel, Bordeaux
Diana and Peter Sichel, Château d'Angludet
Lovers of wine – loving spirits
You have kept a place for me in your hearts
for over twenty years
and have made me know that your houses are also my home
from
'Lady P'

Contents

Alcohol is: *an emanation of divinity* ... [*an element*] *newly revealed to man, but hid from antiquity, because the human race was then too young to need this beverage designed to revive the energies of modern decrepitude* ... *the true water of life will come over in precious drops, which, being rectified by two or three successive distillations, will afford the wonderful quintessence of wine*

RAMÓN LLULL (1233–1316)

Preface

The author of any book such as this must express indebtedness to many people and firms who have helped with its compilation. But my own thanks must be voiced in warmer terms than conventional acknowledgements. When I began to assemble the material, I approached a number of leading members of the spirit trade; some of them were already friends, others I did not know at all and at least a few must have wondered whether I might be going to waste their time.

However, just as I have always found the wine trade to be infinitely courteous, patient and helpful, the spirit trade, as I have met them while writing this book, have without exception been veritable distillates of all these qualities! Heads of world-renowned businesses made themselves available to answer questions, provided privately-printed books for reference and enabled me to make many visits to their installations, thereby better to understand my subject. Several of them have read parts of the text, have sent portions to be checked by their top technicians (and been almost protective towards me when my mistakes had to be corrected). Requests for information have been dispatched all over the world, laboratory staff have been deputed to answer my queries, press and public relations officers have been involved in ferreting out obscure data and historical details. In addition, the secretaries of all these authorities have equally involved themselves by meticulously passing on my requests – sometimes telephoned in great haste and frenetic tones – and have never even momentarily allowed me to feel that the writing of this book was not as important to them as it has been to me.

My friends in journalism and those whose writings about wines and spirits have made them become friends have also been lavish with their help, frequently supplying me with material to which I might not easily have had access and giving me information that they acquired subsequent to their own published works. Those who work in the libraries and archives of many firms and institutions have also expended much of their own time in helping me to find out things, even, on occasions, enlisting the help of their competitors on my behalf.

Information has come from so many sources that I risk omitting some from even a long list. It may be assumed that the mention of any firm or product in this book means that the producers of the drink, their U.K. representatives, their publicity organizations have all contributed a substantial amount of material. When I have asked for lists of those who should be thanked, I have been told that there is no need to mention names – but I remember them with gratitude.

There are also the fortuitous pieces of luck – because many shared my interest and involved themselves. The owner of a shop specializing in Scandinavian goods gave me a piece of information I might otherwise never have discovered about schnapps. The librarian at one of the great naval museums not only was able to tell me within seconds the number of the officers who would have shared the liquor stores aboard H.M.S. *Victory*, but estimated how many officers from the rest of the Fleet 'Lord Nelson would certainly expect to entertain'. A distinguished folklorist brought back samples of east European brandies for me – some of which leaked all through her hand luggage; the dispenser at a famous London nursing-home (where the deputy matron, also, was an enthusiast on wines and spirits) generously gave me the chance of tasting New Zealand whiskey. The response to all requests for help has been wholehearted and meticulously thorough.

There are, however, those who must be named – because I am so proud of having had their cooperation with this book. First, the editors and writers of many publications, who have allowed me to quote from these and make use of much material. Among these, I am especially grateful to: *Wine & Spirit*, *Decanter*, *Marine & Air Catering*, *Off Licence News*, the *Journal* of The International Wine & Food Society, back numbers of *Wine & Food*, *Drinks International* and *The Compleat Imbiber*. Many colleagues of mine on *The Times* have brought me information about drinks encountered all over the world and have looked up their files for correspondence about cocktails and mixes, famous and obscure. *Harper's Wine & Spirit Trade Gazette* enabled me to make known my intention to write this book and, thereby, put me in touch with many helpful people.

Among those press and public relations friends who have spent time and trouble on my business far in excess of their duties, I would especially like to thank: Miss Hilary Laidlaw-Thompson of the Leslie Bishop Co.; Tony Beardmore of Martini & Rossi; Hugh Mackay of the Italian Institute for Foreign Trade; Derek Williams of Odhams & Gunn; Henry Damant of the South African Wine Farmers' Association; Geoffrey Godbert of Counsel Ltd; Mrs Thelma Seear; David Russell; Miss Catherine Manac'h and her colleagues at S.O.P.E.X.A. and many friends at The Wine Development Board. Robert Fudge, of Seagram U.K., has provided information and guidance about U.S. and Canadian whiskey and other spirits that has been invaluable to me. The Guildhall Library and the firms of Graham Kemp Associates, Forman House P.R., J B S Associates, Burson Marstellar and J. Walter Thompson have all been extremely helpful.

Many sections of this book could not possibly have been completed without the help of Brian Spiller of the Distillers' Company Ltd. Not only did he make available to me material discovered in the course of his own writings and researches, but he offered to read parts of the work himself and, in addition, enlisted on my behalf the advice and comments of many erudite colleagues in various departments of the great firms within this organization. In particular, the chapters on distilling, whisky and gin were read and corrected with authority and impartiality – I hope that the final version is worthy of those who spent so much time on it for me. Stanley Prestidge, of H.M. Customs and Excise, whom I was fortunate enough to meet through the offices of Sir Ronald Radford, was equally generous with advice and encouragement, as were his colleagues and his librarian.

The Scotch Whisky Association, especially Jeffrey Wormstone, have assisted a great deal in one of the major sections of this book and, through them, I was able to be in touch with George Viveash, a great authority on alcoholic strength and the hydrometer. It was many dear friends at William Grant, including David Grant himself, who first taught me about straight malt and they have continued to help me over the years, as well as entertaining me both in London and at Dufftown. In the great firm of John Walker, Sir Hugh Ripley Bt, Francis Jones and Nigel Shattock have been the sources of much information and many kindnesses. Peter Enright, of White Horse Distillers, was also most kind and helpful. Through the good offices of Colin Mackay, when he was with the United Distillers of Ireland, I was able to visit the U.D.I. and learn something from them.

There have been many friends at United Rum who have been of great help, in particular Tony Hart, who on several occasions was a friend in need on the end of the telephone. Clive Williams, M.W., kindly arranged for me to taste a wide range of white rums when he was in charge of the now defunct wine school of Gilbey Vintners. John Lipitch, of R. & C. Vintners, has helped with many parts of this book, especially the section on tequila, and his friendship over many years has been of incalculable value to me. His former chief, Edward Roche, taught me a lot about vodka, as did P. G. Vanetzian of Grivan Products. For information about Bénédictine, I am indebted to Derrick Palengat; and, concerning cassis, I acknowledge the help of A. D. Stevens of Stevens Garnier; Mark Lake of Taylor & Lake; David Gummer of Dolamore; and Anthony Goldthorp of O. W. Loeb; also that of Michael Collings of Percy Fox, concerning Southern Comfort. James Long of International Distillers & Vintners first taught me about 'de luxe' Scotch and he and his colleagues have remained stalwart friends throughout the compilation of this work; in particular, I must thank Doctors A. C. Simpson and D. W. Clutton in the laboratories at Harlow who, with others there, have provided much technical information and explained it to me, also allowing its use in many parts of this book.

With regard to gin, I owe much to Alan Mays-Smith of James Burrough, who once arranged a comparative tasting of martinis for me. C. E. Ashmore of Tanqueray Gordon I met by chance at a wine tasting and he and his colleagues in that organization have given me much useful material, including information about gin in the international markets. Ian Coombs, of Long John International has similarly been of assistance. Sir Guy Fison, M.W., of Saccone and Speed has most patiently answered many queries about spirits and E.E.C. regulations. Most of all, perhaps, my colleague John Doxat, of Buchanan Booth's Agencies, has helped with all those spirits on which he is an authority.

In the City, Bruce Dehn, Clerk to The Worshipful Company of Distillers, has most generously allowed me to inspect documents relating to the history of distillation and the Company, and has been unsparing of his time – as of his wit – in assisting me with this section.

My friends in the world of vermouth have been teaching me for many years: Jimmy Wakeling and Gilbert Wheelock, of Martini and Rossi, have helped me both here and in Pessione, and G.U. ('Bep') Salvi, when he was 'Mr Noilly Prat', was equally helpful also with my visits to Marseilles and Sète. Peter Reynier of J. B. Reynier, gave much assistance about Chambéry. David Rutherford, of Rutherford, Osborne & Perkin, has encouraged me throughout and helped me with several sections of the text.

Thanks are also due to many friends abroad and those who have arranged for me to meet their principals in many establishments. The great firm of Cointreau have been helpful and hospitable to me over many years and Robert and Violette Cointreau are dear and charming friends; Alejandro Cassinello introduced me to those who became very good friends at the Distillerie de la Côte Basque and Clés des Ducs Armagnac; Andrew Henderson made it possible for me to meet and to visit Miguel Torres, in the Penedès region of Catalonia, who makes fine brandy as well as fine wines; friends at the Danish Agricultural Producers enabled me to meet Paul Fabian, of the Danish Distilleries, now an old friend too; Anthony Leschallas and his colleagues at Mentzendorff introduced me to Delamain. John Surtees, many years ago, arranged for my late husband and myself to visit the charming and much regretted Guy Roullet, of Denis Mounié; dear George Peploe, of Hedges & Butler, introduced François and Robert Hine, my hosts at Jarnac when I was only recently widowed – how fortunate I have been to have learned something about Cognac from them. John Baker, another very old friend, enabled me to visit Salignac. Maurice Fillioux, at Hennessy, one of the outstanding personalities of Cognac, was my host there at one time and I hope I may say that he taught me a great deal. Pierre Cordier, of Martell, is another authority whom I should wish to call friend as well as tutor.

Michael Stokes-Rees, of S.A.W.F.A., enabled me to see something of the great brandy establishments at the Cape, and G. Stuart Foulds, of the Australian Wine Centre, was most helpful in obtaining information about Australian brandies and liqueurs. In Cyprus, that most delectable of islands, there are so many friends that I can only express general thanks to The Vine Products Commission, plus the firms of KEO, SODAP and ETKO-Haggipavlu, but the names of many individuals are as dear to me as my respect for their work is great.

It will be noted by anyone who has read thus far that this Preface verges on becoming a love letter – or, rather, a letter of love. For this book has been a hard one to write. I have needed a lot of help and a lot of goodwill. Others to whom I owe thanks for their support during the research and the writing may not think they need naming – but some of them must be included here: my editor, Jill Norman, who has remained a friend throughout the traumas of getting a book of this kind ready for the press; my very dear colleague, Margaret Bird, whose transcription of my tapes and deciphering of my handwriting have been impeccable for many years, plus her daughter, Amanda Hassall, whose work is second only to that of her mother – I couldn't have done this book without both of them. Helen Thomson, of O. W. Loeb, has given much help with many obscure points of reference, often involving the cooperation of her colleagues in the firm. There is also my dear agent, Michael Horniman of A. P. Watt; this was the first book I wrote since he began looking after my literary affairs and his thoughtful advice and encouragement have contributed more than he can possibly know.

Finally, I must express my great gratitude to R. E. H. Gunyon, who died before he could see this book in final form but who helped with many parts of it. He obtained many books for me and, from his own great knowledge, enriched my views on many aspects of spirits. On one occasion when I telephoned him at a time of great worry and perplexity, his response was immediate: 'I'm reading a book on that very thing – would you like me to send it to you?' Everyone whom I have thanked for the help they have given to this book gave it with a generous heart and unstinting hand. Reg Gunyon's memory stands for them all.

Thank you, my dear friend – and my dear friends.

PAMELA VANDYKE PRICE
January 1977–May 1978

Acknowledgements

As well as the many who became actively involved in the compilation of this book there are an additional number of firms who have most helpfully kept me supplied with updated material and information about their products. They are listed here with the thanks and gratitude of the author:

The establishments of Cinzano, Riccadonna, Cora, Gancia, and the Minos Winery of Crete, the installations of Achaia Clauss at Patras, Greece; the Houses of Bardinet and Marie Brizard in Bordeaux; the C.O.D.E. des Rhums in Martinique; Tequila Sauza of Mexico; the House of Cusenier; Bertram's Van der Hum at the Cape; in Denmark, the House of Heering and the Dansk Spiritfabrikker; Mandarine Napoleon.

In the U.K., the firms of J. R. Phillips; Atkinson Baldwin; Grierson Blumenthal; Geo. Idle Courtney; Findlater Matta; Walter Siegel; Luis Gordon; Rawlings Voigt; Clode, Baker & Wylde; L. Rose; the Brönte Liqueur Co.; Giffard Liqueurs; Lamb & Watt; Grants of Maidstone; Ross of Leith; Hedges & Butler; Berry Brothers; Corney & Barrow; G. F. Grant; Grants of St James's; Stowells & Threshers; Balls Bros.; The Merchant Vintners; Jarvis Halliday and Matthew Clark.

The publishers wish to thank International Distillers and Vintners for permission to use the illustrations on pages 28, 29, 141, 145 and 163; also to the House of Hallgarten for the chart on page 256.

Introduction

This book is a layman's guide to those drinks that are collectively known as 'spirits' – that is, those that are either the direct result of one of the several processes of distillation, or else beverages that incorporate some form of distillate.

As all these drinks vary considerably, it is not surprising that equally varied views are held about them, even by the seriously interested drinking public. The images conjured up by certain names may be far removed from the processes actually associated with those names. For example, the words 'gin' or 'whisky' tend to be associated with some kind of monstrous factory, controlled by computers and staffed by grey-faced laboratory technicians. The word 'liqueur', on the other hand, evokes candlelit monastic dispensaries, in which saintly-visaged religious compound recipes from old parchments, apparently by guess and by God. The one sort of 'spirit' appears to have sprung, already mechanized, from the bowels of the Industrial Revolution; the other, still handcrafted and clogged with legend, is wafted from the pages of a medieval 'herball'.

Both these impressions are wholly wrong – indeed, they have always been wrong. To believe them in any way is unfair to the distinguished spirit producers of the past and the skilled manufacturers of today.

There is another difficulty that may deter the drinker from knowing much about spirits. They have no easily understood international language, although it would be quite easy to evolve one. In the U.K., for example, the alcoholic strength of spirits has, up to now, been expressed in terms that are absurdly complicated, for, to the person wanting to know whether a drink is high or low in alcohol, the expressions 'over proof', 'under proof', 'degrees Sykes' have virtually no meaning at all. For years I had a vague notion that 'Sykes' somehow related to Bill Sikes, the burglar in *Oliver Twist*!

Bewilderment is increased when the drinker realizes that the U.S. 'proof' scale is different from that termed 'Imperial', and that tables of reference that might be expected to enlighten the seeker for information may include 'alcohol by weight, Germany', and 'alcohol by volume 60F Tralles, Italy, Russia'; the amount of liquid contained in the bottle may be expressed in terms of Imperial gallons, American gallons and Imperial and American cubic inches – measures that are unlikely to mean anything at all to the ordinary drinker.

The basic information that most people require when buying a bottle of spirits is not much: they wish to know the liquid content of the bottle, expressed in terms that relate to something, such as fluid ounces – with which the average occupant of the kitchen is familiar, as is also the buyer of bottles of table wine – or metric terms. Then they wish to have an idea of the approximate alcoholic strength of the liquid – spirits are known to be 'stronger' than table wine and fortified wine, but it is only vaguely realized that there are some spirits that are much stronger than others.

Fortunately, the adoption of the metric system in the U.K. in the near future will simplify the problems of the would-be buyer of spirits. People like me who, since Britain 'went metric', can at last cope with their change in shops and can appraise the weight of one commodity in terms of another will get more help from the label on a bottle of spirits than the 'contenance' or fluid capacity which must, by law, be given already; it will now be given in litres and centilitres instead of the archaic measures – pints, quarters, gallons – which are as out of date in the drinks trade as the groat in coinage and the peck in pickled peppercorns.

As far as the United States is concerned, metrication is on its way, although not yet arrived. For spirits imported to the U.S. in bottle, the regulations prevailing in the country of origin are naturally followed, with any additional information required by the U.S. authorities, but the California Wine Board would like standard wine bottles, based on the metric system, to be adopted, and obviously

The system of expressing alcoholic strength as percentage of alcohol by volume is well known in the drinks trade and is usually spirits would follow any change of this kind.

casually referred to as 'Gay Lussac', after the French chemist, Joseph Gay-Lussac (1778–1850), who formulated it in 1824. But, unfortunately for us all, the system whereby alcoholic strength is now to be measured is not quite the same, although it is expressed in terms of percentage of alcohol by volume – the system known as 'Reichard', which was worked out in 1951. The essential is that the Gay Lussac percentage, referring to the weight of the alcohol (see pages 315–17) was taken as 15 per cent, whereas the Reichard percentage is 20 per cent. The difference is virtually negligible when wine is concerned, which is why the wine trade will still interchange the terms 'percentage of alcohol by volume' and 'Gay Lussac', which, for them, are almost synonymous. But in the case of spirits the difference is often marked, which is why the Reichard scale will be used here, unless otherwise indicated, when alcoholic strength is concerned. At the time of going to press, a new hydrometer is being produced, which will enable alcoholic strength to be measured even more accurately, but, for the general reader, reference to the tables on pages 318–21 will probably suffice, as long as the difference between the Gay Lussac and Reichard systems is remembered.

Another thing that may, in the past, have been a difficulty to anyone trying to find out something about spirits, is the assumption that the reader of a book about them knows at least some basic chemistry, being able to appreciate what is meant by terms such as 'rectify' and 'infuse', the significance of enzymes, the use of a hydrometer and how to interpret a string of figures, letters and symbols as a formula that means some kind of drink. Perhaps education today does cope with such matters. But forty years ago my chemistry classes appear to have taught me little except how to draw the bunsen burner in cross-section and to recite Boyle's law: 'Heat expands, cold contracts', which in fact was formulated by the Sir Robert Boyle who worked out a system in the seventeenth century for measuring alcoholic content – something I might even then have found more interesting.

Lacking even a slight knowledge of science, many people, like me, must have found their minds sagging under technical references and, as it is not always possible to ask the sort of question that makes an informant realize one's profound ignorance, ignorant one tends to remain. Until I had to tackle this book, I was not really sure exactly what happens in the process of distilling; it had never been explained to me in language that I could easily understand. Being commissioned to write about spirits, I became bold enough to ask questions and persist in getting answers that meant something to me. The long list of those whose patience, authority and disregard of time has enabled me to write about spirits as a lay person for lay people indicates my perseverance as well as their kindness.

Spirits repay investigation. They are far more interesting than most drinkers will have realized. Many have traditions at least as old as many table wines, most have played an important part in the economics of their regions and countries; whether you study them historically, socially, or simply as drinks, it is important to know both something about the way in which they are made and how to serve them for maximum enjoyment.

Anyone who, today, orders a gin and tonic is playing a part in a great saga of science, marketing and legislation, rich in many outstanding personalities. Gin may no longer be 'Dutch courage', the evil spirit of Hogarth's 'Gin Lane' or the 'fuel for flaming youth' of the 1930s, but it is still playing a significant role in the history of drinks.

Spirits are therefore interesting quite apart from and additional to the effect they have on the drinker. They have been with us for a very long time, even if not much notice has been taken of them. Since they were first concocted for medical or cosmetic purposes in a primitive Arab still they have been part of our lives: enhancing the reputation of some religious houses with plague remedies; smuggled across the Channel so that Parson Woodforde heard 'a thump at the door', later finding a tub or two 'but no one there'; being used as the ancestors of disinfectants, sedatives, anaesthetics and antibiotics. They have been vaguely involved with magic, have caused riots and even wars, served as currency, changed legislations and are argued about constantly in today's permissive society. Except for the strictly Muslim communities, a life without spirits is now hard to imagine.

The best way to use this book is probably to root about in it at random, maybe starting with a reference you wish to consult. Within the relevant section you will probably find other references to other sections, so that you can gradually assimilate the patchwork of the whole. Inevitably, many sections overlap; as I myself do not like to turn to and fro constantly in a book when I am following one consecutive narrative, I have not hesitated to repeat certain basic information where I think it may be helpful. Spirits cannot be tidied neatly into categories but in general the full entry concerning a particular spirit will be found in the section that deals with the predominant base or ingredient or flavour: thus, liqueurs based on whisky are all together, anise-flavoured spirits are all together and so on.

The basic spirits are explained generally and simply. Space does not permit the inclusion of details of variations in methods and procedures, although it should be borne in mind that each firm in production will have its own individuality – and that it will make spirits according to 'the style of the house'. If you understand the basics of a spirit, then your own experience will add to your information. If the method by which brandy is made has been understood and reference is made to any particular exceptions to the general practices, plus some indication as to which are the firms most likely to be known in world markets, then this, in my view, is enough to start the reader off. Anyone able to visit a particular distillery will of course learn more about that firm. Sometimes, however, there is not much in the way of general information that can be given: the history of the firms making whisky in North America, for example, is short, even though they are so commercially important. Statistics, even when these are available, are seldom directly conducive to the greater appreciation and enjoyment of a drink, so I have tried to avoid them cluttering the pages of a general guide – also, nothing can date a book faster than the citing of figures that will have changed even by the time the volume gets into print.

Every writer on wines or spirits has the problem of deciding which names should have capital letters. To my mind, a name that is a proper name should have a capital letter. (To put down something such as 'it is in the Cognac region that cognac is made' makes old sub-editors like me feel that the author and publishers haven't read the proofs – it looks odd.) So, the name of a place gets a capital letter, whether the place or the wine or spirit named for it is being referred to. Words that merely derive from proper names, such as hock, claret, sherry do not; but Bourbon, Scotch, Tequila, get their capitals. Brand names of course must have capitals – they are registered as such: Cointreau, Tia Maria, Chartreuse, Rhum Negrita, Drambuie and so on. Specific grape names are also proper names to me. Riesling, Muscat, Chardonnay are in my view rightly dignified by capital letters. References to them are also facilitated if they stand out somewhat on the page.

In attempting to make clear the account of the spirits I describe, I have, when in doubt, used a personal system that seems consistent and that I would find helpful if I were reading this book for the first time. My publishers have indulged me by letting me do what I have thought is both easily understandable and likely to cause least confusion. The reader should, I think, be able to follow our procedures.

For reasons of space, also, this cannot be a directory of mixed drinks. The main mixtures made with the basic spirits are briefly included, with recommendations about serving them; uninformed service spoils many an otherwise good drink. But there is no absolute 'right' and 'wrong' in the making of a mixture; one can learn from everybody else. This is why I have quoted generously from friends and other writers, and instanced my own quirks so as to stimulate an adventurous and experimental attitude.

There are also variations that accord with climatic and social conditions – whether a country is hot or cold, the times at which meals are taken, the forms of entertainment and whether or not there are locally produced forms of drinks. My American friends eat, drink and, often, mix their drinks in ways that are quite different from the practices of my friends in France, Germany, Italy, the Iberian Peninsula and the Mediterranean countries – and they all have many practices that differ again from those that are conventional in the various parts of the United Kingdom. There is no sense in slavishly following one set of habits when it is possible to learn so much and enjoy so much more by trying others. This, too, is where spirits are interesting social commodities: the way in which they are used varies a great deal even in these days when increased communications are ironing out the differences between many ways of life – but both palate and mind need the stimulus of change, even if this involves the risk of a temporary disappointment. The person who 'really knows', once and for ever, has a closed mind; he might as well take a pill as a good drink.

No one human being can ever know anything about all spirits but, in the compilation of this book, I have been fortunate enough to have had the advice and help of many of those who are acknowledged authorities in their separate fields. They do not necessarily always agree with each other and it is probable that some readers will not agree with them. As regards matters of opinion, both parties to an argument may be right. I have tried to write the sort of book that I should have found helpful and interesting had I wanted to learn about spirits. When this book was first planned, I could not have anticipated how much more I had to learn, but I trust that I have indicated how enjoyable my task has been.

PAMELA VANDYKE PRICE
December 1976–January 1978

2. Distillation

Distillation is a complex process, but its essentials are easy to grasp if the non-scientific reader refuses to be deterred by the use of some technical terms. Being non-scientific myself, I propose either to explain those few that have to be used or to avoid them and give an approximate explanation in simple language.

The Shorter Oxford Dictionary gives the definition for 'distil, distill' as 'to trickle down or fall in drops; to exude' and the word, from the Latin 'distillare', appears as recently as 1609 in the sense of 'to pass or flow gently'. The process of distillation is recorded in 1598, the distiller in 1577, the distillator in 1576 and a distillatory as early as 1460.

Translated into kitchen terms, distilling becomes easier to understand. Anyone who has done even a little cooking will know that if a liquid is heated, it eventually either boils away and evaporates, or else – if the heating is carefully controlled – it will be concentrated and a proportion of the water it contained will be given off in the form of steam and aromas. But if an alcoholic liquid, in which there must inevitably be some water, is heated, then the alcohol, having a lower boiling point than the water, is given off in the form of vapour; it is the water and such various constituents of the original that are not as volatile as the alcohol that remain behind.

You can distil from a liquid that has undergone some process of fermentation, either one that takes place naturally, as when the wine yeasts work on the sugar in the grapes to convert this into alcohol, or one in which fermentation has been induced, for example, the action of added yeasts to a liquid extract of germinated barley in making malt whisky. This means that the process of distillation must be carried out with a liquid consisting basically of water and alcohol in some form. This is not the place to discuss the process of fermentation in detail, but it is relevant to mention that this occurs, as far as some substances are concerned, quite naturally and far more easily than might be supposed: for example, many people will have had the experience of tasting an apparently delicious ripe melon which gives off a slightly 'beery' smell and, although seeming sweet, has a very definite 'prickle' or even sharp additional flavour – the fruit has begun to ferment. Certain forms of food left aside for too long may also develop this slight sharpness that is the beginning of the process of fermentation and, as this will go on inside the stomach of anyone who eats them, this is as good a reason as any for throwing away anything in which this touch of prickle is detected. Foods forgotten in pantry or even refrigerator can eventually begin to ferment and little bubbles will be noticed on the surface.

But through the action of fermentation a vast range of alcoholic beverages can be produced from fruits, vegetables, barks, peels, seeds and even flowers. Cereal grains are probably the most important in this respect, but essentially nearly everything that undergoes germination can be fermented, even if considerable assistance has to be given to the original base material. Some of the products of the sort of stills with which the more fortunate prisoners of war were able to pass the time and enliven their captivity were curious in the extreme, but man's ingenuity in these matters is great and the history of distillation is enriched by experiment.

A scientific definition of distillation has been given to me as 'the separation of the constituents of a liquid mixture by partial vaporization of the mixture and separate recovery of the vapour and the residue. The more volatile constituents of the original mixture are obtained in increased concentration in the vapour; the less volatile remaining in great concentration in the residue. The apparatus in which this process is carried on is called a still.' As, in the ordinary way, an alcoholic beverage will not attain a strength of more than about 14 per cent of alcohol by volume simply as a result of the straightforward process of fermentation (there are exceptions but these *are* definitely exceptional), distillation has to be employed if a liquid that is stronger in terms of alcohol is required. So, in order to extract the interesting and complex part of the alcoholic beverage from the water, the liquid is heated so that the alcohol is given off, captured in the form of vapour and then brought back to liquid form by being cooled. Because no two alcoholic beverages have exactly the same chemical composition, they cannot all be vaporized in exactly the same way and this is where the skill of the distiller is involved.

HOW A STILL OPERATES

A basic still – not one specifically used for any one spirit – consists of
a vessel like a closed-in pot (hence 'pot still'), which can be heated
(in primitive form by a fire underneath) and from which a long neck
carries the vaporized alcohol away from the pot into another vessel,
where the cooling and reliquification is effected, generally by means
of the conveying pipe being surrounded by continuously changing
water, so as to cool the vapour. The resulting liquid comes out at the
end as spirit. But this is spirit in a primitive, coarse form, very high in
alcohol and unlikely to be particularly palatable even after subsequent
maturation, which is why the use of the pot still involves far more
than simply heating up the pot and drawing off the resultant spirit.

The distiller must take care, first, to control the heating up of the
pot, so that the rate at which the spirit comes over the pipe (often
called the 'swan neck') is appropriate; he will then switch the flow
and direct the main part of the newly made spirit into another channel
so that it does not mingle with the first part of the distillate. This first
part of the run will be particularly fierce and full of all types of
'impurities', which are elements in the original liquid before it is
distilled. It is these that give individuality to the great spirits made in
pot stills, but their presence must be controlled. The distiller will
survey and check the subsequent spirit coming over until, towards
what experience will have told him is the end of the run, the distillate
becomes weak and equally unsuitable for the spirit required; this too
will be channelled away. These 'heads and tails', as they are usually
known, will subsequently be redistilled from the beginning in the
pot; the main product of the first distillate will then be distilled all
over again with the heads and tails of the second distillate. In many
instances two distillations are all that will be carried out, but in some
(as for Irish whiskey) the process will be repeated three times.

Once a still has begun to heat up and the distillate is coming over,
the process cannot be stopped and even today, with scientific instruments able to record the state of progress of the heads and tails,
the responsibility for controlling the still must still be that of the
individual distiller, whose experience and skill must be of the highest
if a satisfactory distillate is to result from his operations. The distiller's skills are often passed from father to son for many generations.

The pot still

The pot still is the original means whereby liquids were distilled.

Although stills of this sort, used by medieval alchemists, are perfectly recognizable in pictures, and, indeed, would be at least possible to use, the pot still is capable of certain modifications, according both to the region in which it is employed (the specific type of Armagnac still being the most noticeable example of this) and the quantities it has to handle. The bulbous shape, the swan neck and the receptacle in which the vapour is cooled are the constant factors, the still and its

Pot Still

The pot is filled with the 'wash' of barley (malt whisky) or wine (brandy). When heated the vapour rises and, being condensed in the tube, which is encased in a cooling jacket, becomes the liquid distillate. The feints are removed during distillation and the 'heart' of the spirit is redistilled in order to obtain a higher degree of alcohol.

components being made of copper for reasons which will be obvious to anyone with experience in cooking – for copper is the ideal metal for heating, especially if detailed control must be kept on this process, and its advantages in use outweigh the careful maintenance that is necessary for it to function perfectly.

Despite the modifications, the great gleaming bulbous vessels, nowadays fitted with various taps, controls and, usually, the keys and seals of the relevant Customs and Excise Authorities, all have a family resemblance. In some types of still, there is an additional device known as a '*chauffe vin*', which seems to be chiefly in use in certain types of French brandy manufacture and in some Cognac establishments; the *chauffe vin* gives the wine a preliminary heating before it goes into the kettle or pot for the first part of the distillation process.

Rectifying

The process of rectification means, as its name implies, that the distillation is adjusted, purified or refined; as the dictionary says, 'a repeated distillation'. In this context, rectification is 'a distillation carried out in such a way that the vapour rising from a still comes into contact with a condensed portion of the vapour previously evolved from the same still. A transfer of material and an interchange of heat result from this contact, thereby securing a greater enrichment of the vapour in the more volatile components than could be secured with a single distillation operation using the same amount of heat.' A pot still may be fitted with a rectifier, in which the least volatile portions of the distillate are condensed and returned to the still, while the more volatile portions of the vapour pass on into the condenser.

The patent or continuous still

This type of still, often referred to as the Coffey still after its inventor (see page 45), is slightly more complex. The process, as one of its names, 'continuous still', implies, goes on all the time, thereby making the still more economic than the pot still to operate, both in terms of time and labour. In some ways, the inventor's name makes this type of still a little easier to understand, for its operation is indeed somewhat akin to that of a complex coffee percolator.

Instead of the basic 'wash' or starting liquid being heated up in a

Patent Still

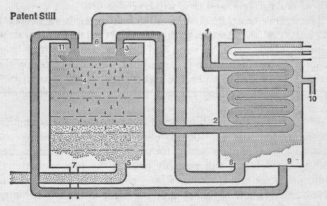

The continuous still takes a steady stream of 'wash' into (1) and is heated. At (2) it emerges and goes to (3) where it flows into an open trough. This overflows, the wash falling onto perforated plates (4). Steam entering at (5) rises, causing the volatile elements* to pass as vapour at (6). Excess water drains away at (7). Spirit vapour re-enters rectifiers (8). As this vapour rises, cooled by wash pipes, the 'feints'** fall back to (9); they are then pumped to join fresh wash at (11). Pure neutral spirit flows out at (10).

*The volatile elements consisting of the alcohol which boils at a lower point than water.
**The feints being undesirable distillates containing impurities.

kettle or pot, it is spread in layers or storeys over a large surface, heat being supplied by steam from an outside boiler. The liquid comes in at the top of the still, which can be toweringly tall and, like the pot still, is mainly made of copper. The liquid or wash then trickles from the top of the still over perforated copper plates, while, at the same time, steam is pushed in at the base of the still, rising up through these copper plates. As the liquid trickles down, the alcohol is vaporized; by the time the wash reaches the bottom copper plate virtually all the alcohol has been given off, the residue being discharged from the still, while the vaporized alcohol plus its volatile impurities in the steam rise to the top of the still. During this process the temperature becomes lower and more steam is condensed, so that the vapour becomes richer in alcohol. The section of the still in which this process takes place is called the analyser.

The vapours which have risen to the top of the analyser now pass to the base of the rectifier, which is another column of perforated copper plates alongside the analyser. In this there is a pipe which, zigzagging through the length of the rectifying column, condenses the vapour which, rising, finally reaches the top of the column and can be taken off. The liquid at this stage is very strong in alcohol.

Various things collect in the bottom of the rectifier, and are returned to the analyser for processing; these include weak impure alcohol and fusel oil, and they will be redistilled.

The curious term 'fusel oil' is often inadvertently spelled as 'fuel oil', but is nothing whatever to do with this! Certain forms of alcohol, including those found in wine and brandy, are known as 'higher alcohols'; when distillation is carried out, these can be concentrated so that, when added to water, the higher alcohols will separate into an 'oil layer'. It is this oil layer that is 'fusel oil' and, with rectification, it will be removed.

As the end of the distilling process approaches, the strength will decline and the ends of the distillation are run off into a receiver, often referred to as a 'feints receiver' for subsequent redistillation. Reference to the diagram will possibly explain the process better than additional description; anyone who is able to visit a distillery will at least be able to sort out what is taking place in the two columns of each still, though of course there may be several of these in operation at the same time.

MATURATION

Some spirits are ready to drink as soon as they have been made, the white ones, such as gin, vodka, aquavit being probably the most notable examples. They are usually bottled and offered for sale within a comparatively short time of coming from the still.

With other spirits, however, a tremendous influence is exerted on them by both the vessel in which they mature and the surrounding atmosphere, as well as the length of time they are left. Spirits kept in glass vessels may change only slightly, though they may indeed change, as for example happens with certain types of fruit spirits, where the spirit will eventually overpower the fruitiness. This also occurs with certain types of cassis liqueur (see page 285).

Whether or not a spirit is subjected to maturation after it is made depends on what it is like when it first comes from the still and what type of spirit it is proposed to make. In many instances, this young distillate is not only of an extremely high strength – so that, in order to make it drinkable in more than sip-sized portions, it has to be broken down with water (usually soft water) – but may also be coarse and harsh, quite unsuitable in any way as an enjoyable beverage. Of course, the maturation period of the great spirits is nowadays governed by legislation, but this has evolved mainly with the interests of the customer paramount – there would be no point in everyone quickly getting blind drunk or becoming ill as the result of even the finest spirit, which would in consequence rapidly become unsaleable. The processes of enjoyment associated with social drinking must never be forgotten – it may be possible, in times of great shortage, to market an inferior product but the public are not easily persuaded to go on buying such a thing once they have an alternative choice, even when advertising and promotional pressures are great.

Even the greatest devotee of spirits that are virtually palatable straight from the still and require little subsequent maturation would not, I think, contest the assertion that it is those spirits requiring a significant period of maturation which, eventually, provide the drinker with the most subtle and complex experiences associated with spirit drinking. This is why the use of particular types of cask and vat and the siting and climatic conditions of any warehouse designed for maturing this type of spirit are all factors of the greatest importance.

COMPOUNDED DISTILLATIONS

In addition to spirits produced by either the pot still or continuous still and the blends of both, there are spirits that may certainly be based on distillates as described, but that are chiefly associated – and often named – for the flavours that are then added to them; these additions may be made by macerating or infusing other substances in the spirit, or they may be incorporated by actually distilling, say, a fruit, as well. Some of the loosely named 'fruit brandies', such as cherry brandy, come into the former category. The actual distillates of fruit, however, make the 'white alcohols', which include spirits such as kirsch. The spirits in which such things as herbs, barks, peels, spices are involved are generally known as 'liqueurs', although there is no legal definition of these at the time of writing, and possibly the more accurate term for many is the French 'digestive', as they serve mainly for this purpose. And there are many drinks in the class of 'aperitives', also containing spirits but taking their name from the Latin word *'aperire'* – 'to open'.

There is no set of internationally accepted definitions which enable these drinks to be neatly categorized but, in the relevant sections, I have indicated such controls as may apply in the U.K. and main producing countries to these and other basic spirits. It should be borne in mind that a spirit may legally bear one name in a particular country and be obliged to be called something else in another. Quite recently there was an attempt by the French at the E.E.C. negotiations to impose the term *'vins de liqueur'* for what we should call 'fortified wines'; France does not make fortified wines (high strength wines are produced there but they are not 'made strong' by the addition of spirits) and it had to be firmly argued that countries either making or buying such fortified wines as sherry and port in quantity would have found the description 'liqueur wines' wholly misleading and confusing.

BLENDS AND AGEING

The 'art' of the blender is a term rightly employed in relation to many aspects of the spirit trade, for it is the blender who will maintain the consistent quality of a well-known brand and, if he thinks fit, evolve a new one for the specific requirements of a particular market. Tastes change and fashion influences spirits as much as anything else, so that shades of colour, distinctiveness of aroma or lightness of bouquet, assertiveness or blandness of flavour and different strengths may all be adjusted and altered if required. But, for the most part, it is commercially unwise to alter a brand that has already won popularity – people want one bottle of a particular spirit to please them in the same way as the previous bottle they bought, and a customer may be lost if some novelty is substituted for an established favourite. This is one reason why many large-scale producers of spirits evolve new styles, with new names, rather than radically altering anything already well established in the market, and also why they may continue to produce a few lines that in fact have a small but loyal following, possibly from a fashion of former times.

Even in the very largest spirit concerns, equipped with the most up-to-date fully automated machinery, there will, somewhere, always be a man or a few men who will rely quite as much on their own noses as on any scientific readings or laboratory reports in order to maintain the quality of the spirits for which they are responsible. What the blender apprehends and registers when his nose and, sometimes, his palate, register a smell, aroma and bouquet, will be a far more detailed and even essentially different experience from the 'nice' or 'nasty' registered by the ordinary person; even the layman accustomed to using his nose may only register a few impressions from a spirit – the blender may register dozens. Experience will enable the blender to distinguish the proportions of separate elements requisite in a blend so as to achieve the ultimate harmonious whole. He will be able, if necessary, to correct the possible deficiencies of one element in a blend by the addition of something else, for raw materials and even the most carefully processed basic elements in spirit production cannot always be constant.

Nor must the blender be content with making one type of spirit to exactly the same formula, no matter where in the world it is to be sold. True, certain spirits, notably the more neutral ones, promote their products precisely on these lines – that they are exactly the same, wherever in the world you may buy them. But this is not always enough. Differences in climate may condition local taste; when spirits are destined to form part of mixtures, the local water supply, which can vary enormously from that of an individual spring to the recycled tap water of a great city, will radically affect the way in which a liquid makes its impact on nose and palate. In some instances, therefore, it is necessary to alter the basic formula for a particular line simply so that it should *seem* to taste the same in certain export markets; this is all part of the blender's task.

There is a general and erroneous impression that 'old is good'. But age is a relative thing. Some spirits require little or virtually no maturation, others quite a lot, and this can give them a particular character that pleases; but there is a lifespan, as far as spirits that are matured in wood are concerned, beyond which they will not improve and, once they go into bottle, they will not change radically (with only few exceptions) until they are opened. Their peak drinking period may be when they are a few years old, with others, it may be after they have undergone a fairly long period of maturation. It is their individual age, not, except in rare instances, the particular year in which they were made, that is significant. Obviously, the date when a spirit was made indicates how old it is, but the process of distillation itself, especially by the continuous still, and any subsequent blending will level any variations that may have been in the original components of the basic liquid. The exceptions to this, such as vintage brandies of various sorts, are not commercially significant today, although interesting to the lover of this type of fine spirit lucky enough to find them. However, as the spirit will not improve once it has been bottled, there is absolutely no point in labelling it with a vintage, though its label may bear an indication of age.

In no way should any sign, symbol or date on a bottle of spirits be confused with the vintage date on a bottle of wine; if a bottle of spirits does bear the date of a year, this may be when the firm or distillery was formed. Symbols indicating quality may vary enormously – the 'three star' type of French brandy (as will be seen, the term has no defined legal indication as regards quality, only a vague, traditional implication of the brandy being of a certain kind) may be a very raw, coarse brandy in, say, a Mediterranean country. Any mentions of the age of the parts of blends in Scotch are rigidly controlled, but the terms 'superior', 'reserve' and many others have negligible significance.

3. A Brief History of Distillation

It will never be known who first evolved the process of distilling. Wine and other fermented beverages probably developed from the chance discovery that, for example, a liquid from the juice of fruits that had been forgotten had undergone the process of fermentation – whereby the sugar in the fruit and its juice had been acted upon by yeasts – and thus become an alcoholic beverage. But distilling is a more complex process: the liquid has to be heated, the vapour arising from it drawn off and then cooled, this resulting liquid being the distillate – how tortuous this process seems, especially when the distillate might well have been highly unpalatable!

But distilling probably had its origins in liquids intended for medicinal or at least cosmetic purposes. Physicians in ancient times knew about concentrating liquids. The ancient Egyptians, in the recipes extant in preserved papyri, often recommend heating wine with additives and infusing it as well. Hippocrates of Cos (469–399 B.C.), known as 'The Father of Medicine', includes recommendations for 'boiled down wine' in many remedies, and many Greek, Roman and Byzantine physicians appear to have made frequent use of concentrates of wine, although the first definite reference to a distillate seems to be that by Pliny the Elder (A.D. 23–79), who in his *Natural History* refers to a distillate of the 'fruit' – which is possibly the resin – of the cedar tree, boiled, with the resulting condensed vapour caught in a fleece of wool and pressed out; this oil was 'generally known as pisselaeon'. Pedacius Dioscorides, a Greek army surgeon who became physician to the Emperor Nero, wrote a great deal about wine infused with various substances and in concentrated form, and so did Galen (A.D. 131–201), possibly the greatest of all Greek physicians, who had acted as doctor to gladiators.

It was, however, the Arabs who gave distillation to the world, even though the Koran forbids any use of wine. A few Arabic physicians suggested the use of wine in various treatments and they certainly knew about the earlier work of Hippocrates, Galen, Dioscorides and similar great physicians. The word 'alcohol' comes from the Arabic '*al-kohl*', meaning the powder used for outlining the eyes by Arab ladies, and the word elixir comes from the Arabic '*al-ixsir*', a word first used in English in alchemy to refer both to preparations which it was thought might transform base metal into gold, such as the famous 'philosopher's stone', and also to a preparation which was capable of prolonging life. The Arab scientists were both erudite and liberal, studying the works of their predecessors and contemporaries in Greece and Syria, and in the Hindu and other Arab cultures. In A.D. 754, the first apothecary's shop was set up in Baghdad and by this time it is just possible that distilling was known to the more learned in the Arabic world. It could have been part of the evolution of medicines and drugs or it might originally have been a means of preparing scents and cosmetic preparations. The 'Arabian Nights' Caliph, Haroun-al-Raschid (A.D. 766–809), may have been familiar with the use of wines as medicaments and possibly therefore with distillates. The great Jewish physician Maimonides (1135–1204), born in Cordova, who was Court Physician to Sultan Saladin, referred to wine in his *Regimen Sanitatis*, and may also have known something of distillation.

There is also a reference to 'roses of Iraq' being macerated, then: 'put in a distilling flask and place a grain of musk in the spout of the *anbîq* . . . Then they distill over a soft fire. The distillate is preserved in a glass phial the neck of which is closed.' The Arab Ibn Al-Bhaitar, surgeon, botanist, herbalist, who, perhaps significantly, was born at Málaga, studied in Seville and travelled extensively, describes a similar process in his huge collection of remedies. But, as one authority points out, none of the Arab scientists actually mentions distilling alcohol until about the thirteenth century, and then the word used is not 'alcohol' but '*al-raqa*', from which the word 'arak' derives, and which means 'sweat'. This term is the first one to be used in references to a distillate and only in a later period are terms such as 'spirit of wine' found.

The Arab form of still, the *anbîq*, was simple: it could be cooled simply by air, or by the application of wet sponges or rags. Improvements such as the spout of the still and the condenser were evolved in the western world and adopted by the Arabs. A primitive Arab still is quite recognizable and might even produce a recognizable distillate.

It should be remembered that, even in the Dark Ages and throughout the early medieval period, members of religious orders, scholars and physicians were able to travel fairly freely, staying *en route* in the religious establishments and hostels which were the only accommodation available, where they naturally shared their knowledge and their discoveries with those running the house. Wine was of course necessary for sacramental purposes and was also used as a disinfectant, particularly when the water supply was not above suspicion. Even during periods of war between kings and sultans, the interchange of opinions and spread of knowledge around the Mediterranean and even to the far north had a considerable effect on the use of alcoholic beverages in medical as well as social contexts, so that it is probable that the awareness of a particular type of alcoholic beverage, the distillate, might have been talked about, challenging and fascinating the early scientists, even as early as the tenth or eleventh century. Distilleries were established at Sabur and at Damascus in the Arab world, and the great medical treatise *Regimen Sanitatis Salernitanum*, the rules for health of the School of Salerno, was certainly known to everyone attempting to treat any form of disease after the eleventh century. The *Regimen* is very practical: 'Porke without wine is not so good to eate' – nor would it have been in a country knowing nothing of refrigeration, unless one had some sort of disinfecting liquid by way of accompaniment.

Religious establishments and other medical schools, notably those of Naples, Palermo, Montpellier and Bologna, made extensive use of herbs, spices and an enormous variety of infused, macerated and compounded liquids; in 1300, there appears a recipe for distilling wine, with the addition of sulphur, salt and tartar extracted from a white wine, which are put in a copper alembic (still) with a 'black wine' (such as the famous black wine of Cahors, so called because of its depth and strength as well as its deep colour). The recipe states: 'place all in a copper alembic and distil off the *aqua ardens*.' Thaddeus of Florence (1223–1303), who founded the Bologna medical school, wrote a book about using distillates, *De Virtue Aquae Vitae, quae etiam dicitur aqua ardens* (concerning the qualities of the water of life, which is also named fiery water); he is referred to by Dante in the *Divina Commedia* as 'the great doctor'. And at the beginning of the fourteenth century the great Arnaud de Villanova wrote the *Liber de Vinis*.

Arnaud was a Catalan, from that region which produced so many creative personalities. He was educated by the Dominicans and may have been trained in medicine at Naples and possibly Valencia, where he would have been able to study the work of Arab physicians. He became a teacher at the Montpellier medical school and was consulted by the King of Aragon and later by several popes, who in fact protected him when the Inquisition began to suspect him. Most of his writings were destroyed, but Arnaud himself escaped and, in about 1310, wrote his book; his numerous additional writings vanished when he was drowned in the Mediterranean in 1311.

Arnaud refers to '*aqua vine*' (water of wine), to which he added the comment 'but some name it ... *aqua vitae* [water of life], or the water that preserves itself always, also golden water ... It strengthens the body and prolongs life', adding that 'fresh wounds washed with the spirit of wine attain the desired healing faster than any other.' It is probably correct to say that Arnaud was the first physician to record a concentrated alcoholic solution as an antiseptic for wounds. He did believe that a water of life could be made out of wine and in his search for the way in which base metals could be turned into gold he was followed by such eminent scholars as Roger Bacon, Albertus Magnus (Albert the Great), and even Thomas Aquinus, however strange this belief may seem to us today.

The alembics or stills that had been used on a small scale in monastic pharmacies, medical schools and apothecaries' shops, began to be employed for making alcoholic beverages of a higher strength. These were small pot stills, in which only limited quantities of spirits could be made at a time. The production of distillates on a large scale came slowly – in wine-producing regions the wine sufficed as a drink, but the distillation of pot ale by Irish monks certainly took place in fairly early times (not to be confused with the term 'pot ale' which, until comparatively recently, referred to an illicit distillation), and it seems astonishing to me that anyone should have gone to the trouble of attempting to do this by the fermentation of grain. But it is perhaps pertinent to be reminded that, at a time when there were few social distractions and comparatively little to read, even for those who were literate, the mind that had been trained according to the traditions of medieval scholarship was a fairly formidable instrument, which sought activity wherever it might be. Clerks were trained to think methodically, analyse and test theories and propositions; the study of the basically simple processes of fermentation and distillation might subsequently have been applied to processes involving other substances and modifications of previously successful procedures. Someone who started by making a perfume, a medicine or some other form of distillate must have gone on to speculate about making a beverage.

Anyway, as will be seen in the different parts of this book, the various spirits began to be made in different parts of the civilized world, sometimes as remedies, sometimes as a means of disposing of gluts of foodstuffs, sometimes as a refinement of another alcoholic beverage. With the end of the Middle Ages and the decline of the international influence of the religious establishments, the interchange of knowledge became more difficult, and the distillers who worked in the Renaissance do not appear to have achieved more than slight additional knowledge of their product. Science advanced in other ways and for the time being distilling did not markedly progress. But the advancement of medicine did spread the knowledge of the value of many distilled beverages in the treatment of wounds – also in the stimulation of the drinkers. Hieronymus Brunschwig (c. 1450–1533), an Alsace army surgeon, famous for the discoveries he made about treating wounds, wrote *The Vertuose Boke of Distyllacyon* in which he strongly recommended *aqua vitae composita*, a mixture of strong Gascony wine, herbs and brandy. This he said was 'wonderfull good, excellynge many other soveraynge oyles to dyvers dyseases'. Now the daisy family is the *Compositae* and wormwood belongs to it – was Brunschwig's *aqua vitae composita* a type of primitive vermouth? And was the 'composita' on which Darnley, second husband of Mary Queen of Scots, made a visitor drunk, the same sort of drink (see pages 121–2)? It is possible.

Ambrose Paré (1510–90), another surgeon who had worked with war wounded, also used brandy for dressing wounds, and surgeons on board ship made extensive use of it: 'at least a hogshead or two of French wine and one of brandy' being required by the surgeon of one ship for a single voyage in 1658. In the days prior to the evolution of anaesthesia, of course, there are numerous records of large quantities of spirits, notably rum, being given to those about to undergo amputations or other operations, but it seems that this was a mercy extended mostly to the rank and file; there are no records that I have been able to trace of monarchs and members of the nobility being treated in this considerate way when they were under the knife – perhaps it was assumed that they had greater fortitude than common folk.

THE WORSHIPFUL COMPANY OF DISTILLERS

The Worshipful Company of Distillers received its Charter in 1638, being founded by Sir Theodore de Mayerne, physician to King Charles I, with a colleague, Dr Thomas Cademan, as Master. The Company was empowered by its Charter to regulate the procedures of all those distilling and making vinegar and of those engaged in the preparation of 'Artificial and Strong Waters and of making Beeregar and Alegar, in the Cities of London and Westminster, the Suburbs and Liberties thereof and within twenty-one miles thereof'. The references to 'Beeregar and Alegar' are to making beer and ale – as with vinegar. There had been many abuses because, says Stowe's 'Survey of 1583 (revised by Strype and cited in 1754), 'the ordinary Makers of those Liquors made them of Hogwash, and Dregs, and the Washing of Coolbacks, which might occasion many infectious Diseases . . . even the Distillers of Aqua Vitae, and Vinegar-makers, did engross it up; and with it work secretly in their Houses.' Those handling drinks were to have controls imposed as to what they might use and were instructed to keep their products in 'good Bonds'.

Of course, many traders said it was too expensive for them to observe all these ideal conditions; they could, they said, sell their products to the Low Countries and to the Spaniards (an early example of merchants pleading special circumstances because they were boosting the export trade). Even 'Twenty Years before this, one Dr Baily sought to have the Survey of corrupt Vinegar, Beeregre, and Alegre, among other corrupt things, as Oil, Sope, and Butter.' But consumer protection had a struggle at this stage, for: 'The Trade concerned so many poor Men's Livings, that it was impossible to bring it into one Man's hand by License. These things were argued in point of Law against Drake, who by his Patent assumed a Power over the whole Distillers Trade.'

Those trying to get some sort of quality control attempted to link bad drinks with outbreaks of plague and other epidemics, but they seem to have failed in their efforts until Mayerne founded The Worshipful Company of Distillers, which, at this stage anyway, was – as will have been noted – primarily concerned with drinks other than those that we know as 'spirits'.

Mayerne was a remarkable man. Son of a French Protestant historian of Swiss origin, he took his M.B. after four years at Heidelberg in 1596 and his M.D. in 1597 at Montpellier. He was amazingly cosmopolitan, even by the easygoing international notions of medical men, being appointed Royal District Physician in Paris in 1600 and, in 1606, receiving an M.D. at Oxford and being appointed physician to the Queen (Anne of Denmark, consort of James I of England); in 1611 he became first physician to James I, he was a Member of the Royal College of Physicians in 1616 and, in 1618, he wrote the dedication of the first *Pharmacopaeia* published by that body.

Mayerne was a much-loved doctor; indeed, his appearance in his portraits, with a fine bushy white beard and shrewd glance, categorizes him as the sort of physician in whom the sick would easily have had confidence. 'Mayerne, for love of me, goe to my wife', is one of Charles I's touching notes when, in the middle of the Civil War, Henrietta Maria was expecting a child. He must have had more than passing interest in the *Book of Instructions to the Distilling Craft*, which was issued in 1639, and he himself wrote a cookery book, which appeared three years after his death, at the age of eighty-two, in 1655. The preface begins: 'It was an odde saying of a mad fellow, who, having first well dined, clapt his hand upon the board, and protested, that this eating and drinking was a very pretty invention, whoever first found it out.' To him is ascribed the reason for The Distillers' Company at that period sharing the premises of The Cooks' Company. There is a story that he died as a result of drinking wine at a tavern in the Strand – but one later account says "twere best to leave unnamed the ill-fated hostelry', and I would doubt that an experienced doctor and practical cook could easily have been gulled into eating or drinking anything obviously bad, though it could easily have been a chance infection.

The Worshipful Company was granted another Charter by King James II in 1688 and in 1774 the Court of Common Council passed an act imposing a penalty on all within the City of London, unless free of the Company, who should exercise the trades over which the Company had jurisdiction by reason of its Charter. The members were still primarily concerned with seeing that vinegar, beer and ale were wholesomely made and that those distilling for medical or cosmetic purposes did not pervert their craft. But as the consumption of spirits increased, the Company became more seriously involved with controlling them. (Although, it should be stressed, they are and always have been a quite separate body from the Distillers' Company Ltd, originally formed by several of the great firms engaged in producing Scotch; see page 114).

The Distillers do not possess a hall and never have done. But they still restrict membership to those who are actually concerned with the craft of distilling; even though the connection may be slight, it still must be there. In the wine and spirit trade they are of great distinction and importance.

Drinks higher in alcoholic strength than wine seem to have become part of the social drinking scene from about the sixteenth century onwards, the more northern countries, where wine was not made, possibly being in advance of the wine-producing areas, for the simple reason that those who were able to afford to partake of stimulating, warming beverages to counteract the cold climate were anxious to do so as often as possible.

In countries and regions where the wealthier members of the middle as well as the ruling classes could buy spirits or make them up in their own homes, these people began to take over the role of the medieval religious houses by using such spirits as remedies, semi-medicinal drinks and digestives, often quite outside the context of meals.

In the seventeenth century, as the relevant sections of this book indicate, the findings of the scientists and the expansion of markets in the New World, as well as the Old, contributed to spirits being known elsewhere and being made in a greater diversity – and better. It was becoming possible to make a distillate on a scale larger than that required for immediate personal use and to make this in a form that, because of the informed control of the way it was made, could travel. At this time some of the great spirits of the world emerge as distinctive. Then, in the eighteenth century, enormous quantities of mixed drinks began to be consumed, in the form of punches, cups and other large-scale compounds, frequently involving the addition of spirits. This seems to introduce a complication to drinking, but man is always seeking for something new, and it must be remembered that only at the end of the seventeenth century had the use of the bottle and cork for the long-term laying down of fine wines been satisfactorily evolved, so that those who considered themselves highly civilized, and who were in a position to buy novelties and vary their entertainment, could now elaborate on their drinks. This too is the era when the syllabubs, possets, early versions of the egg nog, and similar beverages begin to feature in cookery books.

The eighteenth century was a time of great political activity all over the world, and, although it is a simplification to say that in most major towns and cities little groups of men were sitting around plotting, it is not altogether inaccurate – and they had something to drink while they were doing so. Even before the French Revolution, society in many European courts was beginning to strain after less formality and for drinks that would stimulate within a short space of time, as compared with the long sessions of heavy drinking associated with table and fortified wines. It was at the higher levels of society – when discussion was sometimes truly a matter of life or death and usually of an excited intensity that attracted the brilliant among the intelligentsia as well as the nobility – that social interchange required a swift stimulus, hence spirit-based drinks that need not take time to consume. These were the ancestors of the business drinks, the dry martini or double gin and tonic.

Again to simplify a distinct trend, the beginnings of industrialization also stimulated spirit drinking; in Britain, the as yet unexplained explosion of the population, coinciding with the beginnings of the Industrial Revolution, resulted in huge numbers of people being virtually herded together in appalling conditions, suffering nutritional deficiencies, new hazards to health, and dreadful depression – so that they naturally turned to the reviving and sedative spirits available to them. It is one of the tragedies in the history of spirits that the wretches depicted by Hogarth in 'Gin Lane' would at least have gained some nourishment had they stuck to beer, ale or wine, instead of the dreadful versions of spirits with which they sought to deaden their sufferings or the 'wet and warm' pseudo-sustenance of tea. During the nineteenth century, spirit drinking was to gain an evil reputation in many quarters as well as achieving a remarkable commercial success.

Glasses began to be of importance, too: the great English factories made glasses valued throughout the civilized world. In the spring number of *Wine & Food* 1937, E. F. Armstrong (about whom I know nothing whatsoever) writes on 'Cordials and their glasses' and makes the important point that in the eighteenth century the quality of English glass and the skill of the glass makers complemented the

> desire for luxury which during the eighteenth century rapidly extended throughout large classes of society ... It is probably correct to say that to be in the fashion one had to use the glasses of the moment, the old ones being discarded in their favour. The habit of yesterday to retain the remnants of the set which formed one of the customary wedding gifts did not then exist. So the glassmaker and seller received full encouragement to produce glasses of decorative value and individual merit.

This is a notion I have never encountered anywhere else, although it would seem logical, in all but the most extravagant type of household, to retain glasses capable of being used, whether they had formed part of a wedding present set or not, until they were broken. The fact that the writer is probably referring to an Edwardian or late Victorian custom and, in his denigration of 'today there seems to be no taste in glass, little desire to drink out of glass of quality', indicates to me that he was one of those for whom the 'old days' are always qualified with the adjective 'good'. But he has some interesting things to say about the shapes of the glasses used for the short drinks and social drinks of the period, for example that:

For cordials there were very small bowls on tall stems or similar bowls on shorter stems. For ratafias a trumpet shaped bowl was *de rigueur*. Syllabubs were appropriately drunk from an elegant glass cup with one handle. For other spirits the smaller stemless glasses without handles sufficed: many of these are to be seen in Hogarth's pictures, and so they have come to be named Hogarths . . . Probably the glasses with handles were used for hot drinks, the Hogarths being for cold drinks such as cold punch and spirits.

This is the period when the toastmaster's glass, of much smaller capacity than it seems and with a thick foot, for rapping on the table, was made, and the toasting glass, with a particularly thin stem that might be easily snapped (so that no less worthy toast might be drunk from the glass – less exciting but more practical than shattering the crystal on the floor). There were 'solitaires' for rinsing a glass to be used for several wines (these look like deep fingerbowls and have a lip to support the glass stem); coolers, somewhat deeper; toddy lifters, like a pipette, to portion out the mixed drinks, and all the superb products of the British silversmiths that catered for the punches and cups – the coolers, the bowls and the scalloped-edged 'Monteith' with indentations to hold cups or glasses and supposedly named for a man who wore a scalloped coat.

All this time, stills had remained essentially the same as when they had first evolved. They might of course vary in detailed construction from region to region and, to a certain extent, might also vary as to the way they were built inside; much depended on the resources and experience of the distiller. Portable or travelling stills were very common, and indeed these are in use today. But the superbly gleaming copper stills, hand-beaten and polished to setting-sun brilliance, that we see today would have been rarities in the more primitive distilleries; their distilling was very much a cottage industry and the craftsmen, if they were available, may have been restricted to working with such materials as could easily and economically be obtained. The pot still of such times might be comparatively small, and therefore its capacity and yield would be considerably limited; indeed, a large still would have been neither thrifty nor practicable if the country or area in which it was operating were suffering from any form of famine or food shortage, when a distillate obviously would be considered a luxury.

Spirits became important articles of commerce when improved communications and the creation of markets for them made their export a means of making money on a large scale. So it is not surprising to find a number of attempts being made at the beginning of the nineteenth century to speed up the distilling process and enable it to be carried out on a large scale. Some of those experimenting in the earliest times were also concerned with trying to avoid the comparatively wasteful amount of fuel involved in firing a pot still. Sir Anthony Perrier of Cork was granted a patent in 1822 for a type of continuous still. A Frenchman called St Marc actually brought a type of continuous still to England in 1823, but he could not get anyone to adopt his idea, and the patent was sold to a man called J. B. Sharp, the still made according to the patent being set up in Ireland. As early as 1813 a still named for its inventors, Cellier–Blumenthal, really did come near the continuous still as we know it today and, in London, gin distillers began to use a type of continuous still in the 1820s as a result of the work of a man who had been a veterinary surgeon in Napoleon's armies.

Then, in 1828, Robert Stein, a member of a Lowlands whisky-distilling family (with whom, it will be noted in the section devoted to Scotch, the Haig family was allied by marriage), was permitted to set up a continuous still at Attlee's Distillery in Wandsworth; in 1829 he put a still of this kind into his brother's distillery at Kirkliston, near Edinburgh. A still of this type was also installed at the Haig distillery at Cameron Bridge, where in fact it remained until as recently as 1928.

In 1831 Aeneas Coffey patented the still that bears his name (also referred to as a patent or continuous still). Coffey was an Irishman, a former senior excise official, who was given permission in 1832 to use the still at Dock Distillery, Dublin. Coffey originally aimed at making a 'pure' spirit. He did not succeed – his still is the factor that enables patent still whisky (and other spirits) to retain sufficient impurities, or congenerics, to establish its character, according to the base of the distillate. Coffey's still was of the greatest value to distillers in Britain as well as those in Ireland. It enabled spirits to be made on a large scale and popularized at rates which, in spite of the duty, still keep these spirits within the purchasing power of the public. From this time on, too, many spirits could be quickly distilled. The coming of the railways and the development of the merchant marine meant that they could reach world as well as regional markets.

The way in which the strength of spirit is judged is another landmark in the history of distilling. In the early days various primitive methods were used: linen was soaked in the spirit and then burned – if the linen did not burn the spirit was bad; oil could be added, the spirit being considered strong if it floated on the surface. Gunpowder moistened with spirit would be ignited and, if it burnt slowly, the spirit was good, if it merely spluttered it was weak. The 'bead test' was used at least up until the middle of the nineteenth century: for this, the spirit was shaken in a phial and an experienced observer was able to estimate the spirit's strength by timing the period taken for the beads that had formed on the surface to finally break and disappear. With matters as primitive as this, it is surprising to find that the present 'proof standard' was fixed in 1816 for excise duties and two years later for the customs.

As early as 1675, Robert Boyle had noted that: 'the greater the proportion of alcohol in a liquid, the lower was the specific gravity', and Samuel Pepys in 1668 refers to Boyle who, 'Did give me a glass bubble to try the strength of spirits with' – this was a glass instrument, rather like a fairly thick thermometer, with a bulb at the end containing mercury; this 'aerometer' was put into a liquid and would float higher or lower in it according to the spirit content, so that a series of marks on the glass stem would indicate the amount of alcohol. This was the ancestor of the hydrometer and saccharometer which are in use today.

John Clarke evolved a metal hydrometer in 1725, which could be used to measure the different specific gravities of wines. It took some time for this hydrometer to be adopted and there were lengthy arguments between authorities arguing the differences between the readings of Clarke's hydrometer and the hydrometer as used in Ireland. But Clarke's hydrometer was officially recognized in 1787, and in 1833 the Royal Society reported on its use with approval. Then followed complex proceedings between a number of people, including a lady whose father had made the hydrometer adapted for the U.S., the widow of a Bordeaux distiller, and Bartholomew Sykes, the secretary of the English Board of Excise; the Sykes hydrometer was legally approved in 1816 and tables of weights per gallon corresponding to the indications on the Sykes instrument received legal sanction in 1852. They continued in use until 1915.

This is not the place to consider the history of H.M. Customs and Excise but it is worth mentioning that it was customs and excise officials who had a considerable effect on improving, organizing and regulating spirits in a benevolent manner; they were not merely concerned with getting as much money as they could from the distillers.

During the nineteenth century the major spirits began to form part of the general social drinking scene, as well as playing a part in medicine, acting as occasional stimulants and sedatives, and providing an economic way of disposing of gluts of certain types of crops.

Although we may raise our eyebrows over the hypocrisy of many aspects of Victorian life, there were an appreciable number of producers and consumers who, while not going to the length of wishing to ban alcoholic drinks, did realize that casually produced spirits were a potential danger to health and might inflame many social ills. They were determined that spirits should be good and not be abused.

At the beginning of the twentieth century, and particularly in the year 1909, many different forms of legislation in a number of countries came into force, with the aim of defining what certain spirits should be, where they could be made and maintaining their quality by specifying their methods of production and, when relevant, maturation. It is interesting that this legislation seems to have been introduced at almost the same time in the major spirit-producing countries, without, necessarily, involving international cooperation. The power of industry and the development of advertising and promotion made spirit production very big business and the need for some controls was widely recognized.

Prior to 1914, spirits did not feature much in the formal entertainments offered by polite society, although of course they were drunk casually in enormous quantities. The continental, with or without his 'little friend', or even with his wife and family would visit a café, men drank spirits at their clubs, at the music hall, in a pub, or outside the context of a meal in even the modest households offering between times refreshments. It will probably never be known how many women, too, discreetly partook of some form of spirits 'for medicinal purposes' at this time, but millions must have had reason to be grateful to the cheering, soothing effect of a spirit upon them – hence the brandy bottle in the medicine cupboard of even comparatively abstemious households.

The 1914–18 war and the subsequent appalling aftermath, culminating in the world depression, brought many spirits into the lives of those who might have hardly been aware of them before. The 'quick lift' is the descendant of the 'Dutch courage' of earlier times and many certainly needed it during this period. It must have been additionally hard, therefore, when the United States in 1920 prohibited the sale of alcoholic beverages; the ban itself led to the horrors of some of the drinks produced under Prohibition, and to the rise of gangsterdom profiting by the customer's reasonable wish to be able to purchase a commodity that he was not necessarily going to abuse.

The various centres for unloading spirits and wines to be smuggled in by the bootleggers were highly organized: the Bahama head-quarters was known as 'the Isle of Rum' and Saint Pierre, 'the Isle of Champagne'. Al Lillien, one of the greatest operators of the time, had a fleet of seven vessels, which brought in £2-million worth of Scotch to the U.S. in a year; one of his ships, actually called the *Cask*, is recorded as taking on 20,000 cases of whisky in Glasgow, going to Le Havre and unloading – to claim Customs' rebate – then reloading the whisky overnight, after which the *Cask* sailed for the Bermudas to unload for the U.S. In December, sea-planes helped bring in liquor for Christmas and ships even had advertisments: 'Buy here – Scotch $25 – why go further?', in large letters on their sides.

As with smuggling in the eighteenth and nineteenth centuries, people at the highest levels were involved, including every grade of officer supposed to enforce the law, from mayors and sheriffs down; the bootleggers by this time were far removed from the Mexicans who had used their topboots for smuggling. The amount of smuggling from Canada into the U.S. was enormous and there were constant battles. Canadian officials signed clearances for spirits supposedly going to various destinations throughout the world, which, they were well aware, would simply be run over the border into the U.S. Once, a gigantic furniture van arrived from Canada to deliver spirits to a smart Broadway restaurant during the evening; because the manager dared not leave the van outside all night, he took the customers into his confidence, they promptly left their dinners and formed a chain to get the smuggled liquor into the cellar without delay, a nearby policeman taking not the slightest notice.

Also at this time, Finland, Norway and Sweden were 'dry' and spirits could not be sold in Belgium – with the inevitable result that enormous quantities were smuggled in from various sources. Fortunately for the inhabitants of most of these countries, the attempts to stamp out smuggling were worse than half-hearted, so that there was no incentive to make 'bath-tub' spirits. In Helsinki, for example, the wine waiter would ask diners if they wished to have any *smugler varen* as a matter of course, putting bottles of non-alcoholic beer on the table (sometimes even empty ones) to draw attention away from any wines.

By the time the world depression had begun to lift, spirits were firmly established and in fact in my own childhood in the early and mid 1930s, those who would have thought it quite extravagant and indeed unsuitable to serve table wines with food, certainly had various forms of cocktail or 'gin and' mixtures to offer to guests. The cocktail cabinet was something of a status symbol, as was the home bar in the U.S. During this time, too, the custom of offering drinks before dinner or luncheon had become established, whereas prior to 1914 it was comparatively rare. Then, the company would assemble, people would be introduced to each other and ladies shown who would escort them in to the meal; but the process would not take longer than about a quarter of an hour, for there were servants who would ensure that the meal was on time and the company were able to keep to a strict timetable. In many French households (not necessarily of the nobility) to this day, and even in wine-producing regions, there may very well be a mere ten to fifteen minutes of preliminary conversation, sometimes without any refreshment, before one goes in to the meal. There are still those who can come in to say *'Madame est servie'*, without Madame apparently concerning herself in any way with what is being prepared for dinner or lunch. I have never seen the theory advanced that it was the unpredictability of the guests and the necessity for the hostess to preoccupy herself with what was going on in the kitchen that has prolonged the preprandial sessions and necessitated the offering of several rounds of liquid refreshment, but I think this must be so.

Today spirits are completely respectable drinks, whereas it was quite daring to ask for them in company as late as the 30s, even among the brightest of Bright Young Things. Until she had attained the respectability of marriage, with consequent built-in chaperonage, and reached an age when she could no longer be called a 'girl', I doubt that a middle-class young woman would have easily gone by herself into a public house and ordered a spirit drink. The 'cocktail era' and the general social acceptance of gin drinks in entertaining are typical of the period between the wars. The casual ordering of gin was one of the barriers that finally came down in the 1939 war.

Young people today find it hard to imagine a time when spirits were either unobtainable or so limited that the 'quota' system of the suppliers was often extended to regular customers of wine merchant and pub alike; during the war, the armed forces had priority and, after them, such export markets as still might be supplied – and this continued for some time after hostilities ceased. The 1930s idea of a 'bottle party' when each guest brought his own contribution was revived – and some of the bottles brought were of curious provenance. The 'orange juice' – a very nasty version of the real thing – issued to infants was often coveted and some of the 'cocktails' one would be offered at a dance might be strange indeed, simply mixtures of whatever the barman had been able to assemble.

American ships, of course, were 'dry' and there are endless stories of high-powered conferences at sea when special arrangements had to be made to get adequate supplies of acceptable liquid refreshment for those of other nations who might be taking part. But 'export spirits' often came back to Britain through the kindness of those who were able to buy them freely and this must have been the time when many Europeans had their first taste of Bourbon and rye. It seems odd, on reflection, that the vast stocks of wine in the cellars of such great houses as often sold them later at auction in the 1960s and 1970s apparently didn't include vast stocks of spirits too, but I suppose these were bought little and often, as required; certainly everyone in civilian life appeared to be short of spirits. Of course, most large properties were taken over for various official purposes anyway, so maybe the cellars would have been sealed – or even walled up, as happened in many of those in occupied France.

Prisoners of war in Germany, however, often managed to do their own distilling. There are hilarious accounts of the equipment involved with making wine and beer, but a still posed far greater problems, for it had to be dismantled when not in use – distilling could only be done in secret; fuel could be obtained, so could various ingredients from food parcels, such as fruits and sugar, and the various tins and containers that could be assembled were made into primitive types of condensers and other sections of the still. One ingenious group even made a hydrometer from a glass toothbrush holder. Bottles used for medicines and hair tonic were used to take the distillate. One set of prisoners formed themselves into a company, running off the first 'heads' of the distillate into bottles for 'People's Plonk', which they would sell, subsequently using the heart of the distillate for 'Directors' Special Reserve', which generally was consumed at once, in the middle of the night, around the working still. In this particular camp there appear to have been several stills operating and one day a prisoner fell over at roll-call, moaning that he couldn't see; one of the 'Directors' of the more reputable distillery immediately went to see who it was, returning with the reassuring report 'Not one of our customers.' (The man recovered in minutes and, understandably, transferred his custom.) The still, cherished in the memories of its directors to this day, was only discovered after a gigantic celebration when victory was known to be in sight; on this occasion the 'Directors' Special' is reported nearly to have wrecked the hydrometer, and, in the aftermath, the 'Revenooers', or German guards, swooped and discovered all, like excisemen of old.

Doctors, who of course had access to medical alcohol, were much in demand to 'help' such mixtures as could be compounded for parties. Wynford Vaughan Thomas, who was with the allied forces in the Italian campaign and up through the Rhône Valley and Burgundy, describes a liberation get-together in Dijon, when the top brass of the British, French and American troops were formally entertained; from hidden reserves, the Burgundians had brought out the best wines they had to assist in the celebration, and all eyes gleamed as elegant crystal glasses were proffered on silver salvers. Wynford, in attendance near one of the French field marshals, a man of infinite refinement and a true lover of wine, was waiting for a comment on what was certain to be a superlative drink, when an equally high-ranking U.S. officer joined them. 'Hi, general,' said this delightful warrior, 'isn't this just great? And we've made our contribution too – I got the doc to pep up this frog liquor with some medical alcohol!' The Frenchman turned pale but courtesy impelled him to go on lifting his glass to his lips. However, just before drinking, he was heard to murmur, quoting the words of Madame Roland on the steps of the scaffold, 'Liberté, liberté, what crimes are committed in thy name!'

In the period after the Second World War, spirit consumption in general has risen, in spite of economic pressures and increasing taxation. But people drink differently today, and this, in my view, affects spirit consumption in two main ways: first, timetables are far more casual, so that there is much more between-times drinking; secondly, it is accepted that it is perfectly respectable to admit to times of stress, when the 'quick lift' that can be produced by a reasonable amount of good spirit is both beneficial and social. But people want simple things, both to save time and because we are all more conscious of the reactions of our own systems to different substances, so that nowadays complicated mixtures are often viewed with suspicion and an eye cast round for the nearest pot plant. Also, advertising and promotional campaigns have made people very much more aware of the differences according to brand as far as the major spirits are concerned and, although it is doubtful whether the proverbial man in the street knows very much about the different flavours of the different brands of the major spirits, nevertheless there is a proportion of the buying public who will now ask for a spirit according to brand and insist on getting it. The increased and increasing interest in wine, encouraged by more foreign travel, has naturally increased interest in spirits – people want to know what they are, the types that they drank when they were abroad on a holiday, the sort of 'status symbol' drink that they are offered with some ceremony at a special party. There is a definite interest and desire for information.

It must also not be forgotten that, in addition to being commodities increasingly in demand by the public, all spirits are a double source of revenue: because of their sales they make money for the producers, and because of the taxes levied on them they provide revenue for whatever government may be concerned. As far as the world-famous spirits are concerned, they are of enormous importance in the export trade, those making them often being able to wring concessions of various kinds from otherwise unwilling governments simply so that these valuable products should continue to earn foreign currency. The benevolent foundations and the various forms of cultural patronage emanating from the big spirit concerns throughout the world are of enormous importance too. This should not be forgotten, although it is usually the more obvious sponsorship of sporting events, prizes and spectacular presentations that get the publicity.

It is impossible to predict what may be the future of distilling and the great spirits – but that there will be changes, both in what is made and how, I have no doubt. Everyday life in any country where the standard of living enables spirits to be bought for social drinking has altered so radically in the last fifty years that it must do so as well in the future. What use will be made of spirits in the twenty-first century is as yet anyone's guess – but it seems fair to say there appears to be no reason why it should not be beneficial and enjoyable.

4. Brandy

Brandy is a distillate of wine. It can, therefore, be made wherever wine is made, also wherever an alcoholic beverage that can loosely be defined as wine is made – as it may be from fruits other than freshly gathered grapes. Other sections of this book deal with brandies made from distillates of fruits and berries.

Brandy, says *The Shorter Oxford English Dictionary*, is 'an ardent spirit distilled from wine or grapes; but also a name for other similar spirits'. It is important to bear this definition in mind, because, as the Dictionary also points out, the English word 'brandy' derives from the Dutch '*brandewijn*', anglicized as 'brandy wine', a term that the English began to use in the seventeenth century. They certainly understood 'brandy wine' to mean 'burnt wine', in other words, a distillate of wine; but in fact *brandewijn* is not necessarily a distillate of wine at all, any more than is the Dutch 'maltwine' – the result of three pot distillations of a mixture of rye, maize and barley – which is the basis of genever (see page 105). In Holland, the term *brandewijn* means a distillate, but the basis for this need not be a spirit resulting from distilling wine. According to the region or country, the term for the type of spirit that was used as a reviver, warmer or stimulant varied, although its name usually signified what it was: thus, *aqua vitae* in Latin, *eau de vie* in French, *uisge beatha* in Gaelic (the language of Scotland) mean, in general, 'spirit' – not necessarily a particular spirit. The seventeenth-century Englishman who referred to 'brandy wine' or 'brandy' was probably using the term as loosely – and being as ignorant about the product – as those who today use such terms as 'fresh', 'freshly picked', 'garden fresh', 'fresh frozen', and 'morning fresh'; the food in such instances may be far removed from what the purist would require the word 'fresh' to imply and the term 'brandy' might then, to the averagely ignorant, have signified virtually any foreign spirit which wasn't actually gin (which would have been termed Hollands).

The lack of precision in references to spirits is exemplified by an Act of 1690 stating that 'good and wholesome brandies, aqua vitae and spirits may be drawn and made from malted corn' and in an attempt to discriminate against the import of French brandy, the British were then inclined to call the product of any distillation from other liquors than wine 'brandy'; 'British brandy' seems to have been one of the more horrible drinks of the seventeenth and eighteenth centuries. The Honourable John Byng, later Viscount Torrington, regularly drank brandy when travelling, stating that his daily consumption was sometimes half a pint or even a pint; he found that, 'I must send decent liquor to these inns, else when I am tired and faint, I am forc'd to drink British spirits called brandy – or medicated sloe juice call'd port.' In 1782, a German visitor to England commented that, 'the insatiable lust for brandy, especially among the common people, goes to fantastic lengths', and he described how 'the propensity of the common people to the drinking of brandy or gin is carried to a great excess . . . in the late riots . . . more people have been found dead near empty brandy casks in the street, than were killed by the musket balls of regiments.' (What, we may well ask, were all those brandy casks doing in the streets anyway? Perhaps the mob broke open any available stores of liquor.) But this type of 'brandy' was probably something akin to 'brandy cowe', which is described in the early nineteenth century as being the washings of brandy casks.

Today, however, the term brandy does mean a spirit distilled from wine, and most wine-producing regions also make some form of brandy, as well as other types of distillate or flavoured brandy. As the word 'brandy' is English, however, it is usual for many brandies to be presented to the would-be drinker as 'Cognac', the name often being spelled in ways that are hardly recognizable as the same as the supreme brandy: for example, *coñac*, *koniak* and so on. The word Cognac in these forms is not protected, except in France and a few other countries, and cannot be until the formation of an international wine and spirits authority; the word simply happens to be more easily pronounced in all types of language than *eau de vie*, brandy or anything else.

Brandy is not distilled from fine wines – this would be wholly uneconomic – but, according to the region and traditional practice, the distillate may be made from the pressings of the residue, or of grapes, with all their skins, pith and pips, that remains after the making of the actual wine. It is often not realized that, as far as the finest red wines of the world are concerned, the grapes are not in fact pressed at all, merely stripped by various mechanical means from their stalks. When the fruit has been broken up in this way and the juice comes out, the remaining pulp, still moist and squashy, can be subjected to several pressings to extract every drop of moisture; these pressings, which take place in what is like a large-scale version of a domestic press, such as is used in making tongue, are seldom added to the main wine of a great estate, except in occasional small permitted quantities of the first and lightest pressing. They are concentrated and could make the wine harsh and unattractive. But, if this *vin de presse*, or the final pressing, is not required for domestic consumption, then it can be the basis of a distillate. (The stalks and stems of the bunches of grapes are also used for pressing sometimes, but the result can be very harsh indeed and often serves only to make industrial alcohol.)

In such regions as concentrate on brandy production, it is the brandy that is the important thing and not the wine, so that the wine is made with the specific purpose of distilling. It is not usually a wine that could be made more than passably pleasant for drinking anyway. The types of grapes used are generally not the great classic wine grapes, the wine does not have to be made in the same way as for the finer table wines; the quality and character of the spirit are determined by the method of distillation, the skill of whoever is in charge of the process and the final maturation and blending. It is not possible to make a wonderful brandy simply by being a clever distiller, but it is certainly possible nowadays to make a palatable spirit, even one that can attain liqueur quality as well as doing good service in a mix, by the right use of modern distilling techniques and, most important for any type of brandy, the understanding of the fact that, like wine, brandy must be granted a period of maturation if it is to be anything other than a coarse, strong spirit that can give little pleasure except rapid intoxication to the drinker. If you just want the effect of a very strong drink without any of the associated pleasures of aroma, flavour, aftertaste and general charm, then a good brandy is not for you – it might be better to drink a sound brand of one of the instantly ready white spirits.

Why brandy was originally made is a matter that never seems to have been satisfactorily decided. Some authorities assert that, in times of a glut of wine, it was found that the spirit distilled from it was a useful way of disposing of the surplus; others think that the distillate was first made in large quantities because it took up less room than wine and therefore shipping costs were lower, although the price of the spirit might be higher. A variation of this theory is that, in certain areas, taxes on wine were so heavy that the exasperated growers turned to distilling so as to avoid the wine taxes as much as possible. The Spaniards and Italians were making a type of spirit from wine as early as the thirteenth century, the northern countries – Ireland, Scotland and many parts of Germany and Scandinavia – were all making spirits at an even earlier date, although the regions in which this distillation was done are not, as far as I know, those where wine was also produced. But the French did not begin to make a spirit from wine until much later and where they started to do so is not precisely known. There was a shipment of brandy from La Rochelle in 1529, which indicates that distilling had become a significant commercial activity some time earlier, but the document-ation is sparse.

What puzzles all who write on this subject is the fact that, although one can see that northern countries, where wine was not produced or certainly not to any large extent, turned to distilling in order to make themselves a warming drink of some sort, the French do not seem to have felt the need for this until later. Even if the claims made for brandy being easier to carry, taking up less storage space, attracting less taxation (in those days), and as a means of disposing of surplus or unusable wine are all admitted, it is still a strange thing that brandy, such an enormously important spirit today, should have evolved from wine, a product that might well be expected to satisfy both the senses and the pockets of the makers.

This is not the place for detailed speculation, but I think it is relevant to indicate a few of the ways in which brandy is unique as a spirit. First, it is the only spirit which derives from an already alcoholic beverage: the grain, potato and similar spirits come from products that are, primarily, processed to make foodstuffs. True, the *alcools blancs* or real fruit brandies are distillates of fruits, which might themselves be used to produce drinks, albeit non-alcoholic, but these distillates are the result of a process whereby the fruits are directly converted into an alcoholic beverage, whereas with brandy the grapes have previously been made into wine. As far as I know, no fruit brandy is made commercially as a result of having previously made a wine from that same fruit.

Then, although many other spirits appear to have derived either from the preventative or remedial products of the religious estab-lishments or, later, the early scientists in their laboratories (it should not be forgotten that it was the monks who made the first versions of both Scotch and Irish), brandy appears to have evolved mainly from secular sources. Anyone who makes wine can make brandy, whereas

I do not think that you would get more than a vaguely acceptable spirit, even employing all the assistance of science, from distilling the juice of grapes purely intended to be eaten as fruit. So, although it is unlikely that it will ever be determined exactly who made brandy for the first time and where, it seems reasonable to assume that anyone making wine in a quantity superfluous to the needs of his own household had the opportunity to make it. It is possible that before the days of wine in bottles, any wine maker might have used his surplus at the end of the winter as a warming drink by heating it. The use of concentrated must or unfermented grape juice which was boiled down, has been known since very early times – for example, in ancient Egypt. And, as Edward Hyams pertinently remarks, 'it is not claimed that the alchemists of the Eastern Roman Empire were the first to distill wine into brandy; only that they had stills in their laboratories. But would it not be rather odd if they had never had the curiosity to see what happened if you put wine into the still?'

Brandy must certainly have been a somewhat crude spirit in its early form, else there would not have been the confusion between brandy made from the distillate of wine, as we know it, and other spirits; 'ew ardent' is often a general reference, from which it is impossible to deduce what the spirits referred to may actually have been. But brandy does seem to have been particularly used in connection with travel: the cut glass and ornamented small flasks, designed to be fitted inside portmanteaux, dressing cases, and to be slotted into private travelling carriages were far more likely to have been intended for holding brandy than as 'scent bottles', under which name they are now often sold. From the seventeenth century onwards certainly, flasks to hold brandy were designed for travellers and could be attached to saddles, even to top boots, and military uniforms often included the flask slung over the shoulder or round the waist. Brandy of course was useful for washing wounds and served as a disinfectant for water – very much as wine did in wine-producing countries. Indeed, in the sixteenth and seventeenth centuries, brandy might be said to be the T.C.P.-cum-chlorodyne of the traveller. Early editions of John Murray's *Guides* for travellers stress the value of spirits as preventive medicine and recommend brandy as useful 'in marshy situations'. The queasiness brought on by the jolting of an unsprung coach often required a stomach-settler and, in 1760, Dr Somerville, writing about Scottish hospitality, says: 'when visitors called in the forenoon, ale or brandy was usually offered; and, to persons of importance, claret and brandy-punch.' Punch, in its various forms, became traditionally associated with the

Whig party in England, whereas the Tory drinks were sack and claret. The snob appeal of brandy was naturally much enhanced when, in the Napoleonic Wars, brandy became difficult to obtain in England and the smuggled version of it, whether or not it had been adulterated, was endowed with the glamour attached to a commodity in short supply.

In 1815, Thomas Moore described a dinner with Lord Byron at Watiers; Byron ate lobsters and, in between eating them, drank 'a small liqueur glass of strong white brandy, sometimes a tumbler of very hot water and then pure brandy again'. The poet may have been doing this as some form of preventive medicine against the risk of a bad lobster; after this course the company all drank two bottles of claret without ill effects. Disraeli, going to Maidstone in 1838, stopped to break his journey at Rochester, in what seems to have been typical English July weather, 'to drink a glass of brandy and water and to scribble a note to Mrs Wyndham Lewis'. And there is a most interesting reference in a letter of Monsieur Auguste Hennessy in 1849, commenting on the changes of the drinking habits of the British:

> The fact is that the public originally took to drinking Brandy and Water for medical reasons and, having found it both pleasant and effective, they are likely to continue. The original Brandy drinker is now being joined by those who drink wine, and also by far more numerous an entirely new class, namely the Artisan and Workman who formerly drank 'porter' and ale and who now find that they are offered Brandy and Water at almost the same price. They were telling me for instance that the average Coalheaver, who does an almost Superhuman task substituted Brandy and Water for 'porter' and finds that he works better on it.
>
> It is the general opinion over here that, in spite of the virtual disappearance of Cholera and, on the other hand, the appearance of the new Patent Still Whisky, that the consumption of Brandy will continue throughout the winter and that, even if the figures of the last few months are not maintained, one can look forward to a great and permanent increase.

And by the middle of the century, when Gladstone reduced the duty on French wines (1860), the wine writers of the day were much engaged in discussing whether or not brandy should be added to wine; this was also extremely important *vis-à-vis* the port trade of the time. In 1860, Cyrus Redding, talking about sherry, declared: 'for England, however, no wine will do without brandy . . . brandied and adulterated wines are the bane of Englishmen . . . Pure wine was not made for men who can drink two or three bottles of brandied wine at a sitting.' Redding was also aware of the possible medicinal value of brandy and water: 'in a large company, where the individual is thrown off his guard by speeches, toasts and claptraps of all kinds, it is far better to order, if it agrees with the individual, a decanter of weak brandy and water and pass the wine bottles as they come round. Many would this way escape a fearful headache.'

This is a side reference to the use of brandy as a hangover remedy, something that the fathers of many who are today high in the wine trade would have recommended. In 1814, Byron, staggering back to his rooms in Albany, 'desired Fletcher to give him a tumbler of brandy', and drained it to the health of Mrs Wilmot, who had been the star at the evening's party, although wearing mourning. The poet remained 'in a sad state all night' but the next morning was able to write the beautiful verses 'She walks in Beauty like the Night'. In 1847, Throne Crick, in *The Diary of a Commercial Traveller*, draws the portrait of a perennially-flushed commercial, Grogram Rummy, who had to begin the day with 'soda water repeated a time or two and sundry squibs, with warm water and sugarless, of his favourite seldom-failing restorative brandy, to enable the stomach and palate to return to their usual tone.' In *Orley Farm*, Anthony Trollope's novel which began to appear in monthly instalments in 1862, the travellers in the commercial room of the Bull Inn, Leeds, had brandy and water before dinner, but when, later, the formidable Mr Moulder takes too much brandy – followed by whisky, lemon and hot water – he recovers: 'at twelve o'clock the next morning, after the second bottle of soda and brandy, he was "as sweet as sweet".' Dickens's Mr Pickwick liked brandy and water and Thomas Love Peacock's Reverend Dr Opimian in *Gryll Grange*, 1860, took brandy and hot water in winter as a nightcap, but brandy and soda in the summer. Towards the end of the nineteenth century, George Augustus Sala tells of a young man who when drunk would be 'conveyed on a stretcher to St James's Watchhouse, where his servant would "wait upon him there with a change of linen and a small silver flask of brandy"', which must have been a beneficent drink as the young man afterwards married a widow 'of enormous wealth'. George Saintsbury, who has impressed his name upon many aspects of wines and spirits in spite of having been the most intolerant and boring of writers about both, liked hot brandy with hot water as a nightcap and said 'all alcoholic drinks, rightly used, are good for body and soul alike; but as a restorative of both there is nothing like brandy.' He was discussing a currently fashionable marque of

Champagne with a friend who was a Pall Mall wine merchant; the man in the trade said, in response to Saintsbury's disapproval: *I'd nearly as soon have a bra-a-andy and sod-a-a!*'. This comment suggests that, even then, the mixed drink was a rather common thing – somewhat on a level with baked beans on toast or corned beef hash or cottage pie – if one were in the rarefied company of someone vaunting himself as a gourmet.

Significantly, although Alexis Soyer invented a 'Crimean cup à la Marmora' when he went out to the Crimean War as the companion of Florence Nightingale and specified 'one pint Cognac brandy' in the recipe, the references to brandy do not make the difference between brandy as such and Cognac. It is possible that our ancestors in Britain took brandy as being synonymous with Cognac – but they don't say so.

The boost, as far as the fashionable world was concerned, came when the then Prince of Wales, later Edward VII, preferred to drink brandy after dinner, both because he liked smoking a large cigar and because he preferred to join the ladies at mixed dinner parties, instead of sitting for several hours over the port. And the writer T. G. Shaw, at the beginning of the nineteenth century, might have been describing country house habits of the beginning of the twentieth:

> Five o'clock dinners require substantial suppers, when ladies 'of a certain age' were privileged – and did not neglect their privilege – to have a 'tumbler', with the choice of wine, whisky, brandy, rum or Hollands, which were on the sideboard. Before retiring for the night, the practice was invariable to have a tray brought up with the various kinds of spirits.

It is probably a fair generalization to say that, as far as brandy drinking after dinner was concerned, it would have been the men who opted for the brandy, the ladies being given a liqueur, until very recent times; even a quarter of a century ago, a woman who went into a bar or a restaurant and was asked what she would like to drink, might opt for a whisky or a whisky and soda, but, if she asked for brandy, the implication would be that she was not feeling very well, had had a shock, or needed a restorative, in the old-fashioned sense of the word.

COGNAC

It is pertinently stated that there are two French words known to people throughout the world who are hardly aware that they are

French – 'Cognac' and 'Paris'. The Cognac region has been under vines for centuries, the wines being shipped to export markets from La Rochelle, Saintes and Cognac itself, for the river Charente could formerly accommodate small boats of shallow draught up to this point. The Dutch in particular were big customers and, in his masterly book *Cognac*, Cyril Ray indicates that it may have been their influence on the wine producers, whom they were able to educate in various methods of handling and sweetening, that eventually resulted in the entire region devoting its produce to distillation.

In 1909 a decree of the French government marked out the Cognac area and the regions within it in parts of the *départements* of the Charente and Charente Maritime: these spread out in vaguely circular shapes from the axis Cognac–Jarnac, rather like the shading from a blot of wine on a white cloth. The innermost region and the one that produces the very finest brandies is Grande Champagne, the

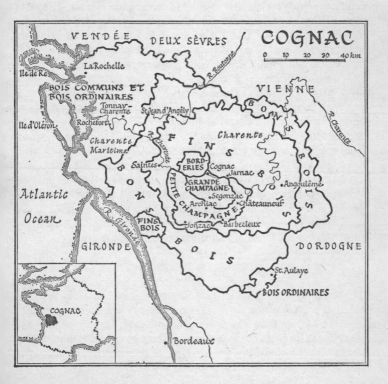

word 'Champagne' being the French version of the Latin word
'*Campania*', signifying open countryside, as in Malvolio's ex-
clamation in *Twelfth Night*: 'Daylight and Champain discover not
more'. The soil is chalky and crumbling, and there are twenty-eight
communes or parishes in which about two thirds of the area able to
be planted is under vines and destined for distilling. Petite Champagne is an area including sixty communes, of which about a third
of the suitable region is under vines, the soil being slightly less
crumbling. Brandies from the two areas, when combined, with a
proportion of at least 50 per cent of Grande Champagne, are allowed
by law to call themselves 'Fine Champagne'. (This is a term not to be
confused with '*une fine*' for which see page 78.) The Borderies region
is fairly small, just north and slightly west of Cognac. The area is
more wooded and there is less chalk in the soil; it has a higher
proportion of suitable ground under the vines than any of the others
in the Cognac region. The brandies made here can have a definite
firmness, which makes them valuable in the finer blends. They can
occasionally be sweet, with a particular character that can be extremely pleasant for those who are able to taste them as single
unblended spirits. The Fins Bois is the largest Cognac area, extending throughout 278 parishes. As its name implies, there are woods –
and also considerable farming – so that a comparatively small
proportion of the region is under vines. The soil tends to have a lot of
gravel and the brandies, because of this, tend to age quickly, and can
be extremely useful elements in a blend. The Bons Bois region
encircles that of the Fins Bois, is more exposed to the sea breezes
from the Atlantic, and has a rather more obviously earthy soil, with
the result that the brandies are inclined to be somewhat coarse, but
again they can be very useful in cheap blends, as are those of the Bois
Ordinaires, which includes the region along the coast around La
Rochelle and Rochefort and Royan and the offshore islands of Île
de Ré and Île d'Oléron. These brandies are considered harsh by
comparison with those of the central regions of the area.

Making Cognac

The vines used for making Cognac are mainly the Folle Blanche,
St Émilion, Columbard; a certain proportion, not exceeding 10
per cent, of Sémillon, Sauvignon, Blanc-Remé, Jurançon Blanc and
Montils is also permitted. It is not permitted to assist the fermentation with any additional yeast strains. The wine these vines make,
white, ideally high in acidity and thin and shrill in style, can, even at

its best, be no more than a lightly refreshing drink on a hot day. The use of sulphur dioxide (possibly the most usual form of disinfectant in any process of fermentation) is forbidden, because it has been found that it comes over in the process of distillation in the pot still and affects the quality of the ultimate spirit. Some of the Cognac producers own vineyards, but may also buy in the wine from peasant growers; the work of distillation may be carried out by a large establishment or else by a cooperative, buying from the small-scale grower, or be effected by the small distilleries which operate in the area and subsequently sell the result of their distillations to one of the large establishments. Among those who make the wines to be distilled in the Cognac region, around 2000 of them are *bouilleurs de cru*, a term which means that they can distil their own wines for brandy but may not buy in other wines to distil; these growers will then sell their brandy to another concern, although a very small percentage of what an individual *bouilleur de cru* makes does occasionally reach the market. A *bouilleur de profession* is someone who is allowed to distil wine bought in for the purpose and who can also undertake the process of distillation for other growers. The operations of these *bouilleurs de profession*, who are around 300 in number, account for more than a half of all the brandy made in Cognac.

It is, however, the big firms, the Cognac shippers, such as Martell, Hennessy, Rémy Martin, Salignac, Courvoisier and Hine that are the concerns that most affect the general public buying Cognac. Whether they own vineyards or not, and whether they undertake distillation or not, their main function is to acquire brandies, age them and then make up the blends that have made their reputations. The distillation of the wine must, by law, be carried out in the pot still of the type particular to the Charente region; the big Cognac Houses may have installations of them out in the vineyards, although the most impressive and largest are in the firms' town establishments.

The pot still today is in fact the same type of still as was used in the sixteenth century. It consists of a big copper 'pot', polished to brilliancy, its head either tapering slightly to a point or being dumpy and in fact rather like a brandy glass of the right shape reversed. From this head, a tapering 'swan neck' leads down into the adjoining container or 'pipe' which is a receptacle inside which there is a twirly continuation of the swan neck leading from the original container for the wine, for which the French word is *'chaudière'*. The basic principle is that the fire under the *chaudière* causes the wine to boil and the vapours rise into the head, subsequently passing over the narrow pipe or swan neck into the *serpentin*, or twirly pipe, in the second container which holds cold water. The vapours condense and come out (about 26–32° Gay Lussac), this liquid being known as the *brouillis*. The *brouillis* are then put back into the original still for the second distillation, known as the *bonne chauffe*; once again the liquid comes to the boil and passes over the swan neck, for subsequent cooling in the *serpentin*, but this is a stage in the production of Cognac far more delicate than it may sound when explained in this rough way. The first part of the distillate that 'comes over', in other words passes through the swan neck to emerge as infant Cognac, is known as the 'heads' and this can be strong and even unpleasant in aroma; it is therefore diverted, before it can be put into the 'heart' of the brandy, and set on one side. The end of the distillate, 'the tails', is similarly treated, because this part of the brandy will be weak. An instrument constantly checks the alcoholic strength, but it is the distiller who decides the exact instant when the heads or tails are to be diverted from the heart of the spirit, and his judgement about this is affected by the original alcoholic strength of the wines being used, their particular character, the temperature of the day in which the distillate is being made and the type of fuel being used. Instruments nowadays indicate the alcoholic strength of the liquid that is coming over, but in former times the still was struck (i.e., the distillate was diverted) *à la perle*, which Dr Simpson has described as 'the point at which air bubbles induced in samples drawn in the glass rose slowly and persisted at the liquid/air interface'. Of course the distiller today has constant reference to his instruments, but I should be surprised if he does not rely equally on what he sees, tastes and smells, and on the experience he has acquired as much as on what the scientists and their systems of measurement are able to tell him.

The fuel too is subject to control, wood no longer being either practical or economic, and coal, which is still in use, giving a heat that is not always easy to control and gauge within a matter of seconds. The law requires that Cognac can only be distilled with an actual fire, so that electricity is not permitted, and it is thought that oil firing might affect the fragrance of the brandy. So the big distilleries nowadays use gas. The exact moment when the process of distillation is started and the stages at which it is cut require enormous skill and experience on the part of the distiller; the families of many distillers have been in the business for generations, and, even in these days of the utilization of every modern technological improvement that is legally permitted, it is still quite usual for the distiller to spend the night sleeping or watching by the still when it is running. The process of distillation overall takes about eight hours.

The heads and tails of the distillate are redistilled, and the way this is done is equally strictly controlled.

The brandy that emerges from the still – which has to be cleaned out thoroughly each time the process takes place – is a colourless liquid, about 70° Gay Lussac, and is ready for maturing in wood. The taster of the establishment that is considering buying it subjects it to the most critical survey. Again, this work has often passed from father to son for six or seven generations. The taster's room will contain a 'library' of specimens of brandies from different sources of supply and different years, so that the samples submitted may be compared against the type of brandy required; again, the great firms have often been buying from the same small distillers for generations, as well as distilling for themselves. To see anyone tasting Cognacs, either when buying or planning to combine them in the ultimate blend, is to watch a great artist at work.

The maturation of Cognac in wood is another stage that requires many allied skills. The cask gives something to any wine that it houses during its development and this is even truer of fine brandy. Traditionally, only oak from the Limousin Forest was used, but nowadays Tronçais oak is also utilized. The oak trees of the two forests are not identical; they are taller and more elegant trees in appearance than the stockier trees that the word 'oak' evokes in the mind of Britons. The wood has to be seasoned before it is made into casks, otherwise an unpleasant flavour would be imparted to the brandy. As it takes up to six years of exposure to the air in suitable conditions to season the wood for a cask, it will be appreciated that the cask itself is a precious item and the coopers in the big Cognac houses are highly skilled workers. For example, for 'stave wood' the wood is cleft not sawn and, if a cask should be damaged in any way, it is important that a repair should be made with a suitable piece of wood, whether this is in the head or the sides of the cask.

The placid maturation in cask provides the brandy with such tannin as it requires to give it definition, and the spirit takes on the delicate amber colour as well as developing its unique aroma and taste. During this period of maturation the brandy is subject to evaporation because, even in the most tightly sealed cask, the porousness of the wood in the generally dry atmosphere of the Cognac region causes between 2 per cent and 4 per cent each year to 'go to the angels' as the Cognac saying has it; or, putting the expression of loss another way, 'the sun is our best customer', according to other brandy firms. Another odd thing about Cognac – which is also sometimes noticed in other regions making spirits and also in

Oporto – is that a black deposit will form on the roof of the warehouse where the brandy lies; anyone able to look down on Cognac or Jarnac will see this quite plainly in the panorama of roofscapes, and, as will be appreciated, this is something that can never be a secret from the customs or tax officers!

According to the type of brandy being made, the rate at which Cognac matures in cask and the period during which it may be expected to improve both vary; but Cognac in wood does not improve indefinitely and in general thirty to forty years is the average life of an ordinary type of brandy; exceptional brandies may have longer lives, but they too may eventually become thin, the spirit showing less than pleasantly through the delicacy of the matured Cognac. If it is wished to keep such fine brandies for any length of time beyond their reasonable life in wood, they are transferred to glass *bonbons*, large bulbous vessels like a type of carboy. The section of the brandy warehouse where the finest brandies are kept is generally known as the *paradis*.

The casks of brandy are not just left alone to mature. Constant supervision is necessary, not only to ensure that the warehouse itself is in good order (and it can be imagined that the precautions against fire are elaborate and the insurance premiums gigantic) but because the contents of each cask will vary slightly and must be watched throughout its life. Samples drawn direct from the cask are usually fished out through the bung-hole with the aid of a small cup on a wire or cord, which is known as *une preuve*. It is legally permitted to add a very small percentage of cane sugar dissolved in brandy to soften a particular cask that may be making a raw, coarse spirit, and the same may be done with caramel, which adds colour to the resulting blend – this is something much affected by fashion and also by the particular market which is being catered for: obviously, customers like a continuity of style. It should be stressed that neither of these minute additives should distort the resulting brandy in any way. There are two ways in which to note the difference between a really fine Cognac and a pleasant but nevertheless rather ordinary grape brandy: after the glass is empty, move it around in the air and then smell it again – the lingering aroma will be of a most definite character and enable you to distinguish the individuality of each of the spirits. Or, as is commonly done in tasting brandy, put a little of the spirit in the palm of your hand (which of course should not have been washed with scented soap or treated with any lotion), rub your palms together so that the spirit evaporates and then smell them. You will be surprised at the impression of the brandy that remains. But you may be somewhat taken aback, because you will certainly smell any obvious sweetening or additional flavouring that has been used in producing the spirit with the possibly erroneous idea of making it 'better'. A brandy that smells strongly of vanilla when appraised in this way has almost certainly been touched up in a fashion that the lover of the spirit at its aristocratic best and certainly the student of fine Cognac cannot approve.

All the time the supplies of brandy are being blended to make the various 'marques' of the great houses, the huge stocks being drawn upon at regular intervals. This marrying of different ages and types of brandy is the masterpiece and life work of the taster of a great establishment. Each Cognac will contain a large number of different brandies, which harmonize into the desired single Cognac at the end; usually, in the finest blends of all, there will be a high proportion of really old brandy, but there is need, too, for some of the more vigorous younger spirits to make their contribution.

When the Cognac is bottled, it is ready for sale. It will not improve in bottle and there is absolutely no point in letting it get old. It is not quite true to say that it will not change in bottle, because the fact that it is stoppered with a cork means that, over many years, some air will inevitably get into the bottle and slightly alter the spirit, but this is an infinitesimal difference; remember too that, unlike wine, bottles of spirits must be kept upright, else the spirit will rot the cork. But the supposition that the old, cobwebby bottle may contain something finer than the perfectly clean modern one still persists; readers of Evelyn Waugh's *Brideshead Revisited* may remember how the narrator takes the parvenu Rex Mottram to a great Paris restaurant, where Rex makes a fuss about the pale, delicate Cognac in a simple bottle 'free from grime and Napoleonic cyphers. It was only a year or two older than Rex and lately bottled. They gave it to us in very thin tulip-shaped glasses of modest size.' The ignorant Rex condemns the colour and the glasses, insists on a huge balloon glass warmed over the spirit lamp and pronounces the Cognac as 'the sort of stuff he put soda in at home. So, shamefacedly, they wheeled out of its hiding place the vast and mouldy bottle they kept for people of Rex's sort.

'"That's the stuff," he said, tilting the treacly concoction till it left dark rings round the sides of his glass.' This sums up all that is important about how – and how not – to drink good brandy.

The thing to remember is that whatever age a brandy is when it goes into bottle, and whatever style it is, so it will remain throughout its life in that bottle; a brandy kept for very long indeed would probably deteriorate – hence the absurdity of vaunting the 'Napoleon brandy' (readers will probably share my astonishment that anything gastronomic or delicate as regards drink can pertinently be associated with the Little Corporal). A young, rawish brandy put into bottle early in its life will be raw if it is not so young when it is opened, even after fifty years. The evaporation from the casks of Cognac means that they must be topped up and, whereas the system of controls that regulate the labelling and sale of Cognacs requires certain certificates of minimum age, it is impossible to be precise about this, the details of the requirements merely specifying that to be able to comply with the regulations the various brandies must be more than so many years old, the top age being as low as five.

Nor do the stars or other differentiating names on Cognac labels have any precise legal significance; they relate solely to the different grades of Cognac produced by the individual houses, who may use these as they wish, without making claims as to age, of course – but the price gives the clue to the quality of the Cognac. The customer may be quite sure that any name or description that a Cognac house puts on its label will have been subject to official approval before being passed.

Vintage and old or early landed Cognac

Up to 1963 it was possible for a Cognac establishment to market a vintage Cognac, the brandy of a single year, and for the date to be given on the label. But fashions for particular vintages led to abuses and consequently French law now prohibits Cognac from being marketed under a vintage label; though, of course, in the 'libraries' in the tasting rooms vintage brandies are stocked for reference purposes.

And until 1973 it was rare, but not unknown, for a British shipper to bring over a single vintage of unblended Cognac of any specific type and mature it in the U.K. (In the spring of 1973, Britain became a member of the European Community and consequently had to comply with the E.E.C. wine and spirit labelling regulations.) The British climate, damp, with the atmosphere somewhat thick, is totally different from that of Cognac or most of France. In consequence, the problem of rapid evaporation from the cask hardly arises, and in the case of 'old landed' Cognac stored in a British bond, one of the securest places in the world, it is impossible to top up the casks anyway. But the alcoholic strength of the brandy gradually declines, and the spirit takes on less colour from the wood than it might have done in its homeland.

An interesting comment made by one of the most respected personalities in the South African wine and spirit world makes this of added relevance to the maturation of brandy in general. As he remarked, the porous nature of the cask means not only that the atmosphere – the air – gets in, but that the spirit gets out; there is therefore brandy outside the cask as well as in. The atmosphere in a brandy distillery where maturation is proceeding acts like a jacket around the cask: the air is thick with the brandy, even more so in a damp climate. This two-way traffic of the spirit and the air plays a part that is only just beginning to be recognized but which has been demonstrated by the results of 'old landed' Cognacs – exclusive, as far as I know, to the U.K. – so that many brandy warehouses now are not merely air-conditioned but humidified.

The maturation of 'old landed' Cognac is naturally affected by where the bond is – a northern bond will be quite different in climate and humidity from one in the London docks, for example – and the date and place where the Cognac was bottled will therefore make it different too. In principle, all these details ought to be stated on the label of this rare form of brandy. But as it is not only rare but now of extremely high price, even if any is obtainable, this is perhaps only of academic interest. It is interesting, though, to know that one can take a cask from Cognac and, when the brandy inside it is matured in a British bond, without topping up, the result will be something quite different from the brandy in the cask next to it in the original warehouse in the Charente. 'Old landed' or, as it is sometimes labelled, 'early landed' Cognac has great charm for some people, including myself, but there are many who cannot see its attraction.

The great Cognac Houses

There are endless fascinating stories, both of families and businesses, for anyone who has time to study Cognac. The two biggest firms are Martell and Hennessy, the first being dominant in the U.K. market, the second in the U.S.A., but both running each other close in every way and certainly possessing the most enormous stocks – they claim to hold the biggest stocks of brandy in the world between them. Martell is also probably the oldest of the great Cognac houses, founded in 1715 by Jean Martell of Jersey, whose widow formed a company after his death and who was succeeded by her sons in turn. The firm became J. & S. Martell in 1805 and is still very much a family business.

Hennessy was founded in 1765 by Richard Hennessy, third son of the Squire of Ballmacmoy, County Cork, who had been in the Irish Brigade fighting with the French against England for the Stuart cause; he spent part of his convalescence, after being wounded, in Cognac in 1740 and appreciated the brandy, shipping several casks back to friends in Ireland, who liked it so much that he eventually went into business and settled there. Richard's son James later re-formed the company as Jas. Hennessy & Co. and today the Hennessys, French and English, still run the concern, in addition to exerting a strong influence in the racing world.

Rémy Martin was founded by a wine grower and merchant of that name in 1724, and in 1924 the firm was taken over by André Renaud, another vineyard owner in the Grande Champagne district, whose family still own it. Rémy Martin specialize in V.S.O.P. Fine Champagne Cognac and for their two hundredth anniversary they made an anniversary blend of Grand Champagne grade, none of the Cognacs in this being younger than fifty years old, the oldest having been laid down over a hundred years ago. Only 2000 bottles were allowed on quota to the U.K., and these were sold at £50 each.

The establishment of Otard-Dupuy dates from 1795, and there is an impressive portrait of Jacques Otard de la Grange, deputy and mayor of Cognac, who was one of the founders. Otard are fortunate in owning the Château de Cognac itself in the centre of the town, a very picturesque building, where François I, king of France, was born in 1494; the castle had a history even before that, probably dating from the ninth century, and, during the period that the region belonged to the English, the Black Prince lived there from 1365 to 1370. The lavishly decorated rooms were used for many important official receptions, but when the building became public property during the French Revolution, Otard were able to buy it.

In Jarnac, the firms of Delamain and Hine are most interestingly linked with the U.K. In the early seventeenth century, a Delamain came to London from France with Henrietta Maria when she married Charles I, and he finally settled in Ireland; his nephew eventually went back to France in 1760 and into the brandy trade.

Thomas Hine was born in Beaminster, Dorset, in 1775, the family having been Protestant supporters of the Monmouth rebellion; surviving the subsequent reprisals, Thomas went to work in Jarnac, in the Delamain establishment, and married one of the daughters of the house, setting up in business in 1817. He had refused to become French, and during the Napoleonic Wars underwent some privations, but survived, dying in 1822. His son, still British, became Mayor of Jarnac. Later generations of the French Hines run Cognac

Hine today, with the trademark of a stag – originally a hind, a play on their name. But this still presents problems to the French, especially those of competing establishments: the first time I visited the house of Hine on the quayside at Jarnac, none of the employees of Bisquit Dubouché next door could apparently understand any version of the way in which I pronounced the name of their neighbours! The Hines have kept up with their English relations and, in fact, during the Second World War came under particular suspicion by the Germans because of their name.

ARMAGNAC

Armagnac takes its name from what was formerly a defined French province, in the south-west of France. It is often called 'the brandy of the Gascons', because part of this region was the former area of Gascony, home of many swashbuckling characters of whom the most famous must certainly be Alexandre Dumas' d'Artagnan, in fact a real person: Charles de Batz Castelmore, Seigneur d'Artagnan, who led the King's Musketeers under Louis XIV in the seventeenth century. These were men known for their swordsmanship, aggressive manners and tendencies to exaggeration in speech. Rostand's Cyrano de Bergerac is a typical fictional Gascon. (All Gascons of this kind, of course, also have tender, loving hearts, are utterly chivalrous and will die serving a cause in which they believe.)

There are many curious misconceptions about Armagnac, in particular that it is 'weaker' and 'more feminine' than Cognac. As it has remained very much a small-scale business with many installations out in the country (unlike the large-scale organizations of the Charentes), it is not always easy for people to find out much about this other great brandy unless they know where to go.

Significantly, there is a written reference to Armagnac as early as 1411 and again in 1461; this is much earlier than the first references to Cognac, but if one thinks of the proximity of the Armagnac region to the Pyrenees and to Spain, it does not seem unreasonable that the art of distillation might have been brought to Gascony by the Moors before it was known elsewhere. Arnaud de Villanova was, after all, a Catalan, and, although the kingdom of Catalonia is at the eastern end of the Pyrenees, mountain people tend to move about independently of frontiers. So it is at least possible that the distillate made by Arnaud and his associate Ramón Llull in the thirteenth century might have been heard of in France and even that the method of making this type of distillate of wine could have been made known there too. In addition, the route through the Pyrenees at the western end was one of the great pilgrims' roads to Santiago de Compostella, and pilgrims came through Languedoc Roussillon on the same pilgrimage down from Burgundy and Germany, so that there was constant coming and going of travellers of all kinds throughout the Middle Ages, enriching in many ways the regions passed.

Armagnac seems to have been used more for medicinal purposes at the beginning of its life, but by the eighteenth century it had become popular as a drink, possibly due to the improvement of communications and the way in which the Gascons moved around France in the various wars. The region then under vines was very much larger than it is now and the majority of the wines made were distilled; indeed, the Armagnac of those days was often sent up to the Charentes for blending with Congac. The southern spirit had always been quite different in character, owing to the cold winters, with strong winds coming in from the west and the sea, plus the rather rich hilly landscape, near to the mountain range of the Pyrenees. In 1909, controls began to define what Armagnac is, where it may come from and how it should be labelled.

The main grapes used for making Armagnac are traditionally the Piquepoul, the local variety of the Folle Blanche, and, in the production of Armagnac, today the St Émilion and Colombard, also the Jurançon, Blanquette, Mauzac and the Clairette Meslier, called Plant de Graisse. The student of wine will note that, whereas some of these varieties are also used in the Cognac area, much use is made of varieties that also make wines of the Pyrenean region.

Controls specify the handling of the wines in detail: they must not be subjected to sugaring, sulphuring nor may they be racked off. The distilling is done from wines still on their lees, which enables the subtlety of the spirit to develop to the full.

Up to the nineteenth century, the still used in the Armagnac region was essentially the same as that of Cognac: two distillations were carried out in a pot still. But there were many attempts to improve this type of still and even to evolve another – scientists whose names are associated with instruments, processes and foodstuffs known all over the world today, pursued this aim: Baumé, Chaptal, Parmentier among them. Then at the turn of the century, a former cavalry captain, Antoine de Mélet, achieved outstanding success with a new type of still and, subsequently, a Montpellier chemist, Édouard Adam, perfected a still that was able to produce a spirit to a determined strength in one continuous process of heating and cooling. The Armagnac still evolved from these and, by the end of the nineteenth century, a peasant of the region, named Verdier, established the final version that is now in use. It should be stressed, however, that this Armagnac still is not identical with the patent or Coffey still, though it is natural to wonder whether the Armagnaçais, experimenting at the beginning of the nineteenth century, ever heard of or exchanged views with the Irishman Aeneas Coffey, pursuing the same end at the same time.

Because of the simplicity typical of the production of Armagnac, much distillation is done by stills that actually travel about in the region; these look a little like a small steam engine on a cart. The still is entirely of copper. There is only the single distillation and the spirit comes over at a strength which, to meet legal requirements, must not exceed 63° Gay Lussac; both the way in which the still may be used and the resulting strength are subject to controls put into force in 1936. But the strength of the Armagnac itself is often much lower than 63° and it is this that gives rise to the misapprehension that Armagnac is 'weaker' than Cognac.

But, as will have been realized, it is not primarily the alcoholic strength of spirits such as Armagnac and Cognac that endows them with their charm: both can be of the same strength. This can be broken down or, indeed, kept high when the bottling is to be done. But the important thing about the Armagnac low strength is that more of the non-alcoholic elements in the spirit come over into the distillate, which accounts for the outstanding fragrance of even a fairly ordinary Armagnac. This can surprise the drinker, who may expect Armagnac to be a somewhat withdrawn, reserved spirit, like Cognac and who will be immediately astonished by the bouquet of the Armagnac; this bouquet, however, should never lead the drinker to assume that the subsequent flavour may be less attractive or that the constitution of the brandy is 'weaker' in terms of alcohol.

Armagnac must be distilled by the end of the April following the vintage of the wine. Its age is worked out from the end of August in the year of its vintage, when it is given a rating of 0; on 1 September in the year following the vintage it gets a rating of 1, and these ratings go up by one on the 1st of every succeeding September. The spirit is of course matured in oak, *au pièce*, these casks holding 400–420 litres, ideally of wood from the forests of Monlezun, although producers may get casks of oak from other regions. It is said that this particular type of oak ages the spirit faster than Limousin oak, but I have no knowledge of this. In a recent edition of Alexis Lichine's *Encyclopedia* (Cassell, 1974), however, a most interesting experiment is described, in which freshly distilled brandies from the Bas-Armagnac, all run from the same still in 1952, were put into casks, half of which were the black oak of Armagnac and half Limousin, as used for much Cognac. The casks were sealed and not tasted again until 1956; then it was found that the brandy in the Armagnac oak was as it should be, but the spirit in the other casks was, somehow, unsatisfactory. This is yet another instance of the casks giving much to the resulting drink.

The age of Armagnac itself is rather roughly worked out: Armagnacs marked as three-star or XXX will be three years of age, those marked V.O. from five to ten, and V.S.O.P. Armagnacs from ten to

fifteen. The expression *'hors d'age'* will mean that the brandy is twenty-five years old or even more, but Armagnac will not go on improving in wood and it is generally agreed that, after about thirty years in cask, the spirit will begin to be too assertive and the balance of the Armagnac distorted. Vintage Armagnac may still be found, although, of course, if casks are topped up, it cannot truthfully be said that every single element in that cask is of the same year; if the Armagnac label does bear a date, and the brandy has been blended, then the date must be that of the youngest in the blend, as with luxury Scotch.

The placid maturation and skilled blending of Armagnac is traditional. The three regions making it produce rather different types of wine and, consequently, the resulting distillate will vary. The area now defined are Ténarèze, Bas-Armagnac and Haut-Armagnac. It is the Bas-Armagnac that makes the finest brandy because, it is thought, the soil of the vineyards is a satisfactory mixture of both sand and clay. Legislation requires that if an Armagnac should be labelled with any of the three regions, then the brandy in the bottle must be only from that region – if the label simply says 'Armagnac' then the contents will be a blend. As regards the strength, this is up to the individual Armagnac establishment to determine, for, whereas the strength of the distillate is controlled, the resulting spirit, when matured and prepared for bottling after blending, may be broken down to the required strength, just as Cognacs may be.

Armagnac vis-à-vis *Cognac*

One of the things that may confuse the person tasting Armagnac is that it really is not like Cognac at all. Some people have tried to describe it, using very flowery terms, and I myself once wrote that the appeal of Armagnac tends to be emotional whereas that of Cognac is intellectual. But the delicate shades of aroma, flavour and aftertaste of Armagnac are a challenge to anyone's powers of description. A contemporary producer refers to the *'goût fauve'*, or untamed flavour. Other writers have said that Armagnac is feminine, Cognac, masculine – it is for the drinker to evolve helpful descriptive tags.

Each of the Armagnac establishments will make a slightly different individual type and only personal choice can determine which is the best. The range of Armagnacs produced by a firm will of course include both the ordinary ones, where the brandy can be used for a drink diluted with water or in a mix, and those of liqueur quality.

Bottles

The bottle used is mostly of a squat flagon-like shape, known as a *basquaise*, from the adjacent Pays Basque. The origin of this is certainly the goatskin used in former times to carry wine, and would certainly have been equally practicable for spirits, although I wonder whether the brandy might eventually rot the skin? In this permissive age it will probably not shock anyone to learn that the shape of this bottle does in fact derive from the scrotum of the goat, and it is logical that shepherds, mountaineers and certainly smugglers would find this a most convenient portable vessel. This bottle can be globular or slightly triangular. Today, other types of bottle may be in use for Armagnac, according to the policy of individual establishments, and the *pot gascon*, which contains 250 cl (the *basquaise* contains only 70 cl or 150 cl) is like a large, square-shouldered Bordeaux bottle.

Armagnac should be served like any other good brandy and in the same sort of glass (see page 85). One of the makers suggests emptying the glass, then covering it for a few seconds with the palm of the hand, then inhaling the concentrated smells that will remain – this is as good a way as any of judging the general character of this brandy. You can serve Armagnac, according to its quality, as a simple short or long drink, or, with the finest types, as a liqueur. The Pousse Rapière is a drink that began to be popularized some years ago in the region: this is a measure of Armagnac in a tulip-shaped glass, topped up with the slightly sparkling Vin Sauvage of the Gers region, which is very dry, almost harsh. The result is garnished with a slice of orange, the peel of which, squeezed over the Armagnac first, gives a delicious zest. The name – 'swordthrust' – is said to relate to the last stroke when the swordsman, having spitted his opponent on a long Gascon rapier, needed just that extra bit of energy to twist his wrist ('Thews of iron, wrists of steel,' says Dumas describing the musketeers) and withdraw the blade. Prosaically, one feels that it would have been the unfortunate victim who would have benefited from the drink even more – but it is a good mixture anyway.

Visitors to the Distillerie de la Côte Basque, in Bayonne, which produces Armagnac Clés des Ducs (and Izarra) can see how Armagnac is matured. It is also possible in the local shops to buy packs of orange-flavoured Armagnac and the Gers sparkling wine, to make up a Pousse Rapière, although personally I prefer to compose my own mixtures of this kind.

A final point: it should never be assumed that Armagnac is cheaper than Cognac, or indeed that the liqueur-quality brandy of any region is cheaper by comparison with Cognac of the same standard. Armagnac and other brandies may be cheaper in certain export markets, simply because they may not have to bear the costs of the great internationally-known Cognacs as regards advertising and marketing. But no quality brandy can ever be low in price.

MARC AND SIMILAR BRANDIES

Marc (pronounced 'mar') is a colourless spirit, the result of distilling the final squeezings of the mass of compressed grapeskins, pips and stalks that remain after making wine; the most usual procedure is for the 'cake' of debris to be subjected to pressure then for it and the resulting liquid to be distilled, after which it can be matured in wood or kept in glass. At one time, probably every wine-producing region would have used up their final pressings in this way; nowadays it is scarcely worth while for wine makers to bother with distilling, when they can sell their final pressings, if they wish, for use as industrial alcohol and use the grape debris as cattle food. But in some regions a little spirit of this sort does continue to be made.

Marc de Bourgogne is the most famous in France, but there is a marc made in Champagne and, in Alsace, the pressings of the Gewürztraminer grape are used to make a marc de Gewürztraminer. This type of spirit is usually extremely strong and a very little generally suffices even the enthusiastic drinker. Much depends on the skill with which the marc is made, and the way and length of time that it has been matured.

The Italian version of marc is *grappa*, the Portuguese version, *bagaceira*. In Spain, *aguardiente* is the term used for a distillate that can be made from any type of vegetables or fruits, including potatoes; *aguardiente de orujo*, which is strictly the type of *aguardiente* made as marc is made, is the type to order if a grape-based spirits is required. Pisco, a spirit made in several South American countries, is best known in the form that it is available in Peru, where it is, as far as I can ascertain, made from the debris of Muscat wines. (It is possibly most associated with the 'Pisco Sour', a cocktail of 2 ounces Pisco, a teaspoonful of sugar, the white of an egg and three quarters of a 'pony glass' or small wine glass of lemon juice, shaken with crushed ice until foamy, and served with a few drops of Angostura Bitters on the top.) Pisco gets its name from the port of that name in Peru, and the spirit is made in the Pisco, Ica and Chincha Valleys near by. In Chile the cocktail is apparently called an Elqui Sour. The source of my information describes Pisco and elqui as having a 'grapey' flavour

and smell, and being like a 'very new semi-dry white wine'. As I have
never tried Pisco, I cannot vouch for this, although I should not
have supposed a spirit would have smelled and tasted like a wine in
this way – unless one had already drunk quite a lot of it!

FINE

A '*fine*' (pronounced 'feen') is brandy distilled from wine. It is made
in France – hence its name – and distilled from suitable wines to make
an acceptable spirit, as with Cognac, but it must not be confused in
any way with Cognac, Armagnac or any spirit entitled to the name of
a particular region. Although the process of distillation is naturally
subject to various controls, the use of a particular kind of still, or
similar procedures, is not to be assumed with a spirit simply offered
as *une fine*. The English translation of the term is approximately
'grape brandy', and it is perfectly suitable for use in mixtures, or
just with water. In France, *une fine à l'eau* (brandy and water) should
be made with Cognac if one is in a good restaurant, hotel or smart bar;
elsewhere, ordinary grape brandy may be used. Occasionally, however, a *fine* may be specifically designated by its origin, such as Fine
Marne, which comes from the Marne region – and is not to be
confused with Fine Champagne, which (see page 62) is the type of
Cognac from a specific area. In Burgundy, the spirit Fine Bourgogne
is often a distillate made from the lees of the wine. In case anyone is
sufficiently captious as to query why the French require a separate
term for 'brandy', the answer is that, if anyone in France uses the
term *eau de vie* for 'brandy' they may get a choice of a wide range of
spirits, from *alcools blancs* (see page 309) to a variety of digestives and
liqueurs; if they want a brandy, they ask for *une fine* – unless they
specify either Cognac or Armagnac, which of course they may get
anyway! In the type of international bars frequented by those who do
not speak French easily, 'un brandy' will have no need of translation, but out in the country, it may mean nothing – which is why
the term *fine* is a useful addition to the traveller's vocabulary.

OTHER BRANDIES

Because brandy is distilled from wine, it therefore can be and often
is made wherever wine is made. It must, if it is to be of any quality,
be made from wine produced from freshly gathered grapes and, in
these days when Cognac and Armagnac are inevitably expensive as
the result of economic pressures, many people have been able to

utilize good grape brandy, at a lower price, in mixed drinks and in the kitchen, and even for drinking with water or soda. There is no reason why this type of brandy should not be a pleasant drink in its own right, but always, in appraising a spirit of this kind, it is important to bear two things in mind. First, the type of the wine from which the brandy is distilled will be very influential on the end product: the full, flavoury wines such as are often made in southern countries tend, in my experience, to make rather scented, open-textured and possibly slightly superficially appealing brandies. They can be admirable holiday drinks and make a pleasant change from anything more austere.

Second, there are the methods of distillation and maturation: a pot still brandy will be a more individual and subtler product in general than one made in the continuous still. Sometimes a firm will make brandy by both methods and combine the two in a blend, rather like the great blends of Scotch whisky. But the only way to make up your mind about brandies of which you have had no previous experience is to try them – taste is too personal and brandies to varied to generalize.

For example, Asbach, the huge German brandy concern, respected for fine quality, buys wine from wherever they think suitable throughout Europe and distil in a pot still, afterwards maturing the spirit in Limousin oak casks. Asbach-Uralt is their best-known exported brand. Eckes, a giant firm, make a range of brandies in Germany, their brands Chantré and Mariacron being widely known. Fundador is made in Spain by Domecq, the huge sherry firm that dominates Spanish brandy. Domecq had supplied 'Holandas', or Jerez brandy, for the Dutch market from the beginning of the eighteenth century and their particular brandy of this kind came to lead the market. In 1850, an Amsterdam merchant ordered a special consignment, with many stipulations to improve the quality. The various processes involved with making this superior spirit took a long time and eventually the Dutchman refused to take delivery of his brandy, which was virtually forgotten and simply remained in its casks in Jerez. Some time later, Pedro Domecq tasted this remnant and found that the brandy had developed enormously as regards both flavour and bouquet, so in 1874 the first consignment of Fundador was offered for sale. Domecq own a number of distilleries and use both the continuous and pot still methods, employing the continuous still to make the higher-strength spirit and the Cognac-type still for lower-strength brandy. After an initial maturation in wood, brandies are taken to Jerez itself for blending and then undergo a longer period of maturation. Other well-known names of makers of Spanish brandies include Terry, Osborne, Gonzalez Byass of the sherry establishment, and the fine table wine firm of Torres at Vilafranca del Penedés, in Catalonia.

The Italian brandy, Stock (Stock Original 84 V.S.O.P., which has been distilled in Trieste since 1884), is the world's top-selling brandy. Like all other Italian brandies, it has to be aged for at least three years in wood. Stock has establishments in Austria, North and South America, Australia and South Africa as well as eight in Italy. They use both pot and continuous stills. There are other Italian brandy concerns of importance, including Buton – famous for its several styles bottled under the 'Vecchia Romagna' label.

The Greek brandy Metaxas is very well known to holidaymakers. They make a range of different quality brandies, as do the other Greek wineries. All the wineries in Cyprus make brandy, but that of Haggipavlu is the oldest to be made for this market and different from all the others – good though they may be; indeed, a Cyprus Brandy Sour, possibly the most famous mixed drink of this island of wine, can only be made to the satisfaction of critics such as myself when the brandy in it is ETKO-Haggipavlu's Anglias, not even their liqueur-brandy quality.

South African and Australian brandies, different again, are consumed in huge quantities in their homelands and can be excellent. They are made as the various concerns responsible determine, and usually a range of qualities is available from each establishment.

U.S. Brandy

Brandy has probably been made since wine was first made in various parts of the U.S., but today the most important source of American brandy is California. Here the original stills were, as might be expected, pot stills, and the grape used for making wine for distillation the Mission grape; the first brandy may have been made well over two centuries ago, but it is certainly a spirit that has been documented since the latter part of the eighteenth century.

In the nineteenth century, the continuous still was introduced and today this type of still predominates, for obvious reasons: it can produce large quantities of brandy that can be adjusted to the taste of the market. There are, I am informed, some pot stills that remain in operation, but the distillate they produce is mostly used for blending with the continuous still brandy. The grapes used, too, are now drawn from the wide range of varieties cultivated for wine production but, if a brandy is labelled as the product of California then the California Brandy Advisory Board requires that the grapes should have been grown and the spirit distilled in California only. The brandy must be aged in wood – usually in American oak, which gives a particular character to the spirit – for at least two years, but finer quality brandies will be aged for four years or more.

Styles naturally vary considerably, according to the establishment making the brandy, and any permitted additives employed for sweetening and giving more flavour are strictly controlled and are the secrets of the brandy producers. A few 'straight' brandies, which have no additives beyond the caramel which is used for colouring, are made and these, according to Hurst Hannum and Robert S. Blumberg's *Brandies & Liqueurs of the World* (Doubleday, 1976), may sometimes be bottled in bond – the strict control of the bond is a virtual guarantee that the brandy will have been untouched except by authorized authorities: brandies of this kind will have been matured in wood for a minimum of four years.

The fourteen members of the California Brandy Advisory Board produce the bulk of all U.S. brandy, some of them being large-scale producers of wine as well, others concentrating on distilling. Most make a range of brandies, some of them marketed under different labels according to the part of the U.S. in which they are to be sold. Guild Wineries & Distilleries is extremely important and other names include Schenley Distillers, The Christian Brothers, United Vintners, East-Side Winery, Paul Masson, California Growers Winery, California Wine Association; the Beaulieu establishment makes good brandies as well as fine wines and the Cresta Blanca Winery has begun to market vintage brandy. Hannum and Blumberg describe California brandies as 'light, clean, grapey' and stress that they should not be compared with European pot still brandies, but be appraised in their own right.

It is worth knowing, perhaps, that the brandy used for making various kinds of liqueurs and other alcoholic beverages, also for the fortification of port and sherry and wines made in a similar way, is not usually the sort of brandy that one would much enjoy drinking; production of this type of brandy, usually strictly controlled, is directed towards fortifying or strengthening the wines or other beverages, but the brandy in such instances must be subordinate to the other elements, underlying them, and not obtruding itself either by colour or too pronounced a smell or taste. Indeed, when certain fortified wines begin to age and are 'over the top', it is possible to detect the brandy 'coming through', as the fruit and flavour of the wine decline. People who buy fruits in brandy and see a matured spirit used for this purpose are often surprised when they are shown the colourless spirit that is utilized for the purposes I have briefly described.

BRANDY DRINKS

Brandy is traditionally very much a drink associated with medicinal uses. It is not, of course, ever to be considered as a substitute for prescribed medicines, but in certain circumstances, especially in the past, its therapeutic value has been admitted if the ideal medical resources were lacking. For example, in certain forms of shock, loss of blood and snakebite, it used to be found that a very large quantity of brandy, such as would have normally produced complete drunkenness, could be efficacious for stimulating and reviving the system. People usually find it immediately easy to like the smell of a good brandy, whereas many spirits tend to be rather an acquired taste.

Dr Johnson's much quoted remark: 'Claret is for boys, port for men, but he who aspires to be a hero must drink brandy', is a double-edged comment – it is precisely the congenerics or 'impurities' that make good brandy fascinating and attractive that can wreak havoc on the system of anyone who takes too much; a brandy hangover is an experience that no sensible person would willingly risk twice! But brandy, either with water or something else, was a traditional 'morning after' remedy almost up to the present day. 'Nelson's Blood' is more of a stomach-settler and is supposed to have been made up for Lord Nelson, who was a prey to sea-sickness; it consists of half-and-half port and brandy, ideally Cognac, or one-third Cognac to two-thirds port.

The most famous drink based on brandy is probably the Sidecar, which is a cocktail made of half brandy with a quarter of freshly-squeezed lemon juice and a quarter of Cointreau, all shaken together. But a brandy cocktail, which of course can be made with brandies other than Cognac, as taught to me by the late Hon. Frederick Hennessy, consists of $1\frac{1}{2}$ ounces Cognac, 1 ounce Cointreau, a half teaspoonful of sugar syrup and two dashes of Angostura Aromatic Bitters, stirred and then strained into a glass. A Stinger is a drink seldom asked for these days, but if you have rather a coarse brandy available for making a cocktail, it consists of two parts of the brandy and one of white crème de menthe, shaken and then strained. The aperitive that Madame Killian Hennessy evolved and serves at the

Château St Brice, in the heart of the Cognac country, is a particularly refreshing mixture, albeit strong: three parts of Cognac to one of freshly-squeezed lemon juice, plus a little sugar syrup if a slightly sweet drink is liked. All the ingredients must be really cold and, if you like a very crisp drink indeed, omit the sugar syrup.

The Brandy Sour is, according to most cocktail handbooks, 1 ounce brandy, the juice of half a lemon, about half a teaspoonful of sugar and, if you wish, a teaspoonful of egg white, which is then shaken thoroughly and strained into a large glass. But the Brandy Sour of Cyprus, which is a long drink, is neither as sophisticated nor as complicated; it is a generous mixture of Cyprus brandy in a tall glass, about half as much fresh orange juice, a squeeze of fresh lemon, a dash of grenadine or sugar if liked, all of which should either be well chilled or poured over ice cubes; this is topped up with fizzy lemonade or, ideally, 7-Up. In some bars, bottled fruit juices are used, but the result is not the same.

The Alexander is a rich and yet delectable drink that really substitutes for a sweet course. I defy anyone to use it as a cocktail and then be able to eat anything! Shake together equal parts of Cognac, crème de cacao and absolutely fresh, thick cream, then strain into glasses.

HOW TO DRINK BRANDY – ANY BRANDY

The majority of brandy firms with whose products I am familiar make a range of several brandies. Whether they use the symbolism of stars to signify quality, or some form of fancy bottle as well, as a more immediately obvious sign, it must be remembered that these symbols have no international significance. For example, the Briton accustomed to a three star Cognac, for brandy and water or soda, will cause surprise by ordering a three star brandy in, say, Greece – for this will be the sort of tough spirit of the workman's cafe and it's a five star brandy that the traveller will probably prefer.

There may be the straightforward 'brandy' made wherever wine is made, many ordinary types of which, even as far as Cognac and French grape brandy are concerned, will be unlikely to be seen outside their country of origin. This type of brandy will be used for inexpensive drinks and also often in the kitchen.

Then there may be the brandy that is intended to be drunk with water, soda, ginger ale (I understand there are some people who drink brandy with tonic and also brandy with 'coke', but the very notion of such mixtures appals me) or as the basis for a more complicated mixed drink or cocktail involving brandy that should have some distinction. So the quality of this should be good, especially in the simpler mixtures, where no additives except water in one form or other, carbonated or still, is the diluent. You may weaken a coarse, raw brandy by diluting it but you won't change its character. At the same time, there is no point putting a fine liqueur brandy into a cocktail, unless you simply want to show off – it is surprising how many people still do. For brandy and water or brandy and soda a very good brandy, but certainly not a liqueur brandy, is the type that is best to choose.

Finally, there are the liqueur brandies which are intended to be drunk by themselves. Even if, tasting some speciality of this sort in a remote part of the world, you eventually decide that it is really only acceptable with the addition of soda, water or indeed anything, it is fair to try a supposedly top quality brandy alone first. A pertinent instruction is given by the French writer Paul de Cassagnac, who was once told by a Cognac maker: 'Chew your brandy, my son, chew it as if it were a mouthful of beefsteak.'

Anyone seriously interested in drinking brandy – and the spirit is expensive enough to warrant some discrimination in its selection and service – should also consider whether, for the simpler brandy drinks, the spirit seems more agreeable with ice or without. It is a matter of personal preference as to whether you like this or not and also somewhat depends on whether you want a long, refreshing drink or a short, more stimulating one. Of course, the ice cubes will dilute the brandy and any added water or soda should therefore be measured in smaller quantities, but it will also change the impression that the brandy makes on the palate. Ice cubes made from tap water may actually impart a flavour, however slight, that can adversely affect a good brandy. At one time I drank a great deal of brandy and water with ice and eventually had to make all my ice cubes with Malvern or similar still spring water, because the recycled London tap water, used straight, resulted in scum on the surface of the drink and the ice cubes made from this tap water had much the same effect.

It is worth bearing in mind that, because brandy is the spirit of wine, it is possible to serve it before a meal at which rather special wines may accompany the food, without the clash of 'grape with grain' occurring. At the same time, brandy in its finer qualities is in itself demanding and the greater brandies may make such a remarkable initial impression at a meal of this kind that they 'wipe the eye' of the wines to follow. This can happen if, for example, you serve a liqueur brandy before a meal – and it may be too strong for subsequent appreciation of the food and wines anyway. Similarly, if a brandy from some region or country that is not already familiar to you is used for a preprandial drink or in a cocktail, it is worth trying the drink in various forms beforehand; some of the Mediterranean brandies, for example, can be very assertive as regards fragrance and tend to be on the sweet side. This can mean that they risk throwing out of proportion any carefully measured mixed drink and also that they may seem too much of a good thing by way of an aperitive; better for a drink between times.

The brandy glass

For cocktails and long drinks use a large or small glass, of virtually any reasonable suitable shape and size; even cut glasses and tumblers, which do not really help the spirit much, may be used if you wish. But for brandy in the liqueur category, there is only one basic type of glass, to show off this superb spirit and justify its cost. Unfortunately, it is still rare to find brandy served correctly. Because of the many occasions when ignorant glassmakers, stupid sommeliers, idiotic hosts and conceited guests insist on serving and drinking brandy in a wholly ridiculous and degrading way, it is worth condemning the apparatus with which they complicate this otherwise enjoyable procedure – and destroy the brandy as well.

The use of a gigantic glass for fine brandy is wrong. As François Hine says, 'I do not wish to float a goldfish.' Not only are these huge balloons ostentatious and out of proportion but, by over-aerating the brandy, they result in the fragrance being thrown off within the globe of air they encircle before it can easily reach the nose of the drinker and certainly before he can enjoy the fragrance at the same time as the flavour. As the spirit has to crawl to him across a desert of glass, the experience of drinking brandy out of such a vessel is virtually confined to the way it looks (appalling to the sincere lover of brandy, who also wants to smell and drink it: see page 67).

The ideal brandy glass has a stem and, although it will be about the size of an 8-ounce wine glass, the shapes may vary: some are like goblets, with rather more incurving rims, others resemble the sherry copita, and have a slightly funnel-like shape, the top of the globe or bowl of the glass straightening up. But the purpose of a good glass for brandy is that the aroma should be directed towards the drinker's nose, either being swirled towards this by the incurving sides of the glass which will direct it in an upward spiral, or, with the more funnel-like shape, concentrating the fragrance in the bowl and then sending the smell straight up the sides, towards the point at which the lips will meet the spirit. The essential is that the glass should not be too big to be held in the palm of one hand – or between the palms of someone with small hands. It is the warmth of the hand alone, gently conveyed through the thin glass – ideally crystal – that will release the initial fragrance. The thinness of the glass is really important; it should just veil the spirit from the drinker, never obtruding its own feel and texture. This is why cut glasses are to be avoided. They have to be thickish to sustain the cutting and it's almost impossible to forget this thick rim in your lips. There are, I know, those who like the appearance of drinks in a faceted glass, but I prefer to see the contents of my glass without any distortion of its colour and shades of tones.

It is only fair to say that one firm, Rémy Martin, do not approve of warming brandy even by the heat of the hand. They assert that, as this slight warming will accentuate the aroma of the brandy, it will distort the experience of the spirit's bouquet. They assert that their own Fine Champagne V.S.O.P. can be best appraised in a glass that is almost straight-sided and that the brandy can be enjoyed at its best even by adding an ice cube to the glass, but certainly not by warming it. I happen not to agree with this as far as the finer liqueur brandies are concerned, but it is a point of view worth investigating and one can only make up one's mind by experience.

Anyone accustomed to wine drinking will know that no glass from which a bouquet and aroma are to be enjoyed should be filled more than by a half or two-thirds. As far as fine brandy is concerned, the proportions are probably for one-third in the glass.

The point on which every single person who knows anything about brandy is unanimous, however, is that the glass should never be heated by a flame or other artificial means. Not only does this risk the drinker actually burning his hand and the stink of the spirit lamp interfering with the bouquet of the brandy, but the violent shock to the brandy itself, put into a glass heated like this, causes it to fling off all its subtle smells and, by the time the drinker even begins to get at it, these are gone. Make the comparison if you wish – you can't revive a cooked brandy once you have subjected it to violent heating and if you simply want the experience of a spirity liquid from which the smell and most of the taste have been forcefully flung, go on heating the brandy glass. Otherwise, simply use the palm of the hand, like any civilized drinker.

5. Gin

Gin has a far more interesting history than those who merely think of it as a basis for many mixed drinks might suppose. It seems to be the only spirit that has progressively risen in the social scale from humble beginnings. Even though many people who would have ranked as at least moderately superior certainly did drink it, they did not usually publicize the fact, nor did they often order it in company or include it in the drinks served as refreshments in their own houses when they entertained their equals. It was what may be categorized as a 'fish and chip' type of drink until very recent times.

Because gin is made all over the world today and because, in most people's minds, it is primarily intended to be used in mixtures, it tends to be a somewhat disregarded spirit. However, its traditions are as impressive as the scale of its production.

As we know it today, gin seems to have been first made by Franciscus de la Boë (1614–72), Professor of Medicine at Leyden University in Holland; his name is sometimes given as 'Sylvius', a play on the Latin word for 'wood' and the French 'bois', which is similar to Boë. It was he who evolved a spirit from rye produced in a pot still; this was then redistilled with juniper and other ingredients.

Juniper (*Juniperus communis*), a member of the cypress family, has been known from early times as a diuretic (something that increases the excretion of urine) and physicians had therefore begun to associate it with the treatment of diseases of the kidneys, liver and heart, and also to use it in cases of dropsy, to avoid the retention of fluid in the body. 'Juniper wine' had in fact been made in France somewhat earlier than de la Boë's distillate, its composition being credited to one of the bastard sons of Henri IV.

As early as 1575, a type of gin seems to have been sold by the firm of Lucas Bols of Amsterdam. This establishment was not allowed to carry on business inside the city, because the use of a still was regarded as a fire risk among the many wooden buildings in the town, so Lucas Bols set his still up in the outskirts, in what was known as 'the little shed' (in Dutch, the expression is *'t Lootsje*), on the banks of a stream which was used for cooling the distillates. By 1612, Amsterdam had extended to include 'the little shed', and the stream was enlarged to form 'the Rose Canal'. This suburb seems to have been a pretty place, and the Dutch liked to take walks out to the Bols distillery where they could then have a drink. Later, when the invading French troops occupied the area, they referred to this part of Amsterdam as 'Le Jardin', which is why the Dutch began to call it 'Jordaan'. Lucas Bols have moved to more up-to-date premises now, but they still retain a little bar at 106 Rosengracht (Rose Canal) dating from the seventeenth century, on the site of the former 'little shed'.

It is possible that the juniper flavouring used in gin was originally adopted because the distillate of rye tasted unpleasant. Anyway, the spirit swiftly gained in popularity, especially as this period – the late sixteenth and the seventeenth centuries – was the time of enormous expansion in trade in Holland to export markets. The Dutch were also renowned explorers, but those travelling to the East Indies were easy victims to fevers and similar tropical diseases; a strong drink, either as a stimulant or a warming draught in case of chills, would have obviously been popular, and the juniper in such early gins could also have been regarded as therapeutic.

The French word for juniper is *'genièvre'*; the Dutch word is *'jineverbes'*. It is therefore quite easy to see how, before there was any attempt at the regularization of spelling, the word for a juniper-flavoured spirit became, variously 'jenever', 'genever', 'geneva', sometimes with capital letters – which resulted eventually in some people assuming that it had something to do with the Swiss city, Geneva. There is, of course, no connection of any sort. However, the extreme forms of Protestantism – Lutheranism and Calvinism – which did have their strongholds in liberal Switzerland, were linked in sympathy with many Protestant Dutch during their struggles against the Catholic Spaniards and French, who from the sixteenth century were striving to dominate what eventually became the powerful Dutch republic. I think, therefore, that 'geneva' was possibly an emotive word for many people at this time, the use of it casually implying something good – with about as much significance as the expressions 'French perfume', 'Swiss watch' or 'German camera' do today. Anyway, the term for the Dutch spirit was easy enough for the foreign troops, mercenaries and armies on the side of

Protestantism, to pronounce. Queen Elizabeth I, albeit with reluctance, allowed English troops to fight for the Dutch, and it was in 1585 that Sir Philip Sidney died of gangrene after being wounded at the Battle of Zutphen. So it is easy to see how English soldiers returning from these and subsequent wars in Holland, where they had learnt the value of the spirit-created 'Dutch courage' both in bad weather or at times of short rations, would refer to the spirit as 'Hollands' or, more simply, abbreviating its Dutch name, as 'gin'. Polite society used the term 'Hollands' until at least the middle of the nineteenth century, and this term is still included in the 1976 edition of *The Concise Oxford Dictionary*, *The Shorter Oxford Dictionary* citing the first use of the word as in 1788. But 'gin' is noted in this dictionary as being used as early as 1714.

The English then began to make a type of gin for themselves, but it seems to have been mostly of dubious quality. They had a reputation for drinking quite heavily in Tudor times, but it was not then considered good manners to get drunk except: 'in some private gentlemen's houses, and with some captains and soldiers, and with the vulgar citizens and artisans, large and intemperate drinking is used; but in general the great and better part of the English hold all excess blameworthy and drunkenness is a reproachful vice', said Fynes Morison, in 1617. However, 'foreign influences' were blamed for many trends of which the more conservative English disapproved, for, said historian and antiquary William Camden (1551–1623), 'The English, who hitherto had, of all the northern nations, shewn themselves the least addicted to immoderate drinking, and been commended for their sobriety, first learn'd, in these Netherland wars, to swallow a large quantity of intoxicating liquor, and to destroy their own health by drinking that of others.' Camden was possibly super-patriotic. But even Thomas Nashe, the poet and playwright (1567–1601), who was certainly no killjoy, commented that, as regards 'Superfluietie in drink', it was 'a sinne, that ever since we have mixt ourselves with the Low-countries, is counted honourable'.

Gin was not, in the Elizabethan, Jacobean and Caroline periods, considered particularly smart as a drink, because French brandy was the dominant spirit (being both cheap and easy to get from across the Channel). It was only after the accession of William of Orange in 1688 that it became patriotic to follow the example of 'Dutch Billy' and drink gin. Adherents to the Stuart cause still drank brandy.

In 1690, however, the import of French brandy and other foreign spirits was forbidden and, although it is only possible to cite figures for gin legally produced (there may have been as much again illicitly on sale), the English drank 500,000 gallons. Shortage of grain crops caused the authorities concern over the quantity being used for distillation, yet, by 1727, gin consumption totalled 5 million gallons and it was 11 million by 1733. From 1690 onwards, anybody was allowed to distil and sell gin or spirits in general if a notice was posted on the house advising of the intention to do so and, after ten days, the premises were automatically 'licensed'.

The Worshipful Company of Distillers, founded in the reign of Charles I (see page 39) had been granted the exclusive right to distil gin both in London and for twenty-one miles around. But Queen Anne ('Brandy Nan', who liked her tipple in the form of 'cold tea' poured from an apparently innocent teapot – some of the very large teapots dating from this period were certainly intended to hold more potent hot beverages than tea) cancelled the privileges of The Distillers' Company just at the time when the huge increase in gin drinking would have benefited from widespread and strict controls. Most unpleasant types began to be sold, from almost any outlet – stalls, barrows, itinerant pedlars, tobacconists, people ostensibly running stables or some form of 'shop', and also at the barber's shop or in the brothel. Can it be that it is from this time that gin begins to become associated with 'women's complaints' and as a means of aborting? Certainly gin seems to have acquired a vaguely 'sexy' set of associations – not as an aphrodisiac, but as a female fortifier. Other spirits do not seem to have been so associated, although I do remember that, before 1939, a piece of advice sometimes given to young girls who found themselves in an isolated place with an importunate man, was to make him drink copiously of brandy (if it were available) so that 'desire should outrun performance'. Gin, however, was probably the original 'tart's tipple' simply because it was easily bought and cheap.

The ingredients of much of this eighteenth-century 'gin' were often fearful. They might include aniseed, turpentine and even sulphuric acid. It was estimated that, in the Cities of London and Westminster, one house in four was selling spirits. Hogarth's famous picture 'Gin Lane' portrays both the excesses and tragedies of wretched people pawning anything they possessed to pay for the spirit, and above the door of a dram shop is the famous sign 'Drunk for 1d. Dead drunk for 2d. Clean straw for nothing'. The appalling ingredients, as much as the quantity of gin consumed, were responsible for the shocking effect of gin on the poor, and those in authority attempted to improve matters by imposing a tax on gin and requiring those who sold it to purchase a licence. This, like many repressive methods intended to remedy ills, merely resulted in a fall in the sales of such gin as was reputable and the evolving of another frightful spirit known as 'Parliamentary brandy', which one contemporary writer described as 'a fiery lake that sets the brain in flames, burns up the entrails and scorches every part within'. But gin had by this time become part of the British economy; the abundant grain harvests of the early part of the eighteenth century – which were common in other countries in Europe and resulted in much distilling there, too – meant that it was necessary to make use of at least part of the crop for distillation, in order to dispose of the surplus.

The British 'Gin act' of 1729 was repealed and, in 1733, another one introduced, which stipulated that spirits could not be sold outside dwelling houses – with the result that every house immediately became a potential dram shop, selling gin! Successive legislation thereafter slowly began to curb the indiscriminate sale of gin by licensing premises that might be used for drinking; this encouraged such distillers who were already properly licensed, but there was still an enormous quantity of illegal gin made. A gin licence cost £50, but a wine licence only a few shillings, so that all types of gin, good and bad, tinged with wine and possibly flavoured, would therefore be sold by a 'wine merchant', who was really an outlet for illicit gin. As a 'medicinal drink' it could be obtained at the chemist, and it seems that it was from this time that the many sobriquets for gin came into the common speech – The Cure for the Blue Devils, My Lady's Eye Water, Daffy's Elixir, Mother's Milk, Lap, Cuckold's Comfort, Ladies' Delight, Blue Ruin. It has been estimated that the English consumed about six gallons of gin a head per annum at this period.

Gin had definitely acquired an accepted place in the home by this time, especially the 'real thing', even if this were not bought in the usual way. True, many people would have said in public that they kept it for their servants or merely as a semi-medicinal spirit. But I don't suppose that the nobility were wholly indifferent to it, and even the most respectable of ladies might have heard that this spirit was 'helpful'.

Parson Woodforde, the country vicar in Norfolk, whose diaries from 1758 to 1802 give an illuminating and charming account of ordinary life, paid 3d for gin and water at Quantrell's Gardens in 1774, and, in 1776, took a bottle of gin on a winter fishing trip; he appears to have used it as a reviver and warmer for, in 1779, his 'boy Jack [a servant] had another touch of the Ague about noon. I gave him a dram of gin at the beginning of the fit' – though he goes on rather alarmingly: 'and pushed him into one of my Ponds and ordered him to bed immediately and he was better after it and had nothing of the cold fit after, but was very hot'.

The Parson certainly kept gin in his house, for, on 29 March 1777: 'Andrews the Smuggler brought me this night about 11 o'clock a bagg of Hyson Tea 6 Pd. weight. He frightened us a little by whistling under the Parlour Window just as we were going to bed. I gave him some Geneva and paid him for the tea at 10/6 per Pd.' Again, in 1786: 'Had a Tub of Gin brought me this Evening from Robt Buck of Honingham by my Man Benn Leggatt', and, the following day: 'Bottled of my Gin this morning – 19 bottles.' The duty on these imported commodities made it almost respectable for countryfolk, whose lands and gardens often afforded a private route for smugglers (as happens at parts of the French–Spanish border today), to buy such items as reasonably as they could. Crabbe describes the activities of the smugglers in *The Village* (1783), in which he mentions that, if detected, they would disperse and try to escape in different directions or else try by

> . . . yielding part (which equal knaves demand)
> To gain a lawless passport through the land

– in other words, giving their pursuers a share of the smuggled goods as a bribe to be allowed to escape.

Woodforde received regular supplies of spirits, for, on 29 December 1786: 'Had another Tub of Gin and another of the best Coniac Brandy brought me this Evening abt 9. We heard a thump at the Front Door about that time, but did not know what it was, till I went out and found the 2 Tubs – but nobody there.' Indeed, 'Moonshine' John Buck, one of the Parson's tenant farmers, appears to have been operating on a large scale in the neighbourhood of Weston Longeville, in Norfolk, and there are references to several 'Bucks', including his son, who one supposes would have helped him. Moonshine Buck was unlucky enough to break one of the Parson's decanters at a tithe audit supper early in his ministry, but the Bucks apparently remained his friends and, accompanied by his niece Nancy, Woodforde visited John and his wife. The Parson was apprehensive – as must have been most of his parishioners – when Buck was informed on to the excise by someone, relieved when he got off with a small fine and grieved when 'poor Mr John Buck was buried in Weston Church about Noon' in 1800. Woodforde was then too ill himself to take the service (he died in 1802) and it was conducted by his curate. In 1788 there is a practical note to one of Woodforde's transactions:

'June 6: To my Man Ben for things pd. £4.4.8, that is £1.18s.od. for a Tub of Coniac Brandy of four gallons by Moonshine Buck and £2.6s.od. for two Tubs of Geneva of 4 Gallons each by ditto and the odd 8d. for Horse Shoes removed.' (So that the 'Five and twenty ponies, trotting through the dark, Brandy for the parson, baccy for the clerk', as in Kipling's 'Smuggler's Song', should make less sound than if shod with iron shoes) In March 1789 (the year of the French Revolution), Woodforde's entry indicates a possibly typical personal, even English attitude: '. . . the happy restoration of His Majesty's Health. [George III, whose periodic fits of what seemed madness but which are now thought to be the illness porphyria, had alarmed the nation.] I gave to our People in the Kitchen on the Occasion a Bottle of Gin to drink the King's Health this Evening after Supper, and the Queen's to Morrow.'

Woodforde made a charitable and medicinal use of gin when, in 1790 in July, 'a poor Woman . . . with a small Child with her was taken very ill with a violent Pain . . . by my great Gates and was laid down in the road. I went out to her and gave her a good Glass of Gin.' And it is probable that he had recurrent need of the spirit, for, on 13 December 1794: 'Busy all the Morning almost in bottling two tubs of Gin, that came by Moonshine this Morn, very early.'

A domestic item that Parson Woodforde may have known about is also associated with the smuggling of gin in the eighteenth century – the rolling-pin. Traditionally, rolling-pins were made of glass and, being hollow, were also used to hold salt; the pin was hung up in the kitchen fire-place – the alcove where fire-irons, stores, spit and implements were kept – not as some comic 'weapon' for the house-wife, as in a Punch and Judy show, but so that the expensive salt might be kept dry. Salt was not merely a condiment but a preservative and hams would have been hung in the kitchen chimney for smoking after being soaked in brine or salted. Towards the end of the eighteenth century, however, the development of British glassware firms resulted in their making many ornamental rolling-pins, in coloured, striped or decorated glass; these were used almost as decorations, – and certainly as love tokens – very much like the hand-carved spoons, which gave the verb 'spooning' to the language, because a man would give the spoon to a girl, much in the same way as the fraternity pin is given in the U.S. today. The hollow rolling-pins could be used to hold more luxurious commodities than salt, and sweetmeats, tea and sugar were some of the lines 'gift packaged' in a pretty pin, which would have been a very acceptable present. Sometimes a motto or loving message might be inscribed on the pin.

When the pin was in use for making pastry it would be filled with water – to keep the dough cool, just as many modern glass pins are filled with iced water today. Sailors in the eighteenth century, finding that British glass pins were popular both at home and abroad, bought them in vast quantities as little gifts for their girls in every port. When they came back from abroad, however, they would fill up their surplus pins with duty-free gin, which of course, being colourless, looked like water even if the customs officers did notice that the ratings were coming home with a lot of love tokens in hand.

Gin is also associated with Admiral Lord Nelson. It is related that, using the island of Minorca as a harbour, he gave the inhabitants the idea of making gin to provide for the needs of the sailors wanting a spirit drink, there probably being a shortage of rum on the Mediterranean station. It may be possible that Admiral Collingwood, Nelson's second-in-command, who took over after Nelson's death at Trafalgar in 1805, was more influential in this, but anyway there is still gin made on Minorca and one brand bears Nelson's name. Those who have tasted it tell me that at least one of the types still sold resembles Dutch gin rather than London gin, as it has a more distinct flavour of juniper.

In the eighteenth century the availability of gin for the general public had become, in a way, associated with the happiness of the poor – so that those who wanted to curb the consumption of gin were hated as interfering with liberty. Informers on those who transgressed the restrictions governing sales were so loathed that the authorities were almost powerless to prevent them being attacked once they were known – some were thrown into the Thames, and a magistrate who upheld the laws might be pelted in the streets. Dr Johnson, who, as researchers into social matters must sometimes feel, said something about everything, is reported to have been against the taxing of gin.

One man who informed against those breaking the law turned the mass craving for gin to his profit, once he realized that the prisons were crammed and that he might find his occupation gone at any moment by continuing simply to report. This was Captain Dudley Bradstreet, who rented a ground-floor room in the City of London and put the sign of a cat in the window; people outside in the street would put coins into the slot in the cat's mouth and ask it to give them some gin, this – or a fluid passing for gin – was then trickled through a pipe that was hidden underneath the cat's paw. Customers could hold a cup or jug under the concealed pipe but some simply bent down and opened their mouths to catch the gin. Bradstreet made as much as £220 in a single month by this trade, would-be customers blocked the street – Blue Anchor Alley – and he only gave up his business when many people began to copy him. (But he probably retired comfortably.)

By the nineteenth century, the establishment of many licensed premises selling beer – the first 'pubs' – also promoted the building of often elaborately decorated 'gin palaces', of which there were more than 5000 in London by 1830. (Remember that the area of even Greater London was really small – Hampstead, Kensington and many areas of the modern metropolis were country villages and the great estates in Mayfair had acres of parks and gardens, so that the total of outlets for gin was enormous in proportion to the area of London as it was then.)

The poor of the Industrial Revolution were desperate for some form of warmth and stimulus; the inexplicable population explosion of the early nineteenth century, prior to the real period of industrialization, meant that thousands thronged to the public places of refreshment. Dickens, in *Sketches by Boz* (1836), described a gin palace, the brilliantly lit interior, furnished with polished mahogany and brass, glittering engraved glass and mirrors – such as may sometimes be seen in many old-fashioned British public houses to this day – and 'gas lights in richly gilt burners . . . perfectly dazzling when contrasted with the darkness and dirt we have just left'. (The streets were still hardly lit.) Dickens's characters Fagin, Bill Sikes, Mr Bumble and Sairey Gamp, the horrible midwife, are all described drinking gin, Mrs Gamp taking it from a teapot. No wonder the poor were drawn to the glittering places where light, company and even illusory and short-term cheer were to be had at low cost. Cruikshank, the most famous illustrator of Dickens and an ardent temperance worker, wrote that 'gin is become a great demi-god, a mighty spirit dwelling in gaudy gold-be-plastered temples.'

Also, by the beginning of the nineteenth century, gin had become a more openly respectable drink, hospitals made use of it instead of brandy as a stimulant, and Lord Byron casually stated: 'Gin and water is the source of all my inspiration.' Gin's medicinal properties were certainly useful in 1815, when the aged Field-Marshal Blücher, hastening from Quatre Bras to the assistance of Wellington at Waterloo, fell off his horse and received a reviving massage of gin and onions; after this he went on to join the Iron Duke and achieved their joint victory over Napoleon. The use of gin on this occasion, of course, was a chance one; almost any spirit would have served as a rub – but the Prussians carried gin as a multi-purpose spirit.

King William IV gave the Royal Arms to Sir Felix Booth's Distillery in 1833, and Lord Kinross mentions the 'Sailor King's friendship with Booth (see page 113) thinking it possible that the monarch could have acquired a taste for gin in the Royal Navy, where it had by now begun to be drunk by the officers, although the lower deck still kept to rum, which was issued daily to them (see pages 183–4, 185).

Later Victorian writers make a number of mentions of gin: Thackeray refers to it rather slightingly in *Pendennis*, Hazlitt is reported to have drunk far too much of it, but Artemus Ward mentions gin and tansy, and Ruskin 'gin and bitters for breakfast'. Scott refers to it in rather a disreputable context in *Guy Mannering*, though Thomas Hood is more enthusiastic:

> Gin! Gin! a drop of Gin!
> When, darkly, Adversity's days set in,
> And the friends and peers
> Of earlier years
> Prove warm without, but cold within.

The invention of the Coffey or continuous still (see page 45) enabled a better-quality spirit to be made, and gin now began to be served with soda water and bitters, as well as being drunk straight. Gin and soda, garnished with lemon, was known as 'the British soldier's delight'; gin and ginger beer was called 'Hatfield'; and the Thames watermen liked 'Purl' to warm them on cold mornings – this was gin and hot beer. Flashman, the bad boy of *Tom Brown's Schooldays* (1851), drank gin punch.

The new type of gin coming on to the British market in the mid nineteenth century was what eventually became known as 'dry', the former type of sweetish gin that was most popular being exemplified by one called 'Old Tom'. I cannot find whether or not this relates to Captain Bradstreet's cat in any way (see page 94), but the label of the brand Old Tom showed a tomcat on a barrel and it is supposed to have been first made by Thomas Chamberlain, of Hodges' Distillery, hence Old Tom; Boord's of London, who were founded in 1726, adopted the Old Tom label in about 1849 (see page 113). This sweetened type of gin is still popular in some northern countries, notably Finland, and also nowadays in California.

Drunkenness directly attributable to the consumption of gin was, however, a serious problem in the nineteenth century. Thomas Carlyle described gin as 'Liquid madness sold at tenpence the quartern', and the French visitors Taine and Besant remarked on its influence everywhere, Taine noting that men were 'dead drunk on the pavement in Chelsea', and Besant commenting in horror at the appearance of the drinkers who turned a 'ghostly, ghastly corpse-like kind of blue'. (Someone who served in the Mediterranean in the Second World War told me that after a copious intake of Italian gin he and all his colleagues also turned blue, in spite of the spirit apparently being at least potable.) The temperance movement had a hard and long fight against such appalling excesses; working people counted on even the transitorily cheering effect of gin in many conditions of hardship, and consumption at a high level continued. Billingsgate fishmongers, for example, drank quantities of gin and milk.

Gin arrived in the drawing-room in the nineteenth century, forming part of the refreshments offered openly during respectable social activities. It was still rather a modest, even socially inferior, sort of drink; in Trollope's *Ayala's Angel* (1881) the high-minded heroine looks down on her uncle, who drinks gin instead of port, and Richard Jefferies (1848–87) refers to the type of English county town that had only a 'gin and water market', the gin being the spirit taken to confirm a deal – the tradition of 'sealing the bargain' in a commercial version of a loving cup being a tradition that persists even today, when the persons involved in a deal say 'Let's have a drink on it.' By the time Bernard Shaw wrote *Pygmalion* (1912) it was quite in keeping that Eliza Doolittle's mother should have been reported by the heroine to have been a gin drinker. The music hall song of this period 'Don't have any more, Mrs Moore' warned that 'too many double gins give the ladies double chins'. Indeed, I remember, as a teenager in the Second World War, that my contemporaries and I shared a vague notion that gin produced bags under the eyes, and therefore was supposed to result in one looking old before one's time.

The Victorians, with their odd squeamishness about concealing the legs of furniture and disguising the existence of almost all natural functions, had silver decanter labels with 'Nig' on them, so as to prevent servants knowing that there was actually gin in the house. The Victorians also had labels for 'White wine', which used to puzzle me: why should they have kept white wine in labelled decanters in this way? But 'white wine' was a euphemism for gin.

The great gin distilleries, of which Booth's is the senior still to be in operation (Robert Bowthe was a vintner as early as 1569), became bigger with the 'cocktail age' of the 1930s. When, after the First World War, the United States prohibited the sale of alcoholic beverages (see page 47) the quantity of 'bath-tub gin' made illicitly there recalled the horrors of the frightful period of the mid eighteenth century in England. For fourteen years, the bootleggers selling gin into the U.S. did fantastic business, even though the 'gin' they sold might contain less than 1 per cent of the real thing: for all kinds of bases were used to make the spirit, including wood alcohol – which was a true killer. Even Eau de Cologne and the antifreeze from cars were used. Gin that might have started life as the genuine article might be diluted and 'stretched' before it ever got into the U.S. either via Canada, or the French islands of Saint-Pierre-et-Miquelon, off the Newfoundland coast, from which cases of the spirit could be floated ashore and recovered by the bootleggers from the sea. The revolting 'gin' of this period was certainly a major factor that contributed to the popularity of and fashion for mixed drinks, because the flavour of the additives could conceal the horrible taste of the base spirit. All this, however, only increased world demand for London dry gin – the 'real thing' – and the market for this boomed when Prohibition came to an end.

The vogue for mixed drinks, especially the dry martini, influenced by the popularity of fashions in everything stemming from the United States, became tremendous throughout the world in the years immediately before 1939. Barmen of certain fashionable hotels, restaurants and clubs quickly became world famous for their cocktails. Travel was then becoming possible and enjoyable even for those who were not particularly wealthy, so tourists, especially the more conspicuous members of what might be somewhat disparagingly referred to as 'café society', could find something familiar by way of refreshment when they walked in to Harry's Bar in Paris, or the Savoy in London. The term 'American bar', which has never, as far as I know, been defined, implies that a wide range of mixed drinks is available there (whether they really are or not) and the phrase still possesses a vague glamour, trailing from the cocktail age of the twenties. Clubs, in which people could order alcoholic drinks outside the more limited licensing hours of ordinary bars and restaurants, now enabled members to spend an evening (also sometimes with dancing) without incurring the expense of a large meal; sometimes they merely had 'breakfast' of bacon and eggs, kedgeree or kippers, in the small hours, as well as a drink. This was an economical attraction for the London set of youngish men and women who might be 'smart' in the columnists' and magazine sense of the word, but who, in the depression of the early thirties, before 'ladies and gentlemen' all had jobs that were taken seriously, might not have much money in their pockets. The night-clubs of the various capital cities appreciated the publicity value of such members, whose activities were chronicled in the social columns of glossy publications – and who liked to lead fashion by drinking mixtures that the ordinary person had never tasted and might never think of trying.

Except for pre-mixed bottled 'cocktails' which were not very highly thought of, although drunk copiously, I suppose the ordinary middle- or lower middle-class household, whether in the suburbs of London or the provinces, such as that in which I grew up before 1939, seldom mixed anything more exotic than 'Gin and It' (Italian sweet vermouth), or 'Gin and French' (dry vermouth). Sometimes in a smart bar or club one might have gin and lime (Rose's Lime Juice conducted a huge advertising campaign linked to the newish craze for the boyishly slim figure); gin and orange or peach bitters, or 'pink gin'; and, just possibly, gin and Dubonnet. But for the ordinary person, and certainly the ordinary woman, this was about the most exotic limit. Robin McDouall, one time secretary to the Travellers' Club in Pall Mall and an authoritative gastronomic journalist, was secretary to a rich and well-born (though not aristocratic) couple living in the English midlands in the 1930s. He writes that, in those days 'drinks before luncheon or dinner were a post First War innovation and still thought rather dashing'. He remembers that the household did have 'whisky and soda on the sideboard – though the takers were rather frowned upon [by the older members of the family] . . . After tennis or squash we young ones might creep into the dining-room and find some whisky . . . the next drink was five minutes before the eight o'clock dinner gong. No suggestion of a cocktail and no time to make one.' It seems unlikely that the lady of that household would have ever seen gin 'above stairs'. Novelist Barbara Cartland, who was a débutante in the 1920s, notes in her autobiography, *We Danced All Night* (Hutchinson, 1971), that:

English drinking habits had been very conventional for a long time. No drinks were ever offered before meals. If a man wanted a whisky and soda before dinner, he went to the smoking-room, or sought out the butler in the pantry. It was unthinkable for a woman to drink at such a time. Even in 1937, in my father-in-law's house, if I wanted a glass of sherry before dinner my husband had to fetch it for me up to my bedroom. There was no question of my being offered one downstairs.

It was therefore not surprising that cocktails being drunk in night-clubs was all part of the atmosphere of sin now being played up by the newspapers until it rose into an angry denunciation of 'flaming youth'.

Middle-class young 'ladies' would never have gone into an ordinary public-house bar unaccompanied; indeed, they probably wouldn't have been allowed in by the licensee! Older women might use bars and pubs, usually in company, but these were not casually visited by respectable young females, except, of course, a few of the fashionable haunts of the big cities. And the young woman in any place of refreshment would have hesitated before ordering anything based on spirits, unless she was really of the 'smart set', a foreigner – or on the stage. Enid Bagnold, who, both as journalist, playwright and wife of Sir Roderick Jones, head of Reuters for many years, knew many worlds and their ways well, gives a significant line to a character in her novel *The Loved and Envied* (1951): in this, which takes place after the Second World War, a woman in her late forties remarks, apropros of drinking a cocktail, that, 'In my youth, only people who wrote about the slums mentioned gin.' In Angela Thirkell's novel *A Double Affair* (1957), two young men taking out to dinner the girls to whom they are engaged, drink beer while the food and wines with it are ordered; the girls (who do drink sherry at parties in the homes of family and friends) have nothing to drink by way of aperitive, even though they are sitting in the hotel lounge, not the bar, in a country town.

In Noel Coward's revue of the 1930s, *Words and Music*, a chorus of debutantes sang:

> 'For gin, in cruel
> Sober truth
> Supplies the fuel
> For flaming youth.'

The idea of 'hard liquor' was that of a formidable drink, that might affect you in many ways – and even lead swiftly to intoxication and addiction. The sort of scenes depicted in F. Scott Fitzgerald's novels (and his life) and much American fiction of this period between the wars were not, however, usual – they attracted attention mainly because they were exceptional. By this time, of course, gin was widely available all over the world and, once the period of Prohibition was over in the U.S., people went on drinking gin because they liked it.

After the Second World War gin began to be more widely featured in the simpler mixtures such as gin and tonic that are now served everywhere. It is interesting to remember, however, that when T. S. Eliot's *The Cocktail Party* was first produced in the early 1950s it was slightly unusual to order gin and water, as the strange guest does in the play; the setting is that of a well-to-do and fairly smart household, but I can remember a slight rustle of surprise and 'What an odd drink!' when Sir Henry Harcourt-Reilly asked for it. Gin and water, however, with the addition of sugar and lemon (the recipe is sometimes varied as gin and brandy) was a Victorian tipple, called Gin Twist, half and half', and William Maginn wrote 'A Thirstimony' in favour of it.

This is the point at which the most famous cocktail in the world should be discussed because, even if it did exist in some form prior to the twentieth century, it certainly came to dominate the mixed-drinks scene throughout the world in this century. The dry martini, since a court judgement, has been declared such an internationally known mixture as not to require capital letters. It is certainly the world's most discussed cocktail. (Though I have a suspicion that, if it ever were possible to take a poll of gin-based drinks consumed in the 1970s, the gin and tonic might rival it in the U.K.) Endless arguments have been and doubtless will be devoted to how it originated as well as to its composition. My friend John Doxat has written an entire book about it (*Stirred – Not Shaken*, Hutchinson Benham, 1976). It never seems to have had the slightest success as a pre-mixed made-up drink in bottle, and in many of the more trivial novels of North American life in which young people, trying to get on in the social rat-race, entertain important guests, the stress on whether or not the martinis are approved of is astonishing; as an achievement and status symbol it appears to dominate U.S. suburbia. If the mixing of the drink were as much fun as John Doxat makes it sound, this might not matter – but I was astonished to find that, in the 1960s in London, a dinner given in a well-staffed flat by an American businessman was delayed a considerable time while the host would mess around making more martinis – it seemed quite unnecessary, especially to the youngest and hungriest present!

The dry martini is a twentieth-century creation: there are certainly recipes for drinks before that period (in the 1860s, for example) that include vermouth and gin (as well as many other ingredients), but then the gin itself tended to be Old Tom or a sweet type and the recipes contain many other sweetish elements. This use of a sweetish gin might seem to dispose of the assertion that the vermouth with which the first dry martini was made must have been that of Noilly Prat (see page 241) and not Martini Dry (see page 239) because, in the 1860s, Martini & Rossi were not exporting this type of vermouth to the U.S. But John Doxat tells how Martini de Arma de Taggia, who was the head barman at the Knickerbocker Hotel in New York in the pre-1914 period, made a drink that became extremely popular; this happened to have Martini Dry Vermouth in it, but the drink was named, he thinks, for the man who made it, not the vermouth.

A much earlier barman and compiler of a book on mixed drinks, Jerry Thomas, who wrote *The Bar-Tender's Guide* (Dent & Fitzgerald, New York, 1862), still cited by many drinks writers today, actually did invent a 'Martinez cocktail' but this is unlikely to have been the direct ancestor of the dry martini, simply because of its sweetness. The Martinez cocktail, made in a 'small bar-glass', consisted of a wine glass of vermouth, '1 pony of Old Tom gin', a dash of Baker's bitters and two dashes of maraschino, with '2 small lumps of ice'. It was shaken (not stirred) and strained into a 'large cocktail glass' plus a slice of lemon. Those who wanted a 'very sweet' drink had an additional two dashes of gum syrup. More significantly, perhaps, John Doxat says:

> Not until after World War I did the proportions of equal amounts of dry gin and vermouth start to vary in favour of a higher percentage of spirit. In my early Martini days, the rule was about one-third vermouth to two-thirds gin. Orange bitters were usually added ... It was really only in the later 1940s that Martinis started getting drier and drier.

There are lengthy descriptions of the preparation of the cocktail in most drinks books, some of them making even the most elaborate and complicated procedures associated with wine seem positively casual.

The intelligent use of the dry martini as a pleasant refresher and appetite creator is obviously something to appreciate. But I admit to being unable to understand how people can find lasting enjoyment in standing around for hours drinking the same fairly strong drink, though apparently some do. The use of what is truly an 'occasional' drink as an end in itself seems odd – indeed, boring – and the drinkers appear to confuse social drinking with actually getting drunk. This, to me, seems wholly stupid and, in the view of any civilized drinker, anti-social. Good gin should be more than a drink that is taken to stultify the drinker. Its properties deserve intelligent use and consumption.

HOW GIN IS MADE

Gin can be, and once was, made by simply taking pure spirit and soaking flavourings in it. This, however, is a primitive method and the making of gin is now a highly complex procedure. Naturally, each of the great gin manufacturers will have their own individual formulae and follow their own particular methods, but for London gin, possibly the most famous in the world, I am going to describe the procedures as they are recounted by the Distillers' Company Ltd of London (abbreviated to D.C.L.), as this is the explanation that I myself have found easiest to understand.

The spirit on which the gin is based is made originally from cereal grains; these are fermented and then distilled (see page 26 for a basic description of distilling). A continuous or Coffey still is used for this process. The spirit resulting from this distillation is colourless and has virtually no flavour at all – it is distilled at a strength of 96 per cent or, in the terms formerly used in the U.K., 68° over proof.

The next stage in making London dry gin takes place at the gin distillery. It might seem logical to expect a gin distiller to operate under a distilling licence, but in fact he operates under a rectifying licence. This rectification of the alcohol he purchases (i.e., the colourless spirit produced in the continuous still, as described above) is customarily carried out in a pot still before any botanicals, such as juniper, are introduced and is a batch process – that is, a batch of spirit is produced at a time, as opposed to the continuous still process, in which the spirit can go on being made as long as the still is operated. The stillman in charge of the process watches the spirit throughout, sampling it at intervals. A booklet supplied by Gordon's says, of this stage in the making of gin: 'The resulting spirit is a colourless, crystal clear, absolutely pure liquid, having sufficient body and characteristics to receive and blend with the flavouring ingredients introduced in the next and final stage.'

The third stage of gin making also involves the old method of distillation – the pot still. The D.C.L. say: 'A quantity of rectified spirit is pumped into the still, flavouring ingredients are added, heat is applied to the still, and the distillation process begins. During this distillation the delicate flavour characteristics are imparted to the spirit.' Although juniper and coriander seem to be the botanicals constant to all gin recipes, other herbs, spices and root flavourings may be used, according to the products of each particular gin establishment.

Meanwhile, the distiller must observe the running of the pot still constantly. The initial liquid that comes over (which is usually referred to as 'foreshots' or 'feints') is put into a special receiver for distillation again later; when the 'run' seems finished, the final distillate coming off this is also put aside, for subsequent redistillation. The middle of the 'run' will be the gin as the distiller wishes it to be.

This distillate is then pumped into blending vessels, which may be glass-lined or of stainless steel, where it is sampled again and subjected to stringent tests; in addition, the strength is adjusted – specially treated water is used for breaking down the high strength of the spirit – for the requirements of various markets. The strength of gin for the U.K. is usually 98 per cent or 70° proof. For export markets, however, the strength may be higher: this, it should be borne in mind, is not simply because customers outside the U.K. may prefer a higher-strength gin, but because the different rates of excise duty in other countries may affect this higher-strength gin, which is to be sold at prices the market in any one particular country may be prepared to pay.

TYPES OF GIN

London Dry

This is probably the best known style of gin in the world. It is made according to the basic method described in previous pages. The name is generally taken to refer to the character of the gin, although French law requires that the word 'London' cannot appear on the label of a gin if that spirit is not actually distilled in London. It is generally accepted that London dry gins, bearing English names, made under licence or by subsidiaries of the original distillers in many export markets, are the finest gins in the world.

Plymouth gin

This had its origin at Plymouth and, hence, it has always been popular with both the Royal Navy and the Merchant Navy. It is today the exclusivity of Coates & Co., of Plymouth, and is reputedly slightly more aromatic than London dry gin, although rather less so than Dutch gin. This is the gin that, traditionally, should be used for 'pink gin' (see page 107).

Dutch gin

Still referred to by H.M. Customs as 'Hollands', it is also sometimes called 'Schiedam' after the district outside Rotterdam which is a centre of distilling operations. It is usually made from a spirit distilled from barley or maize, and can be lower in strength than London dry gin. The smaller amount of rectified alcohol and the flavourings used give it a more definite taste and aromatic smell, too. The main brands are made by De Kuyper and by Lucas Bols. The two main types of gin made are *oude genever* and *jonge genever*, old and young gin. The names refer to the age of the original recipes, and in no way to the age of the gin – gin does not benefit in any way by ageing, indeed, it can lose flavour thereby. The 'old' type is pale yellow and on the heavy side, the 'young' is white and lighter in style. In fact, says an authority at Booth's Distilleries, 'the heaviness of the "old" results from the type of alcohol used for the product. This is not so highly rectified as the London type gin and therefore contains more congenerics and appears to have a "heavier" flavour.'

Because of the definite flavour that Dutch gins possess in general, it is often stated that they probably resemble the original spirit more closely than the gins made elsewhere, which tend to be lighter and more neutral. It is obviously impossible for any definite pronouncement to be made about this, although I think it likely that all gins, in the early part of their history, would have been sweetened if possible – not only did people crave anything sweet as a luxury in the days before sugar became cheap, but any form of sweetening is the easiest way of disguising the imperfections of a drink.

In the De Kuyper establishment the 'young' Geneva as opposed to the 'old' Geneva is differentiated by the proportion of 'maltwine', which is the spirit base. Maltwine is produced by three pot still distillations of a mixture of rye, maize and barley, and, to quote *Wine & Spirit*, February 1977: 'the original Geneva, or Hollands gin, would be made by distilling this maltwine with juniper and the other flavouring agents used in the production of gin. This gave it a much more powerful flavour than London or dry gin for which a neutral grain spirit would be used as the base.' Maltwine, however, costs twice as much to produce as normal grain spirit, and so, catering for a market that prefers rather lighter spirits, 'young' Geneva now contains as little as only 5 per cent maltwine or even none, whereas 'old' Geneva contains only 30 per cent maltwine today.

Citroen Jenever, also made by De Kuyper, is lemon peel distilled with alcohol – it is not strictly a gin at all, but it is very popular in Holland, and may be drunk straight (like all Dutch gins) or made into a long drink with dry tonic and ice.

Dutch gin tends to be drunk straight, instead of being an ingredient in a mixture, and is usually served very cold or at least chilled. (It is particularly good with smoked fish, such as smoked eel.) It is never used in Holland as the basis for mixed drinks.

American gin

This is all of the London dry type, very dry and most strong, but Grossman (*Grossman's Guide to Wines, Spirits and Beers*, Charles Scribner's Sons, 1974) makes an interesting comment on North American gins. He asserts that the difference in the water used in Britain influences 'the character of the fermented mash and the spirits distilled from it'. This is certainly possible, although I have unfortunately not been able to find anyone who could describe this difference as if they perceived it.

Sloe gin and fruit gins

It is possible to make a fruit-flavoured gin simply by infusing the fruit or peel or berries or citrus fruits in gin. Orange gins, lemon and other gins (see also pages 258–9) have all had a vogue in the past, although purists would term them gin cordials rather than true gin. Sloe gin tends to be very much a British, or more precisely an English, speciality; making it was an activity common to many households in former times, when gin was cheap and sloes could be gathered for nothing.

The sloe, *Prunus spinosa*, is also known as blackthorn, or, sometimes, wild plum. Its flesh, high in acidity, is particularly suitable for steeping in gin, when, with time, a wonderfully pungent, silky, subtly warming liquid results; sloe gin seems to have excellent digestive properties and is always drunk by itself, often as a cordial at the end of a meal. It is traditionally much associated with the 'stirrup cup' served to huntsmen and those preparing to follow hounds before they all move off; the term refers to the type of glass that might be handed up to someone already on horseback, with a knob or rounded base instead of a foot, so that it couldn't be set down until, empty, it was turned upside down and replaced on a proffered tray. The type of glass used for a stirrup cup is also sometimes known as a posting glass, because it was often handed up at coaching inns to the postboy or postillions, who remained mounted on the horses drawing the coaches that maintained a regular service for the public or, if privately employed, were usually being hurried on by their employers. The postillions hadn't time to dismount if they were to keep to their timetables.

Several brands of sloe gin are made commercially in the U.K., but the best known is certainly the Pedlar brand, made by James Hawker of Plymouth, who have supplied the British Royal Household for 300 years.

Banana gin is another 'courtesy' gin, and similar spirits are encountered in Africa. 'Trade gin', however, is a crude spirit, used John Doxat says 'to placate tribal rulers, notably in Africa. Probably origin of custom of pouring gin on ground where distinguished visitor going to alight: custom virtually discontinued.'

GIN DRINKS

Pink gin: There are recurrent bursts of correspondence about the way a 'pink gin' should be made, and in 1975 *The Times* Diary reported on the various methods. The Diary's editor had a session with a Chief Petty Officer teaching trainees at Chatham, who advised the use only of Plymouth gin; he put two drops of Angostura Bitters in a glass, swirled it around the sides, then threw out the surplus Bitters (see page 218) before adding a measure of gin and a measure of iced water (not ice) to the glass. The resulting drink was very pale indeed. Readers followed this report with many of their own suggestions, stressing that the most common fault is to make the drink too 'pink'. Some recommended setting light to the Bitters before putting in the gin, and then rotating the glass both clockwise and anti-clockwise, tipping out the Bitters only when the flame had died. But all were unanimous that the drink should never be darker than pale pink; one reader advocated exactly four drops of Bitters per helping of gin. Some readers also stated that Plymouth gin should only be used with orange bitters, not insisting on Angostura except when London gin was used; others thought that the general use of Plymouth gin was 'a naval quirk'. It became clear that making this aperitive is as great a matter of individual skill and preference as the dry martini.

The Singapore gin sling: This drink has also aroused animated correspondence in *The Times*. It is said to have been evolved by the barman, Ngiam Ton Boon, in the Long Bar of Raffles Hotel, Singapore, in 1915. The recipe, as given on one of the hotel's postcards, is: two measures Tanqueray gin, one of Peter Heering Cherry Brandy, one each of orange, pineapple and lime juice, a drop or two each of Angostura Bitters, Bénédictine and Cointreau, the whole being combined in a shaker and then served topped with fresh pineapple and a cherry. But readers disputed this recipe. One cited a version that omitted the orange and pineapple juice, and substituted ginger ale. Another reader reported that the gin sling was not uncommon in the east prior to 1915, the ingredients basically being gin, fresh lime juice, cherry brandy, Angostura Bitters, ice and soda, so that the Raffles Hotel recipe might have merely been a version of this. In

1899, however, Mrs Beeton's *Household Management* gave the very simple recipe of: one wineglassful of gin, three lumps of sugar, two slices of lemon, and ice, the mixture to be stirred and drunk through a straw.

The Tom Collins and the John Collins: At the beginning of the nineteenth century, a quatrain commemorated an ancestor of the modern barman:

> My name is John Collins, head waiter at Limmer's,
> Corner of Conduit Street, Hanover Square.
> My chief occupation is filling the brimmers
> For all the young gentleman frequenters there.

John Doxat suggests that a 'brimmer' might have been what would today be termed a 'Sour', that is, a spirit-based drink also including fruit juice, sugar and mineral water, and he thinks that the Tom Collins would have been this type of drink, made with the Old Tom brand of gin – hence its name. In the 1930s and even earlier, according to the Handbook of the U.K. Bartenders Guild, a John Collins was stated to be made with Dutch gin and a Tom Collins with Old Tom gin. David Embury, another authoritative writer on mixed drinks and an American, confirms that a John Collins is made using Hollands or Genever, and a Tom Collins either with Old Tom or London Dry. The booklet of the D.C.L. called *London Gin* states that today both drinks are almost always made with London dry gin and differ only in name. Tom Collins, however, appears to be the established form of the drink in the U.S., where the John Collins seems never to have been popular. Basically, however, these drinks consist of two measures of gin (of whatever sort is preferred) plus the juice of a lemon and some sugar syrup, stirred with ice cubes and soda water. There are all kinds of 'Collins' drinks, the first name varying according to the spirit involved: for example, a Colonel Collins is made with Bourbon whiskey, a Mike Collins with Irish whiskey, a Pierre Collins with Cognac, a Sandy Collins with Scotch.

Pimm's: For many years the lable on the bottle of this preparation carried the slogan 'the original gin sling'. It is a true Cockney creation (that is, it was 'born' within the sound of the bells of St Mary-le-Bow, in Cheapside in the City of London, the church whose bells told Dick Whittington to 'turn again').

James Pimm was trading as a shellfish-monger in Lombard Street in the City in 1823–4, but he later removed to Number 3, Poultry, near the Mansion House, Royal Exchange and Bank of England; here he established Pimm's Oyster Warehouse. The site was already a historic one, as well as being commercially very well placed. In 1499 the Hogshead Tavern had occupied the position and, later, The Three Graces, where, in August 1661, Samuel Pepys noted in his diary that, 'We drank a great deal of wine, I too much and Mr Fanshaw until he could hardly go.'

Brian Spiller, who has researched the history of Pimm's, thinks that it was unlikely that oysters would have been accompanied by anything resembling a gin sling and I entirely agree. But James Pimm's successor, Samuel Morey, is recorded as having taken out a retail liquor licence in 1860, which is indicative that spirits were henceforth sold to the oyster bar customers – so this may have been when the bar began to sell a mixed drink, a type of cup, using wines and spirits plus other ingredients, such as liqueurs and, maybe, fruits and herbs. The goodwill of the original James Pimm was maintained, so the drink appears to have been named for him, even though he had by then left the business. Pimm's Restaurant became extremely popular Frederick Sawyer, who acquired it in 1865–6, is described as 'Late [in the sense of recently] Purveyor to the Crystal Palace'. Sawyer's successor, Charles Bell, sold Pimm's to Horatio David Davies, a wine merchant in the City, owner of cafés in both Regent Street and Golden Lane in the West End of London. Pimm's is entered in a directory of the times as a firm being 'oyster growers, wine merchants and refreshment contractors' and, when Horatio David Davies bought the Ship and Turtle Restaurant, a popular eating place with aldermen and City gentry, the suffix 'turtle merchants' was added to this description of Pimm's. It became smart as well as successful. Horatio Davies, now 'Sir Horatio', rose progressively in the world to become an M.P. and Lord Mayor of London from 1897 to 1898; he turned Pimm's into a private company in 1906, and, after his death, family trusts that he had set up kept control of Pimm's in the family for another fifty-seven years.

It is not certain exactly when Pimm's as a drink began to be generally marketed in bottle form, outside of the restaurants and bars that were controlled by the company. The first bottled version was based on gin, the second on Scotch, the third on brandy. The first case exported went to the Galle Face Hotel, Colombo, Ceylon, well before the turn of the century; Pimm's was being sent to the Sudan in 1898 – going to Khartoum with Lord Kitchener's forces, and also to Omdurman (the scene of the battle at which Kitchener defeated the Mahdi and Dervishes who had killed General Gordon, and where the young Winston Churchill took part in the great cavalry charge). Pimm's has always been popular with British regiments; as Brian

Spiller pertinently comments, the success of the drink 'owed more to the British officer's regard for creature comforts than to sustained export effort'. When, a few years ago, some of my friends in the wine trade who were doing their period of service in The Honourable Artillery Company went on manoeuvres to Cyprus, I was amazed to hear that a plane-load of Pimm's No. 1 had to be flown out, as they had consumed the island's supplies within a few days! (To my query as to why they had not drunk the Brandy Sour, Cyprus's speciality, see page 83, the reply was airily 'Oh we drank that *as well*!')

Pimm's began to be markedly popular in the Britain of the 1920s, but only after the Second World War did it make much impression on export markets outside those of the British colonies and armed forces. London clubs and hotels began to feature the drink between the wars, although there were no sales representatives until comparatively recently – the directors and staff of Pimm's did all the original promotional work and selling. Other versions were introduced: No. 4 was based on rum, No. 5 on rye whisky, No. 6 on vodka and No. 7 on Bourbon. But No. 1, the gin-based version, remained unquestionably the most popular and for a time it was the only one made, although recently vodka-based Pimm's has been reintroduced. In 1969, Pimm's as a family business ceased to operate and became part of the mighty D.C.L. who have henceforth been able to introduce it and even make it in many parts of the world.

The recipe for Pimm's (all the versions) is known only to the 'Secret Six', the top executives of the company, but all employees of Pimm's sign an undertaking that they will never divulge anything that they may happen to learn about the ingredients. The flavour of the mixture is regularly checked against the original recipe. Although Pimm's can be drunk as a 'short' drink, in other words, neat (although chilled), it is usually made into a medium or long drink with fizzy lemonade – a drink that will be familiar to any Briton; however, this vaguely lemon-flavoured sparkling beverage is not known in either France or, more significantly in the commercial sense, the United States. So the Pimm's exported to these countries is made with the addition of citric acid to the recipe, so that the diluting agent can simply be soda water.

The basic recipe for Pimm's as printed on its label simply states: 'A long drink, requiring the addition of 3 to 4 parts of aerated lemonade to 1 part of Pimm's. The addition of a slice of lemon and a sliver of cucumber rind (or a sprig of borage) is recommended. Serve well iced.' Alas, as borage is only briefly in season in the U.K. in midsummer, to use it is a counsel of perfection – but the cucumber rind makes a surprising difference. Too many extras in the form of fruit can not only try the maker's temper, but can nullify the freshness and appeal of the basic drink. People who like experimenting with drinks may try varying Pimm's by substituting ginger ale instead of lemonade to dilute it, or, for very special occasions, using non-vintage Champagne, or possibly a good dryish sparkling wine for the purpose. (Curiously, guests will be unlikely to notice that any sparkling wine has been used if they are simply offered an apparently ordinary Pimm's – although they will certainly feel the alcoholic effects of the 'King Pimm's' sooner than usual!)

Gin cocktails: It would take far too much space to give recipes for all the cocktails in which gin is a main ingredient. In addition to the dry martini (see page 101), gin and tonic, and other drinks that have been previously mentioned, these are possibly the best known classic mixtures:

Bronx – half dry gin, plus one quarter each of dry and sweet vermouth, with a little fresh orange juice, all shaken and then strained into a glass.

Gimlet – half and half Rose's lime juice and dry gin.

Negroni – two measures dry gin, one of sweet vermouth and one of Campari Bitters (see page 221), topped up with soda water.

White Lady – half dry gin, one quarter each of Cointreau (see page 272) and lemon juice, shaken and then strained into a glass.

A Ginn Fizz is a measure of dry gin, the juice of half a lemon, plus half a tablespoonful of powdered sugar, shaken, strained into a wine glass and topped up with soda. In recent years, a mixture of gin and vintage cider was launched as the Mod 'n Rocker, but among the post-war drinkers I think this was more appropriately named Virgin's Ruin.

Specifying whether a gin-based cocktail is stirred or shaken is important; not only can the method of mixing alter the appearance of the drink which may thereby be made cloudy rather than slightly opaque, but some gin devotees think too much agitation can 'bruise the gin'. You have to experiment and find out for yourself.

SOME MAKERS OF GIN

Reference has already been made to the old-established house of Lucas Bols (see page 87) in Holland. De Kuyper, another famous Dutch firm, was set up at Schiedam, near Rotterdam, by John De Kuyper in 1695, and is still a family concern. There are a number of others, such as Warnink and Fockink, but the former are the best-known in export markets.

The top-selling gin in the world is Gordon's. They were first established in Finsbury in London, where, as is often forgotten today, there was a 'spa', due to the pure water of a supposedly medicinal spring; indeed, there were several London springs, some used since Roman times, others being discovered and favoured by the medieval religious (hence 'Clerics' Well' – Clerkenwell), and, most famous of all, the 'Wells' of Dr Sadler, now the well-known theatre.

Alexander Gordon began to make a spirit 'as pure as the waters of Finsbury' in Goswell Street, now Goswell Road, in the City in the eighteenth century; he may also have used the various herbs and plants that would then have been growing in Finsbury Fields. In 1769 his success enabled him to form a company and, by 1800, his gin was widely known and liked. Today, the company stress that the recipe for Gordon's gin remains unchanged; some of his original huge copper stills that survived the serious bombing of London in 1941 remain in use and are as effective today as they were in the eighteenth century.

In 1898, Gordon's and the Bloomsbury Distillery of Charles Tanqueray united and they now trade as Tanqueray Gordon. A huge distillery and bottling plant was set up by them in New Jersey in 1933 (when Prohibition was repealed), another plant was built in Illinois in 1965 and a third in California in 1971. There are also distilleries making Gordon's gin in South Africa, Brazil and other lively export markets, which include Spain, Canada, New Zealand and Venezuela. Tanqueray's gin is mainly an export gin; it is very dry and strong even by U.K. standards – 47·4 per cent or 83° proof.

The Gilbey brothers set up as wine merchants in 1865, but it is possible that they had associations with gin long before that; some confusion exists as to their origins, but it is thought that one of the Gilbey ancestors who was a coachman augmented his job by distributing illicitly distilled gin that was made by another brother, who was officially a miller. This gin was so popular that the two brothers made their fortunes. It is certain that Gilbey's began to distil gin in 1872 and they were particularly successful in getting their brand into the U.S. market, even during the period of Prohibition; they evolved a square bottle, sand-blasted on three sides, with a label printed on both sides and visible through the one clear side. In spite of this bottle being so expensive, it was hard to imitate and therefore afforded some protection to the original gin. Gilbey's gin is made under licence in many export markets today.

The House of Burrough, world famous for its Beefeater brand of gin, was established by James Burrough at the beginning of the nineteenth century in Chelsea; the founder chose the name 'Beefeater' because he wanted something traditionally British, associated with quality and standing – his shrewd choice of brand indicates his abilities. The firm prospered so that, in 1908, a new distillery had to be built at Lambeth. Some of the first exports of Beefeater went to the U.S. and, by 1963, Burrough's could claim to be the biggest U.K. exporters of gin. They possess what is probably the largest rectifying still in Britain. Burrough's is still a family firm.

Booth's, however, is the oldest British gin firm. Members of the family were in the wine trade as early as 1569, having come to London from the north-east of England. They were engaged in brewing as well and, by 1740, were distilling. Felix Booth, later made a baronet, set up another distillery at Brentford in the early nineteenth century; he was a remarkable man and financed the expedition of Captain John Ross to discover the North-West Passage, 1829–33, which is why part of Arctic Canada is marked as 'Boothia'; other of both the family and first names of the Booths recorded this venture, although Felix's own involvement was supposed not to be revealed. He became a personal friend of King William IV, and in Barham's *The Ingoldsby Legends* (1840–47) there are the lines:

> Though I own even then I should see no great sin in it
> Were there three drops of Sir Felix's gin in it.

Booth's became a limited liability company when the last male Booth died in 1826. The Red Lion Distillery was opened in 1959 and in it, still working, is a still made in 1828, brought from the original Booth gin premises.

Booth's London gin, Finest Dry, is quite distinctive, because of its pale golden colour; this came about when some gin was stored in sherry casks and forgotten – the gin, when rediscovered, was found to be so good that for some time afterwards it was given three years' maturation in cask, although today this effect is achieved by other means. The absolutely clear High & Dry is another Booth's gin, delicately flavoured and sometimes termed the world's driest gin; House of Lords is another dry gin made by the firm.

Booth's, whose U.K. sales have been handled by Buchanan Booth's Agencies since 1969, also now make Boord's gin (and other spirits). Boord was founded in 1726 and was, as I mentioned earlier, famous for the brand Old Tom, with its Cat and Barrel trademark; Boord do not sell under their own label in the U.K. but are well known in export markets and today deal solely in gin, much of it the traditional sweetish type. The gin has, I am informed, a following in California.

Coates & Co., sole makers of Plymouth gin, own what may be the most unusual headquarters: in 1793 they bought what had been the Blackfriars Monastery, founded in 1425. This building was turned into a debtor's prison in 1536, when the monasteries were dissolved by King Henry VIII but the refectory of the monastic establishment, with a particularly fine beamed roof, henceforth became the official hall or meeting place of Plymouth. It was here that the Pilgrim Fathers were said to have held their final gathering before setting sail for North America in 1620, and, a little later, the hall was a meeting place for the Huguenots who took refuge in England, after the Revocation of the Edict of Nantes in 1685 made France no longer a free country for them. Although the hall was bombed in the Second World War, it has been carefully restored. Coates once belonged to the firm Seager Evans, themselves controlled by Schenley of New York and the American ownership resulted in the gin formula being altered, so that the produce became virtually the same as London dry gin. Coates now belongs to Whitbread, the English brewers.

The 'Squire' from whom Squire's gin gets its name was Squire Osbaldeston, 1786–1866, known as 'the Squire of All England' because of his numerous achievements in country activities, although he had nothing directly to do with gin. Osbaldeston owned huge estates in Yorkshire, played championship tennis and cricket, rowed, hunted and was a crack shot – once killing ninety-seven grouse with ninety-seven cartridges and forty partridges with forty shots, and being able to put thirty pistol shots straight through the ace of diamonds at thirty yards! In 1831 he rode 200 miles 'against the clock', taking twenty-seven horses and finishing in 8 hours 42 minutes – a record that still stands. Squire's gin was evolved by a number of British brewers to be the 'house gin' of their various outlets. Cornhill is a slightly coloured version of it, only sold in the U.K.

The Distillers' Company Ltd (again, it should be stressed that this Company is not in any way part of The Worshipful Company of Distillers, see pages 39–41) was registered in 1877, as the result of a merger of six lowland Scottish grain distillers – the malt distillers were accustomed to make gin spirit, which they then delivered to the rectifiers who produced the finished spirit. The six Scottish firms were supplying spirit to London and, in 1883, Menzies, owners of the

Caledonian Distillery in Edinburgh, applied to join, bringing with them the rectifying business carried on by a firm called Drysdale, of Tooley Street, London. So the D.C.L. henceforth became rectifiers of gin as well as suppliers of spirit. In 1922 Tanqueray Gordon joined the D.C.L., as did Booth's in 1937, with its subsidiary, John Watney of Wandsworth.

Each gin firm within the D.C.L. sells its brands in competition with others, and acts independently as regards production and house styles; they do not own shops and, in the U.K., sell mainly to whole-salers. But on export markets they are of enormous importance, selling generally to sole distributors appointed for particular terri-tories, except for those areas where the distribution of alcoholic liquor is a government monopoly. The D.C.L. is rightly referred to as a 'giant' for it should be remembered that it markets other spirits in addition to gin, and is one of the largest commercial concerns in the U.K. At the end of 1977, the D.C.L., by withdrawing the most successful brand of Scotch in the world – Johnnie Walker Red Label – made a significant stand against the E.E.C., which had been attempting to coerce U.K. producers to raise their prices while many European countries were discriminating against Scotch in favour of locally produced spirits. At the time of writing it is not clear what may result – but the influence of the D.C.L. is enormous throughout the whole world of spirit production.

6. Whisky

It is inevitable that this should be the longest section in this book, because whisky, in its various forms, is commercially the most important spirit in the world. Until recently, when vodka began to jostle the several best-selling U.S. whiskeys for top sales, it was these whiskeys that dominated the world market; even now, with both vodka and white rum consumption rising sharply throughout the whole American continent, the combined volume of the various U.S. whiskeys outstrips other spirits overall. In the U.K., 50 per cent of all spirits consumed is Scotch (even though the world's top-selling gin comes from Britain). Of course, in countries that traditionally make other spirits, whisky may start with a handicap, especially as regards its cost, but once it gains a hold in a foreign market it appears to increase steadily in popularity.

The U.S.A. is the most important export market for Scotch; Japan is second on the list, with single malt Scotch representing around 60 per cent of its total imports. But the top export market in the world for single malt is Italy, which is fourth in overall Scotch imports, coming after France. Australia, Venezuela and Spain are other substantial consumers of Scotch, but it is Brazil that comes second only to Italy as a buyer of single malt and, in 1976 the most remarkable rise in imports of Scotch of all was in Cyprus – 873 per cent up on the previous year's total!

Even in Muslim countries, where breaches of the 'no alcohol' rules enforced by the religious observances of Islam can result in severe penalties, there are often still means of getting whisky – which is usually Scotch. The oil-producing Middle East sheikdoms manage somehow to let in whisky for drinking by foreigners; on the level where these executives do business, there is no quibble at per-bottle prices that sound to Europeans like the rates for half a case or more. There are reports that even those who are officially abstainers are a growing market for this sought-after spirit; with so many Arab businessmen being educated and trained abroad and frequently travelling outside their countries, it would be surprising if none ever displayed any interest in whisky – even if only to provide it as hospitality for visiting foreigners.

As will be seen (pages 166–81), whisky of perfectly good quality is now made in many countries to cater for what seems a world-wide liking for this spirit. In France, of all proudly gastronomic places, 'le whisky' has been a smart drink, even in wine-producing regions, for many years.

Whisky, throughout its history, has had considerable direct and also far-reaching influence on the regions and in the countries where it has been and is made; its production has affected fiscal legislation and government policies way beyond the circumstances of its giving work to millions of people in certain areas. I do not think that the producers of any other single spirit exert the sort of pressure – albeit benevolent – that can be brought to bear by, in particular, the makers of Scotch (although the importance of the U.S. and Canadian firms is considerable). It was the D.C.L. who, in 1977, stood up to the European Economic Community (see page 115). Those who make whisky assuredly make history.

There are several problems, however, about dealing adequately with the spirit in a book of this size. The main difficulty is one of compression and proportion: Scotch whisky is nowadays the subject of continuous research and is so well documented that an abridgement of its history and even a sketchy account of the processes whereby it has become the spirit that is known today is very difficult to make. The history and production of North American and Canadian whiskey, however, is scantily recorded for the general reader, in spite of its commercial significance. Scotch whisky has a long, appealing story, rich in personalities; other whiskies began to be of great importance at a time when, thanks to improved communications and increased literacy, industrial records could be kept in detail. It is easy for anyone to be interested in the poor farmer's son who became a 'whisky baron', or the ways in which illicit distillers outwitted the excise, or the comedy of the confrontation of a Prohibition gangster with an old established St James's Street wine merchant. It is harder to understand the technicalities of the various mighty U.S. distilleries, the great mergers and the economics of the biggest business in the spirit world. So this part of the book is inclined to stress Scotch and Irish, simply because it is easier to put tags on these for the unscientific and 'unbusinessminded' reader.

Spelling: Every writer has an individual scheme for making terms easier for readers, although sometimes, by the too-subtle use of 'a capital initial letter for the place but an ordinary letter for the drink named for the place', I think that they complicate the reader's understanding and make the page look as if someone has done a bad job on the proof-reading! So, if a word has its origin in a proper name – Scotch, Irish, Bourbon, Canadian – I have kept the capital letter when using it. Other words relating to different types of whisky: malt, rye, blended, de luxe – do not have capital letters, as they refer to a general category and have nothing to do with a place name.

Scotch whisky is spelled 'whisky', Irish is spelled 'whiskey'. What should I have done about the other whiskies – or whiskeys – of the world? As far as I can see, from fairly wide reading, the trend is to use the word 'whiskey' for all such allied spirits as are not Scotch; the plurals of the words are 'whiskies' when the spirits are any form of Scotch, otherwise, 'whiskeys'. Except in this intro-duction to the section, when I refer in a general sense to all the spirits of this kind in the world, the plural will be 'whiskeys' – *pace* the Scots. The latest (1976) edition of *The Concise Oxford Dictionary* indicates that the 'ey' ending is 'esp. of U.S. and of Irish', so I have followed this – although that respected work of reference is by no means wholly reliable, as witness its definitions of 'sherry', 'cham-pagne', and 'cognac' (*sic*), none of which would be acceptable either by the U.K. wine and spirit trade, or by the E.E.C.

STRENGTH OF WHISKY

Because of the world importance of whisky, the strength of the particular type and brand that the drinker may be considering is of special relevance. Readers are therefore referred to the tables (pages 318–21) if they are uncertain as to the interpretation of the in-formation on the label of the bottle. But it should also be stressed that alcoholic strength is not synonymous with quality as far as this type of spirit is concerned, any more than that the most expensive bottle must always be the best; it depends on why and how you are drinking.

WHAT WHISK(E)Y IS

It is unlikely that many people would be able to define whisky in general terms. Nor can I. The definitions of the particular types will be found in the sections devoted to them. But it may be generally agreed that it is a spirit – that is, the result of distillation – based on various types of grains, which may be malted (see page 141), unmalted, or a blend of the two. After that, to quote from the House of Seagram, 'All that is needed to produce a simple beverage alcohol product is water, sugar, yeast and a government licence. If you plan to produce a quality product, however, then you would be wise to pay particular attention to the character of the water, the source of the sugar and the type of yeast.'

Because there are so many whiskies and whiskeys, it is certainly impossible in so short a space to do more than indicate approximate differences between them as regards what they taste like. The interested reader must investigate and form individual preferences and opinions. Even books on Scotch can do no more than indicate the styles of the different distilleries as these appeal to the writer and attempt to give some description of the individual malts. It will be appreciated that the different ways in which any form of whisky may be drunk will affect the way in which it appeals to the palate: before or after a meal, late at night, in a bar, as part of a mixture and so on. Even if the thousands, possibly even tens of thousands, of whiskies could be assembled in one place for tasting, I doubt that one person could appraise more than a few of them at one time. So categorizations, however much some readers may want them, are impossible to the honest – and misleading if the less scrupulous try to compile them.

As regards the processes involved with production, it would be a waste of space to repeat definitions of 'malting', 'diastase' and so on in each different section. If you refer to the detailed discussion of these under 'Scotch' – where all the main processes are mentioned – then it should not be difficult to relate them to other whiskeys.

SCOTCH

The word 'Scotch' has been referred to by Professor David Daiches in his book *Scotch Whisky* (André Deutsch, 1969) as an adjective that can be applied only to whisky and broth; the Scots refer to themselves as Scots and use the same word adjectivally, or use the word 'Scottish'. Jack House, the literary editor of a Scottish newspaper, in a privately published book on White Horse whisky, says with feeling: 'My imagination boggles at the number of occasions on which I have been informed that the first mention of whisky in the country of its origin was in the Scottish Exchequer Rolls of 1494. It runs "Eight bolls of malt to Friar John Cor wherewith to make *aquavitae*".' But Scotch of a sort was certainly being made in Scotland long before that date, according to all records – too numerous to detail here, but references to them will be found in many of the books listed in the relevant section at the end of this book.

The Irish were distilling in some primitive way for at least two hundred years before the 'bolls of malt' were ordered and it was the missionary monks from Ireland who probably brought distilling to Scotland. A knowledgeable friend of mine in the whisky business thinks that the 'pot ale' made in the religious houses may have been the earliest form of Irish whiskey and he also points out that it is significant that, to distil this pot ale, barley was used. Barley is an excellent food for cattle and was therefore an essential crop in these early times. It seems significant that barley is also one of the earliest grains to have been put to domestic use: the ancient Egyptians made beer from it and the ancient Greeks valued it as a food. There are some theories that, in ancient Crete, the cult of the 'corn goddess' might have more accurately been that of the 'barley goddess' – the spirit that brought the harvest to fruition and thereby fed people and animals. Several Scots ballads are about 'John Barleycorn' and Burns's famous poem of the same name describes a man subject to ploughing, reaping, 'wasted o'er a scorching flame', crushed between two stones. When his tormentors have 'ta'en his very heart's blood' as a drink, 'Their joy did more abound'. The similarity between this and all the legends of the slain hero who revives to bring back life to the earth is obvious.

Perhaps the most significant fact about barley that may originally have led to its associations with magic and legend, is that it is a self-fertile cereal, and actually lives off its own starch. It is not often seen as a basic foodstuff in more affluent societies today, but in fact has a variety of uses, all of them supplying basic needs that would have been much appreciated in early times. Travellers intending to remain for any time in one place would certainly have brought barley with them if possible.

The Irish missionary monks settled in such places as Dufftown, Islay (famous names in the world of Scotch today) and around the Mull of Kintyre, where there were thirteen religious establishments and, later, thirteen distilleries, for this is where the Campbeltowns are made. The knowledge of distilling may have reached southern Ireland from Spain, but anyway it would not have been a great step from distilling pot ale to making a spirit from barley. In simple terms – using language the monks would not have known – the production of whisky had begun. For, when barley is germinated and malted (Professor Daiches describes this process as barley that has been allowed to germinate by soaking in water and has then been dried by the application of heat), enzymes are secreted which turn the starch in the grain to sugar. These enzymes are referred to as diastase. This sugar content is contributory to the flavoursome by-products of the grain, and it is these which produce the eventual plus factors or congenerics – the allied 'impurities' that give charm and individuality to a spirit of this sort. The monks would have found the spirit nourishing as well as stimulating in the rather poor land in which they settled.

It was the maturation in cask that enabled the spirit to refine itself. The soft, often humid atmosphere where many of the distilleries are sited, permeates the wood of the cask, causing some evaporation and disappearance of the impurities. This process of evaporation also inevitably results in a certain loss of strength, but, in a climate such as that of Scotland, not an excessive amount, if the spirit is given time in wood. The use of the cask would have been known to the monks and some cellarers might have noted that whereas wine kept in cask too long would become sour and vinegary, a spirit would definitely improve. It is easy to realize how the spirit produced in individual homesteads, even of quite a modest sort, and certainly in large houses after the influence of the religious establishments had waned, would have soon become something to attract admirers and those who wished to buy it. Whisky began to be a sought-after commodity.

In 1505 the surgeons of Edinburgh were given an associated monopoly of making and selling aqua vitae within that city – the spirit, of course, was of medicinal value. It is not known exactly what this type of aqua vitae was like but there were certainly individual producers: in 1555 the Bailies of Edinburgh ordered 'Besse Campbell to desist and ceis from making *aqua vitae* within the burgh' without permission of the surgeons.

Fynes Moryson, who wrote *An Itinerary* in 1617, says that there were three different types of spirit distilled in the Western Islands of Scotland, and, using their Gaelic names, refers to them as 'usquebaug, testarig, and usquebaug-baul'. *Uisge beathe* is of course the Gaelic for 'water of life', the first word of which gives us 'whisky'. Ross Wilson, who has probably written more about Scotch than anyone else, thinks that the spirit distilled domestically would not always have been made only from malt and suggests that unmalted grain or barley might also have been used. He relates the Gaelic terms to the Latin ones *simplex*, *composita* and *perfectissima*: simplex (*usquebaug*) being distilled twice, composita (*testarig*) three times – hence its name – and perfectissima (*usquebaug-baul*) being distilled four times and reported to be so strong that 'two spoonfuls were alleged to endanger a man's life. Darnley, second husband of Mary Stuart, made one of his French friends drunk on *aqua composita*. Holinshead in his 1577 *Chronicles* also notes the three different types of spirit and gives the famous praise of whisky – how strange that Shakespeare, who borrowed extensively from Holinshead, omitted to include it!

> Beying moderatelie taken, it sloweth age, it strengtheneth youthe; it helpeth digestion; it cutteth fleume; it abandoneth melancholie; it relisheth the harte; it lighteneth the mynde; it quickeneth the spirities; it cureth the hydropsie; it healeth the strangury; it pounceth the stone; it repelleth grauel; it puffeth awaie ventosite; it kepyth and preserveth the head from whyrling – the eyes from dazelyng – the tongue from lispyng – the mouth from snafflying – the teethe from chatteryng – the throte from ratlying – the weason from stieflyng – the stomach from wamblyng – the harte from swellyng – the bellie from wirtchyng – the guts from rumblying – the sinowes from shrinkyng – the veynes from crumplyng – the bones from soakyng … trulie it is a soueraigne liquor.

The spirit at this stage in its history would certainly have been very varied and the triple-distilled *composita* stronger than the ordinary type.

It is possible to know a little more detail about the history of Scotch after 1643, when Parliament began to tax spirits for the first time. Beer, ale, cider and perry were taxed as well, and of course wine had been subject to duty before this. There was an outcry, as might be expected, but spirits still appear to have been distilled domestically and, perhaps significantly, the excise duty was merely on the amount of spirit distilled, without any reference to the strength of it. Some historians suppose that in this period when, it will be remembered, the brandy trade was developing considerably in France (see page 69), the traditional interchange of trade between Scotland and the French west coast may have resulted in some influence of the Scottish distillers affecting the production of what was later to be Cognac. This can never be proved or disproved; personally, I think that it seems unlikely.

The history of Scotch is henceforth bound up with the history of the various problems connected with duty, those who tried to evade it and those who tried to get more revenue from its imposition. Although it could be profitable to make and sell whisky, the use of grain that might otherwise have served as a foodstuff could mean hardship for many in times of bad harvests, so that various forms of legislation attempted to control the amount of distillation that was done.

In 1688, King James II had fled from England and William of Orange landed at Torbay, later being proclaimed with his wife Mary, daughter of James II, as joint sovereigns of the British Isles. Legislation was now brought in to tax spirits according to their strength and at this period occurs the first mention of a single Scotch, for the 'ancient brewary of aquavity' at Ferintosh (or Farintosh) in Ross-shire belonging to Duncan Forbes of Culloden, a Whig and therefore no friend of the Stuart cause, was destroyed by Jacobites. By way of recompense, in 1690 Parliament allowed him a 'privilege' – to distil grain free of duty, on payment of a fee of about £22 a year. 'Ferintosh' became a widely known and esteemed whisky, though envious neighbours complained – well they might, for it was worked out that Duncan Forbes had paid a mere £22 instead of an annual excise duty of £20,000, and other distillers regarded this as too much of a good thing. Forbes's descendants remained loyal to the Hanoverian kings, being influential in keeping the peace in the rebellions of both 1715 and 1745, and the fame of Ferintosh whisky, reported as 'strongly flavoured with the smoke of the peat', spread. Duncan Forbes was proud both of it and of having spent a large sum in suppressing the 1745–6 rebellion. His 'privilege' did not last, however, for the British government had to give way to protests in 1785 and withdrew it. Though they paid Forbes's son, after his death, £21,580 compensation for the original payment, the Forbes family considered it was insufficient.

The Scots were big drinkers – of anything apparently. As well as imported spirits, such as gin and brandy (smuggled in) being in demand, the fashionable trend of drinking tea began to take a hold in many homes; this aroused so much disapproval in the church in Scotland that the clergy publicly averred that even whisky was preferable – true, it had also become traditional to 'qualify' the last cup of tea by adding a little whisky. This, of course, was justified because the spirit would 'correct all the bad effects of the tea'.

Two other interesting mentions of whisky occur at the time of the Forty-five Rebellion (the rising after Prince Charles Edward Stuart had landed in Scotland in 1745). The story of Drambuie is better known (see pages 262–3), but the Prince is known also to have expressed a preference for oat bread and whisky and actually bought a bottle of the spirit when he was sheltering at Portree on the Isle of Skye. It is also recorded that a minister of the Episcopal Church of

Scotland, who was attached to Lord Ogilvy's regiment on the side of Bonnie Prince Charlie, gave holy communion to the dying Lord Strathallan 'on the Culloden field, it is said, with oat-cake and whisky, the requisite elements not being obtainable'.

Dr Johnson and James Boswell toured parts of Scotland in 1773, often being offered whisky in the very humble surroundings where they stopped for refreshment. Johnson only tried it once. He said:

> I thought it preferable to any English malt brandy. [This type of spirit (see page 64) sounds so vile that I assume any clean spirit would have been obviously preferable.] It was strong, but not pungent, and was free from the empyreumatick taste or smell. What was the process I had no opportunity of inquiring, nor do I wish to improve the art of making poison pleasant. Not long after the dram, may be expected the breakfast.

The toad-eater Boswell, however, was a better reporter and did taste whisky several times, even though, when he could, he drank rum. The travellers were offered whisky in a shell at Coll, in the Hebrides, though the Doctor would only drink water from it, but at Inverary, where he did try 'what it is that makes a Scotchman happy' and made the comment previously quoted, he drained all but a drop from his glass, which Boswell tipped into his, 'that I might say we had drunk whisky together'. Boswell then proposed a toast to Mrs Thrale (the courageous and able woman who was 'adored' by Johnson until she married for love for a second time, when he wrote her monstrously spiteful letters and never saw her again). At this period Johnson was still a 'friend' to Hester Thrale and said he 'would not have *her* drunk in whisky, but rather "some insular lady"'.

It was at the end of the eighteenth century that Robert Burns wrote 'Freedom and whisky gang thegither'! But legislation was making it as profitable for the whisky smuggler in Scotland as the brandy, rum and gin smuggler in England. Closer controls of the way the distilling was done and the duty was applied came into force; the duty was different in the Highlands from that of the Lowlands, and there was another 'Intermediate' district established in 1797, between the Highlands and Lowlands, this too having its individual duty. But none of these controls worked satisfactorily, illicit distilling was on the increase and, in addition to the problems within Scotland itself, there were enormous differences between the spirits that were distilled in England and those in Scotland. Eventually, thanks to an organized Customs and Excise and improved scientific instruments, the strength of spirits being handled could be both constantly and easily checked, and therefore controlled, and the authorities gradually began to establish the systems of strength that govern spirits today. Illicit distilling continued, however, on a grand scale. Indeed, without it, the vast quantities of spirits that the Scots consumed could hardly have been supplied, except to very rich people. It was drunk on every possible occasion. At funerals, for example, enormous quantities of whisky were consumed, the bearers being traditionally supposed to take five glasses before 'the lifting' – it is not surprising that they very often dropped the coffin or even sometimes arrived at the church without it! In 1825 at the funeral of the Honourable Alexander Fraser of Lovat, some of the mourners toppled into the vault.

At the time of the war with Napoleonic France, the First Regiment the Royal Edinburgh Volunteers were specifically ordered to get their feet dry every night, and 'in case of being very wet, it is highly useful to rub the body and limbs with spirits, warm if possible, taking at the same time a mouthful and not more inwardly, diluted with warm water.' When in 1811 the poet Shelley eloped with Harriet Westbrook and took her to lodge at 60 George Street, Edinburgh, the landlord banged on the bedroom door to tell the couple that it was customary for wedding guests to come in during the night and wash the bride with whisky! Shelley threw the man out, actually threatening him with his pistol, or so one account says, although, as this story does not appear in one 'Life' of the poet, it may merely be the sort of tale that he was inclined to invent.

One of the heroes of the excise was Malcolm Gillespie (1779–1827), who engaged in numerous battles with the smugglers after his entry into the service in 1799. In the course of his twenty-eight years' service he was wounded forty-two times. It is sad to relate that, having seized a record number of spirits (other types as well as whisky), also stills and equipment, he was eventually put to death for forgery after getting seriously into debt. The excisemen risked many dangers and, even when they were successful in seizing the illicit spirit, the magistrates themselves might well be suborned by the smugglers: one woman testifying turned to the sheriff and said that she hadn't made a drop of whisky 'since youn wee keg I sent to yesel'! There were even female smugglers, one of whom ran a still in the Lomond Hills and another who pretended to be a witch as a cover for smuggling.

Of course, with knowledge and scientific control of the operation of distilling being scanty, the resulting spirit produced was often frightful. Even if the distillate began by being good, it was rare for a

smuggler to be able to mature it. But the underground distillers of
the early nineteenth century used great ingenuity in concealing their
activities, often actually having their premises underground; it was,
of course, a problem to conceal the smoke coming up from the still
and sometimes this was disguised by making a fire up above, or
appearing to wash clothes actually over the chimney of the still. One
ingenious character diverted the chimney of his still so that the smoke
blended with the spume of a near-by waterfall! But people, such as
shepherds and sportsmen, often actually fell into these concealed
stills while out in the country and so some smugglers preferred to
hide their stills in towns; one was under a church in the High Street
at Edinburgh, and another actually inside the clock tower at Dufftown, where the smoke went up a chimney so constructed as to look
like a lightning conductor; the waste went down a drain into the
public sewer. The excise supervisor, constantly about in Dufftown
where he had his office and which even today is a small, compact
township, never noticed anything unusual about the clock tower;
if he did pick up the smell of the still when it was in operation, he
probably simply thought that the wind was blowing from one of the
numerous licensed distilleries near by! One band of smugglers used
to sink their still in Loch Druing and another gang persuaded the
beadle of the church at Nigg to store theirs in the pulpit! Very often,
the whole business of smuggling became almost a sport, the smugglers luring on the excisemen to places where there had never been a
still at all, diverting attention from the real illicit operations. The
wives of the excise officers often enjoyed regular gifts of food (and
even whisky) from the smugglers' wives, to whom they passed on
information about the possible plans of the 'Riding Officers' in the
locality. Women played active parts in the smuggling, hiding
quantities of whisky under voluminous skirts and cloaks.

There are plenty of references to whisky in the novels of Sir Walter
Scott. He himself drank Glenlivet and is recorded as having served
whisky to guests in the traditional quaich, a small wooden cup with
a silver inlay. For himself, he reserved a cup that had been reputedly
the property of Bonnie Prince Charlie; it had a glass bottom – so that
anyone drinking could still keep an eye on what was going on around
him. Whisky was used lavishly in the punches and mixed drinks that
were popular at the time. Individual household recipes for a good
mixture were proudly demonstrated, and women as well as men
shared in this. When George IV visited Edinburgh in 1822, Elizabeth
Grant recorded that her father 'sent word to me – I was the cellarer –
to empty my pet bin where was whisky long in wood, long in un-

corked bottles, mild as milk and a true contraband *goût* in it.' The reference to uncorked bottles is odd, but I assume that there would have been some form of light sealing of the bottles, which in the cold damp atmosphere of the cellar would not have allowed the whisky to deteriorate to any great extent. Elizabeth Grant was only one of the many women who exerted a considerable influence on the production of whisky. One of the tougher characters was a certain Mrs Watson. The gauger employed by the excise to look for illicit stills usually had his approach announced by the hoisting of a flag. But one gauger, who had lain in wait overnight, emerged only when the men of the area had gone off to work and then tackled Mrs Watson, whom he found with the equipment for distilling in her home. Saying, 'I have clean caught you this morning', he received the reply: 'Did anybody see ye come in?' to which the imprudently truthful answer being 'No', she merely replied: 'And by the Lord Harry, nobody will ever see ye gang oot.' Indeed, the gauger was never seen again.

Scotch was becoming respectable. Queen Victoria, visiting Scotland in 1852 and 1855, appreciated drinking whisky with her husband Prince Albert, and in 1859, when she had gone up the mountain Ben Muich Dhui, her journal records: 'I had a little whisky and water, as the people declared pure water would be too chilling.'

In 1831, a patent was entered for a new kind of still by Aeneas Coffey, of the Dock Distillery, Dublin, distiller. This took a little more time to be approved for general use, but it was a turning point in the history of Scotch. This 'Coffey still' was the continuous still (see page 45) and, after initial difficulties, its use began to affect the production of spirits everywhere in the world and significantly in Scotland.

Distilling within Great Britain now became big business indeed. There was the trend to a different type of blend: previously, blending had really only concerned malt whiskies, the product of individual pot stills being combined, but from now on blending was to be concerned with the blend of pot still whiskies and those that were produced in the patent or continuous still.

Another important change occurred when Scotch began to be sold by the bottle. When it was drawn from a cask, this cask was naturally topped up – and the resulting blend might be good or bad; the various malts could be thus combined and patent still whisky might also be tipped in. All very well for writer Charles Tovey to say, in 1864, that in a 'gentleman's cellar ... the cask is filled up again with any whisky that is particularly approved, and thus the spirit becomes well matured and perfect'. But anyone ordering whisky in a public house might get almost anything and even a wine merchant might not make the distinction between Scotch and Irish, although a reputable firm would do so.

Consistency of quality is something that the drinker of today takes for granted, but it was as recently as 1878 that Jameson and Roe of Dublin:

> determined to bottle from four- to six-year-old whisky in bond, and to secure every bottle with a mark or capsule which it will be felony to forge or imitate. The whisky thus bottled will be supplied to the trade by the usual channels, and may be purchased by the public from any retailer of wines and spirits. Such whisky would be of guaranteed age, genuineness and excellence.

The Scots were able to defeat the potential serious competition of Irish whiskey at this time, and it began to decline as far as the English market was concerned; even the popularity of brandy began to suffer by the competition from Scotland. Business in Scotch began to boom and among the Scottish distillers themselves there was violent competition. This competition, between what were becoming the major distillers of Scotland, did in fact stimulate trade, simply because, in order to avoid wasting their time and energies on squabbling about the English market, they began to turn for more business to the export field. At this point in the history of Scotch several things happened.

The first event was that the vineyards of Europe and therefore much of the wine regions of the world, were severely affected, first by the disease of *oïdium* or downy mildew, and then, in the 1870s, by the aphis *phylloxera vastatrix*; this attacks the roots of the vine so that, had it not been found possible to continue vine growing by grafting classic vine stocks on to phylloxera-resistant American vine stocks, wine as we know it today would virtually have disappeared from the world. During the terrible years of these plagues, the brandy regions, where the grapes were used to make wine for distillation were producing virtually nothing. So the time was ripe for the killing that was to be made by those whom Allen Andrews has described as 'the 'Whisky Barons'.

In 1877 six firms amalgamated and, seven years later, another joined them, forming the 'Distillers' Company Limited' (see page 114). Now began the great spread of Scotch.

Scotch in the twentieth century

Once Scotch had become big business, it was inevitable that it should also be subject to court rulings and legal definitions. As early as 1905, the keen rivalry between firms engaged in distilling grain whisky and those producing malt whisky resulted in a court case; the grain distillers could, of course, produce more whisky in a shorter time than those distilling malt in the pot still, and these last felt themselves threatened by the competition of the grain distillers. The magistrate gave judgement against the grain distillers, saying that, 'Whisky should consist of spirits distilled in a pot still, derived from malted barley, mixed, or not, with unmalted barley and wheat, or either of them.'

The grain whisky distillers lodged an appeal after this, but fortunately both sides in the dispute now realized that their interests would be better served by their combining to do business, instead of fighting each other, so they appealed to the government of the day and, as a result, a Royal Commission was set up in 1908.

In 1909, the Commission pronounced that:

'Whiskey' [this spelling was the most usual form of the word at this date, although now it signifies Irish or other whiskeys] is a spirit obtained by distillation from a mash of cereal grains saccharified by the diastase of malt; that 'Scotch Whiskey' is whiskey, as above defined distilled in Scotland ... We have received no evidence to show that the form of the still has any necessary relationship with the wholesomeness of the spirit produced.

The last sentence refers to the claims that some people had been making to the effect that the patent or continuous stills made a 'purer' type of whisky than the product of pot stills. From this time all those making whisky in Scotland accepted the definition.

The Whisky Association was formed in 1917, handling the Irish whiskey interests as well as those of Scotch, but the Scotch Whisky Association, concerned solely with Scotch, was formed in 1942; there is also the Malt Distillers Association of Scotland, members of which are usually also members of the Scotch Whisky Association. The definition of the two types of Scotch whisky, according to this Association, is: 'Malt whisky which is made from malted barley only and grain whisky which is made from malted barley together with unmalted barley and maize.' Scotch can only be produced in Scotland and, according to an Act of 1969, 'the expression "blended whisky" or "blended Scotch whisky" shall mean a blend of a number of distillates, each of which separately is entitled to the description whisky or Scotch whisky as the case may be.'

Thanks to the promotional efforts of the great whisky firms,

Scotch progressively became a generally acceptable drink throughout the British Isles although it tended to be a 'man's drink' at least up until 1939 and, often, is a drink enjoyed between times rather than directly in relation to a formal meal. The great country houses in the north of England and, as might be expected, in Scotland, often provided travellers with small carafes (holding several drams) in their bedrooms and this practice was followed by certain of the luxury hotels.

Now, however, something happened in the United States that radically affected the history of spirit production in general and Scotch in particular. This was the enforcement of Prohibition – the prohibition of the making and consuming of alcoholic beverages.

As early as 1917, the U.S. Congress had forbidden the making of alcoholic beverages – this was when the U.S. came into the First World War on the side of the Allies against Germany. The aim of the ban was to ensure that grains that might be used as foodstuffs would not be diverted to distilling. But the temperance movement had been active in the U.S. for a long time – the 'Prohibition Party' was founded in 1869 and such were the activities of the anti-alcoholists that, by 1906, eighteen of the states of North America were officially 'dry', the State of Maine having become so as early as 1846. But this kind of ban on alcohol was not rigidly enforced although in 1918 half the states were officially 'dry'.

In January 1919, the notorious '18th constitutional amendment' was ratified by three quarters of the states and became law when the Volstead Prohibition Act was passed in October 1919, in spite of the veto of President Wilson. This Act put a ban on all drinks having an alcoholic content more than one half of 1 per cent. The period subsequent to the Act, until the repeal of the 18th amendment in 1933 (ratified in December, in time for a Christmas celebration) was the Prohibition era.

Prohibition resulted in the rise of gangsterdom, when criminals defied the law to supply alcohol to a market that could make their trading highly profitable; this influence was far worse – and lasted longer – than a little social drunkenness might have been. Many ills had their origin at this time, as might be expected, for people who think themselves fairly entitled to obtain a commodity do not usually meekly accept a ban on it. A forbidden commodity has glamour and appeal; in the post-war years, the American public felt it needed and had a right to its liquor. So did the otherwise law-abiding spirit producers in other countries.

Once liquor production was forbidden in the U.S., except for medical purposes, it was obvious that those who wanted to go on drinking would plan to import the stuff. Many ingenious ways were devised for getting Scotch ashore in North America – although, once there, it might well be adulterated with other spirits of the most horrible kind. This proved a challenge to another outstanding personality. Francis Berry, one of the partners in Berry Brothers and Rudd, a St James's wine business founded in the seventeenth century, had already achieved much on behalf of Scotch overseas, having realized that this was the spirit possibly best able to stand up to the severest vicissitudes of travel, changes in climate and ignorant service. In 1921, he crossed to the United States on a liner that also carried 'Pussyfoot' Johnson, the famous advocate of Prohibition, and even talked with him.

The significant circumstance was that it was possible to ship in all kinds of contraband cargo to the U.S. through Nassau, which was British, just as had been done by the blockade runners in the American Civil War. The problem that concerned all those trying to get their Scotch through the twentieth-century blockade, however, was that of quality – the spirit producers were well aware that those trading in the precious illegal cargo in the U.S. would 'cut' the spirit with all kinds of appalling additives, illegal distillates and poisonous wood alcohol. As the merchants knew, this would do the names of their brands no good once Prohibition was abolished – which they were certain that it must inevitably be. Meanwhile, the U.S. government warehouses held on to existing stocks of drinks, but millions of gallons were also pumped literally into the street gutters. With the production of the U.S. spirits rye and Bourbon halted in this way, the underground market was beginning to clamour for Scotch. The opportunity was there – and the right man seized it.

In Nassau, where he stayed, Francis Berry was introduced to a Captain William McCoy. This man had great experience as a rum runner. (Rum, it will be remembered, was the spirit traditionally drunk in the U.S. until whiskey began to be made there on a large scale.) McCoy's name has been added to the English language to signify genuineness – 'the real McCoy' was his guarantee to his customers that the produce he sold them, across the blockade, was completely genuine when it left his hands, no matter what the gangsters on the other side might do to it thereafter. Captain McCoy and Francis Berry planned a special type of Scotch, which should appeal to a public previously used to the flavour of rye; it should contain rather soft malts and have a light colour – indicative of its light style. This Scotch was 'Cutty Sark', the brand sold by Berry Brothers as their finest blend. It made a tremendous impact on the Mexican and South American markets as well as in the U.S.

The account of the gangster Jack 'Legs' Diamond, attended by his henchmen, coming in to the London premises of Berry Bros, to buy Scotch in the Prohibition period, is like a Damon Runyon story. But the Berrys didn't sell him Cutty Sark – for that blend was only entrusted to those whose handling might be sure of guarding its reputation. In 1961, Cutty Sark became the brand leader of all Scotch in the U.S. market and is one of the top-selling Scotches there to this day.

Although the whole civilized world had begun to drink Scotch in the form of the great blends, it was not really until after the end of the Second World War that the single malts came back into their own. Up to the late 1950s I had never tasted a single malt and was under the impression that both its strength and its assertive character was such that I would be laid low by a mere sip! It was only when the man who taught me wine gave me a single malt and I guessed it to be a particular kind of Cognac that I became interested in the subject. This was also the time when it was becoming possible once again to buy straight malt south of the border from several London retailers.

As Scotch had been a valuable export during the war and continued to earn dollars afterwards, the British public were inclined just to ask for 'whisky' in a generally hopeful way; there were many occasions when they couldn't get it at all. It took many years before the buying public in the U.K. ventured to specify brands, and even longer to ask for the de luxe Scotches (see page 152) and the malts. Although a malt whisky is still considered a drink for a special occasion and the average consumer of Scotch may not necessarily know the names of more than one or two malts, straight malt is now to be found in some variety in London and so are the de luxe blends of the great distilleries; each of these will incorporate a high proportion of malt and they are also asked for by name in smart bars. But Scotch is still not invariably the 'aperitive or when in doubt' drink in England, as far as I know, that it seems to be elsewhere.

Gentlemen who made Scotch

The personalities of the whisky trade in the nineteenth and early twentieth centuries are picturesque and remarkable. They fit into the era when the Scots were making world-wide reputations in many fields and their achievements are endowed with considerable panache.

There was Peter Mackie, nicknamed 'Restless Peter', of a family whose records go back at least to the seventeenth century; he studied at the family distillery, Lagavulin, on the Isle of Islay and was a partner in the firm when his uncle formed James Mackie in 1883; he later bought the malt distillery of Craigellachie on Speyside. Peter Mackie realized the importance of a brand name; his family still owned the house in the Canongate that had been conveyed to them in 1650. This house was on the site of the White Horse Inn, supposedly named for the white horse that Mary Queen of Scots used to ride down the Royal Mile, from Holyrood House. So, in 1891, the brand name White Horse was registered, a whisky blended to appeal to drinkers who liked the distinctive flavour of malt (Lagavulin is used in White Horse), plus the light-coloured, fresh, zingy spirit that was made in a patent still. Peter Mackie, like his contemporaries, fought Lloyd George over the enormously increased tax he imposed on whisky. Peter's only son, James Logan Mackie, who was killed outside Jerusalem in 1917, brought the direct line to an end.

Then there were the brothers Dewar, John Alexander and Thomas Robert, sons of a crofter born in 1806 who became a wine and spirit merchant in Perth and prospered, blending and bottling his own whisky. 'Whisky Tom', the youngest son, later Baron Dewar, tackled the English market for Scotch in a bold and creative way: in 1886 he literally stopped the Brewers' Show at London's Agricultural Hall by having bagpipes played – and wouldn't halt their performance. Dewars leased one distillery on upper Tayside and, in 1896, built their own at Aberfeldy, near the croft where their father had been born. Whisky Tom put up an electric sign of a Highlander drinking a dram at Dewar's Wharf, near Waterloo Bridge in London, and to extend the sales of his Scotch he went round the world, taking two years to do so, promoting the whisky. He was a friend of Sir Thomas Lipton, the grocery magnate and ocean-racing enthusiast, who was called 'Tea Tom' to distinguish him from 'Whisky Tom' and both the Toms were also friends and patrons of comedian Sir Harry Lauder. It was in Dewar's that the great blender Alexander John Cameron worked – still a legendary and quoted personality in the history of Scotch. Dewar's White Label brand has forty different whiskies in it and Cameron established the delicate intricacy of blending these elements in appropriate order, marrying them according to style and maturing at each stage in the blend when requisite. The blend still includes the malt from Aberfeldy.

It was White Label that Tom Dewar sent to Andrew Carnegie, when asked to supply something special to be presented to the

President of the United States, and this brand is among the top Scotches selling in the U.S. today; Dewar's comments on his travels in the U.S. are pawky (a term *The Concise Oxford Dictionary* describes as 'humorous, amusing', for those who are not familiar with this delicious Scots adjective) and, when he explored Canada (where he spoke to the train-driver in British Columbia in Gaelic) he noted that the crofters who had emigrated to the Rockies 'have one very bad habit: they *will* distil their own whisky'. Tom instituted many sporting trophies and was also an amateur artist; in the great Dewar House he set up in the Haymarket in London he was proud to display a picture by Raeburn and also the actual table from the tavern at Ayr at which Robert Burns wrote many of his poems. Dewar's is still a family firm, although Tom remained a bachelor; his brother (later Lord Forteviot) continued the line.

John Walker went into the wine and spirit business in 1820 and within a shortish time was also tackling the English market, his son Alexander opening a London office in 1880. Alexander's son, another Alexander, commissioned the popular artist Tom Browne to draw the likeness of 'Johnnie Walker' and Lord Stevenson, a colleague of Alexander, wrote the famous slogan 'Born 1820 – still going strong' alongside the first sketch; from this time the firm sold their whisky under this name, instead of 'Walker's Old Kilmarnock Whisky'. Johnnie Walker is the top-selling Scotch in the world, the Red Label being enormously popular in both the U.K. and U.S. (But in December 1977 the D.C.L. withdrew this brand from the U.K. market in their stand against the attempt by the E.E.C. to dictate their policy as regards pricing. To quote the *Sunday Times* of 15 January 1978: 'Johnnie Walker Red Label becomes a high-priced drink and remains a heavily promoted export spearhead.')

The stories are legion: Andrew Usher – whose son endowed the City of Edinburgh with the Usher Hall – is claimed by some to have been the first to evolve a successful blend of whisky; he acquired a small pot still, having already built up connections with other distillers. In 1852 he combined pot still single malts in a blend together with Lowland grain whiskies from the patent stills. Once it was made possible to blend malt and grain whiskies satisfactorily, the way was open for the creation of an infinite variety of different brands, each with its own individual character, able to be maintained consistently because of the process of blending.

William Sanderson of Leith, who had previously produced 'aqua shrub', containing whisky, the juices of fruits and sugar, also made 'whisky bitters', which was an infusion of herbs in whisky; in 1882, prompted by his son, he made up nearly one hundred different blends of whisky, each of which was put into a miniature cask with a number. The Sandersons then held a comparative tasting, to which they invited friends and even other blenders, all known to be connoisseurs of Scotch. At the end the opinion of the tasters was unanimous and coincided with that of William himself – the finest blend came out of vat number 69 and Vat 69 has remained its name; the dumpy bottle, incidentally, is modelled on an old one traditional in the Leith bottle factories, and the 'Talbot Hound', the Sanderson family emblem, guards the great blend.

It is impossible to do more than mention many other firms. Long John Macdonald, 6 feet 4 inches tall and a descendant of the Lord of the Isles, built the Ben Nevis Distillery in 1825. Today, however, Long John International is no longer associated with this distillery, which is currently owned by Whitbread the brewers. This firm also own Tormore in the Speyside 'Golden Rectangle' of distilleries and Laphroaig on the Isle of Islay. Long John is among the best-selling Scotches in Europe, notably in Scandinavia.

William Shaw pioneered the brand Queen Anne in Canada and the U.S.; his firm is now a member of Glenlivet Distilleries. Arthur Bell started in 1825, selling wines and spirits in a shop in Perth. He was made a partner in 1851 and the firm was registered as Bell's in 1865. Today's Bell's is the biggest independent whisky company in Scotland and they have set up their own company in the United States. Bell's is the best-selling Scotch in Scotland and among the top brands in the U.K. William Teacher, born in 1811, opened his first Glasgow shop in 1830 and was famous – some might even have said notorious – for his refusal to tolerate drunkenness or smoking. He eventually owned eighteen shops and his customers asked him to make up a blend specially for them – this was the start of Teacher's Highland Cream; Teacher's now belong to Allied Breweries and is one of the best-selling Scotches in Britain.

The Chivas Brothers, originally 'Italian warehousemen' (dealers in general groceries), started in business in Aberdeen in 1801; the original blend of Chivas Regal was one in which none of the whiskies was less than twenty-five years old. Today, the firm belongs to the Distillers Corporation of Canada, owning three distilleries as well as giant installations for maturing and bottling Scotch. And Justerini & Brooks must not be forgotten – their history is given elsewhere (see page 251) but the blend J. & B. Rare is particularly popular in the United States, where it was the top brand of Scotch in 1977.

One of the greatest personalities in the later history of Scotch was certainly James ('Jimmie') Buchanan. He was born in Ontario in 1849 and was supposed to have delicate health, so he returned to Scotland to work in a shipping firm (when aged 14) and then became a clearing clerk in a Customs House. But his pay here was poor – £20 a year – so he joined his brother, who was a grain merchant in Glasgow. When James was thirty he came to London as agent for whisky merchants Charles Mackinlay & Co. After five years, Buchanan decided to go into business on his own and, borrowing capital and having supplies guaranteed by a firm already owning distilleries and blending whisky, he launched himself with 'The Buchanan Blend of Fine Old Scotch Whiskies'.

This was an age of keen competition, when firms were fighting for business in society, music halls, hotels, the Houses of Commons and Lords, and with owners of bars and restaurants. James Buchanan, strikingly attractive, immaculately dressed, driving a smart pony and carriage through the fashionable parts of London, where, later, his daily parade of horse-drawn vans was an impressive spectacle, was light-years ahead in his concepts of promotion and advertising. Buchanan had the idea of making 'a blend sufficiently light and old to please the palate of the user'. This introduction of a whisky that seemed to have been specially created for urban dwellers was a masterstroke. He got the prima donna Adelina Patti to permit him to state that she drank 'exclusively at her meals whisky and water'; of course it was Buchanan Blend that was the whisky associated with her. His whisky won a gold medal in Paris and then, when whisky began to be sold out of bottles rather than drawn from casks in bars, the public began to ask for the Scotch in the black bottle with the white label – which resulted in the registration of the Buchanan brand Black & White. Buchanan received a Royal Warrant from Queen Victoria and, later, one from King Edward VII; he turned his firm into a public company in 1903 and, having already been made a baronet, he was created Lord Woolavington in 1922 – the year he won his first Derby with Captain Cuttle.

Then there is the House of Haig. They were Norman by origin and early versions of the name are given as del Hage, de Haga; it is possible that they took it from Cap de la Hague, the most northerly point of the Cherbourg peninsula. But they had their roots in Scotland at least as early as the twelfth century, when Petrus del Hage witnessed a Lowland charter; a century later Thomas the Rhymer, seer and poet, wrote prophetically that 'Tide what may, whate'er betide, Haig shall be Haig of Bemersyde'. Indeed, they have now owned Bemersyde through twenty-nine generations.

In 1627, Robert Haig had to leave Bemersyde after a family quarrel and he settled in Stirlingshire, where he seems to have been some kind of bailiff to the Earl of Mar, eventually owning his own farm at St Ninians, where he did some distilling. In January 1655 he was summoned before the Kirk Sessions charged with Sabbath breaking, because distilling had been carried out at St Ninians on the Lord's Day. Fortunately 'the goodwife' (his wife), away at church at the time, was able to establish that it was only the servant girl who had 'played some afterwort', so that Robert and his wife escaped with a severe warning.

Robert's great-great-grandson set up in distilling in Clackmannanshire and when he died suddenly in 1773 his widow kept on the business. This Mrs Haig was by birth a Stein, a name highly significant in the history of distilling (see page 45) and her father, who owned two distilleries, helped bring up the orphaned Haig children, so that the sons had a good grounding in the business, which they continued, setting up distilleries in other regions. One of the daughters married a local distiller, another married John Jameson, founder of the Irish whiskey firm of that name (see page 161). The five Haig sons were all remarkable. At this time, just before the French Revolution, the populace tended to riot if food ran short and in 1784 the bread shortage in Edinburgh led to a serious rising, the mob threatening to destroy any distillery where, they thought, oats and potatoes were being used for distilling, instead of these foodstuffs being released for their own nourishment. The Haigs and their servants repelled a savage onslaught on the distillery – the military had to be brought in later – and then issued a statement affirming that no ingredients suitable for human foodstuffs were being used by them.

In 1826, one of the Haig cousins, Robert Stein, owner of the Kilbegie Distillery, evolved what was possibly the first patent still, which the John Haig of the time immediately installed at his Cameron Bridge premises; it was this John Haig who became a founder of the Distillers Company Limited when this was formed in 1877. The youngest son of this John and his beautiful wife, Rachel Veitch (herself the daughter of another family much involved with the history of Scotch), was Douglas Haig, born in 1861, famous in the 1914–18 war and for creating the tradition of the poppy to commemorate 11 November, Armistice Day. Because of his family traditions, Douglas took the title of 'Bemersyde' when he was created Earl Haig and, when he died in 1928, he was buried in Dryburgh Abbey (alongside Sir Walter Scott) in accordance with a privilege claimed by the Haig family from the time of Petrus del Hage.

In 1919 the Distillers' Company Ltd acquired the share capital of John Haig & Co. Ltd, and in 1923 that of Haig & Haig, a business that had been built up in the U.S. by John Alicius Haig, brother of Hugh Veitch Haig, who had started in the States in 1888. The firm went from strength to strength in the period between the wars, chiefly being known for 'Dimple Scotch' and 'Gold Label' and Haig became the top selling whisky in the U.K. Its position is of even greater importance since December 1977, when the D.C.L. withdrew Johnnie Walker from the U.K. Market. In 1938 the firm of Haig moved its London office to Distillers' House in St James's Square. This is a beautiful building, with lofty, elegant rooms, which are still maintained in virtual eighteenth-century style.

One tragi-comical episode in the Haig story took place during the Second World War, when the S.S. *Politician* went aground off the Isle of Eriskay, with 2000 cases of export Haig & Haig on board; this episode was the inspiration for Sir Compton Mackenzie's story *Whisky Galore*, which tells of the effect of such a shipwreck on a whisky-starved community.

Finally, even though omitting many other firms of great interest that cannot be mentioned for reasons of space, there is William Grant, who provides one more example of the perseverance of the Scot in achieving commercial triumphs apparently in the face of great odds. (I describe them last because they were the first whisky firm I got to know and because they have probably taught me more about Scotch than any other.)

The family – it is still very much a family firm – is first remarked in 1745, when brothers Alexander, Daniel and William Grant were survivors of the Battle of Culloden. Alexander returned afterwards to his croft at Gighcot, and he is supposed to have lived to the age of 103; his Gaelic name, 'Auld Cearnach' can mean either 'hero' or 'freebooter'. William, the youngest brother, was also a farmer but he had bad luck, and in 1783, although almost ruined, he set out for the south to aim for England, where he gained success in the Lancashire cotton boom of the period. It was his two sons who were the originals of the Cheerybyle brothers, in Charles Dickens's *Nicholas Nickleby*. They became eminent members of the Manchester cotton trade.

It was the sole surviving son of Alexander Grant who perpetuated the whisky line, even though this man, also named Alexander, died at the age of thirty-seven. One of his sons was William Grant, born in 1784. William originally trained with his brother to be a tailor, but went off to join the 1st Battalion 92nd Regiment of Foot (later the Gordon Highlanders), and took part in the Battle of Waterloo in 1815. As this William was only 4 feet 11 inches tall, he boasted that 'all the bullets went over my head' and when he was discharged from the army in 1817 at Newcastle he walked the 320 miles to his home in Dufftown where, appropriately, he was henceforth known as 'Old Waterloo'.

William Grant married twice. By his second wife he had a son, another William, who was born in 1839. This second William began life very humbly as a herd, before being apprenticed to a cobbler; he gave up this job to become a clerk at the Tininiver lime works at Crachie and, being adventurous and energetic, he too hoped to find satisfactory deposits of lime; once he even walked the 120 miles to Balmoral and back in two days so as to examine promising outcrops. But the local laird was afraid that the kilns of William Grant's proposed limestone quarry might adversely affect the nearby woods, valuable to him for the preservation of game, and so he refused to grant the concession for development to young William. Therefore, at the age of twenty-seven, William Grant became first, a book-keeper, later the manager, at the nearby Mortlach Distillery. He had married by this time and had nine children, yet, in spite of his having less than £100 a year to live on, five of his seven sons went to university, another went to sea and the seventh was able to train in another distillery. All the sons shared in William's dream of having a distillery of his own and all contributed what they could throughout the years to the fund that was destined to achieve this purpose.

In 1886, when William Grant was forty-six, the owners of the Cardow Distillery decided to install new plant and William bought the old one for £119.19s.10d. That autumn he resigned from being the manager of Mortlach, and, within a year, he and his sons built the Glenfiddich Distillery. The first whisky ran from the still on Christmas Day 1887 and the copper cup in which this first whisky is said to have been drunk is still preserved. Five years later, William Grant had prospered so as to be able to start another distillery adjacent to Glenfiddich, at Balvenie, and also became owner of near-by Balvenie House, which he used for his malt barns.

The early struggles of the firm were complicated by various economic pressures affecting Scotch in general for at the end of the nineteenth century many whisky firms had serious problems; some of them were involved and even ruined in 1898 by the bankruptcy of Pattisons, formerly a spectacularly successful whisky concern. But the Grants had prudently cut back on their production just before this disaster and, from now on, they extended their activities from being mere distillers to becoming blenders, wholesalers and exporters as well. Charles Gordon, up to then headmaster of Cabrach Public School in Upper Banffshire, was now brought into the firm and sent to Glasgow to build up sales of the Grant blend, which was called Standfast; this was so named after the war-cry of Clan Grant, which most certainly would have been heard over the field of Culloden in 1745. Gordon had sold only one case of Standfast after 181 calls and he had had no more success when his visits had totalled 503 – to promote a new brand at the beginning of the century in the teeth of fierce competition required great perseverance. However, successes on the home market were eventually sufficiently satisfactory for John Grant to go to Canada and the United States in 1904 and for Charles Gordon to undertake adventurous and lengthy trips to the Far East, selling William Grant's whisky.

William Grant opened their London office in 1927 and established their bottling plant and export headquarters at Paisley in 1956. In 1957 they adopted the triangular bottle used for Glenfiddich and Standfast and this was also to be used for Balvenie. In 1963 an enormous grain distillery was built by the firm at Girvan; this makes Ladyburn, which is a Lowland malt, also gin and vodka in addition to the grain spirit.

In 1970, the United States firm of Popper Morson took on the distribution of both Grants and Glenfiddich for the U.S., the company's name being changed to William Grant and Sons Inc. This was not only an important step in terms of business but part of another family saga, for Joseph Popper, who had founded his business on Coney Island in 1889, was a descendant of a man of the same name who had been a distiller of various spirits in Prague in 1750. The firm had always been resolute about preserving the quality of their products and Charles Morson, head of Popper Morson, was already respected as a blender of fine whiskies. The original Joseph Popper had been associated with the saying, 'Wherever his liquors were sold, his fame spread', and the traditions of this firm were therefore similar to those of William Grant.

A list of the larger distillery groups and the distilleries that these firms own will be found on page 323. It is, however, worth pointing out the achievements of a Canadian firm in the world of Scotch. In 1930, the firm of Hiram Walker-Gooderham & Worts (see page 168) of Ontario began to acquire shares in the Stirling Bonding Co., and also in J. & C. Stodart, who owned Glenburgie-Glenlivet Distillery, near Elgin. In 1936, Hiram Walker bought the rest of the shares in these firms, also the very traditional firm of George Ballantine of Dumbarton and purchased Milton Duff Glenlivet Distillery from the Yool family. The barley used by these two distilleries is now supplied by an associated company of Hiram Walker, that of Robert Kilgour, in Kirkcaldy, Fife. In addition, Hiram Walker have added a huge grain distillery to their Scottish headquarters at Dumbarton, where they also own the Lowland malt distillery Inverleven.

In 1954, Hiram Walker took over Glencadam Distillery at Brechin and Scapa Distillery on Orkney; the next year, they took over Pulteney Distillery at Wick, Caithness, the most northerly distillery on the Scottish mainland, and in 1970 they bought Balblair at Edderton, Tain, in Ross. Balblair was founded in 1749 and, because of the abundant streams and supply of special quality peat (the region is sometimes called 'the parish of peats'), used to be a great centre for illicit distilling.

Hiram Walker's best-known whisky is probably the blend called Ballantines, but, through the members of its group, it markets a de luxe blend called Ambassador as well as several others.

How Scotch is made

Malt whisky. Although today the consumption of single malt represents only about 2 per cent of the total production of Scotch, as malt is the ancestor of all whisky it is important to understand how it is made. If in this section I draw largely on the information given to me by William Grant, this is because they were the first to introduce

Malt Whisky

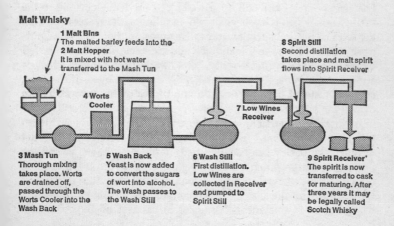

1 Malt Bins
The malted barley feeds into the
2 Malt Hopper
It is mixed with hot water
transferred to the Mash Tun

4 Worts Cooler

8 Spirit Still
Second distillation
takes place and malt spirit
flows into Spirit Receiver

7 Low Wines Receiver

3 Mash Tun
Thorough mixing
takes place. Worts
are drained off,
passed through the
Worts Cooler into the
Wash Back

5 Wash Back
Yeast is now added
to convert the sugars
of wort into alcohol.
The Wash passes to
the Wash Still

6 Wash Still
First distillation.
Low Wines are
collected in Receiver
and pumped to
Spirit Still

9 Spirit Receiver'
The spirit is now
transferred to cask
for maturing. After
three years it may
be legally called
Scotch Whisky

me to a detailed appraisal of single malts – from other distilleries as well as their own; the Scotch Whisky Association, with the Distillers' Company Ltd, have also been able to explain in lay terms what might otherwise have seemed difficult technical processes, so I quote freely from their written material.

The barley, which is the base of malt whisky, has to be carefully selected: it must have, for example, a high germination, a suitable moisture, nitrogen and protein content. When the barley arrives at the distillery it is carefully checked for quality and purity and then steeped; this means that it is soaked in water for two or three days. The importance of the water supply becomes evident, for the barley will absorb about 44 per cent of moisture. This is why so many distilleries are in picturesque surroundings where running streams provide one of the basic ingredients for Scotch – the water.

The mystery – in the true sense of the word – of the spirit, however, remains. To quote an example familiar to me, the water supply for William Grant's Glenfiddich and Balvenie Distilleries at Dufftown is all from the Robbie Dhub (Black Robert) spring, itself a stream resulting from seven springs. It is said that an old Catholic priest recommended the spring to William Grant when he founded the distillery, because it had previously been used for illicit distillation with much success. This water comes at least partly from the melting snows of the Conval Mountains, which are subsequently filtered through peat and granite; the stream also flows through gravel, sand, peat and heather. There is no filtration or addition to the water at the distillery, so the water simply has the natural liveliness of a true hill stream, which can be delicious and refreshing to drink. (Middle Eastern countries still sell open water categorized according to the spring from which it has been drawn – a refinement greater even than the sales of bottled spring water in Europe and the U.S.). At Dufftown, even though the Glenfiddich and Balvenie distilleries are fed by the same stream and are only a short walk apart, the two whiskies are quite different, the difference being apparent even to the most ignorant taster. I have been told that a distiller who once wished to extend the operations of his establishment had the original still copied in minute detail so that another distillery could be reproduced alongside the original – but the two whiskies were appreciately different!

When the barley has been steeped, it is spread out on a malting floor, where it germinates during eight to twelve days. During this time it will create its own heat; if you put your hand into it, you feel the warmth and the starch in it is modified by certain enzymes (the definition of an enzyme is 'the protein catalyst of a specific biochemical reaction') and the enzyme called diastase is secreted. It is the diastase that, later on in the whisky making process, changes the starch in the barley into a sugar, which is maltose. At this stage the malt barn is a beautiful place: the 'couch' of barley on the floor is regularly turned by workers using a wooden 'shiel', a type of shovel; the patterns made by this regular turning make the barley look like a petrified pale golden-brown sea, with curling waves. The head maltman supervises the transformation of the dormant barley into living malt, until the green malt reaches the required state of growth. The term 'green' does not refer to the colour of the barley, which is still golden-brown; the grain is now soft and chalky, the process of germination has gone as far as is required and the growth of the grain is stopped. This is done by taking it to the kilns for drying, thus arresting the germination process.

The drying kilns have a ventilator at the top in the Chinese-looking 'pagoda head'. Grant's traditionally use peat to give flavour to the barley, but nowadays anthracite is also used to bring the kiln up to the higher temperature necessary for drying the malt in a wholly satisfactory way. At Dufftown the barley remains in the kiln for about forty-eight hours, half the time being dried by peat and half on anthracite, but malts made elsewhere may have longer on peat.

In many distilleries today, however, malt is not made 'on the floor', as described here, but is mechanically processed. Aerating the barley by hand is obviously time-consuming and therefore many distilleries use either huge revolving drums, that take air to the centre of the drum, so that the barley inside is aired – this method takes up little space – or what are called 'Saladin boxes', after their inventor, a French engineer called Saladin; these boxes are long metal containers in which the barley is, as it were, combed by revolving forks that pass up and down each box. Saladin boxes began to be used in the early 1950s. But in some distilleries all three methods of airing the barley will be used, according to the notions of the establishment as to which will be both best and most economical for their purposes.

The dried malt is taken from the kiln and allowed to cool down. Its rootlets are taken off to be sold as cattle feed before the grinding takes place in the malt mill after which it goes to the mash tun. Here it is mixed with hot water, which starts up the action of the diastase in it and completes the conversion of the soluble starch into maltose. The liquid resulting from this – which is called the 'wort' – is then drawn off and the remaining husks, known as 'draff', are also sold as cattle feed. The herds of the regions around the great distilleries produce champion beasts, which is not surprising.

The wort cools down and is then sent into the tun-room. Here the 'wash backs', which are enormous vessels, receive it and yeast is added; this goes into action to convert the sugar in the wort to alcohol, the process taking about forty-eight hours. The resulting liquid is known as 'wash'. The temperature of the wash rises so that the yeast cells gradually die, the bacteria that remain after they have done so being one of the factors that makes each malt subtly different. During the process of the yeast's action, the liquid churns violently, as if paddles were agitating it, and gigantic foamy bubbles, of a loose texture, form like lace on the surface.

The wash is now to be distilled. It is pumped from the wash back to the wash charger, which is where the wash stills draw their supplies; these wash stills are huge copper pots shaped like cones – hence the name pot still – which taper into a pipe running sideways, known as the swan neck, or the 'lyne arm', which goes into the worm; this is an ever-decreasing coil which winds through a tank kept cool with cold running water. At the bottom of the worm tank there is the 'tail pipe' and the 'spirit safe' which is where the sampling equipment is sited. First the liquid is heated so that the alcohol vaporizes, rising from the liquid, and is driven off to be cooled and then condensed; in the first distillation the alcohol is separated from the liquid, leaving behind the unfermentable matter and yeast, and goes on to the second distillation, which takes place in a separate still, called the 'low wines' still.

The first and last runnings of the first still are returned to be redistilled as they contain substantial amounts of impure spirit. The first part is known as the foreshots; the second part of the runnings is the middle cut and is the part which becomes whisky, and the third part is called feints.

The run of the first distillation takes about five hours, that of the second from nine to ten hours. It will be realized that the stillman has a highly skilled job in deciding when to run the still 'on spirit' for maximum quality. (In quoting the time these processes take, I am citing what is done by William Grant. It should be appreciated that other distilleries will have their own individual schedules.)

After the whisky has been made it is put into oak casks. It is colourless at this stage and will acquire any colouring from its cask. It is also subject to the strictest control by the Customs and Excise, who have been concerned with it since it became low wines at the second distillation. It has previously been stressed (see page 121) that the action of the atmosphere on the whisky in wood is important, due to the climate of Scotland being a soft, often very damp one;

because of this, although there is some evaporation of the spirit during the maturation period, plus a slight loss of alcohol strength, this loss and decline is nothing like as great as, for example, would occur in the maturation of a brandy made and matured in a hot dry region (see page 65).

Scotch must be kept for a minimum of three years, but a malt will continue to mature with marked improvement for as long as fifteen years, although after about twenty years it may take on a slightly woody character. This depends on the character of the whisky itself; some malts reach their peak faster than others. Whisky matured in a very large cask will mature more slowly, but the action of the atmosphere on the contents of the cask is always of great importance and naturally varies from region to region. The blender who controls the stock at this stage will also know that some of his malts are destined for blending instead of remaining straight malts and therefore may be required to attain a slightly different character from those that are to be drunk straight.

Patent still whisky. The basis for this, the mash, consists of a proportion of malt plus unmalted cereals. These unmalted cereals are ground and cooked under steam pressure, the grain and water being agitated by stirrers during this time, so that the starch cells in the grain burst. Subsequently, in the mash tun, the diastase proportion of the mash that consists of malt will change the starch into maltose. The worts are collected at a specific gravity lower than that found in the pot still process, as the patent still is best fitted to take a mash with a proof spirit content of about 9–10 per cent. The continuous still

Grain Whisky

1 Maize Storage Bin The maize feeds into the Cooker.

3 Malt Storage Bin After weighing and grounding the malt passes to
4 Malt Hopper Here the malt is mixed with hot water and passed to the Mash Tun

6 Worts Cooler

2 Cooker Here the maize is mixed with hot water and pressure steam cooked before being drawn off into the Mash Tun

5 Mash Tun The malt converts the starch in the maize to sugar. The resultant worts are then passed through the Worts Cooler to the Wash Back

7 Wash Back Yeast is now added to convert the sugars of wort into alcohol. The wash after fermentation passes through a complex system of distillation and rectification columns from which the grain spirit is transferred to the Spirit Receiver

8 Spirit Receiver The spirit is now transferred to cask for maturing. After three years it may be legally called Scotch Whisky

distils a liquid and the resulting spirit comes off at a much higher strength – although this strength is reduced before the spirit is put into cask and it is matured at a strength similar to that of malt whisky. Grain whisky, as it is known, does not need as long a period of maturation as malt whisky made in a pot still; it is quite different in character from malt, also being lighter in style.

Blending. It must be clearly understood that, except for straight malt whiskies, all other whiskies are some form of a blend of whiskies. The blending of the malt and grain whiskies is a highly skilled task. When it is undertaken, the various whiskies are run off into large vats, after which the blender will decide how they are to be combined.

Some firms will vat together the malt whiskies and grain whiskies they are going to use at this stage of the proceedings. Others, for various good reasons, prefer to vat malts separately from grains. It is at the stage when the blend of the different whiskies is drawn off from the vats to go into casks for maturation (prior to bottling) that the essential 'marrying' or unifying of the constituents takes place. Again, it depends on the individual establishment as to whether the various malts and grains are married separately or together at this stage; it is a task of great skill to decide the order in which the different whiskies are blended, how much of each is required for the ultimate blend and how long each whisky in the blend needs for its maturation. After the final maturation period, the whisky is bottled.

It is necessary to realize that each blend of Scotch may contain a great number of different whiskies; it is quite impossible to generalize about how many. The blender will determine how these whiskies will react on each other so as to achieve the desired harmonious blend in the bottle. Naturally, different markets have different preferences and there are various fashions in whisky: for example, the creation of the blend 'Cutty Sark' (see page 131) catered for specific U.S. preferences. In order to achieve continuity of the blend, the colour of the whisky also has to be consistent – there is a preference for palish Scotch in some markets – and, as with other spirits, the strength of the whisky may have to be reduced by the addition of water, to bring it to the strength at which the spirit is to be sold.

The different Scotches

The products of each of the great firms will be wholly individual, both as regards the malts and grains they use. It is worth noting that in some of the most popular blends the proportion of malt may be high, but, as malts themselves vary so much in character, the layman can only establish preferences by trying as many as possible.

Until around the middle of the twentieth century, straight malt was thought to be a drink wholly unsuited for anyone other than those leading an active out-of-door life, such as the fortunate Highlanders who made it. But malt is not necessarily 'strong' in the alcoholic sense. Of course, the straight malts are not drinks to toss off in quantity anyway, and knowledge and appreciation of them is one of the most interesting developments in the history of Scotch today. Each is as different as, say, a different classed growth claret.

Highland malts. These are made north of the Highland line which runs approximately from Glasgow to Dundee, and are sometimes subdivided into Glenlivets and Highlands. The Livet is a tributary of the Avon and itself runs into the Spey, so it is truthfully said that Glenlivet is 'the longest glen in Scotland'. The whole of this region is extremely beautiful and the curious effect of the pagoda-topped distilleries in the majestic landscape is remarkable. Of Dufftown, sometimes referred to as 'the capital of malt', it is said:

> Rome was built on seven hills,
> Dufftown stands on seven stills.

A reference to the map will show the number of distilleries clustered here.

'The Glenlivet', however, deserves a note to itself. It was the child of George Smith, who was born in 1792, the son of a Glenlivet farmer; he began both to distil and smuggle whisky around 1817, while running a farm, but he was shrewd enough to see that ultimately distilling under licence might be more profitable, so he took one out in 1824. This was the origin of The Glenlivet Distillery. George Smith had considerable opposition at the outset from his former allies, the illicit distillers and smugglers, but eventually the 1822 Act requiring distilling under licence triumphed – and the only man in Glenlivet to remain distilling was George Smith. The whisky was taken in carts, drawn by the gigantic Clydesdale horses, from Upper Drumin to the coast, for shipping south. The advent of the railway was a tremendous boon, and so was George Smith's skill and success in farming; this resulted in his buying more and more land from the Duke of Richmond and Gordon on Speyside, where Smith began to grow his own barley and where he eventually established another distillery, in addition to breeding prizewinning cattle. George Smith's elder son died in 1846, so the younger son, John Gordon

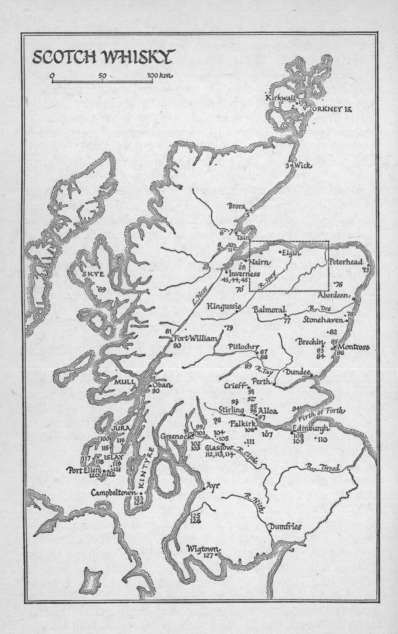

SCOTCH WHISKY

0   50   100 km.

Kirkwall
1
2
ORKNEY IS.

3 Wick

Brora
5
4

6 7
Tain
8 10
9 11
29
Nairn
2 8
•Elgin
Peterhead
73

Inverness
43, 44, 45
70
R. Spey
•76

Aberdeen

SKYE
69

Kingussie
Balmoral
77
R. Dee
•78

81
79
Stonehaven
82
Fort William
80
Pitlochry
87
88
Brechin
85
83
84
Montrose
86

89 R. Tay
Dundee

MULL
Oban
90
Crieff
Perth
91

93 92
95
98
96
Alloa
97
94
Firth of Forth
Stirling
Falkirk
106
107
Edinburgh
108
109
•110

99
101
98
104
•105
111

JURA
100 116
Greenock
102
103
Glasgow
112, 113, 114
R. Clyde

117
118
ISLAY
115
119
121
Pott Ellen
120 122

KINTYRE

R. Tweed

Campbeltown
123
124

Ayr
R. Nith

125
126

Dumfries

Wigtown
127

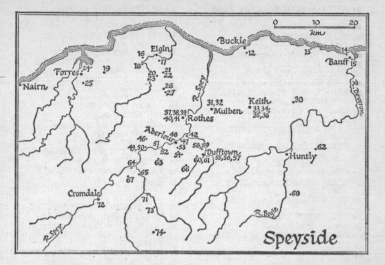

Detail from map (opposite) showing Speyside distilleries

GRAIN

11 INVERGORDON Invergordon
80 BEN NEVIS Fort William
86 LOCHSIDE Montrose
94 CAMERONBRIDGE Windygates
95 CAMBUS Cambus
96 NORTH OF SCOTLAND Cambus
97 CARSEBRIDGE Alloa
101 DUMBARTON Dumbarton
108 CALEDONIAN Edinburgh
109 NORTH BRITISH Edinburgh
111 MOFFAT Airdrie
113 PORT DUNDAS Glasgow
114 STRATHCLYDE Glasgow
125 GIRVAN Girvan

LOWLAND MALT

102 INVERLEVEN Dumbarton
103 LOMOND Dumbarton
104 LITTLEMILL Bowling
105 AUCHENTOSHAN Dalmuir
106 ROSEBANK Falkirk
107 ST MAGDALENE Linlithgow
110 GLENKINCHIE Pencaitland
111 MOFFAT Airdrie
112 KINCLAITH Glasgow
126 LADYBURN Girvan
127 BLADNOCH Wigtown

ISLAY MALT

100 BUNNAHABHAIN Islay
115 CAOL ILA Islay
117 BRUICHLADDICH Islay
118 BOWMORE Islay
119 ARDBEG Islay
120 PORT ELLEN Islay
121 LAGAVULIN Islay
122 LAPHROAIG Islay

CAMPBELTOWN MALT

123 GLEN SCOTIA Campbeltown
124 SPRINGBANK Campbeltown

HIGHLAND MALT

1 HIGHLAND PARK Kirkwall
2 SCAPA Kirkwall
3 PULTENEY Wick
4 BRORA Brora
5 CLYNELISH Brora
6 BALBLAIR Edderton
7 GLENMORANGIE Tain
8 DALMORE Alness
9 TEANINICH Alness
10 BEN WYVIS Invergordon
12 INCHGOWER Buckie
13 GLENGLASSAUGH Portsoy
14 MACDUFF Banff
15 BANFF Banff
16 GLEN MORAY-GLENLIVET Elgin
17 LINKWOOD Elgin
18 MILTONDUFF-GLENLIVET Elgin
19 GLENBURGIE-GLENLIVET Forres
20 MANNOCHMORE Birnie

21 BENRIACH-GLENLIVET Elgin
22 LONGMORN-GLENLIVET Elgin
23 GLENLOSSIE Elgin
24 BENROMACH Forres
25 DALLAS DHU Forres
26 GLEN ELGIN Longmorn
27 COLEBURN Elgin
28 ROYAL BRACKLA Nairn
29 ORD Muir-of-Ord
30 KNOCKDHU Knock, by Huntly
31 AUCHROISK Mulben
32 GLENTAUCHERS Mulben
33 AULTMORE Keith
34 GLEN KEITH-GLENLIVET Keith
35 STRATHISLA-GLENLIVET Keith
36 STRATHMILL Keith
37 CAPERDONICH Rothes
38 GLEN GRANT-GLENLIVET Rothes
39 GLENROTHES-GLENLIVET Rothes
40 GLEN SPEY Rothes
41 SPEYBURN Rothes
42 CRAIGELLACHIE Craigellachie
43 GLEN ALBYN Inverness
44 GLEN MHOR Inverness
45 MILLBURN Inverness
46 CARDOW Knockando
47 MACALLAN Craigellachie
48 ABERLOUR-GLENLIVET Aberlour
49 KNOCKANDO Knockando
50 TAMDHU-GLENLIVET Knockando
51 IMPERIAL Carron
52 DAILUAINE Carron
53 GLENALLACHIE Aberlour
54 BENRINNES Aberlour
55 CONVALMORE Dufftown
56 GLENDULLAN Dufftown
57 MORTLACH Dufftown
58 BALVENIE Dufftown
59 GLENFIDDICH Dufftown
60 DUFFTOWN-GLENLIVET Dufftown
61 PITTYVAICH-GLENLIVET Dufftown
62 GLENDRONACH Huntly
63 GLENFARCLAS-GLENLIVET Ballindalloch
64 CRAGGANMORE Ballindalloch
65 TOMINTOUL-GLENLIVET Ballindalloch
66 ALLTA 'BHAINNE Dufftown
67 TORMORE Advie
68 ARDMORE Kennethmont
69 TALISKER Carbost
70 TOMATIN Tomatin
71 THE GLENLIVET Glenlivet
72 BALMENACH Comdale
73 TAMNAVULIN-GLENLIVET
74 BRAES OF GLENLIVET Dufftown
75 GLENUGIE Peterhead
76 GLENGARIOCH Old Meldrum
77 LOCHNAGAR Balmoral
78 GLENURY-ROYAL Stonehaven
79 DALWHINNIE Dalwhinnie
80 BEN NEVIS Fort William
81 GLENLOCHY Fort William
82 FETTERCAIRN Fettercairn
83 BRECHIN (NORTH PORT) Brechin
84 GLENCADAM Brechin
85 HILLSIDE Montrose
86 LOCHSIDE Montrose
87 BLAIR ATHOL Pitlochry
88 EDRADOUR Pitlochry
89 ABERFELDY Aberfeldy
90 OBAN Oban
91 GLENTURRET Crieff
92 TULLIBARDINE Blackford
93 DEANSTON Doune
98 GLENGOYNE Killearn
99 LOCH LOMOND Alexandria
116 ISLE OF JURA Jura

Smith, was brought back from Edinburgh where he was studying law, to help his father. Business both profited and was extended. John Gordon Smith was particularly proud of the casks of whisky that he sent to the beleaguered officers in Ladysmith, during the Boer War, which arrived in time to celebrate the relief of the town in 1900.

In 1880 the competition of other near-by distilleries calling themselves 'Glenlivet' brought about a law case and this is why 'The Glenlivet' can be only Smith's Glenlivet, the sole whisky made in the parish of Glenlivet. In 1978, The Glenlivet was bought by Seagram (see page 176). Other whiskies can use the name Glenlivet if they add it to their own. The ones that do are: Macallan, Glen Grant, Dufftown, Longmorn, Glenburgie, Glendronach, Glenfarclas, Glen Keith, Strathisla, Glen Rothes, Glen Moray, Aberlour, Tomintoul, Milton Duff. But, as the map shows, there are many other distilleries here.

Lowland malts. These are made south of the Highland line. Only four Lowland malts are now available as such: Rosebank, Bladnoch, Auchentoshan and Littlemill. All the others made near Edinburgh and Glasgow go into blends.

Islay malts. These come from the Isle of Islay (pronounced 'Eyela' with the stress on the first syllable) off the Mull of Kintyre; but, as Islay is essentially part of the region of Strathclyde, sometimes the malts made there are categorized as Strathclyde or referred to as Island malts. Of the distilleries on the Isle of Islay itself, Laphroaig (pronounced 'Laffroyg') is possibly the best known, much of its production going into the blend Islay Mist. Lagavulin is another famous Islay malt, which is also the basis of White Horse (see page 133), and the distillery is probably among the oldest on the island. The Isle of Jura is the site of a distillery of that name, closed for some time, reopened in 1963, the whisky only recently being available again as a single malt. On the Isle of Skye the great name is Talisker, and on Orkney, Highland Park at Kirkwall; the distillery here was established in 1789 on the place where Magnus Eunson, a notorious Orkney smuggler, had his bothy (hut). Because he was an officer of the church, he stored his illegally distilled whisky underneath the pulpit.

Campbeltown malts. These were at one time both more numerous and more popular than they are today, but they suffered from unscrupulous producers who often made whisky unworthy of the region and today production is small, the distilleries being Springbank and Glen Scotia.

It is very difficult to generalize about the character of the malts according to regions of production, when each distillery will make a product entirely different from that of even its immediate neighbours. But for the beginner it may be helpful to think of the following generalizations while gaining specific experience.

The Glenlivets have great distinction and clear-cut character, plus a type of assertiveness, varying in depth of style and elegance from distillery to distillery. The Dufftown malts usually seem to me to possess particular elegance, combined with a delicacy of appeal.

Tomatin, near Inverness, is the largest malt distillery of all and had its origin in a fifteenth-century establishment. It is owned by an independent company and is the only single malt distillery to be quoted on the London Stock Exchange. Tomatin has been described by some writers as light-bodied and with a markedly peaty flavour.

The Lowland malts, which were among those pioneering the popularity of Scotch in England, have a very definite style and those from the Dumbarton region are particularly individual – two of the important names here are Littlemill and Auchentoshan.

The Islay malts and Island malts are also of marked individuality, many people claim to note a flavour of peat and seaweed or iodine in some of them. I don't notice this myself, but they are certainly aromatic, with a somewhat weighty style which may be too strong for anyone starting a study of malts; they have many shades of aroma and flavour and sometimes writers term them 'oily', frequently applying this adjective to Talisker. Highland Park is quite different again, with a markedly crisp, compact style and a pleasing lightness.

The Campbeltowns used to be rather heavy, assertive malts, but today they are lighter and, although they are pleasant, I find them a little four-square in style, perhaps lacking the charm of some of the others. But as many books (some of which are listed on page 325) describe the malt whiskies in detail, the enthusiast is recommended to refer to the taste impressions of these writers.

Blends and de luxe blends of Scotch

Each big whisky house will produce its own blended whisky, as has been indicated, and many wine merchants, stores and retail chains may also have their own special brands. An ordinary blended Scotch can be a first-rate drink, taken either with water (the traditional way in Scotland) or with carbonated water or as the basis for a mixture. The strength of blended Scotch is usually 40 to 42·9 per cent or 70° to 75° proof, and this must be stated on the label, as with all spirits. But nowadays, so that some outlets may offer whisky at a slightly lower price, there are some 'fringe' types which may be very slightly lower in strength, which of course makes for a saving to the customer, as duty is charged according to strength. Scotch intended for export is generally a little higher in alcohol than that for the home trade (42·9 per cent as compared with 40 per cent).

The choice of a blended whisky is entirely a matter of personal preference. It is a pity for the interested consumer to stick rigidly to one brand only and thus forgo the experience of seeing the different variations achieved by the master blenders of the great establishments.

But as well as the whiskies for export being usually slightly higher in alcohol than those for the U.K. Market, there are now a number of 'de luxe' blends of Scotch. Some of these are certainly intended to attract buyers overseas, but they can be true luxuries for any lover of Scotch anywhere.

These de luxe blends are, simply, the very best that the individual blender of Scotch can achieve: each blend will probably contain a higher proportion of malt than the more everyday brand and will have been matured for a longer period; the de luxe Scotch may also be higher in strength, some of them being 42·9 per cent, 45·7 per cent or 57·1 per cent, 75°, 80°, or 100° proof, which again must be stated on the label and which, of course means that the price will be high. If any claim to the age of the de luxe blends is made in the words of its name, then the legal requirement is that any figure quoted must refer to the youngest single whisky in the blend, and not just to the average age of the components. It is therefore possible for a Scotch of this type to be labelled as, say, '12 year old', but for there to be whiskies in the blend that have been matured for much longer than this. The special packs and unusually shaped bottles that are often used for these luxury Scotches are all aimed at pleasing the customer, especially overseas, who wants something out of the ordinary of the highest quality. Some of the Scotches of this type that sell in enormous quantities are hardly known in the U.K., but the best known de luxe Scotches for the Briton will probably be Haig's Dimple, and the Black Label of Johnnie Walker. The next important names are Chivas Regal and The Antiquary. The U.S. top de luxe Scotch at present is Chivas Regal, followed by Black Label, which last also leads in many other export markets; in Venezuela, Buchanan's is the leader and in Japan, Old Parr is extremely important. Among other well-known brands in this category are Red Hackle De Luxe and Usher's De Luxe.

Water and Scotch

The water of Loch Katrine is traditionally the perfect diluting agent for good Scotch but the water of any spring will do, although, whether this is still or slightly sparkling, it should be as neutral in taste as possible. When whisky is being professionally appraised it is seldom actually taken into the mouth, as this would fatigue the palate. The blender works mainly by 'nosing' the whisky but he seldom appraises this by simply sniffing the neat spirit: he 'awakes' it – so that it shows off its characteristics – by various means. The most usual method is to add pure water, of the type previously mentioned, not recycled city tap water; then the different attributes of each sample may be more easily distinguished. Whisky blenders often use a tulip-shaped thin glass, or one that has a slightly bulbous bowl, rising to a funnel-like shape, so that the smell is presented to the nose without the blender losing any of it. Occasionally, blenders may rub some of the spirit on the palms of their hands and, when it has evaporated, sniff the lingering aroma, very much in the way that blenders work among brandies, especially Cognac.

Drinking Scotch

Queen Victoria used to drink whisky, and probably not just because she loved all Scottish products: the spirit in moderation is a lightly stimulating 'nightcap' often suggested by doctors to elderly patients who need a little restorative if they are to relax before going to sleep. A friend once showed me a smallish glass, heavily cut and rather vase-shaped, that had once formed part of a set used for the Queen's nightly dram at Balmoral – the glass had been bequeathed by a relation once associated with the royal household. There is also a report that Victoria laced her claret with Scotch, which appalled Mr Gladstone, who was quite conventional about drinking (and knew something about wine. Bertrand Russell records in his autobiography that, as a young man, he was host at a family dinner where Gladstone, the 'Grand Old Man', then very old, commented at the end, as if to himself: 'This is very good port, but why have they given it to me in a claret glass?').

Whisky's stimulating properties have long since made it very popular as a late-night drink. The drinks tray, traditional in the British Isles at least from the nineteenth century, would be brought in – and in many households it still is – just before people went up to their rooms; it would hold spring water and, at a later period, fruit juice, plus, possibly, some other spirits, but almost invariably whisky.

The value of this excellent spirit to those living and working in unhealthy parts of the world was immediately realized from the time that it became commercially available outside Scotland. In the last days of the British in India, between the World Wars, whisky was 'the' drink, although it was unusual for anyone in the service of the Raj to drink anything alcoholic in the middle of the day – six in the evening was when the first drink was taken, usually whisky much diluted with ice and soda. Scotch was by far the most popular drink, even though the gimlet (a longish drink of gin and lime juice) was also liked. The 'chotapeg' was two fingers of whisky, the 'burrapeg' three.

The concept of the 'sundowner', a drink taken in countries where there is only a short twilight or none, is sound. The temperature can drop sharply as soon as the sun goes, and people can even find their teeth beginning to chatter within an hour after they have been luxuriating in a high temperature in a dry atmosphere. The system feels uneasy while adjusting to the rapid change. This is the time to have a slightly stimulating drink – and, once you are in the habit of taking it at this time, there is no more uneasiness, as the body, helped by alcohol, adjusts comfortably to the cool, balmy night.

It is often asked whether one can mix 'grape with grain', in other words, drink grain spirits as well as wine on the same occasion. I would certainly not generally advocate the consumption of large quantities of grain spirits of any sort, either in mixes or neat, before a meal to be accompanied by very fine wines, simply because after several drinks of this sort the palate really cannot appreciate any food or drink that is of a subtle flavour and of lower strength. But, unless the first wine of a meal is to be a very delicate one, I do not see why a fine whisky with water or even soda should be wholly unacceptable as a cocktail – although naturally it should not be taken in more than moderate amounts. In fact, a straight malt or even a de luxe blend of Scotch can be an admirable choice to accompany certain first courses that present problems as regards wine. For example, there is an admirable recipe for kipper pâté, which includes a little straight malt; any fine wine would be quite at odds with this. Other dishes with which schnapps, vodka and similar spirits are served may also be enjoyed accompanied by a little whisky, chosen for quality.

Scotch is the traditional accompaniment when haggis is served and sometimes the hot haggis has some poured over it. It may surprise some readers to know that this wonderful version of the blood sausage, almost a Scottish national dish, can also be served cold in thin slices as a snack, which is a good way to accompany whisky or whisky-based drinks for a casual party. The way in which the whisky counteracts the richness and sometimes the slight greasiness of the haggis indicates that Scotch can also be an admirable partner for other gamey informal dishes, sausages, rich pâtés, blood pudding or some tripe recipes.

There is also a place for serving fine whisky, of any kind, at the end of a meal, which I have not seen included in any of the 'what to drink with what' sections of the numerous books dealing with social drinking. This is with the savoury. This rather odd course, which does not seem ever to have been even vaguely imitated in other countries, evolved in England at the beginning of the nineteenth century, when, in the absence of a formal court, men began to frequent their clubs for supper and the food was quite unlike that of any course of a meal; indeed, dishes of eggs, anchovies, devilled food or marrow bones are mostly quite unsuitable for a course at a formal meal, certainly when fine wine is being served. The savoury fulfilled the role of the 'quick snack' and served to stimulate a jaded palate. The freshness and firm character of a good whisky make it an admirable drink to go with these salty, piquant dishes.

Cookery writers have somewhat tended to ignore the savoury and I think this may have been because the hostess is not much concerned with 'men's dinners' – their ordering would, in the past, have been left to the chef of the relevant club or private house, or of establishments such as that of Mrs Rosa Lewis at the old Cavendish Hotel, where an escape from formality was part of the charm. Today, the savoury may often supersede the pudding or any form of sweet course, although its presence does not mean there is to be no dessert in the British sense of this word, which still, to the conventional, means fruit and nuts, not a sweet dish; dessert is dessert for a Briton, even if it means the 'sweet course' in the U.S.

One thing that may strike the traveller in many parts of Scotland is that the local inhabitants, even those living almost in the shadow of a pot still, seldom drink straight malt! It will usually be the tourists or visitors from England who order this in the ordinary bar. Derek Cooper, an authority on Skye, where he lives for part of the year, reports that the regulars in the pubs there won't usually be ordering Talisker, but a blended Scotch and this seems to be so in other places. One reason may be that, for the occasional bar refresher, straight malt really is too serious a commodity – it requires quiet, fairly concentrated appraisal. Indeed, the aromatic Island malts are perhaps not the type of Scotch that one would wish to drink every day and in quantity, any more than one would – or could – drink a first growth claret with sausage and mash! And the price of a bottle of malt in a supermarket or a measure of malt in a bar is substantially higher than that of a blended whisky. Derek Cooper thinks that the lighter, often more elegant style of Speyside malt, as compared with such malts as Talisker and Laphroaig, may mean that the Speysides can be drunk more casually and frequently, which in turn may account at least partly for the huge success of the Dufftown Glenfiddich in world markets.

The place of Scotch in the drinking pattern in England and Wales today is not rigidly defined. But in conventional households it still tends to be drunk more outside the context of meals than as an aperitive. This obviously dates from the period between the wars, when (as has been noted on page 99) whisky was seldom offered as an aperitive at parties in the 'polite world', though it was of course quite often drunk casually at other times by men – seldom, I think, by women. Certainly I never remember Scotch as a preprandial drink when I was growing up and many older friends have told me that it would never have been served in the grander type of house to which they were invited. The novels of E. F. Benson and some of those of John Galsworthy, which accurately depict the routine of a certain type of well-to-do English society of the late 1920s and 1930s, often refer to whisky as the drink of those who have been abroad in the services and who take it after dinner – rather in the tradition of the late-evening drinks tray, where it still appears. But, when the characters refer to a 'cocktail' (as opposed to sherry) they invariably mean something with a basis of gin – the word 'cocktail' at this period seems to have had the euphemistic significance of the 'Nig' decanter labels of an earlier period (see page 97).

It may surprise the reader who has little experience of traditional English life to find that, even to this day, it would never occur to me or to the majority of my friends over the age of fifty to offer whisky to anyone as an aperitive – unless the guest happened to be from the U.S. or France. *Le Scotch* has been chic in France, even in wine producing areas, for many years now, and *un petit whisky* is often suggested to the British visitor there. The French are often disappointed when they don't get offered Scotch before they dine in an English – even a Scottish – home! But, although the young and trendy will obviously drink what and when they like and guests invited to a restaurant will of course order whatever they want in the bar, the convention in many U.K. households still holds that whisky is mainly a between times or late-night drink in private houses. It is also often the reviving drink taken on returning home, before people get ready for the evening meal.

IRISH – WHISKEY WITH AN 'E'

The spellings of the word 'whisky' and 'whiskey' have been indiscriminately used in the past, but it is true to say that now Irish is always spelt with the 'e' before the 'y'. Irish is also generally accepted as being the first whiskey that was made, although it is probably a legend that it was introduced to the island by St Patrick (? 385– ? 461). The association of the early church with distilling, however, is probable, because 'Holy Ireland' was a centre of learning so that there was much coming and going between the religious foundations there and those in Europe, who naturally exchanged information about such practicalities as food and drink as well as scholarship. The south of Ireland may have first become acquainted with the process of distilling from monks coming there from Spain. There is a record of an Irish chieftain dying in 1405 from a surfeit of aqua vitae, and there are some references to the natives drinking this spirit at the time when Henry II invaded Ireland in the thirteenth century. It seems possible, from primitive distilling apparatus that has been found in bogs in Ireland and thus preserved, that stills were in use from as early as about 1400 onwards, but there is no indication as to the type of spirit that resulted from this distillation.

In 1580, the English government in Ireland declared that, in Munster, 'persons . . . aiders of rebels . . . makers of *aquavitae* . . .' were to be subjected to martial law; another reference in 1584 states that aqua vitae 'sets the Irishry a-madinge and breeds much mischiefs'. About 1600, Fynes Moryson, then secretary to the Lord Deputy of Ireland, referred to 'aqua vitae, vulgarly called usquebaugh', praising it for medicinal purposes, and saying that among other ingredients it was made with raisins. This might have been the first instance of dried fruit being used for distilling. The 'Old Bushmills Distillery Company Ltd', which claims that it is the oldest distillery in the world, possess a grant issued to Sir Thomas Phillips in 1608, allowing him to distil on the banks of the Bush River in County Antrim. In 1617, Sir Walter Raleigh, on his last voyage to the West Indies, touched at Youghal, where he stocked up for the voyage and John Boyle, the first Earl of Cork, then gave him 'a supreme present – a 32 gallon keg of his own Uisce Baugh'. Throughout Ireland distilling gradually became widespread, although of course the stills usually operated on a very small scale.

The history of Irish whiskey is henceforth mainly concerned with the efforts made by the revenue authorities to control both illicit distilling and, eventually, the raw materials used and the way the distilling was actually done. It was quickly realized that controls of this sort were a vast potential source of wealth. Complicating any form of controls, however, were the private stills; these, kept in someone's house for purely domestic purposes, were not subject to the official controls, being considered as much a part of the equipment of an ordinary small estate as a bread oven. A domestic still, supplying a household and the tenants of the estate, could not easily be inspected or its production limited and the line between supplying spirit for the establishment's needs, using it as payment for goods or simply selling any surplus could not be sharply drawn.

In the eighteenth century there was also a tremendous vogue for brandy, smuggled from France, which competed with the local spirit. There was another problem that faced the Irish distillers: frequently, the various grain crops failed or were only available in short supply, so that these cereals had then to be used both for food and animal fodder, instead of part of the yield being utilized for distillation. Thus, there was no assurance of the raw material being available from year to year.

Many Irish landowners then had substantial holdings in the West Indies where their plantations could make more money than their estates in Ireland, and the sugar crop yielded a more immediately profitable cheap spirit, because of the cheapness of black labour. In the 1770s, for example, rum imports to Ireland accounted for about 80 per cent of the imported spirits. Wine, too, naturally competed with the native spirit among the gentry and nobility, many of whom spent years abroad in wine-growing countries. But, by 1777, the amount of spirit distilled in Ireland was very nearly equal to the amount of wine imported.

In 1780, over a million gallons of spirit were distilled, although of course much of this may have been coarse stuff. The results of the excessive drinking of spirits caused well-meaning people to try to limit this, and the brewers, who up to this time had been able to compete successfully with the distillers, backed the anti-spirits campaigners. But the more the authorities attempted to control or discourage distilling, the more the distillers thought up ways to increase the quantities of spirits and avoid paying the various duties and penalties. The distillers were under considerable pressure even to stay in business, but they did, competing fiercely with each other. However, an Act of 1823, which attempted to operate strict overall controls on distillation in Ireland, did enable those distilling to operate more slowly and, therefore, to produce a spirit of superior quality and adequate maturity. For example, although a distiller might have one still for all his operations, should he have more than one, he had to designate the purpose for which each was used and was not allowed to change them. Many details concerning the still itself, and the various controls, such as locks, were also henceforth subject to legislation; the pipes in the distillery had to be painted in colours according to the liquid they were carrying: white for water, red for wash, blue for low wines or feints, and black for spirits. Nor was the distiller allowed to sell direct to the public. The way in which he stored his spirits was equally strictly controlled.

Subsequent licensing laws also exerted stricter controls on the way spirit was sold. The 'spirit grocer' was often able to sell measures of spirit for consumption on the spot if the drinkers could go into a corner behind some of the groceries. It was easier to get a licence for this type of grocery business than a publican's license, so that women, in the course of doing their shopping, had easy access to 'the craythur' as Irish whiskey is sometimes called, whereas the more respectable might have hesitated before entering a public house. It was not until 1910 that in Ireland the type of licence required by the spirit grocer was merged with that of the retail off-licence.

The enormous increases in the duty on spirits throughout the late nineteenth and the twentieth centuries and the decline of the indigenous population, especially after the terrible years of famine, resulted in an overall decline in spirit consumption. The potato blight of 1845 affected the potato crop of the whole of Europe, but the Irish were more dependent on potatoes than anyone else; in addition to the appalling poverty resulting from the famine, there was a rise in disease, notably scurvy, owing to lack of vitamin C previously supplied by potatoes. Deaths resulting from malnutrition and from the hardships caused when landlords evicted peasants depleted the population. Small wonder that the Irish began to leave their homeland: annual emigration had only been about 60,000 prior to the first of the great famines, but more than 200,000 Irish left in 1847 and by 1851 a quarter of a million left each year. Also, for the Irish distiller, a further significant change at the beginning of the twentieth century was the growing popularity of blended whisky, which consisted of the products of both pot still and continuous still.

The intricacies of the regulations that have affected the history of Irish whiskey are lengthy, and sometimes it seems remarkable that the spirit has survived except as a cottage craft; it is certainly extraordinary that it should be a thriving business in both Northern Ireland and the Republic of Ireland today. True, it always seems to have been regarded favourably by outsiders, Peter the Great of Russia liking 'Irish wine' and Dr Johnson's Dictionary describing Irish spirit as 'particularly distinguished for its pleasant and mild flavour'. Interest in Irish whiskey has always been maintained and, today, visitors to the 'Emerald Isle' come to appreciate its individuality – which is worth getting to know.

In the Republic of Ireland it is estimated that about 12 per cent of the *per capita* income is spent on drink – the Irish drink Irish whiskey, of course, but this does not account for nearly half the spirit consumption; vodka, which represented about 18 per cent at the beginning of 1977, and Scotch, which accounted for 16 per cent are the runners-up.

Irish whiskey today

There are today only three companies distilling in the Republic of Ireland and they together form the United Distillers of Ireland (U.D.I.). These are the Cork Distilleries, John Jameson and John Power, the last two firms being based in Dublin. In Northern Ireland, Old Bushmills Distillery is now the only distillery in operation (see page 158). The Tullamore Distillery, from which Irish Mist liqueur evolved, eventually went out of business as a whiskey distillery though they continued to make the liqueur. Tullamore Dew Whiskey was copied and is now successfully sold by the company called Irish Distillers Ltd.

The Cork Distilleries Co. Ltd, famous for 'Paddy', was amalgamated in 1867 from companies founded in 1779 (North Mall), 1793 (Watercourse), 1796 (The Green) and 1807 (John's Street). Later, the Middleton Distillery, founded in 1825, joined the group. This distillery also makes grain spirits for Cork gin and Nordoff vodka.

The firm of John Jameson has been in business in Dublin since 1780, when the first John Jameson, born in Alloa, in Scotland, bought a distillery in Bow Street to take advantage of the water of the near-by River Liffey. The firm are proud that the late-eighteenth-century procedures of 'Old John' are still followed today. The association of this company with the American firm of W. A. Taylor of New York, itself reputedly the oldest of its kind in the U.S., dates from 1890.

James Power founded his distillery in John's Lane, just outside the city walls of Dublin, in 1791. It was registered as a private limited company in 1899 and in 1921 incorporated as a public company as John Power & Son Ltd. The firm pioneered miniatures of whiskey, popularly called 'the baby Power', in the 1870s, and as, up to that time, the smallest bottle that was permitted to be sold contained four fluid ounces, a special Act of Parliament was required to enable the miniature to be marketed – it contained Power's Gold Label, which acquired the nickname of 'Three Swallows'. Power's have bottled Gold Label in their distillery's own bottling plant since 1889 and, in

1960, they began to launch Sarotov vodka. The warehouse of this firm, at Fox and Geese, Clondalkin, near Dublin, was opened in 1965 and is one of the most modern of its kind in Europe.

It must also be stressed that, although the United Distillers of Ireland comprise three companies, the range of whiskeys of each of those companies has been kept in accordance with the style of each individual concern. Each firm makes a particular type of whiskey and the different brands within each range will possess their distinct character too, from the everyday to the luxury style.

The production of Irish whiskey

The basis of Irish whiskey is barley, but wheat, rye, and even oats may also on occasion be used. Some of the barley is malted – that is, it is steeped in water and spread on the floor of the malt house until it sprouts, which it will do after about eight days; it is then dried and the result is 'malt'. This malt contains a high proportion of diastase, the substance which will convert the starch in the grain to sugar – the sugar being subsequently converted into alcohol by the process of fermentation.

The grains that are not malted are kiln-dried to reduce their moisture content, and subsequently ground finely together, except for the oats, which are simply crushed. Then the grains are 'mashed' by being put in a kieve or mash tun, which is a circular iron vessel, with a perforated false bottom, rather like a huge sieve, raised about an inch over the true floor of the mash tun. Water, previously boiled and then cooled to the requisite temperature, is then let in through this perforated base, the meal drops down on to it, being stirred by revolving rakes. More water is added and, during this stage, the starch contained in the grain is changed by the action of the diastase in it to a mixture of maltose and complex dextrine.

The solution that results from this process is called 'worts'. These worts are drawn off from the mash tun, the strong worts coming off first. The kieve or mash tun is then mashed again, with less liquid being used and the water at a higher temperature. This mashing process is repeated so that, in all, it takes place four times. The cool worts are then put into fermentation vessels where the maltose is converted into alcohol by the addition of appropriate yeast strains. The process of fermentation is violent, the liquid appearing to boil up in the huge containers.

After the fermentation is finished, the resulting liquid is known as the 'wash'. It is this wash that is then distilled in one of the gigantic

How Irish Pot Still Whiskey is Made

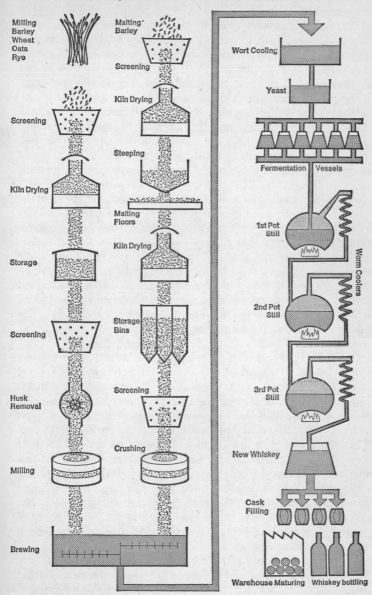

copper pot stills. The large size of these stills is impressive but, although their size is essential in the production of Irish whiskey, it is a matter of great complexity involving intricate technology to explain why they are made on this grand scale, and how the dimensions of different stills and their various modifications can affect the spirit they produce. For the drinker primarily concerned with the enjoyment of the distillate these things must be observed and then taken for granted as part of the intricacies of production.

The process of distilling takes about thirteen hours for each run of the still. The results of the first distillation are known as 'low wines'. When they are distilled for the second time they become 'feints'. The strong feints – strong in the sense of being at the required alcoholic strength in the body of the distillate – are then distilled again, and from this distillation the whiskey is ultimately obtained. (It will be appreciated that this is a very simplified description of the whole process: the most important thing to bear in mind is that this spirit is distilled three times, whereas Scotch and many other pot still products are distilled only twice.)

Once out of the still, the whiskey has to be matured. This is done in wood – mostly oak – casks, where the spirit will remain for at least seven years; for the finer whiskeys, however, in what may be termed the 'liqueur' quality ranges, the age of each whiskey in the final blend will be a minimum of twelve years and often more, although, like other spirits, whiskey does not improve indefinitely by maturing in wood and should be drawn off when it has reached its peak.

The role of the cask is of great importance, as with other pot still spirits; it is said that the cask contributes as much to the spirit as any of the other elements in its production. Anyone who can watch a blender of whiskey at work will be astonished to see how he can detect the type of cask that has been used to mature the spirit without consulting the label of the particular sample drawn from the wood. The influence of the spirit-impregnated wood on the whiskey may seem very slight to the layman when samples are compared at this stage but, once the whiskeys are combined in the ultimate blend, the effect produced by the casks on the range of flavours and smells that go to make up the whiskey that is ready to drink will be marked. The cask, in fact, acts like a subtle condiment in the whiskey's composition, bringing out certain characteristics, suppressing others, uniting and harmonizing the spirit.

Sherry casks are highly rated for maturing Irish; the whiskey they yield will have a pronounced aroma, be fullish in character and rather dark in colour. Sometimes, former sherry casks will have been used on so many occasions for whiskey that all the impregnation by the sherry will have virtually disappeared, but such casks can still be extremely useful for the maturation of Irish. Some casks used will actually be of new wood. The effect this has on the new spirit is also marked, which is why the choice of a close-grained wood, such as oak, is so significant; a spirit must never be obviously 'casky' – as can happen if it stays too long in wood and begins to take on the character of the cask so as to unbalance its own bouquet and flavour. Other casks may be imported after being used in the liquor trade in the United States, either as whole casks or broken down into separate staves for reassembly at the Irish distillery. Occasionally, casks that have been used to mature rum or brandy are also utilized by the Irish distillers. Each cask will endow the spirit it matures with an individual style.

During the maturation of the whiskey the warehouse itself exerts considerably influence on the spirit, because a warehouse situated in a place where the atmosphere is usually dry will mature the whiskey in a different way from one that is known as a 'wet warehouse', situated in a damp atmosphere. As with Cognac (see pages 68–9), a dry warehouse will cause the spirit to increase in strength while losing a lot of its volume, whereas a spirit kept in a wet warehouse will decline far more in alcoholic strength but very little in volume; indeed, it may actually increase in volume if the atmosphere surrounding the cask is so damp that the water in the air penetrates the wood. It is not unknown, in the moist climate of Ireland, for a cask of whiskey to burst, or for its bung to be forced out because of the absorption of the moisture in this way!

What does Irish whiskey taste like?

Comparisons between Irish and Scotch are as inevitable as those between Cognac and Armagnac – and as easily misleading. Of course, both Irish and Scotch are based on barley, but inevitably different types of barley will be used. The type of water by which the still is operated is also of prime importance: generally, it should be soft, and in siting a still any elements in the water deriving from spring or river that has run through peat are considered significant.

Sometimes people say they can detect a 'peaty' flavour in Irish whiskey. This, however, is nowadays unlikely to relate to the fuel used in the kilns or the stills which may not necessarily be peat fired. Any 'peatiness' can come only from the water used. I admit that I would not describe the flavour of Irish in this way at all. All good

Irish whiskey does however have a very pronounced aroma and this is especially to be noted if you can taste the spirit in the clear atmosphere of its homeland; the subtlety of its fragrance can be blurred when it has to cut through the polluted air of a modern industrial city. It might fairly be said that Irish whiskey has an obvious charm, albeit in a good sample this should be elegant rather than obtrusive, also that its flavour is particularly smooth, flowing and lingering on the palate. The experienced taster will probably be able to detect a number of shades of both taste and after-taste.

How to drink Irish

The traditional way of consuming Irish whiskey is with water and of course the better the water, the better the drink. The tap water of many industrial regions will blur the flavour of the whiskey. If, however, people prefer soda there is no reason why they should not drink Irish in this way and the U.D.I. suggest the addition of tonic and a slice of lemon for anyone wanting to experiment. In all the traditional mixtures, Irish may be used instead of another form of whisky, but its different character will change the resulting drink, so a little previous experimentation is worth while if you are not to surprise guests who are accustomed to, say, Scotch or Bourbon in their cocktails or highballs.

Irish coffee. The most famous whiskey-based drink, of course, is Irish coffee, sometimes called Gaelic coffee, so successful that it is now imitated with spirits of different types all over the world. The basic recipe is to pour a measure of Irish over freshly-made hot black coffee, adding sugar only if the consumer likes a sweetened drink, then stirring both whiskey and coffee together. On the top of this a layer of thick fresh cream is poured, although it need not be directed over the back of a spoon held on the surface – the bowl of the spoon will serve perfectly well to prevent the cream sinking into the mixture. But the cream must form a thick cold layer on the top of the hot coffee and whiskey, so that the drinker tastes this through the cream. Tall glasses, often with handles, are now frequently available for this particular drink, which makes an enjoyable finish to a meal and can substitute for a sweet dish.

CANADIAN WHISKEY

Canadian whiskey is often simply referred to as 'rye whiskey' or 'rye' and, somewhat confusingly, it is not subject to the same legal definition as U.S. rye whiskey (see page 179). The definition of the Canadian spirit is simply: 'Canadian whiskey (Canadian rye whiskey, rye whiskey) shall be whiskey distilled in Canada, and shall possess the aroma, taste and character generally attributable to Canadian whiskey.' What that really is, only the habitual drinker of Canadian whiskey can be assumed to know! But it is erroneous to assume that rye is the only grain used for Canadian whiskey. Corn (which the British refer to, more precisely, as maize) is usually the main type of grain used, together with rye and some wheat, plus some malted barley. The proportions of the grains are the affair of the individual distillery.

The first Canadian whiskeys were made in pot stills as might be expected – there were many Scottish emigrants arriving in Canada in early times. But today the continuous still is the only one in use, although there are several types – again, whichever one is used is a matter for the individual establishment to determine. The whiskey must by law be matured in wood for at least three years, both charred and uncharred barrels being used for the purpose; the finer whiskeys may be kept in casks for even longer – in exceptional circumstances even up to ten years. The casks must be of oak; they are mostly of new wood although it is permitted to use casks previously used for the maturation of spirits. For example, many Bourbon casks, which cannot be used a second time for maturing Bourbon (see page 178) are sold to Canada for maturing Canadian whiskey.

Distilling has been carried on in Canada for at least two centuries. The region was claimed for France in 1536 and it was only in 1759 that General Wolfe captured Quebec from the French. Irish immigrants began to arrive in Canada in numbers from around 1798, and there had always been a substantial number of Scots, leaving what was then their predominantly poor country for what they hoped might be the greater and more rewarding resources of a new one. So many of the early settlers would have been familiar with distilling. There is a record of a French Canadian operating as a distiller on a commercial scale in Quebec in 1769, but he made rum, as did many of the U.S. distillers (see pages 171–2). It seems probable that many homesteads in the vast, young country, where controls would have been difficult to enforce, would have had their own private stills as basic domestic equipment; the medicinal and disinfectant properties of a spirit in a primitive countryside were of obvious importance.

In 1832, two men, named Gooderham and, appropriately, Worts, started a distillery in a town that was then named York, but which is now Toronto; this is the oldest distillery still operating in Canada. The Proclamation of Union of Upper and Lower Canada took place in 1841 and a responsible government was set up in 1846, Ottawa becoming Canada's capital in 1858. The possibilities for making and supplying a Canadian spirit were henceforth immense. It is, as is well known, a great grain country and possesses more than 25 per cent of the fresh water supplies of the world; these natural assets were swiftly recognized by the energetic distillers of the nineteenth century, able now to exploit the possibilities of the continuous still.

One of the big names in this section of the whiskey saga is that of Hiram Walker (the firm later combined with Gooderham & Worts to purchase substantial interests in Scotch, see pages 140–41). Hiram Walker bought a piece of land in Ontario, towards the end of the nineteenth century, where he ran a steam-powered mill and a distillery. His business became highly successful; the original settlement is now the town of Walkerville. This was a period of great economic expansion and Hiram Walker launched the world-famous 'Canadian Club' whiskey, which from the outset was so popular that he began to market it outside Canada; Canadian whiskey had been exported as early as 1861, but this was a sales drive of particular power. Canadian Club began to sell in Great Britain and even in France, though of course the French Canadians had always maintained strong links with their European forebears. The exact formula for Hiram Walker's Canadian Club is still a secret, known only to a few executives of the Hiram Walker company; it is one of the top-selling spirits in the world and, in the U.S. market, competes strongly with the other great Canadian whiskey, Seagram's V.O.

This name – one of the biggest in the entire world of spirits – is that of a virtual empire of distilling. Joseph E. Seagram began distilling at Waterloo, Ontario, in 1857, the site of the distillery having been selected with regard to the two wells of abundant pure water there; the Seagram Beaupré plant, on the shore of the St Lawrence river below Quebec, was later also chosen because of the purity and quantity of the local water supply. (The many other Seagram establishments throughout the world are all near to similarly fine, natural water-supplies.) As Joseph E. Seagram & Sons, Inc., is described under 'U.S. whiskeys' (pages 175–6), it is only possible here to deal with their Canadian products, but it is worth remembering that it was a Canadian, Samuel Bronfman, who rehabilitated and inspired the entire company – which includes more than sixty subsidiaries – after the end of Prohibition and directed it to its position of special eminence in the world trade in spirits.

Seagram's V.O. is a 'premium' Canadian whiskey. The use of the term 'premium' in the spirit world signifies a brand of quality, which may be higher in strength and probably costs more, the expression relating particularly to all types of whisky. V.O. is one of the best-known whiskeys in the world – and certainly the top-selling Canadian whiskey. The blend is made up from whiskeys coming from Seagram's six Canadian distilleries, and as many as 120 different whiskeys may be included.

Also operating under the Seagram banner is Calvert Distillers. They make Calvert Masterpiece, a de luxe Canadian whiskey, and Canadian Lord Calvert, which is sent in barrels from the firm's Canadian distilleries to be bottled in the U.S. – thereby effecting a saving in tax as compared with the whiskeys imported in bottle.

The popularity of Canadian whiskey appears to be growing. Other well-known brands include National Distillers' Windsor Supreme, Brown Forman's Canadian Mist, Heublein's Black Velvet Canadian and Schenley's McNaughton Canadian. It is thought that the lightness, which is characteristic of Canadian whiskey in general, plus the many ways in which this spirit can be used in mixed and long drinks, is one of the factors influencing the enormous increases in sales. In certain regions of the U.S., Canadian whiskey outsells Scotch – something significant in a fairly affluent community. It is, in my opinion, rather a gentle type of spirit, fresh and brisk in its appeal. John Doxat, in his book *Drinks and Drinking* (Ward Lock, 1971), says that it 'is smoother, though less flavoursome, than straight Bourbon, is much superior to ordinary whiskey, but lacks the special character inherent in a fine Scotch ... I am endeavouring to be descriptive when I say that it is a "compromise" spirit.' It would seem that the vast number of consumers are playing safe in choosing a pleasant, adaptable whiskey, that is enjoyable in hot or cold climates.

UNITED STATES WHISKEY

It is difficult for anyone whose ideas about the character and qualities of a spirit have been formed from the beginning by one specific type to be able to be dispassionate about another, when both spirits are essentially of different and definite styles. A native of the Armagnac region finds it a wrench to appraise Cognac, after all!

Similarly, the Briton inevitably finds a problem with American whiskey; maybe it would be easier if the spirit had a totally different name – just as it might often be easier for Americans and the inhabitants of the British Isles to understand each other if both did not suppose themselves to be speaking the same language! The similarities to Scotch do exist in American whiskeys, just as they do in some of the lesser-known whiskeys made in other parts of the world. The differences, however, are strident. The devotee of Scotch, the dominant spirit of the United Kingdom, can, at need, accept and appreciate Irish whiskey, because this is linked to Scotch by what may be called a family resemblance and the differences, although apparent, do not jar. But when the Briton attempts to understand American whiskeys the essential difference – caused by the basic material, the grain used – is so great that nose and palate may be shocked.

This almost inborn preference for Scotch by the Briton may be at least as good a reason as any why U.S. whiskey, often competitive in price with Scotch, has only a small following in Britain, except in places where American visitors are frequent. Another reason may be that, as indicated by a recent company report from the House of Seagram, Americans use both American and Canadian whiskeys as the basis for many mixed and long drinks – both because of life-styles which tend to be very different from those of the British Isles, and also because, in recent years, Americans have become very much aware of health risks associated with alcoholic drinks; consequently, they tend to try and counteract the possibly risky effects of short, strong drinks by diluting spirits with all kinds of additives. Scotch, however, is not often drunk in this way.

In a report in the British publication *Wine & Spirit*, Christopher Fielden comments pertinently that:

> For the average Englishman, it is difficult to understand the importance that the cocktail plays in American spirit sales. The creation of new 'mixes' appears to be a substantial art form in its own right on the other side of the Atlantic. Bourbon has long been a base ingredient for many of these cocktails and serious efforts are being made to woo back the younger drinker ... Why else would Old Forester's latest copy-line read 'The Great Whisky [*sic*] That's Made Like Great Wine'?

Americans, on the other hand, seem wholly capable of appreciating Scotch. It may be that this taste transition is easier to make. It may also be that the two spirits are distant cousins, rather than brothers, and that each has been so markedly affected by its environment that, whereas Scotch can adapt to contexts of drinking all over the world, American whiskey tastes at its best within the frame of an American life-style and within the United States – which is, after all, virtually an entire world.

U.S. whiskey in history

Distilling began early in the vast and varied regions that now make up the United States. Numbers of the Dutch who settled there would have been familiar with the process; there is a record of a Dutch still being in operation in 1640 on Staten Island – New Amsterdam as this then was – although it may have been genever that this still made. From the beginning of settlements in North America, vast tracts of land were devoted to growing grain, so that it was inevitable, in times of surplus, that this grain would be used for distillation. Farmers came to use the home-made spirit as a commodity in which to trade; it was easier to store and transport than grain and, of course, the spirit would not deteriorate if kept.

It must not be forgotten that, in those early days, not only did many settlers naturally miss the numerous alcoholic beverages made in the various European countries from which they came, but they really needed them as staple commodities. Water supplies might not always be safe, especially in townships, where rivers and streams might be easily polluted. People would therefore mix some form of spirit with their water, just as Europeans might have mixed wine, so as to make the water safe to drink. In the eighteenth century, New Yorkers requiring good drinking water bought it in barrels from the Teawater Pump, so called because it made especially good tea. Travellers, of course, needed warming drinks; mailcoach drivers were often drunk, as they tried to keep to their required time schedules in all weathers. Countryfolk valued alcoholic beverages as stimulants, disinfectants and revivers. In 1782, the people of Worcester, Massachusetts, declared that liquor was essential for farmworkers, in order to maintain their morale. Many ailments were treated with alcohol in various forms: it was used as a rub, an emetic and an anaesthetic. Women were given it in childbirth; the aged, especially those confined to the house for many months during cold weather, found it easier to have a drink than to make a meal. So it is no wonder that there were frequent and increasing outbreaks of drunkenness, commented on in records from the seventeenth century onwards. This should be borne in mind because, in due time, the seriousness of this social problem led to the late-eighteenth- and early-nineteenth-century temperance movements, which, later, brought about the banning of alcohol (see pages 130–32). It was the appalling abuses that the eventual prohibitionists were attacking, not always the drinks themselves.

Originally, the northern part of the American continent drank rum in vast quantities. It was easy to import from the producing countries of the West Indies, and it could be made in the southern parts of the country from sugar-cane. Naturally, distillers would use what raw materials were available in their area: in the north, Scots and Irish settlers used wheat, rye, barley, potatoes and Indian corn for distilling. As early as 1620 there was a type of ale made in Virginia from maize (corn). In 1720, Governor Berkeley commented that Virginians of the 'richer sort generally brew their small-beer with malt, which they have from England, though barley grows there very well; but for the want of convenience of malt-houses, the inhabitants take no care to sow it'. The fact that barley was not grown on any large scale eventually led to the spirit of the United States being based largely on corn.

Possibly the North Americans would have gone on importing rum, distilling at home and, for those who could afford it, drinking other imported spirits; but when the American War of Independence broke out in 1775, supplies of rum from Cuba and the West Indies were cut off by the British blockade. It was henceforth natural for those who had stocks of locally produced spirit to exploit its commercial possibilities by making it on a larger scale than the mere domestic. Any reasonably sized household or country estate would have distilled and brewed for its domestic requirements; Thomas Jefferson and George Washington are known to have had stills on their properties.

1789 was a historic year: the French Revolution broke out, George Washington became the first President of the United States – and the Reverend Elijah Craig set up a distillery in Georgetown, Bourbon County, Kentucky. Ministers of religion, unless specifically forbidden by their calling, used spirits as freely as the English Parson Woodforde, for medicinal purpose as much as for enjoyment, and if doctor, midwife, veterinary officer or nurse were not available it was often the minister who coped with such domestic crises as might require the use of alcohol. Craig's distillery was situated beside a limestone creek – important in affecting the quality of the water in what is often referred to as the 'Blue Grass Region'. The product of this distillery was probably the first Bourbon whiskey to be commercially made and its generic name derives from that of the region, Bourbon County – the name of the French royal house 'Bourbon' having been adopted by the locality because of the assistance provided by France to them during the War of Independence.

The minister called the spirit 'Kentucky Bourbon Whiskey' and it was made principally from corn (maize), plus some small amounts of barley and rye. The name Bourbon, incidentally is, defined and protected by a 1964 Act of Congress (see page 178), which also decreed that it is entitled to a capital letter (to which I personally consider it entitled, because it is a proper name). The U.K. reader may not know, however, that the word is pronounced 'ber-bun'.

The popularity of Bourbon was immediate and attracted the attention of the authorities, who foresaw a substantial potential source of revenue. In 1791, a tax was levied by the federal government on all spirits. This annoyed the farmers who, as has been mentioned, had been in the habit of using their whiskey for trading; they naturally resented being forbidden to pay their taxes 'in kind', having now to hand over cash. In Pennsylvania the opposition was particularly fierce; here, as in other eastern states, a distillate that may be considered as the direct ancestor of U.S. whiskey had been widely made from early times by those whose European ancestry had familiarized them with the procedure. Finally, the distillers of western Pennsylvania refused to pay their taxes at all, so that, in 1793, George Washington had to call out troops to quell what subsequently became known as the 'Whiskey Rebellion'.

This action resulted in many of the farmers who had been, as they thought, victimized, leaving the area. They moved westwards when they went, mainly to southern Indiana, Illinois, and further into Kentucky and Pennsylvania. Wherever they could find suitable water supplies and an appropriate countryside, they set up their stills again. Significantly, the site of these early distilleries is usually on chalky, limestone soil with a stream running under the immediate region. These areas, to which the first commercial distillers came, are where the bulk of American whiskey is distilled today. As with Canadian whiskey and with Scotch, it is both the water supply and the type of soil through which this water flows or over which it drains that is instrumental in determining the eventual type of spirit distilled.

Many distilleries date from this period. The label of the big seller Jim Beam bears the date 1795. In 1835 a Scot, Dr James Crowe, built the Old Crowe Distillery in Franklin County, Kentucky, which is still in production, owned now by the National Distillers. It was the first establishment to make whiskey in the U.S. according to procedures that are still followed today. Crowe was followed by many other firms: Colonel E. H. Taylor's Old Taylor and the Old Grand-Dad brand are two other well-known Kentucky whiskeys first made at this time. The Old Forester brand was first made commercially according to a family recipe in 1870; the firm's founder,

George Garvin Brown, was a medical supplies salesman, who offered the whiskey 'for medicinal purposes'. In 1872 Old Forester was sold in bottle – the first American whiskey to be available in this way. Otherwise it was sold by the cask, although this might be of a large or small size and the spirit could be dispensed from the barrel into the jug or mug of the customer. The bottle, however, was immediately recognized as a most convenient way of buying a small quantity of whiskey, whether or not it was for medicinal use. It was in 1897 that the Federal Bottled-in-Bond Act made it obligatory for whiskey to carry labels stating the proof strength, age and type. Bottled-in-Bond whiskey is a straight whiskey, four years old, aged in new charred barrels, distilled below 160 proof and bottled at 100 proof. Brown-Forman Distillers, who own Old Forester, were one of the very few firms who were allowed to continue making Old Forester during Prohibition – on the grounds of its being required for medicinal purposes, an example of a tradition proving highly advantageous.

One of the most famous U.S. whiskeys began to be made in Tennessee in 1866. This is Jack Daniels, made at The Hollow, Lynchburg, Moore County, publicized as 'the oldest registered distillery in the United States'. It must be referred to as 'Tennessee whiskey', not Bourbon – although it is made from corn (maize).

Jasper or 'Jack' Newton Daniel was born at The Hollow, Mulberry Creek, in 1848; this is not far from Davy Crockett's log house. By the time Jack was only thirteen, he was in partnership making whiskey with one Dan Call, who had a distillery at Louse Creek, five miles from Lynchburg; soon after the Civil War, Call, who was a member of the Lutheran Church, was told by his spiritual superiors that he must stop making whiskey, or be cast out from the congregation. So he agreed to be bought out by young Jack, who was a Primitive Baptist and not handicapped in his business by his religion. The distillery at The Hollow was built in 1866 but the whiskey did not become widely known until it was awarded the Gold Medal at the St Louis World Fair, in 1904, in competition with whiskeys from all over the world. The 'charcoal mellowing' used in the production of Jack Daniels, supposed to give a particular distinction and finesse to the spirit, is effected by dripping the new whiskey through twelve feet of hard maypole charcoal packed into huge vats; the makers of Jack Daniels state that this does away with the corn (maize) taste that is associated with much Bourbon. However, I must say that the aroma I think of as typical of Bourbon is evident to me in Jack Daniels, although this brand is certainly of individual style and flavour, and is one of the top-selling de luxe U.S. whiskeys (see below, this page).

Various anecdotes connected with Bourbon include the remark of Abraham Lincoln who, begged by teetotallers to remonstrate with General Grant (who was known to drink whiskey) during the American Civil War, replied, 'I wish I knew what brand he drinks, so I could give some of it to my other generals.' In fact, President Lincoln sent Grant a congratulatory gift of Bourbon after the victory of Vicksburg in 1863. Mark Twain was particularly fond of whiskey and during his stay in London got the Savage Club there to stock a supply for him. And when, in 1939, President Franklin D. Roosevelt entertained King George VI and Queen Elizabeth at Hyde Park on the occasion of their visit to the U.S., he himself mixed Old Fashioneds for them, using Bourbon, while his mother silently disapproved. The President is said to have told the King: 'My mother thinks you should have a cup of tea, she doesn't approve of cocktails.' The King, gratefully accepting his drink, said: 'Neither does my mother.'

U.S. whiskeys dominated the American market from the end of Prohibition in 1933 until the mid fifties, when vodka rose in popularity, and subsequently the increasing liking for white rum made these spirits competitive with the whiskeys. Forecasts as to the future have stimulated the mighty U.S. whiskey concerns to unprecedented advertising and promotional activities.

Today, when there are at least 16,000 different brands of liquor registered in the U.S., it is remarkable that still more are being introduced, a recent trend being for premium Bourbon. Austin Nichols's Wild Turkey brand, the highest-priced Bourbon of all, was originally made for the rich sportsmen who went to hunt the wild turkey in South Carolina; this Bourbon, like de luxe Scotch, is high in strength and has a maturation of eight years. Other brands in this de luxe category are Bourbon Supreme of the American Distilling Company, I. W. Harper's Eagle Rare, Old Grand-Dad and Jack Daniels.

The best-selling whiskey in the U.S., however, is a blended whiskey, Seagram's Seven Crown. Joseph E. Seagram & Sons, Inc., which is possibly the biggest spirit establishment in the world, is of enormous importance and influence. It was incorporated in 1933 in Indiana, although its headquarters are in New York City, in a building of outstanding good looks. The Company had its origins in Canada (see page 168). Seagram companies now include Calvert Distillers, who introduced Passport Scotch to the U.S. in 1969;

Four Roses Distillers, who make Four Roses Bourbon, Four Roses Premium Light Whiskey and Kessler American Whiskey; Frankfort Distillers, who make Paul Jones American blended Whiskey and four Bourbons – Henry McKenna, Rare Antique, Antique, and Mattingly & Moore. Another company, General Wine & Spirits, is perhaps most notable for a de luxe Scotch – Royal Salute, which was made for the Coronation of Queen Elizabeth II. They bought the Strathisla-Glenlivet Distillery at Keith and also Chivas Brothers of Aberdeen, who are the makers of Chivas Regal, a twelve-year-old Scotch that is a best-seller in the U.S. today. Seagram Distillers market Seagram's 100 Pipers Scotch, Seagram's Benchmark Bourbon, introduced to the U.S. market in 1965 and 1969 respectively, and they have just acquired control of The Glenlivet (see page 150). Space does not permit mention of their portfolio of other spirits (and wines) from all over the world as well as in the U.S.

Enormous quantities of whiskey are said to be illicitly distilled in the U.S., but I cannot understand how those who assert this are able to particularize – to the extent that: 'One out of every four drinks consumed in the United States is bootleg' (Alexis Lichine, *Encyclopedia of Wines and Spirits*, Cassell, 2nd edition, 1974) – because how can any record be authentic when it refers to an illegal practice? It seems unlikely that this sort of spirit, like the Irish potheen, would possess any quality – except that of high alcoholic strength.

Types of U.S. whiskey

In this inevitably brief account, it will be appreciated that each of the giant whiskey concerns will have its own methods of making its range of spirits. With so many whiskeys on the market, only general definitions are possible – for, to the enthusiast, the differences between the numerous styles and brands is as fascinating a study as the study of straight malts. This is a field for the appraiser of spirits to explore – and, perhaps, to record, for it seems strange that, so far, no study of American whiskeys has been published.

Although, obviously, such whiskeys as were made in early times were produced from pot stills, today all are made in various types of continuous still. The evolution of this still in the first part of the nineteenth century (see page 45) made it possible for U.S. whiskeys to be made in huge quantities early in their history and to cater for the demands of a mass market. In addition, the improvement in communications made it possible to make whiskey in many regions besides those situated in or near areas suitable for the requisite grain or water supply. For example, in making Bourbon, malted barley may be brought in from Minnesota and the Dakotas.

These are the basic procedures of making whiskey: first, the grain is inspected and cleaned, then ground, the resulting 'meal' is mixed to a slurry with water and subjected to heat, so as to effect the necessary alteration in the starches (see page 145); at this stage a small amount of malt is usually incorporated. The wort that then is produced is put into fermentation vats where, with the addition of suitable yeasts, it becomes distiller's 'beer'. Yeasts, which, Seagram pertinently states are 'the work horses of the distilling industry' act so as to achieve fermentation satisfactorily: Seagram has a 'library' of more than 240 different strains of yeast at their Louisville, Kentucky, establishment, some of these descending from yeasts discovered in various parts of the world nearly half a century ago. Fermentation cannot take place without the action of yeasts, but each type of fermentation for whatever spirit or wine requires different yeasts.

The 'beer' that is made by this fermentation is thereafter distilled in an American whiskey still, or beer still, and later the whiskey made in this is reduced in strength by the addition of pure water; it is then put to mature.

At this stage an interesting difference in the making of whiskey must be noted: straight U.S. whiskey must go into new oak casks, made from a special type of oak, for maturation. These casks will be charred inside; the use of these charred barrels – the origin of which is uncertain – gives a 'something' to the spirit and, for myself, it is this use of charred wood that gives me some of the strongest smell and taste impressions of U.S. whiskey. (Some of the charred casks are sold to Scotland, because they cannot be used twice for U.S. whiskey.) In general, it is the cask that seems to give a particular character to these whiskeys (as happens with Scotch and Irish whiskey, pages 144–5 and 164–5) as well as the grain that is used to make them. Corn whiskey, light whiskey and other whiskeys which do not qualify as straight whiskey may be matured in used barrels.

Another process deserves a little explanation concerning these whiskeys – the different types of mash used. Jack Daniels, for example, is described on its label as 'sour mash'. The term refers to the way in which the yeasts are used to ferment the beer: according to *Grossman's Guide to Wines and Spirits* (Charles Scribner's Sons, 1974 edition), a sour mash is made by 'adding at least one-third the volume of the fermenter of spent beer (working yeast), from a previous fermentation, to the fresh mash and fresh yeast'. A sweet mash is made by using nearly all freshly developed yeast in the mash; this is allowed to work for a shorter time than the sour mash.

The greatest volume of U.S. whiskey consists of the blended type, with Bourbon a close second; rye sales are very low by comparison. American blended whiskey and Bourbon account for about 25 per cent of the total distilled spirits market.

Bourbon. U.S. regulations of 1964 state that: 'Bourbon Whiskey must be produced from a mash of not less than 51 per cent corn grain'; also that 'the word "Bourbon" shall not be used to describe any whiskey or whiskey-based distilled spirits not produced in the United States.' The Americans are not risking any competition from the sort of imitations that, years ago, made the progress of Scotch fraught with litigation!

The mash, in fact, is usually about 60–70 per cent corn (maize). The 1964 Act that defined Bourbon states that the whiskey must be aged for at least two years in new, charred, oak barrels and it established the strength at which it must be distilled and that at which it should be bottled. In fact, most good Bourbon is matured for at least four years.

Straight Bourbon is the whiskey that comes from one single distillery. 'Blended straight Bourbon' is a blend of whiskeys from several distilleries and, if the blended straight Bourbon does not consist of at least 51 per cent of corn, although the whiskey may be used in the blend, the word 'Bourbon' may not appear on the label.

Blended Bourbon is a mixture of Bourbon and what are referred to as 'other spirits'. As will have been gathered from the preceding text, it is the straight and blended Bourbons that are the biggest-selling whiskeys in both the U.S. and the world. Quite a memorial to a county that today doesn't exist, as such! For, although the original home of Bourbon is still the source of at least half the Bourbon that is made, the term can legally be applied to whiskeys made outside the region as long as they comply with the 1964 definition of what the spirit should be. However, to qualify for the name 'Kentucky Bourbon' the whiskey must be both distilled and warehoused in Kentucky for a minimum of a year. This has resulted in a curious moving around of stocks: taxes in Kentucky are higher than in some of the neighbouring states, so, after the first year's maturation in Kentucky, many of the distillers of Louisville move their

Bourbon over the Ohio River to spend the rest of its time maturing in Indiana.

Rye. In the U.S. (as opposed to Canada), rye whiskey must be made from a mash which is not less than 51 per cent rye. If there is less than this, the word 'rye' cannot be used on the label of the whiskey. Most rye whiskey is a blend, although there are some straight ryes and blended straight ryes. This type of whiskey seems to vary very much in both taste and quality; some reports indicate that it is more aggressive, even sharper in flavour than Bourbon, but this is not inevitable – all depends on the brand. Most rye whiskey in the U.S. is made in Pennsylvania and Maryland.

Corn whiskey. American friends of mine have described this in harsh terms, but this may be because it frequently lacks adequate maturation. It is distilled from a mash that must contain 80 per cent corn (maize) and must have been aged in wood – though not necessarily new wood – for a minimum of two years (although a reliable source tells me that he has seen some aged for not more than thirty days).

Light whiskey. This is distilled at a high strength and matured for four years in used casks. The spirit was first made in 1968 and released to the public in 1972. It was made, it seems, with the idea of producing a U.S. whiskey that – on account of the contribution made by the cask, which had been seasoned by being used before – might compete more directly with Scotch and Canadian whiskey. It appears that some of this light whiskey goes into the big blends; blended light whiskey is, according to Grossman, 'a mixture of less than 20 per cent straight whiskey at 100 proof (U.S.) with light whiskey'.

Bourbon drinks

The two most famous bourbon mixtures are certainly the Mint Julep, firmly associated with the 'Deep South' and the Old Fashioned, which has now given its name to the elongated tumbler in which it is traditionally served.

The Mint Julep is as controversial a drink as the martini, but the Bourbon's Institute's recipe for it is as follows: 2 ounces Bourbon, a tablespoonful of water, a lump of sugar, four sprigs of mint and crushed ice, all the ingredients except the Bourbon being put into a tall glass or tankard and the Bourbon being added afterwards. The Institute stress that the drink must not be stirred, although I myself don't see why not; what is the point of having the other ingredients in if you don't want them all to combine? The drink is not a layered '*pousse café*'. The garnish is of fresh mint sprigs.

For the Old Fashioned: one teaspoonful of sugar syrup, three drops of Angostura Bitters, $1\frac{1}{2}$ ounces of Bourbon (rye is an alternative) are put into a glass and stirred together, being garnished with a cherry.

The Manhattan cocktail, seldom ordered today but popular between the two wars, is a short drink of approximately $\frac{1}{2}$ ounce of each of dry and sweet vermouth, 1 ounce of Bourbon, a drop of Angostura Aromatic Bitters, all stirred together and served in a small glass, garnished with a cocktail cherry.

The use of Bourbon for various eggnog recipes is well known, and there are plenty of these to be found in books dealing with mixed drinks.

The Highball started its life as a long drink, based on U.S. whiskey, but non-Americans should be aware of the fact that the name now tends to be loosely applied to all drinks based on spirits – not necessarily whiskey – which are just topped up with water or some kind of carbonated water and served in a tall tumbler.

'Branch water' which is the preferred diluting agent for U.S. whiskey, is a term used to signify spring water – the 'branch' being a rivulet from the main natural source.

OTHER WHISKEYS

The popularity of whisky has encouraged many attempts at producing it, often in what may seem to be unlikely places. James Ross, in *Whisky* (Routledge & Kegan Paul, 1970) reports that he has tried 'Scotch-type whiskies' in Spain, Holland (he praised the Dutch version) and Denmark (he found this very nasty), and a friend of his was offered a 'King Edward the First' whiskey made in Austria. If the spirit can be successfully produced and marketed, there is no reason why it should not be enjoyed; legislation can only control and protect the use of a registered brand name. In the 1920s, for example, the makers of White Horse whisky brought and won a case against a German firm who were marketing 'Black and White Horse Whisky'.

Australia produces whiskey, making both malt and a blend of malt and grain spirit. I have also sampled a good whiskey made in New Zealand. There are many jokes about Japanese imitations of Scotch in former times, with labels claiming that the spirit was: 'prepared at Buckingham Palace under the personal supervision of His Majesty'. But today, I am informed by reliable and travelled drinkers, there are apparently entirely acceptable Japanese whiskeys on the market, each correctly and accurately labelled.

One curious piece of whisky history concerns Welsh whisky. In 1887, an eccentric rich man, Richard John Lloyd Price, set up a distillery at Bala, in Wales. He was a convinced Welsh patriot and did not see why whisky should not be made in his homeland. To achieve this, he went about the venture in a businesslike way, engaging several highly qualified technicians experienced in making Scotch, and checking on the source of the local water supply before siting the distillery; at Bala, the stream feeding the distillery actually did flow through peat, as at many of the famous distilleries in Scotland.

The barley required for the whisky was supplied by local Welsh farmers, although they had a problem because the strong hold on the community of the local Methodist chapels (still very influential in Wales) meant that any association with producing an alcoholic beverage was outspokenly condemned. Methodists, with some reason, have traditionally been opponents of the evils resulting from excessive drinking and condemn all 'strong drink'. So the farmers were obliged to deliver the barley under cover of night, to avoid being denounced in their respective chapels. (It is stated that, by way of a 'thank you', they were given the Welsh equivalent of a dram.)

Lloyd Price gave a sample of his whisky to Queen Victoria when, in 1889, she visited Bala; it was presented in a cask with a silver trade mark. It is not recorded what the Queen thought of the whisky (as was mentioned earlier, she enjoyed Scotch). The Welsh company did not – indeed, it could not – prosper; this was the period when the great Scotch 'whisky barons' were fiercely competing for markets everywhere, pouring money into advertising and promoting Scotch by their publicized and lavish life-styles (see page 136). Any competitor would have had a hopeless struggle against the rising tide of Scotch and, in many export markets, of U.S. whiskey. Lloyd Price's company went into liquidation in 1898 and is now only a Welsh legend; I have never heard of any describing what his whisky tasted like. However, as there seem to be plans to revive whisky making in Wales, it is possible that, in this century, we may be able to try it for ourselves.

7. Rum

Rum is an odd spirit. Many who drink it regularly might nevertheless be hard put to define it, and, although it appears to have had an interesting history and has played a considerable part in the economy of several countries, comparatively little of a serious nature has been written about it. The very word is of uncertain origin. *The Shorter Oxford Dictionary* mentions its first appearance as being in 1654, although it seems probable it was being made earlier than this; other authorities think that it is a shortened form of 'rumbustion', which seems to have signified a loud noise and – by association – a strong liquor, or of the Devonian word 'rumbullion', on account of the large number of Devon men who were among the early merchant adventurers. There are those who suggest that it derives from 'brum', a Malay word meaning a fermented drink, and in the eighteenth century, novelist Tobias Smollett in *Peregrine Pickle* refers to 'rumbo'.

It seems far more likely to me that the word 'rum' is a contraction of the Latin *Saccharum officinarum*, which is the botanical name for sugar-cane. This is the plant that supplies more than half the world's requirements of sugar, with rum as a by-product. It is not certain where this plant was first cultivated, but Grossman (*Grossman's Guide to Wines, Spirits and Beers*, Charles Scribner's Sons, 1974) says that the first mention of sugar-cane is 327 B.C., when Alexander the Great returned from India; the Arabs brought sugar-cane to Europe about A.D. 636, but it was a luxury product, definitely in the caviare category (black teeth through eating sugar were almost a status symbol in the first Elizabethan Age), until Christopher Columbus took cuttings of the cane from the Canary Islands to the West Indies at the end of the fifteenth century. Cane is now widely cultivated in southern Spain and New South Wales, as well as various parts of the United States and, of course, the Caribbean; vast areas are cultivated in Brazil, India, Cuba, Hawaii, Puerto Rico, as well as Barbados, Mauritius and Guyana, where it is a staple crop.

As early as the seventeenth century, a type of spirit distilled from sugar was being made in the West Indies. With the increased trade between the West Indies and Europe, the spread of the popularity of rum was rapid. In 1647, Richard Ligon, writing about Barbados, makes a reference to 'kill-devil', a 'hot, hellish and terrible liquor', which, he says, was mainly drunk by the slave-labour in the plantations. Almost up to the present time and the age of antibiotics, any community in hot or tropical climates would have much use for a spirit as stimulant, disinfectant and many allied medicinal purposes. Rum, as it began to be known, was able to be produced cheaply and in quantity. Molasses had been brought to New England in the seventeenth century and rum began to be popular there, the home product being very cheap and the West Indian rum costing very slightly more; New England rum was even used as a currency for those who were buying African slaves, so that the 1686 comment is pertinent. 'It is an unhappy thing that in later years a Kind of Drink called Rum has been common among us. They that are poor, and wicked too, can for a penny or two-pence make themselves drunk.'

By the beginning of the eighteenth century, rum in Barbados was 'preferred to brandy. It is said to be very wholesome and has therefore lately supplied the place of brandy in punch. It is much better than malt spirits and the sad liquor sold by our distillers.' Father Jean Baptiste Labat, writing in 1694, described a spirit drink made hot and mixed with lemon juice – 'there is no doubt that it is excellent for the chest; it feeds and refreshes them [the workers].'

Not only the inhabitants of cane-producing regions appreciated rum. The Royal Navy found it a cheap and versatile spirit, and in the early eighteenth century it began to be consumed in enormous quantities by crews serving in colder northern waters; at the same time, large doses of rum were administered as a crude anaesthetic for those about to undergo shipboard surgery; indeed, rum was used in British hospitals in this way until the nineteenth century and the development of anaesthetics. Rum is a particularly warming spirit and the Navy consumed vast quantities of the dark high-strength type (which must have been the same as was known in the last war as 'Navy neaters'); whether for purposes of stimulation or celebration, the signal to 'splice the main brace' signified an extra issue of rum. However, by 1740, the British Admiral Vernon found that rum was making too many seamen virtually incapable of carrying out their duties. He therefore ordered that the rum ration should be diluted by the addition of water; Admiral Vernon, whose Navy nickname was 'Old Grog' because he nearly always wore a grogram cloak, thus gave at least two words to the English language: 'groggy', which originally meant too full of rum to work steadily, and 'grog' which today signifies a mixture of spirits and water – in France *'un grog'* is rum and hot water. Interestingly, from 1795, the juice of lemons was added to this watered rum ration, and ships that were at sea for longer than six weeks issued it regularly; this had a dramatic effect in the reduction of scurvy: in *The Englishman's Food* (J. C. Drummond and A. Wilbraham, Jonathan Cape, revised edition, 1951) it is stated: 'in 1760 there had been 1754 cases of scurvy in the naval hospital at Haslar; in 1806 there was one.' By the middle of the nineteenth century, lime juice from the West Indies was added to the rum and water ration instead of lemon juice, and, although this was less efficacious (because lemon juice is higher in vitamin C than lime juice), it gave the nickname of 'Limeys' to British sailors and, subsequently, to Britons in general.

Rum, rather like gin, played an important part in social life in the England of the eighteenth century. Parson Woodforde makes many references to it, offering it on several occasions to those who came to pay their tithes to him and whom he feasted afterwards: 'Dec. 3, 1782 . . . Wine drank 6 bottles, Rum drank 5 bottles'. In 1786 for the same party he made 'six Bottles of rum . . . into Punch, 3 Bowls, 2 Bottles of Rum in each'. When travelling, he might take a 'Glass of Rum and Water', which cost him 4d at Norwich in 1789 and, the same year, he 'bespoke a Quarter of a Pipe of Port Wine and 4 Gallons of Rum of Mr Priest Snr'. He would probably have bottled these himself, and at his tithe audit that December his guests enjoyed 'half a Dozen bottles of Port Wine, 8 bottles of Rum besides as much strong Beer as they wished to have'.

Rum also seems to have been used as a medicine, for when the Parson's niece Nancy was 'blown up as if poisoned, attended with a vomiting', he dosed her with 'a good half pint Glass of warm Rum and Water', and at supper gave her 'Water-gruel with a Couple of small Table Spoonfuls of Rum in it, and going to bed I gave her a good dose of Rhubarb and Ginger. She was much better before she went to bed. – And I hope will be brave Tomorrow.'

Woodforde bought smuggled rum as well as other smuggled spirits, and, in October 1792, 'Had a Tub of Brandy and a Tub of Rum brought this Evening. Gave one of the Men that brought it 1/0.' So the next day, he was 'Very busy between 8 and 10 o'clock this Morn in bottling off Brandy and Rum.' He had reason to want to get them hidden away smartly, because one of his tenant farmers, 'Moonshine' John Buck, obviously a respected smuggler, had recently been informed against. The countryfolk stood by each other, although Woodforde risked a fine of £10 for buying smuggled goods and the supplier was liable for £50; anyone informing against them successfully would be let off any possible penalties.

Rum was featured in smart French society during the nineteenth century in a rather odd way, as a possible *coup de milieu*, or drink taken as a digestive in the middle of a rich meal. Grimod de la Reynière refers to this *coup de milieu* as an alternative to Sillery (the wine of a particular part of the Champagne vineyard, then enjoying a vogue), saying that it could consist of bitters, Swiss 'extract of absinthe', or Jamaica rum or old Cognac brandy. It seems strange that this gastronomic writer, always churning out suggestions for elaborate and fantastic meals for the most precious section of high society, should cite Jamaica rum rather than one of the French *rhums*. But perhaps the Jamaica rum would, in Paris, have been more expensive and difficult to obtain – hence its snob value.

The *rhum* made in the French Antilles also gained greatly in popularity in the eighteenth century, so that in the Crimean War (1854–6) French troops were issued with *rhum* instead of the ordinary army issue of wine and marc; in France in 1916 both British and French forces were regularly issued with rum while they were in the trenches. The Royal Navy continued to have its regular rum ration until 1970.

WHAT RUM IS

British law defines rum as 'a spirit distilled direct from sugar-cane products in sugar-growing countries'; this definition dates from 1909, in a report by Sir Algernon Aspinall to the Royal Commission on Whisky and other Potable Spirits. French *rhum*, however, is by French definition the *eau de vie* of sugar-cane, distilled in a single operation from the juice of the cane, or in the form of syrup of molasses of cane, and made in the country where the cane itself is grown. This is why *rhum* cannot be made on the French mainland, nor may it be rectified or flavoured once it leaves the Caribbean.

Until quite recently, books on this subject and courses of instruction run by various trade associations would say that rum is made by both the pot still and the patent still, and that different regions produced different types of rum: French Caribbean *rhums* were traditionally very scented; Jamaica, Demerara and New

England distilleries were accustomed to make full, rather richly flavoured rums, dark to very dark in colour; Demerara rum was particularly strong in aroma. Barbados and Trinidad rums were rather light in colour and style, Virgin Islands and Puerto Rico rums (Puerto Rico is the top rum-producing region in the world) were moderately full-bodied and South American rums likewise, varying from pale to medium gold in colour. Cuba was famous for white rum. But today it is generally true to say that the rum distilleries, most of which now operate continuous stills, instead of the old and more individual type of pot still, cater for whatever type of rum their particular markets require: the British, as has been indicated, have tended to prefer dark, somewhat pungent rums; the French, the more aromatic type; the North American mainland, rums of what might be called a medium style. Traditions naturally play an important part in the style of spirit produced by any one establishment, but it is difficult to generalize about what type of rum is made where these days.

HOW RUM IS MADE

In rum production, the sugar-cane has the surrounding shoots stripped away, after which the main stem is crushed; the juice that comes out, a syrupy liquid, is then clarified and heated, the actual sugar being separated from the molasses, and this sugar alone is made into rum. It is popularly supposed that rum is 'sweet' because of its association with sugar, but, in the process of distillation, the sugar in the liquid undergoing distillation is changed by the action of the yeast into alcohol, and this is not sweet. If it is necessary to produce a rum with some sweetening, this must be added later. Essentially, rum is no sweeter a spirit than, say, whisky, brandy, or other spirits. There is also a rum described as 'fruit cured', which is an orange gold in colour and is taken in the British West Indies as a long drink, diluted with ginger ale, soda or a similar additive. A sample I have tasted was supplied by Caribbean Distillers Ltd.

The way in which rum is made inevitably varies, both according to the region and the traditions of the distillery. To start with, the spirit is without colour, and it may only acquire this by the addition of caramel or burnt sugar, or by ageing in wooden casks, but the latter process is used only for certain very special types of rum. As might be expected, in order to meet increased demand throughout the world, the procedures involved in making rum in a modern distillery have been considerably varied, modified and improved from traditional methods, such as those still described in many reference books. In a recent article in *Wine & Spirit*, Peter L'Anson makes the point that although in the past most distilleries were attached to a sugar factory, and in many instances the two establishments would be under the same ownership, this is not necessarily so today. He then describes the modern type of still, which has six interconnected columns that work as follows: The first column is known as the purifying column; this treats the incoming wash which, boiling and purified, comes out to be pumped to the analysing column. The analysing column treats the wash with steam, which drives the alcoholic vapours upwards and enables the lees to run off at the base of the column. The alcohol, either as a vapour or in liquid form, passes to the rectifying column. The third column, known as the 'heads' or aldehyde column, is fed with the heads or aldehydes from both the purifying column and the aldehyde column, concentrates these vapours and returns the alcohol back so that it may be processed again. In the fourth or rectifying column, the alcoholic vapours are further concentrated and purified, 'the congenerics or impurities of flavours are removed according to the distiller's requirements and the liquid emanating from the top of this column, usually some sixty-odd distilling trays up, is the rum that is required.' The fifth column is the preconcentrated column, used in the distillation of neutral spirits. The sixth column is the hydro-selection column, in which the low-strength impure mixture from the preconcentrated column is received. Hot water brings the alcoholic strength down to as low as 80 u.p. and the mixture is then distilled in this column at this low strength, most of the impurities being drawn off.

In the case of French *rhum*, after the crushing of the sugar-cane the liquid is fermented, the juice either being kept pure, or mixed with water, or combined water and molasses. The fermentation usually lasts for about forty-eight hours, except for *rhums* entitled to be called '*grand arôme*' which undergo a much slower fermentation. *Rhum industrielle* is made from molasses of sugar-cane; *rhum agricole*, sometimes referred to as *grappe blanche* because of its light colour, is made from the concentrated juice of sugar-cane. This last name recalls the comment of the Dominican Father Labat, who at the end of the seventeenth century mentioned, 'Grappe: it is cane juice or "vesou"; they mix it with the juice of two or three lemons and drink it very hot.'

Rhum agricole and *rhum de sirop* (syrup rum) are both specialities of Martinique. *Rhum agricole* takes on colour from the wooden casks in which it is matured – this is the *rhum* that is most used for making Planter's Punch in the French Antilles. *Rhum vieux* has been matured for at least three years in oak, but many *rhums* sold as '*vieux*' may have been aged in wood for much longer and, while they take on colour, they also develop a delicate, penetrating fragrance of great subtlety and fascination – this is the type of fine *rhum* that can hold its own with any fine brandy or whisky.

WHITE RUM

This is very much 'the spirit of the 70s' and huge amounts are now sold throughout the world. But it has long-established traditions. Appleton White, for example, comes from a Jamaican estate founded by a Yorkshireman, John Appleton, in the seventeenth century. This is now the only pure Jamaica rum blend on the U.K. market; the formula according to which it is made dates back to 1825. Today, Guyana produces a considerable amount, as do other regions, but Cuba is certainly where the first big publicity drive for white rum started, even though the Bacardi company, whose establishment was confiscated by Castro, now has its headquarters in Nassau.

A few years ago I compared the main white rums on sale in the U.K., nosing them (spirits are mostly 'tasted' only by smelling – the palate would soon be blunted by them), first neat and at room temperature, then with the addition of Malvern water and finally using each in my own personal recipe for the Daiquiri (which contains no sweetening because I happen to prefer fresh lime juice and no sugar). Although there was very little marked difference in the neat spirits when they were 'naked', there began to be some when the water was added and the difference between the various Daiquiri mixtures was astonishing. White rum has the property of making all fruit, especially citrus, taste fruitier, and the effect of the rums in the cocktail was that in some instances the drink had a more aggressive flavour, in others it was subtler. As the strength of all the white rums was the same, it was evident to me that the way in which this spirit acts as a catalyst may be the reason for its enormous popularity: the associations of health and well-being with any obviously fruity drink, especially when taken in the close atmosphere of a city bar or simply in the humidity of a damp climate, give such mixtures an obvious appeal. The only way for anyone to decide on a preferred brand is to make a similar comparison. As well as the other rums named here, Tropicana and Dry Cane are well-known brands.

One white rum that came out high in my personal opinion at this comparative testing was the only Cuban sample, Havana Club, which is island bottled; this is an interesting example of how a spirit that might not be expected to have much individuality can vary and be distinctive, according both to where it is made and, maybe, bottled. Havana Club is a product of one of the earliest Cuban distilleries, based on an improved formula for rum production evolved by José Luis Casaseca in the nineteenth century; the first of the distilleries, concentrating very much on quality, was established in 1862. On the label of Havana Club is the bronze weathervane that overlooks Havana.

One curious thing about drinks based on white rum, notably the Daiquiri, is that they appear to have a classless appeal: in dockland, coal-mining areas, university towns and country pubs, almost any type of person is likely to order a Daiquiri if a mixed rum drink is required. And of course, for 'rum and Coke', white rum is also used. As far as preferences for mixed drinks based on white rum are concerned, 89 per cent of the public dilute it with cola and 4 per cent with tonic.

Bacardi

This family business dominates at least 50 per cent of the world market of white rum. Indeed, Bacardi accounts for about 65 per cent of all the rum sold in the U.S. (followed by Seagram's Ronrico brand) and it is tipped to achieve the same kind of success as Smirnoff vodka (see page 196) in the next few years, some marketing people thinking that it may even oust the U.S. whiskeys from their dominance of the continent. This is an interesting example of a new version of a traditional drink becoming popular all over again in a market where, before the American War of Independence (see pages 171–2), it was once the chief spirit.

The Bacardi company was founded in 1862 in Cuba, when Don Sacundo Bacardi y Maso arrived there from Catalonia; all his family were traditionally adroit traders and creative personalities, and Sacundo's son Emilio became a member of the political underground movement which was trying to establish a free regime in Cuba. The Bacardi establishment and Emilio's own visits to the cane plantations provided cover for his activities, including the distribution of an underground newspaper. Eventually he was exiled to Spanish Morocco, but the family business went from strength to strength.

Bacardi began to win awards at various international exhibitions: a gold medal at Barcelona in 1888, in France in 1889 and Chicago, 1893. But the most important event was in 1892, when the heir to the throne of Spain, the future Alfonso XIII, was ill with a fever; the child had always been frail and indeed was considered too weak to live in Madrid. The doctors attending him administered a draught of Bacardi and, the fever beginning to break, he slept peacefully. The Bacardi company received letters of gratitude and were henceforth granted permission to use the Royal Arms of Spain on their labels. In 1900, they won another gold medal at the Universal Exhibition in Paris.

Don Emilio, who had been allowed to come home, had another narrow escape in 1895, when his house was searched during an attempted rising by those who were trying to gain Cuba's independence; his wife stuffed all the incriminating papers into the petticoats and underwear of their baby daughter and the family cook, who then went out to do the shopping under the eyes of the watchful soldiers. Don Emilio endured another exile but when he finally returned he was made the first Mayor of Santiago and, in 1906, a senator of Cuba. A brilliant man, a distinguished literary figure as well as administrator, his death in the 1920s was the occasion for a decree of public mourning.

The Bacardi company moved from Cuba in 1960, when the Castro government confiscated the property; at the same time, the 'loyal palm tree', which had been growing in front of the original building in Santiago de Cuba since the foundation of the establishment, died, fulfilling the legend that the company would survive there only as long as the tree! There are many Bacardi establishments throughout the world today, including those in Puerto Rico, Mexico, Brazil and Spain; the black bat on the label is a reminder of the original Cuban warehouse, which was infested with the creatures. Most of the Bacardi that is sold in Britain comes from the Bahamas, that sold to the United States comes from Puerto Rico.

For maturing Bacardi, barrels that are charred inside are used for ageing the darker type for a long period; plain barrels are used for the ordinary light rum that will not be matured as long.

In recent years there was a court case between Bacardi and United Rum, whose white rum is now Santigo, as to whether the name 'Daiquiri' could be used for that of a rum. The Bacardi firm naturally feel that a Daiquiri can be made only with Bacardi rum, but other concerns equally naturally have other ideas and the name of the drink cannot now be used for the name of a particular rum (see page 192).

RUMS IN THE U.K.

In the U.K., rum suffers from the disadvantage that most of it comes into the country in bulk and then, by law, it has to be warehoused for two years (until 1976 it was three years). This regulation dates from the time when rum was mostly the product of a pot still, requiring a certain amount of maturation in cask to get rid of its impurities, but as a high proportion of rums today, including all white rums, are produced by continuous stills, the cost of this totally unnecessary warehousing merely puts up the price of the rum for the customer.

One of the best-known brands of rum on sale in the U.K. is Lamb's Navy, the brand-leader in the dark category, usually described as 'Demerara' and top seller in the British rum market as a whole. In spite of its colour, it is not particularly pungent as regards smell. The runner up is Captain Morgan; although it comes from Jamaica, it also is really described as 'Demerara style' and is a traditional dark rum. Lemon Hart, light in colour but with a pronounced flavour is categorized as a 'traditional Jamaican' rum blend.

RHUM IN FRANCE

Bardinet

In 1857, Paul Bardinet set up as a producer and distributor of *rhum* at Limoges. He was a skilled distiller and had conducted a number of experiments in making liqueurs, becoming particularly concerned with a spirit called *tafia*, or *guildive*, which he discovered in the West Indies; this became enormously successful commercially and in fact is the ancestor of Rhum Negrita, today the dominant brand in France and in fact of great importance in the kitchen – it has been proved by market research that about 70 per cent of French households keep this brand of *rhum* in the kitchen for various culinary purposes, which include flaming and 'degreasing' meat and fish, as well as making pastries and a variety of sweet things. Paul Bardinet first marketed this *rhum* in a bottle with a partial outer casing of white raffia, and this presentation, which has not been changed, has made it very familiar.

In 1895, Edouard Bardinet, son of Paul, moved the establishment to Bordeaux, where, at the time of writing, there are now two houses making Bardinet products, although the establishment has been taken over by the mighty Cointreau organization and will soon be shifted again to Le Havre. Bardinet's white *rhum*, Old Nick, is also well known throughout France. There are Bardinet establishments

in many other countries, including North and South America and
Mexico, Holland, Belgium, Spain, Italy, Switzerland, Germany and
Australia. Bardinet, as well as specializing in the *rhums* of the French
Antilles, also use those of Réunion in the Indian Ocean.

RUM DRINKS

Daiquiri: In the 1890s the manager of the small Daiquiri tin mine in
Cuba used to please his guests with a mixture of white rum and lime
juice, evolved by his servant. This was not only a useful substitute
when supplies of whisky ran short, but became popular in its own
right – and so the Daiquiri (named after the mine) was first made.
President Kennedy particularly enjoyed a Daiquiri. Until it was
possible to get fresh limes easily in Britain the drink tended to be
made with lemon juice in the U.K., although this is not particularly
satisfactory – one needs about twice the amount of lemon as lime
juice.

The proportions of this drink can vary from one-quarter to one-
third or one half of fresh lime juice (bottled lime juice does not give
the same flavour at all), with the remainder being white rum, plus
sugar or sugar syrup to taste, shaken over crushed ice or poured over
ice cubes. Personally, I like one-third lime juice to two-thirds white
rum and no sweetening at all.

Cuba Libre: This is two parts of a light or white rum, a tablespoonful of fresh lime juice, poured over ice and topped up with
Coca Cola.

Planter's Punch: This is a most interesting drink, certainly dating
from the seventeenth century, when it implied a mixed drink based
on rum with some citrus juice and sweetening plus soda. But, in the
French Antilles today, 'un Planteur' is, basically, one part sugar-cane
syrup to four of white *rhum*, plus such fruit juices as liked – orange,
grapefruit, pineapple, coconut milk. I think that the use of fresh
lime juice makes this drink better than other versions. The traditional jingle goes: 'one of sour (lime), two of sweet (sugar), three of
strong (rhum), four of weak (ice)'; the sweetening in these proportions may be too much for the drinker of today. The essential with
a good 'Planteur', as I found when trying a number in both Guade-
loupe and Martinique, is that the mixture must be made up just
before serving – if the fruit juices and spirit are allowed to combine
for any length of time and all kinds of exotic garnishes are incorporated, as enthusiastic barmen tend to do, then the result can be a
pretty-looking but rather insipid beverage.

In the French Antilles today a Petit Punch or Ponche Blanc is a short drink – one part white rum, one part sugar-cane syrup and a slice of green lemon or zest of lime with a few ice cubes. Vieux Punch is basically the same but uses Rhum Vieux and no lemon, although a little cinnamon or nutmeg can be incorporated. The well-known Rhum St James is the type most often used for this mixture. Both these drinks are definitely on the short side and, although this may be an odd suggestion, I found that I preferred to make my 'Ponches' slightly longer by adding soda. The Distillerie des Rhums Agricoles gave me this recipe for a Martiniquais: 1½ ounces Rhum St James, 2 ounces pineapple juice, plus a dash of Amoretta liqueur, shaken with ice cubes and strained into a glass.

Trader Vic's Punch: This is one of the exotic-looking drinks popularized in Trader Vic's restaurants in the U.S. and London and combines one and a quarter parts of light and dark rum, the juice of half an orange, half a lemon, a little sugar and a dash of grenadine. The mixture is shaken with a slice of pineapple, poured into a tall glass and drunk through straws. Trader Vic's bars have an extensive repertoire of elaborate and strong drinks, all of them looking extremely attractive, and many of them being highly alcoholic for casual urban drinking. One Mayfair 'Caribbean'-style bar even features a drink called a Zombie, supposedly so strong and certainly so expensive that no one is allowed to have more than two! But these are not drinks to suit the context of hospitality in the home – the simpler mixes are preferable.

8. Vodka

Vodka has been known for many centuries, although it is difficult to be precise about its origin. The Russians seem to have been making it since the twelfth century; the Poles claim that Polish vodka, which must have been a very primitive spirit then, was made in the eighth century. Polish vodka is mentioned in a herbal in 1534. There are several references to *zhiznennia voda*, which means 'water of life' in Russian, and this term seems to have become shortened to 'vodka' or 'wodka' meaning 'little water'. Some authorities think that the spirit got the name from the Russian port, Viatka. Anyway, by the sixteenth century, a type of 'aqueous wine spirit' known as *vodnyi vinnyi* was in existence, and Polish distilleries were established at Poznan, Cracow and Gdansk. (It is here that most Polish vodka is made today, the best known on export markets probably being Wyborowa.) It is reasonable to assume that, as with other spirits, a certain amount of vodka was distilled in the religious establishments throughout Poland and Russia. It may well be that, because of the great trade routes that connected these countries with the Arab nations of the Middle East, merchants brought both the original spirit and the recipe for it to the northern countries.

In 1649, Tsar Alexis I, father of Peter the Great, instituted an 'alcohol code' for the regulation of quality in the production of spirits, but the method by which vodka is purified by filtering it through charcoal was only satisfactorily achieved in 1794, by Professor Lowitz of St Petersburg. Vodka does not seem to have been widely drunk elsewhere until after the Russian Revolution in 1917, when White Russian *émigrés* began to make it in their places of exile. But one name in the story of vodka was known long before: Smirnoff.

The most important commercial vodka in Imperial Russia was Smirnoff. The family set up their distillery in Moscow where, after Napoleon's 1812 retreat and the burning of the city, the only two main landmarks that survived were the Kremlin and the iron bridge, so that the distillery was called 'the House of Smirnoff by the Iron Bridge'. This vodka achieved such a success that by 1886 it had won three royal seals, entitling it to use the Tsar's coat of arms on the label, and Smirnoff was the only vodka that could be served at the Imperial table.

The firm exhibited their vodka in the Byzantine-style pavilion at a fair at Nijni-Novgorod, and Tatiana, wife of Vladimir Smirnoff, then head of the firm, described how 'the Tsar drank their vodka and gave it his benevolent approval'. At another fair some years later, the Smirnoff establishment took two pavilions dedicated to Russian folklore, with a walk between them, in which white Russian bears were paraded, dancing, and carrying trays of glasses with vodka; the public thronged to try the vodka and clink glasses with the bears which, Tatiana Smirnoff reveals, were mostly 'men, cleverly disguised. There were a few real bears, securely guarded and chained.' The bears actually drank the vodka, too, holding the glasses in their front paws and knocking back the spirit so that they remained amiable and sleepy throughout the fair.

The Smirnoff sales were at least a million bottles a day before 1914, and the family was fabulously rich. But in the Revolution Vladimir Smirnoff had to flee, first to Poland and then to France, where he set up a small distillery in Paris. Here he met Rudolf Kunett, a Russian-born American citizen, whose family had in fact supplied the Smirnoffs with much of the grain they had used in Russia. Kunett was allowed to try and sell Smirnoff in the United States and, in 1934, started with a small distillery in Bethel, Connecticut. Unfortunately, he found it difficult to sell the spirit and its commercial success was comparatively small; so, in 1939, he sold the rights in Smirnoff to John G. Martin, English-born chairman of Heublein's, a liquor establishment in Hartford, Connecticut. Martin's fellow-directors tried to dissuade him from buying a spirit that was so far from an asset that only about 6000 cases were being sold annually, but he had his way. However, the traditional way of drinking vodka – knocking it back from a small glass – did not appeal to the American public, still very much in the cocktail era (to this day, I am told, the evening preprandial drinking period is known as 'the cocktail hour', a phrase that sounds archaic to the European ear).

By the late 1940s, Martin may have begun to feel that he should have taken his colleagues' advice, but one day when he was having a drink in the Cock 'n Bull tavern in Los Angeles he mentioned the problem of trying to publicize drinks to the owner, Jack Morgan. Morgan sympathized – he was over-stocked with ginger beer, another line that Americans seemed to view with indifference, even at a time when drinks of many kinds were in short supply. The two men pondered the matter and, from this conversation, evolved the Moscow Mule (vodka, fresh lime or lemon juice and ginger beer served in a copper mug – Jack Morgan had a friend who had inherited a company making copper mugs of which he too had an overabundance) and, later, the Screwdriver (vodka with freshly-squeezed orange juice). It was an instance of the right drink at the right time in the right place: the fruit juices appealed to those vaguely aware of their 'goodness', the drinks' kick to those who wanted a fairly strong mixture, and the novelty (even at the height of anti-Russian feeling in the U.S.) to the California jet and showbiz set, who greatly influence social habits in North America.

But it took time to establish vodka thoroughly. Indeed, in the early 1950s, the gigantic drinks combine, House of Seagram, held a week's business convention in Los Angeles, with free drinks available to all visitors to their hotel suite during the period. Every kind of drink was on hand and several thousand guests were entertained but, at the end of the week, no one had once ordered vodka. Seagram's President, General Schwengel, picked up the unbroached case of vodka on the last night of the convention and, remarking, 'So much for the future of vodka in America!' flung it into the hotel swimming pool.

The scene changed, however – and radically. In 1975 the total sales of vodka in the U.S. represented an 18·7 per cent share of the market and, for the first time in history, sales of Bourbon, up to then an easy leader (and the biggest selling spirit in the world) were surpassed, Bourbon having only a 17·1 per cent share of the U.S. market. Today, there are about 200 different brands of vodka selling in the U.S., many of them, of course, made there.

The commercial success of vodka prepared the way for a huge increase in vodka drinking throughout the world. When the great Catalan artist Pablo Picasso was asked in an interview what he thought were the most notable features of post-war France, he replied: 'Brigitte Bardot, modern jazz, Polish vodka'. One of the advantages of vodka is, to quote an advertisement for one brand, that 'it leaves you breathless' – no smell of liquor remaining detectable on the breath. In addition, it was found and appreciated that vodka is low in the fusel oils and congenerics, which are, basically, types of impurity that can lend charm to spirits, but which can accentuate the after-affects of heavy consumption. Vodka therefore acquired the reputation for being among the 'safer' spirits – though it should be emphasized that this 'safeness' has nothing to do with its power as an intoxicant, which, according to the strength, may be considerable.

A type of Polish vodka that is as strong as 140 proof is not described by those handling it as vodka at all but 'Polish pure spirit'; the strengths of 65·5 and 66 proof feature widely on labels for the odd reason that any spirit under 65 proof must by law be labelled 'diluted with water to . . . proof', which naturally looks as if the spirit were somehow inferior because of the dilution. In fact of course all spirits are broken down by water, but, as with whisky, different vodkas really do appear to have a different taste, sometimes perceived when the spirit is drunk neat, sometimes when it is in a mix, though this may be detecting the variations in the water used rather than any secret formula.

HOW VODKA IS MADE

In former times, vodka might have been distilled from a variety of things, according to whatever crop was available in quantity or glut. This could include molasses, potatoes, and even fruits, including grapes. Today, however, most vodka is distilled from grain. Both Poland and Russia are, of course, large producers of grain.

The spirit, once distilled and rectified, is diluted with distilled water until it is broken down to the required strength; the standard strength for most vodkas today is 65·5°, but certain brands are produced at higher strengths, such as 75° and 80° – the strength must, according to current legislation, be stated on the label. The quality of the ultimate vodka is naturally related to the quality of the grain that is used – Polish vodka is nearly always made from rye – and also the water used, vodka in this instance being, like Scotch, greatly affected by the purity of the source of water involved. The vodka is filtered through layers of activated charcoal, in order to ensure its ultimate purity.

TYPES OF VODKA

Basically, vodka is a neutral spirit, both colourless and without flavour. Sometimes, if the vodka is matured in a wooden wine cask, it will take on a tint from this, but in general it is without colour. The advantage of vodka as a neutral spirit is that it combines very well with many other liquids, giving character to the drink to which it is added and enhancing its basic flavour as well, of course, as its strength.

There is a certain amount of snobbery about whether it is 'better' to choose Polish or Russian vodka, but, if a really neutral spirit is required, then there is not much to determine the choice except availability. Vodka is made in many other countries today and there was even a recent instance of the British Ambassador to Moscow taking with him a British vodka, Masquers, somewhat to the astonishment of the Russians! Other successful vodkas made in England are Cossack and Vladivar.

Flavoured vodkas

Vodka can be flavoured with many things: it is even possible to make an orange or lemon vodka simply by allowing the peel of the fruit to steep in the bottle of neutral vodka for some time. Herb vodkas, spiced vodkas (including a pepper vodka flavoured with either chillies or peppercorns) and vodkas flavoured with fruits are also to be found. The use of pepper as a flavouring possibly has its origin in the legend that Peter the Great used to add pepper to his vodka (though why he should be in any way benevolently associated with good drinking, I cannot guess – the link between him and good vodka seems as improbable and indeed unwise as that of Napoleon and Cognac). Some herb vodkas also have an additional flavouring of honey.

Zubrowka is a Polish vodka, each bottle containing a blade of a type of grass (*Hierochooe odorata*), a favourite pasture of the herds of wild bison in the forests of east Poland. This vodka, often described as a 'virile drink' – because, I suppose, the bison, like the bull, is vaguely symbolic of virility – has a slight tint of yellowish colour.

The term *'starka'*, a word that means old, is applied to a high-strength vodka that has been matured for about ten years in oak, from which it has gained a golden colour.

HOW TO SERVE VODKA

The traditional way of drinking vodka is to pour a small quantity into a little glass and toss it off in a gulp. The vodka should be not merely cold but iced, the bottle having been kept in the freezer rather than the refrigerator. It is traditional in northern countries to serve vodka (like schnapps) with caviare and, often, with smoked fish; because of its strength, vodka is seldom served without some form of food to accompany it, such as pickled cucumbers, herrings, anchovies and similar piquant snacks.

There is no particular advantage in having a high-strength vodka, especially if you are going to make a mixed vodka-based drink, but if the spirit is to be served neat it is only fair to warn guests if you do use a vodka that is stronger than they may usually expect. Otherwise, if people think that they can detect differences between one brand and another, then they must follow their individual preferences. The only general quality-assessment of vodka for which one has paid a fair price is that, when poured, it should look very slightly oily as it enters the glass.

Vodka is a good digestive, the spirit assisting in dissipating the heaviness of rich food, and it may well have become popular in Russia and Poland because of this, as much as because of the warming properties; being used as a type of *trou normand* (see page 283) to cut the richness of foods, as well as with various piquant and salted first courses. In mixes, however, both the strength and the possible inimical qualities of the other ingredients make vodka unsuitable for serving before a meal that is to include fine and delicate wines. One place where I think vodka might appropriately be served, however, is with a savoury; this type of food, which often includes a curry flavouring (as with 'devils' of various sorts), anchovies, bacon and so on, is also an enemy to all but the most robust type of everyday wine. Savouries are only served today in the British Isles or in such parts of the world as retain strong and somewhat old-fashioned British traditions of dining, and they tend to feature mostly on the menus of men's clubs (of the St James's rather than the 'working men's' type) or be served at men-only dinners. Vodka could therefore be served with a savoury as a type of digestive and, unless people intend to drink anything else after the meal, it might form a pleasant conclusion – especially if the latter part of the twentieth century sees the decline of the tradition of all-male dinners and of the ladies leaving the dining-room before the men. The savoury, as a unique British dish, is worth preserving and vodka, as a civilized newcomer to the Anglo-Saxon drinking scene, could bring it back into routine gastronomy.

VODKA DRINKS

Vodka can be combined with tonic water or soda, with a little orange or lemon peel if liked. The Vodkatini is a dry martini with vodka instead of gin. Ian Fleming's hero James Bond, whose reputation for knowing about wines and spirits is wholly undeserved, sometimes orders a Vodkatini 'shaken not stirred'; this continues to irritate those who insist that this type of drink, a version of the martini, must be stirred. Bond also drinks straight vodka sprinkled with black pepper which, he says, is 'to carry the fusel oil to the bottom of the glass'. But I do not see that this twentieth-century imitation of Peter the Great's drinking habits has much to be said for it as a drink – nor how it would achieve its purpose.

The Bloody Mary has to be made up in the following order: a little Worcester sauce is first put into the glass, plus a shot of tabasco if liked. Then add a squeeze of fresh lemon juice, pinch of salt, ice cubes, a measure of vodka, tomato juice and, if liked, a sprinkle of black pepper.

The Bullshot, a recently evolved drink, very popular in the United States for brunch, and reputed to have reviving properties 'the morning after', is beef bouillon and vodka, both well chilled, with salt, pepper, juice or zest of lemon and Worcester sauce and/or tabasco to taste. Americans insist the classic bullshot is made from Campbell's bouillon only, although I myself prefer Campbell's concentrated beef consommé; certainly both of these are better than the insipidities of pre-prepared mixes.

9. Other White Spirits

PERNOD AND PASTIS

Although these are two different commodities, they have certain similarities. Both Pernod and the brand leader in pastis, Ricard, are in the huge French drinks combine that includes Gévéor. Pernod is flavoured with aniseed while most pastis, although it does remind some people of aniseed, is in fact mainly flavoured with liquorice. Both types of drink, too, originally contained the herbal spirit absinthe (see pages 229–31).

Pernod was first made in the eighteenth century, by a Frenchman, Dr Pierre Ordinaire. He was a royalist and therefore, in 1790, found himself a refugee from the Revolutionary movement in France, and went to Neuchâtel in Switzerland. There he made an infusion of fifteen different herbs, which he named for the wormwood that was the principal ingredient; he further discovered that this mixture became particularly effective when it was steeped in high-strength alcohol. When Ordinaire died in 1792, he left the recipe for his drink to his housekeeper, a Madame Henriot; she established herself with her daughters in a shop, marketing this 'special' beverage – she thought that her former employer had discovered a remarkable form of aphrodisiac! Scientifically, there is no such thing, but for those who seek to stimulate themselves, it is often a question of it all being 'in the mind' – yet absinthe had begun to be associated with sexual prowess even at this period. One of Madame Henriot's customers bought the recipe for Dr Ordinaire's digestive in 1797 and, with his son-in-law Henry Louis Pernod, opened a small factory in Switzerland, extending this to one in France, at Pontarlier, near the Swiss frontier, in 1805. Very soon Pernod outstripped the sales of all other types of absinthe drink.

The distillery, alongside the River Doubs, began to produce in vast quantities and when, one day, a cask burst and the spirit flowed down into the river, the local inhabitants were astonished to see it foaming a bright yellow. The original formula for Pernod contained certain narcotics and the drink was of a very high strength, causing a curious, dreamy state of intoxication – as depicted by Pablo Picasso during his 'blue period' in 'The Absinthe Drinker'. This led to a campaign to ban it in the public interest.

The ban on absinthe in Switzerland was apparently the result of a *cause célèbre* in 1905, when a farmer, Jean Lanfray, shot his wife and two daughters, after which he attempted to commit suicide. Because he had earlier drunk six quarters of wine, six brandies and two absinthes, the judge at his trial considered that he might have 'absinthe-induced delirium', although local opinion was inclined to think that Madame Lanfray's nagging had provoked him. Lanfray was jailed for life, but hanged himself in his cell, and in 1907 absinthe was banned, first in Switzerland and then, in 1915, in France and subsequently in the United States, although it can sometimes be found elsewhere. Pernod today is merely flavoured with aniseed. In fact, the amount of genuine absinthe in the drinks of the time was always very small, but imitations of the original drink quickly appeared after the ban. As an imitation is *pastiche* in French, the word 'pastis' became associated with the absinthe drink. However, in the south of France there is another explanation for the term (see pages 202–3).

The Pernod factory was sold to the Swiss chocolate firm of Nestlé in 1915, but in 1926 the successors to the original company joined with a rival firm and formed Pernod Père et Fils. In addition to establishments at Lyons, Marseilles and Bordeaux, the firm now have a gigantic complex at Créteil, just outside Paris, La Pernoderie; here more than 300,000 bottles of Pernod are made daily for Paris drinkers by only six men.

In the south of France, throughout the Rhône Valley, in Provence and along the Mediterranean coast, as well as in Corsica, a similar drink is enormously popular. It too derives from an absinthe concoction and the traditional way of taking it is as in the old days: the spirit, which is colourless, is put in the bottom of the glass, then a special perforated spoon is propped across this and either neat water is dripped through the holes or else, for a sweeter drink, a lump of sugar is put on the spoon and the water poured slowly through. As with Pernod, the addition of water to pastis causes it to become opaque and yellow. The spirit is slightly stirred up or 'troubled' by the addition of the water; in Provençal, the word for this stirring is '*se pastiser*' – and so the generic name '*pastis*' came into being. The cloudiness that occurs in these drinks is the result of the herbs and flavouring elements in them being extracted at a high alcoholic strength; they are therefore soluble in alcohol but not in water and so when this is added, they become less soluble and separate, losing their transparency even though they are made progressively weaker.

Nothing is more instantly evocative of the atmosphere of the south of France than someone sitting in the sunshine, surveying players of *pétanque* on the sunbaked earth, while meditatively sipping an increasingly cloudy pastis. I have been told that there are all kinds of games that pastis drinkers play, timing the dilution of their drink, or betting themselves that they won't let the spoon tumble into the glass before they have finished adding the water – if they do then they must pay a forfeit by drinking another pastis!

The production centre of pastis is Marseilles and Ricard is the brand leader, another very well-known pastis being that of Berger. In Corsica, where the pastis is a little sharper and tangier than the French type, Casanis is the best-known brand and it is drunk all over the island. Pastis 51 is made by Pernod, the date referring to when it was first made, 1951, and also to the ratio of water suggested, five to one.

Paul Ricard was the son of a wine merchant and hoped to become a painter. But one day, walking with his father through the Provençal countryside, they met an old shepherd, who made his own pastis, with a particularly satisfying recipe including anise, liquorice and herbs, macerated in alcohol. Young Paul Ricard, at the age of eighteen, went into business with his father and, having remembered the recipe given to him by the old shepherd, worked to perfect the formula for an equally good pastis. On the floor of the factory at Sainte Marthe, a suburb of Marseilles, there is now a star, symbolic of the star-shaped anise flower, marking the site of his original makeshift laboratory. The recipe includes anise, liquorice, Provençal herbs, triple-distilled alcohol and water.

In 1938, Paul obtained legal recognition for his 'Ricard', and sold over 3½ million bottles in the first year he was in commercial production. During the War he and his staff lived in the Camargue, where he introduced the cultivation of rice to this part of France, planted extensive orchards, distilled pure alcohol for Resistance fighters, and sheltered many who would otherwise have been condemned to forced labour either in France or Germany. Progress made after the War resulted in Ricard being responsible for 50 per cent of all the aperitives, spirits and liqueurs consumed in France, and the business interests of the company are enormous. They own the island of Bendor, just off the French Mediterranean coast, where there is a wine museum and, naturally, plenty of pastis on sale.

Ricard now has plants in many other parts of France and indeed all over the world. During an anti-alcohol campaign in France after the Second World War, Ricard were forbidden to advertise their product: Paul Ricard reacted promptly and constructively by engaging in a number of sponsored promotions, such as making deliveries by camel, to draw attention to it. The slogan of the Ricard sales force is that customers should take 'Ricard à la Marseillaise', that is, one part of Ricard to five of water. Paul Ricard is also a prominent member of the Association des Anysetiers du Roy, a fellowship devoted to the promotion of anise drinks. When in 1968 he retired, to breed prize bulls, the event was described in a French newspaper as the 'hara-kiri of Monsieur Pastis'. In 1971 the two giants, Pernod and Ricard, merged; as well as their most obvious products they make a wide range of still and sparkling wines.

Individuals must determine their own preferences as regards brands, but it may be noted that, when the water is added, Ricard becomes a tawny-yellow, whereas Pernod becomes a yellow-green.

Pernod and pastis drinks

The way of drinking both Pernod and pastis is simply with water (dripped through sugar on to pastis if a sweetish drink is liked). In export markets, which are developing considerably for both these drinks, the traditional method is not particularly popular with young drinkers, who, in their discos and clubs, prefer to dilute Pernod with lemonade or bitter lemon. Frenchmen who agree that the ideal dilution of pastis is five times as much water as spirit, stress that there should not be ice in the drink – the water used should be cold water from a spring. This of course is a counsel of perfection.

There are only a few mixed drinks: the Perroquet is a half and half mixture of crème de menthe and pastis, topped up with water (the peppermint liqueur somewhat cuts the sweetness). A Tomate might be described as a southern answer to the Bloody Mary, for it is pastis with grenadine and water, the grenadine giving the mixture a tomato-juice-like tinge. On one occasion, I saw a high-ranking ecclesiastic in Corsica enjoying what looked like a harmless tomato juice with his parishioners. But he was a true Corsican – he was drinking a Tomate!

SCHNAPPS

Inhabitants of northern countries, where the winter nights are extra long, have been spirit drinkers virtually ever since spirits were widely made. The general term used for them was 'water of life' from the Latin *aqua vitae* and this became *aqvavit* in Danish, *aquavit* in Swedish. But these white spirits are also referred to as *schnapps* in both Germany (where, loosely, it signifies almost any strong drink) and Holland, *schnaps* in Denmark and *snaps* in Sweden. The pronunciation is vaguely the same, and the word itself means a 'gasp' or 'snatch', a term evoking the way in which it is drunk and its subsequent effect. The Danes have been distilling schnaps for about 400 years; they may even have done so earlier, as excavations in central Jutland, in 1930, revealed portions of a type of primitive pot-still, dated about 1400.

In 1534, Canon Christiern Pedersen wrote a guide to distilling, using Danish herbs, and in 1555 King Christian III bought up a set of stills that had been pawned in Copenhagen so that he could make personal use of them – with the unfortunate result that his son Frederick II actually drank himself to death; the funeral sermon, in 1588, included a head-shaking mention to 'this all too prevalent drink'. Frederick's sister Princess Anne had a recipe collection of 181 types of schnaps. Frederick's successor, his son King Christian IV, was an equally heavy drinker but of a tougher constitution, and it was he who started the custom of having drums, trumpets and the firing of cannon to accompany the drinking of toasts, as Shakespeare's Hamlet describes. Christian's sister Anne made heavy drinking fashionable in England when she married James I. The Queen brought in her train a champion toper who had won bets in all the courts of Europe – but this man was defeated by Sir Robert Lawrie, a Scottish knight, in a drinking bout that lasted three days and nights (as Burns describes in his poem 'The Whistle'). Christian attempted to control what is described as 'the great Scandinavian intoxication' by forbidding drink to be served during the hours of services, and prohibiting the clergy from leading services with a glass in their hands, but even though he ordained that regional assemblies should start at 7 a.m. (because later in the day no one was really sober), he made no lasting impression on northern tippling. But he did start the taxation of spirits.

Illegal distillation was common and those who made stills would come from all over Europe to sell their copperware. In addition to this unauthorized activity, official distillation continued on an enormous scale; the Guild of Distillers was formed in Copenhagen in 1741, and numbered 337 Master Distillers by 1758. The Danes and their Scandinavian neighbours went on drinking. Years later when, in 1843, people were encouraged to surrender their illegal stills, being paid for the copper and not penalized if they would comply with the regulations within a certain time, about 11,000 stills were actually handed in. The unsympathetic Karl Marx described Denmark in 1848 (the time of the Schleswig rising against the Danes) as 'a half civilized country' in 'a state of permanent drunkenness alternating with berserk frenzy'. A flask of spirits was part of the regular issue to the Danish Army until as recently as 1903.

Grain, from which most Danish aqvavit has always been made, has been referred to as 'the Danish grape' and 'a great living diamond'. Rye and, later, wheat were the types used. Today, however, potatoes are used in large quantities, from September until March or April, grain being used for distillation for the rest of the year.

These white spirits were much home-made in northern countries, and increasingly the customers, who previously had bought aqvavit from the pharmacist, would go and buy neutral spirits from the distilleries to make it. When, after 1860, these establishments began to market their products under brand names, the phrase 'factory bottled' was significant – the consumer knew that he was getting a particularly flavoured product, that had in no way been diluted. But there are plenty of local recipes still on record, the majority using caraway, which was obtained mostly from Finland, although nowadays the cultivated variety, as opposed to wild caraway, is used by the Danish distilleries. It is in fact illegal to distil in Denmark today without a licence, as it is in the U.K., but some people still make their own variations on the classic aqvavit by using ancestral recipes, involving flavourings with herbs, flowers, roots and berries. In Norway, too, I am told, many people do make their own spirits at home in small-scale stills, according to past traditions – even though this is prohibited by law today.

Up to the First World War the Danes were still the world's top drinkers. Then times changed, conditions in industry improved, taxes went up and everyone had to work harder. The twenty-six Danish distilleries were virtually taxed out of existence in 1917, the sole surviving manufacturer of schnaps being the Danish Distilleries, founded in 1881 in Aalborg, the export department of which is Danisco. The Danish name is De Danske Spritfabrikker. Until Denmark joined the E.E.C. in 1973, the firm had the monopoly in the manufacture of aqvavit and other spirits, but since that date some other firms have set up in business. The Danish Distilleries make nine different brands of *aqvavit* (plus liqueurs, gin, yeast and pure alcohol), but the most important are Aalborg Aqvavit (formerly called Aalborg Taffel Aqvavit) and Aalborg Jubilaeums Aqvavit, which is spiced with dill and other herbs. In Germany Danisco make Maltese Cross Aqvavit, and also Kornenkreutz Taffel Aqvavit. The Copenhagen firm of Peter Heering make several types of aquavit, including Christianshavner Aquavit, flavoured with a blend of spices; Gammelholm Snaps, flavoured with aniseed; and Fattigmands (Poor Man's) Snaps, caraway flavoured; and Daglig (Daily) Snaps. In Sweden, the big brands are Skåne, a colourless type, and O. P. Andersen Aquavit, which has a pale yellowish tinge. The Danish varieties are slightly stronger. An interesting Norwegian aquavit is that of Linie of Trondhjem, which has a picture of a ship on the label and, on the back of the label, one can read through the bottle that the contents of the particular bottle have been sent on a particular vessel to Australia and back, with the dates of the voyage. The purpose of this is presumably to mature the spirit and I have been told that those who want to vaunt their expertise when they order a 'Linie' in a restaurant, will insist on seeing the bottle and then, having read the spirit's provenance as regards the ship and the date, may decide that the vessel was of inferior type or, maybe, that there were too many storms at that time! The spirit itself is tea-coloured, doubtless from the wood in which it undergoes its travels.

Serving schnnaps

Schnapps is strong and therefore, like the stomach settlers or cordials which used to be drunk in England, these white spirits are served in small glasses; public measures decree that these must be 2, 3 or 5 centilitres. Although people entertaining at home can use any glasses that they wish, the traditional schnapps glass is always small – necessitated by the strength of the drink, the way that it is drunk, and the fact that it would warm up if poured into a large glass.

Also associated with the service of aquavit is the kluk bottle or *klukflaske*, a type of decanter that has incurving sides that cause the liquid to make a glug-glug sound as it is poured. This type of flask has been in use since the eighteenth century and is supposed to have been first made when a glass blower sneezed just as he was about to make an ordinary bottle – the involuntary gasp he gave caused the sides of the bottle to collapse. Yet another type of container for aquavit is the 'aquavit hound', a dog-shaped container that also makes a noise when the spirit is poured.

There are many conventions about drinking schnapps. In general, the glass is raised in someone's direction, the first drinker says 'Skaal!', to which the one saluted replies with the same word; then the drinkers stare into each other's eyes – this is supposed to be a survival of the practice of drinking in ancient times, when anyone encumbered with the gigantic drinking horn that would take seconds if not minutes to empty, might have his attention distracted, during which moment a nearby enemy could fall upon him. For the same reason, the arm that holds the glass may be linked with the arm of the person being 'skaaled'. Danes are rather less formal about all this than Swedes. In Sweden, the convention is that the hostess of the party must 'Skaal' her guests before they may drink to her, although host and hostess may make a general gesture of drinking to the assembled company. But, though it is discourteous not to respond to a toast given in this manner, it is at the same time rude to 'skaal' the hostess – she must remain sober. (In Denmark it doesn't seem to matter.)

The traditional accompaniment to a skaal is a jingle which may be either said or sung, and which, translated, means 'Skaal to you, skaal to me, skaal to every pretty girl!' and, in the old days, when in the evenings men wore white waistcoats fastened with buttons at the front, it was supposed to be necessary to drink a schnapps for every button on the waistcoat.

Although some authorities, particularly those writing in the period after the Second World War, argue somewhat about the temperature at which schnapps should be served, I think that it simply must be cold, the bottle preferably having been taken from the freezer and ideally served with a jacket of ice around it. This is easy to achieve if you first stand it in a can of water which then freezes and can be slipped off, leaving the ice around the bottle. One of the most horrible drinks I ever had, on a stuffy day in London, was schnapps at room temperature, taken from someone's sideboard! But schnapps is never drunk without having something to eat – Danes will tell you that the ideal accompaniment is herring, or one of the superlative open sandwiches served on rye bread, with a 'chaser' of cool lager afterwards. Schnapps is excellent with all the casual fare traditional in the Scandinavian countries both as a palate cleanser after the piquant and salty foodstuff and to create the spirit of conviviality; you are supposed to knock the whole contents of the glass back in a single gulp, but it is permissible to take the second in two 'bites' –

swallows – and the third in three if you wish. Memoirs record how special family occasions, both celebrations and funerals, were always accompanied by schnapps, some wills actually allocating the amount of spirit that could be served to the different categories of those attending – the bearers, the mourners and the minister each having specific allowances.

Although one would obviously not serve the food traditional with schnapps with fine wine or the spirit with delicate dishes, schnapps is nevertheless so clean that, rather like vodka, it will not seriously affect the sense of taste for what is to follow – it merely makes everything taste better.

Two other drinks which are good are the long drink, called the 'Schnapdragon', which is schnapps and bitter lemon, both chilled, and Kaffepuns (coffee punch), or 'little black', which occurs at the end of a meal: a small silver coin is put in the bottom of the coffee cup, the coffee is poured until the coin can no longer be seen, then schnapps is poured on to the coffee until the coin becomes visible once more – sometimes this works out at about half and half. It is an admirable digestive.

OUZO

Ouzo is a white spirit, of an aniseed flavour, which is made in many countries of eastern Europe and especially around the Mediterranean. Both the strength and the degree to which the spirit is flavoured can vary considerably, although the ouzo available in the U.K., from Greece and other sources, is generally about 39° Gay Lussac.

Ouzo can be made by simply using aniseed to flavour neat alcohol, but the best type is made by distilling the basic spirit twice, after which the aniseed and any other aromatic herbs are added, usually with a little sugar, and the whole is redistilled; the final distillate is then broken down with distilled water to the strength ultimately required. Some types of Greek ouzo incorporate mastika, derived from a resinous shrub of the same name; this type of ouzo is slightly sweeter than usual. The ouzo of E. Tsantalis, of Thessaloniki, Greece, is described as being made from 'sweet grapes, raisins of fine quality, Macedonian anise and nineteen other aromatic herbs'. Most of the wineries of Greece and Cyprus will make an ouzo and each will be individual. In the Lebanon, this sweetish version of the drink is named *arak* and in Egypt it is called *zebib*.

Ouzo is rather a curious drink. In Greece, Turkey and the Lebanon it is popular all the year round, although in Cyprus and Crete it tends to be mainly a summer refreshment. But in all these countries, as well as on many Mediterranean islands, it can also be drunk with food at a meal, although Anglo-Saxons may find it on the strong side for this purpose.

Ouzo should be served cold. Traditionally, it is offered neat, in a small glass, with a larger glass of water by the side. It is a matter of personal taste as to whether you pour the ouzo into the water or sip from the two glasses in turn. In resorts, ouzo may come having been poured 'on the rocks', although this is rather a pity, because it is attractive to see the way in which the spirit becomes milky as soon as water is added: the better the ouzo, the milkier it should become, and the best type will indeed look rather like milk and water when you dilute it or add ice – there is the same blue rim around the edge where it meets the glass as with watered milk. But ouzo should not be kept under refrigeration, because, if it becomes very cold, the oil in the aniseed will coagulate within the liquid and a type of scale is formed within the bottle, detracting from the clarity, though the flavour is not in fact affected.

Ouzo will always be served with something to eat: eggs, a few small pieces of cheese, nuts, slices of cucumber; regular drinkers accept it as 'strong' and realize it is something requiring 'blotting paper'. A refreshing drink, ouzo has nevertheless a reputation for producing the most appalling type of hangover in those that over indulge, because if more water is drunk to assuage the thirst that develops, the effect of the alcohol is increased by a type of chain reaction. For those who like ouzo to the extent that they risk this type of after-effect, I have been told that yoghurt is the only antidote.

TEQUILA, PULQUE, MEZCAL

Comparatively few reference books give detailed information about any of these three alcoholic drinks, although they have a considerable tradition and are interesting in their use and associations. All are made in Mexico and not, to the best of my knowledge, anywhere else.

The source of Tequila, pulque and mezcal is commonly but mistakenly called a cactus. Botanists are still debating the exact classification of this plant. It is more closely related to the sansevieria, yucca and amaryllis than to any cactus. The generic name for it is *agave*, and there are said to be as many as 400 different types. Most agaves are native to Mexico although some also grow in other parts of South and North America, where the agave type most often used for making Tequila is *Agave tequilana Weber*, a succulent plant, sometimes referred to as the century plant; in Mexico itself it is generally simply called mezcal. It is probably because of this confusion of names that some reference books confuse the drinks as well, but in fact they are three distinct types.

Tequila

For making Tequila, the *Agave tequilana* grows well in the states of Nayarit, Colima, Guanajuato, Michoacan and Jalisco, where the town of Tequila is located. The plant takes from eight to ten years to reach maturity, when it reaches a height and girth of about 4 to 5 feet. Its blade-like leaves, so spiky that they have been likened to bayonets by some writers, are of a blue tinge. From the third to the fifth year, shoots are removed from the mother plant, so as to propagate the plant. When the time comes for the harvest the *jimador* (taken from the word *jima* in the Nahuatl Indian Language, meaning harvest) shears off the leaves with a *coa* (a tool specially designed for this) and the heart of the plant appears; this looks rather like a pineapple, and in fact is often referred to as such. When the leaves are cut off, the pine is revealed, its segments slightly separated, looking rather like the separation of mud in a dried-up river bed. These pines can weigh anywhere from 50 to 250 pounds (23 to 115 kilos). Inside the pine the sweet sap has concentrated.

The pines are roughly chopped and roasted to extract this sap. In former times this roasting was done by putting the pines in a pit in the earth sealed with mud and the *bagasse* from the previous grindings; the pit was set alight to heat up the stone walls, with a ventilator in the upper part producing steam by the addition of water. Today the pines are cooked under pressurized steam. The hearts are then shredded and pressed so that the sweet juice runs out. A certain amount of sugar may be added to the juice at this stage, although the amount of this is controlled by law and naturally depends on the sweetness of the original sap. The juice is then deposited in large tanks, the fermentation begins and the result, after thirty-six to seventy-two hours, then undergoes a double distillation in a pot still.

The distilled product is without colour, so it is then considered a white spirit. It is the most popular type of Tequila sold in Mexico and in the export market.

Some Tequila is aged in wooden casks where it acquires the light gold tinge given it by the white oak. The period of maturation varies from one to twelve months and it may be aged from one year onwards, but the finest Tequila is usually considered to be that which has been in wood for about three to five years. As a result, the spirit has become definitely golden.

The most important Tequila producer is the establishment of Tequila Sauza, a family business founded in 1873, by Don Cenobio Sauza. The president today, Francisco Javier Sauza, grandson to the founder, is known in Mexico and internationally as 'Mr Tequila'. He took over the family business on the death of his father, Eladio Sauza, in 1946 and by his innovations revolutionized the Tequila industry.

Another well-known brand of Tequila is Cuervo. This is also a family business. In 1795, José Maria Guadalupe de Cuervo obtained the right to make 'mezcal wine', in other words Tequila, from the civic authorities of Guadalajara. He had become a landowner near the town of Tequila as early as 1758. In 1805, his daughter took over the factory on his death, and in the late nineteenth century the Cuervo company joined forces with that of the Tequila establishment of Jesus Flores; the daughter of Jesus married José Cuervo Labastida, and from this time on the firms's label was 'Tequila de José Cuervo'. José Cuervo Labastida's grandson, Juan Beckman Gallardo, recently became the head of the firm and his house in Tequila actually occupies part of the land first granted to José Antonio de Cuervo in 1758.

There are, however, a number of other producers, and, in addition to the increasing quantities of Tequila drunk in Mexico, export markets have begun to take large quantities. As might be expected, the United States and Canada are at the top of these, but the Sauza establishment exports to no fewer than thirty-eight foreign markets and the spirit is liked in various European and Far Eastern countries.

True Mexican Tequila, produced according to the quality controls now enforced, should have on its label the letters D.G.N., which signify that the Bureau of Standards has approved it. It must contain at least 51 per cent of the fermented juice of the blue agave; once distilled, it comes within the Mexican definition of '*aguardiente*', which is 'an alcoholic beverage distilled from wine, grape skins or other substances'. Such spirits have their ultimate flavour and smell determined by the various substances that are used in preparing the mash before it undergoes fermentation. By law Tequila must be between 38° and 55° Gay Lussac. Most Tequila is sold at about 40° Gay Lussac.

Pulque

The maguey plant is quite spectacular to see in the regions in which it is cultivated, with its greyish-blue leaves sticking up stiffly around the central pine, from which, eventually, a tall stalk rises on which light yellow flowers grow. In the agave plantations the pine is sometimes made into a type of sweetmeat, and I understand that it tastes somewhat like sugar-cane.

Pulque has a long history. Essentially, it is simply the sap of the agave, which, if left, may begin to ferment inside the plant, so that it seeps out as a sweet, slightly alcoholic beverage. This sweet sap is called '*aguamiel*' or honey water. Pulque is not strictly a spirit, but a fermented drink – for it is not distilled.

When the Spaniards conquered Mexico they realized that it would be impossible to prohibit the use of pulque and therefore they imposed regulations governing its use and sale as early as the seventeenth century. For example, bars in which pulque was sold were not allowed to have doors, had to cease business at sunset and were prohibited from allowing both men and women to drink in the same location. In former times, pulque was used as a special reward given by the doctors and priests to those whom they considered worthy by having accomplished some heroic act. However, people managed to find an excuse to drink pulque whenever the opportunity arose. Such occasions, according to the religious calendar of festivals, occurred on many days throughout the year. During these festivals it was more or less lawful to drink pulque, because the Mexicans linked their religion with the use of alcoholic beverages, considering the use of alcohol a tribute to the gods. So, anyone who styled himself 'religious', whether he was of high or humble rank, of priestly-standing or of military rank would honour the gods by inebriety. But punishment was severe for persons found intoxicated during non-festive occasions and people were sometimes put to death for excessive drinking – only religious occasions were exempt.

A traditional pulque bar, in which, today, food may be served, music played and songs sung (some of these songs are particular to this type of establishment, as are special games played in them, somewhat akin to the pub games of England), may still have a floor covered with sawdust or even consisting of bare soil; traditionalists will pour a little of the spirit on the floor, 'to assuage the thirst of the mother earth', before they drink. Greenish glass measures are used for pulque and there is a particular shape, deriving from the clay pot used before the Spanish Conquest, which is also traditional, together with a halved gourd, occasionally used as a measure or type of carafe for conveying the pulque from the cask to the glass. Many regions of Mexico depend or depended almost entirely on making pulque and the large, elaborately decorated houses built by many of those engaged in its production are known as the palaces of the 'pulque aristocracy', although today a number of these are in use as public buildings instead of private houses.

The agave that is most suitable for pulque production is the *Agave atrovirens*, a very large plant, which at the age of about ten or twelve years begins to put out the tall central stalk; this stalk is sliced off, the plant is left for six months and then the place where the stalk was cut is reopened so that a cavity forms inside and the honeyed juice drains into this. Twice a day workers come round with a type of scoop or spoon with which this is removed; approximately two litres of the juice or *aguamiel* will be accumulated daily by each plant.

The *aguamiel* goes to the processing plant and ferments in oak for a week to fourteen days; in the past this fermentation process took place inside cow hides, but wood is obviously easier to keep clean, something of particular importance when making pulque, because, as the fermentation process has already started in the plant itself, there is a certain risk of its going sour while it is in production. Men are obliged to take their hats off if they come in to a pulque plant, and women are forbidden to enter at all, for fear of contaminating the *aguamiel*, rather in accordance with the tradition (references to which may be found in the book of Leviticus) that, if menstruating, they will 'turn' certain delicate things – to this day, there are mushroom caves in France where women are excluded for this reason.

The American writer Grossman describes pulque as having 'a rather heavy flavour resembling sour milk, but it is much appreciated by the Mexicans because of its cooling, wholesome, nutritional properties'. He also says that mezcal has a 'uniquely herbaceous, weedy taste'.

Mezcal

Mezcal is often used as a generic name for the various types of Mexican spirit, including the best known variety, Tequila. Incidentally, some reference books spell the word with an 's', although in Mexican the 'z' is invariable. A monograph written by Virginia Bottorff de Barrios, who lives in Mexico, stresses that mezcal, the Mexican spirit made from a cactus, is nothing at all to do with the cactus mescal, from which the drug mescaline derives; mescaline has no more relationship with mescal than the one cactus has with the other.

A number of cacti of the maguey family can be used to make mezcal, and, in general, they thrive best in low-lying areas, in regions that are slightly warmer than those where the pulque plantations are situated. Although mezcal is mostly drunk where it is actually produced and distribution is not widespread, even within Mexico (it is virtually unknown in export markets), there is so much mezcal made around San Louis Potosi that its consumption actually vies with that of the local wine. There are also two main regions on the Pacific Coast where mezcal is abundantly produced.

In Mexico it is said about mezcal that 'for everything bad, it is good, and also for everything good.' It is generally colourless and high in alcoholic strength, but those who have been able to drink and compare a number of these Mexican spirits admit that mezcal is not much of a quality drink, however pleasant it may be.

Tepache

Another Mexican drink is tepache, a word deriving from '*tepatsin*', an Indian word signifying 'somebody's medicine'. Tepache is not as high in strength as the other spirits, and is based on the fermentation of pineapple peelings and brown sugar.

Drinking and drinks

It is traditional to knock back both mezcal and Tequila in a single gulp from a small glass, like schnapps, which is why it is not inappropriate to call Tequila the schnapps of the south. Pulque is generally drunk mixed with any of the local fruit juices – pineapple is very popular – as a cheap alternative to beer.

The classic way of drinking Tequila, which requires some practice and skill, is for the drinker to put a little salt in the small pocket made by the join of the thumb and forefinger of the left hand (or right, if you are left-handed). Then a slice of fresh lime or lemon is briefly sucked, after which the reflex of the left wrist is struck smartly with the right, so that, as the hand kicks upwards, the salt leaps into the mouth, and then the Tequila, ready in a small tumbler-type glass, is knocked back. Before people acquire the expertise to take Tequila in this way, they simply lick the salt after the lime or lemon.

Tequila drinks. The Margarita is probably the best known Tequila-based cocktail. $1\frac{1}{2}$ ounces Tequila, $\frac{1}{2}$ ounce triple sec and 1 ounce lemon or lime juice are mixed and then shaken with cracked ice and poured into a glass, the rim of which has been damped with lemon juice and then dipped in salt. The Margarita is a very fresh drink, excellent before typically Mexican or spicy food.

Tequila Sangría is made by putting a mixture of fruit (juice of a lemon and two fresh oranges, about five drops of Angostura Bitters and slices of lemons, oranges and a peach) into a jug with plenty of ice. On to this, pour a bottle of ordinary red wine, and a generous glassful of Tequila Sauza Extra Gold, and top up with soda water. The 'Extra Gold' of this particular type of Tequila refers to its golden colour, derived from its having been aged for some time in wood.

There are several brands of Tequila available in the U.K. today and, as with other spirits, it is necessary to establish one's personal preference by trying different ones: this need not be an expensive operation, as it is often possible to get Tequila in miniatures so as to conduct a small-scale comparative tasting.

SAKE

Sake is a rice-based spirit, which has a long history. It is first mentioned in A.D. 712, when the first Queen of Japan actually made her own. It is traditionally associated with both religious occasions and celebrations. The commercial production of the spirit began in the eighteenth century, when the rice crop from around Osaka was particularly important. As spring water is another important element in sake production, as with many other spirits, the streams of the Rokko Mountains near by were also utilized.

Today, a number of types of sake of varying quality are made, together totalling about one third of Japanese production of alcoholic drinks. The traditional sake container is a smallish flask-like bottle, known as a *tokkuri* bottle, which can be warmed so that the spirit is served hot; it is served in small cups which are called *sakazuki*. The spirit should be kept cool and in a dry place, and tends to lose its freshness after more than about a year in bottle. Alcoholically, it is about 17° Gay Lussac.

In the United States, the largest export market for sake, it is drunk chilled or as an ingredient in mixes, as well as in the traditional hot form with meals. A typical sake-based cocktail is a Sakini, one part of sake to three parts dry gin.

10. Bitters

Bitters have a long history and the name itself has only comparatively recently (1713) been applied to liqueurs and strong drinks of a bitter taste. Before this, and even until almost the present day, this type of alcoholic preparation might be referred to as an elixir. This term derives from the Arabic 'al-iksir' and, for the medieval alchemist, it implied the substance that would change base metals into gold; *The Shorter Oxford Dictionary* gives the definition: 'a supposed drug or essence capable of indefinitely prolonging life'. The best-known bitters in the U.K. are: Angostura Aromatic Bitters; the pick-me-ups, such as Fernet Branca and Underberg; the bitters widely used in mixtures, such as Campari and, of the fruit bitters, Law's Peach Bitters. Well-known American bitters are Abbott's Aged Bitters, from Baltimore, and Peychaud's from New Orleans. Boonekamp is a well-known bitters made in Holland. The semi-medical properties of any bitter drink can be refreshing and tonic, certainly when the drinker has had too much by way of food or alcohol. In some ways, bitters are far more the direct descendants of the curative and preventative compounds of the medieval still-room than any other drink, being concentrated, containing various ingredients that have been used by doctors for many centuries and – because they cannot be cheap, as they are high in alcohol – still being endowed with a 'precious' aura. I have known people assume that, because they are used sparingly and mostly as flavourings in drinks, they are light in alcohol or even actually non-alcoholic; this, however, is never the case and provides only one more example of a type of person who is misled into thinking that anything that is small is less effective than something that is big.

Bitters are of two types: those that are aromatic and somewhat 'medicinal' in general character, which are usually intended for drinking either quite by themselves or else just with soda; and those which are used for flavouring, these usually being named after the fruits from which they are made, such as peaches or oranges. It is easy to see how this type of concentrate could have developed from the kitchen and the aromatic bitters from the apothecary. Because both types of bitters are concentrated, they have been much in demand when other forms of alcohol were either bad in quality or unobtainable. For example, during Prohibition in the United States, certain bitters were able to be sold at the chemist or drug store on account of their supposedly medicinal properties. Customers demanded them in vast quantities, either to drink by themselves or in an attempt to make palatable the many dubious concoctions that were, often, literally brewed in bathtubs. Again, during and after the Second World War in the late 1940s, I can remember my godmother, who ran a dining club in St James's, and many of her friends, who would normally have ordered a 'gin and French' (the name of the martini came only slowly into use among the older generation in Britain at that time), drinking gin with orange or peach bitters, due to the shortage or total absence of vermouth. But fruit bitters are not much used today, with the decline of complicated cocktails and the wide availability of good spirits and vermouths.

The latest edition of the standard American reference work *Grossman's Guide to Wines, Spirits and Beers* (Charles Scribner's Sons, 1974) says that bitters are divided into two types – medicinal and non-medicinal. The medicinal ones are severely tested so that, if they pass, they are exempted from the Internal Revenue Tax on regular alcohol. Grossman says that they do not come 'within the province of our alcoholic-beverage regulations. They come under the Pure Food Act and may be sold by grocery stores or drug or department stores, and in many states their sale is specifically prohibited in a liquor store.' He goes on to admit that they do 'often contain over 40 per cent of alcohol'.

Abbott's Aged Bitters has been made by a family firm since 1865, and the Peychaud Bitters are considered essential in the New Orleans' Sazarac cocktail, for which bitters called Sazarac have also been marketed, combining Peychaud Bitters and the Pernod or absinthe the recipe requires. The basic recipe is that of an Old Fashioned (page 180) with Pernod *and* whiskey with the bitters.

WELL-KNOWN MAKERS OF BITTERS

Angostura Aromatic Bitters

Johan Gottlieb Benjamin Siegert was born in 1796 in Crosswalditz in Silesia. As an army surgeon, Siegert took part in the campaign against Napoleon, winning a medal, and later went to Venezuela to join Simon Bolivar who was fighting to achieve independence. Siegert and his companions arrived at the town of Angostura, on the River Orinoco, where Bolivar put the German in charge of the hospital. Siegert spent most of his working life there and made up what was described as 'a tonic to relieve digestive and similar stomach disorders', in 1824. He called this Amaro Aromático and it began to achieve fame, so that by 1830 Dr Siegert's Aromatic Bitters were exported to Trinidad and then to England. However, their source being the town of Angostura, they tended to be known by this name and eventually Siegert himself allowed them to be sold as Angostura Aromatic Bitters. Some confusion has arisen in reference books, because the town of Angostura was renamed Cuidad Bolívar in 1846; certain books account for the name by saying that the bark of a particular Venezuelan tree, Angostura bark, was an essential ingredient, but in fact this is without foundation. One of the ingredients, however, is the bark of *Galipea officinalis*, a wild tree, native to South America.

Siegert kept the secret formula for his bitters within his own family. He married twice, the second Mrs Siegert being the daughter of a well-known naturalist; her nine children ensured the continuation of his name and it is this part of the family who still run the firm. The company was called Dr J. G. B. Siegert & Hijo in 1867, when Siegert took his eldest son, Carlos, into partnership. Carlos and his brother Alfredo continued to run the firm after their father's death in 1870, but in 1875 the situation in Venezuela was so unsettled that they had to leave the country, managing to get aboard a British vessel bound for Trinidad, remaining below decks until the ship sailed, to avoid discovery and arrest. In Port of Spain they began to make Angostura Aromatic Bitters again and this is still the headquarters of the company.

In 1907 the firm were appointed purveyors of bitters to Alfonso XIII of Spain; in 1909 a London company was formed by Alfredo C. Siegert, and in 1912 they were appointed purveyors of bitters to King George V. But the First World War and the ensuing enormous changes throughout the business world brought serious problems. Because of business pressures, the Siegerts lost control of the firm in 1918, the company was reformed in Trinidad in 1921, and the London firm was liquidated.

It must have looked like the end of the Siegert association, but in 1936 Robert W. Siegert joined the firm and set up a research laboratory; he was appointed a director in 1944. The company were appointed manufacturers of Angostura Aromatic Bitters to King George VI in 1947 and, in 1952, were granted the royal warrant of King Gustav VI of Sweden. In 1954, Robert W. Siegert became managing director and in the following year the company received the royal warrant of Queen Elizabeth II. They also began to make Angos gin, the first gin to be produced in Trinidad.

In 1958, Alfredo Seigert, the grandson of the founder, and Robert W. Seigert, his great-grandson, regained full control of their family firm, which now went from strength to strength. In 1960 they began to make a vodka at the distillery and the bitters company produced a coffee liqueur. In 1969, Robert W. Seigert resigned as managing director, though remaining company chairman and, in 1972, John Gordon Brian Siegert was entrusted with the secret formula of the bitters – still very much a family concern.

Angostura was at one time used semi-medicinally by the Royal Navy – hence its associations with that traditional tipple, pink gin (see page 107). It is not possible to state definitely that the ingredients are really preventatives against fever and scurvy – the formula still being secret – but there is a delightful letter written by Mark Twain in 1874 which shows how the touch of something bitter could make an acceptable drink into a very good one indeed.

The American author was staying at the Langham Hotel and, in a letter to his wife, he says:

Lily, my darling, I want you to be sure to have in the bathroom, when I arrive, a bottle of Scotch Whisky, a lemon, some crushed sugar and a bottle of Angostura Bitters. Ever since I have been in London I have taken in a wine glass what is called a cock-tail (made with these ingredients) before breakfast, before dinner, and just before going to bed . . . to which I attribute the fact that up to this day my digestion has been wonderful – simply perfect . . . Now my dear, if you would give the order now, to have those things put in the bathroom and left there till I come, they will be there when I arrive. Will you? . . . I love to picture myself ringing the bell, at midnight – then a pause of a second or two, then the turn of a bolt – 'Who is it?' – then ever so many kisses, then you and I in the bathroom, I drinking my cock-tail and undressing and you standing by – then to bed, and everything happy and jolly as it should be.

The use of the 'cock-tail' before breakfast puts the drink into the category of a morning-after pick-me-up. But the drinking of the cocktail in the bathroom at a reunion with his wife has some suggestion of its being efficacious as an aphrodisiac.

Angostura Aromatic Bitters are not only used as an addition to sauces, savoury mixes and in salad dressings, but even with fruit salad, and apple recipes; of course, only a very few drops are used. As these bitters do not contain salt, they have been found extremely helpful in recipes prepared for those on a salt-free diet, because, to quote the home economist engaged in testing some of these, 'the Angostura Aromatic Bitters do seem to exert a catalyptic effect and compensate for the salt which has been omitted', referring particularly to dishes where fairly strong flavours, such as those of onion and horse-radish, might appear unacceptable without the usual salt.

Campari

Many people probably think of Campari as a contemporary drink, as it does not seem to have been until the late 1960s and 1970s that it made much impression on drinking patterns in the U.K. In fact, it is over a century old. The founder of the Campari firm, Gaspare, was a countryman from Novara, hence his name, evolved from *'campi'* – fields. Gaspare Campari had urban tastes, however, and served his appenticeship in a small Turin café. But he was determined to be more than a mere barman and, while working, pursued his studies in a laboratory, trying to evolve original drinks with which he hoped to make his name known. He married and had two daughters, but unfortunately his wife and children died; he subsequently returned to Novara, to run and then buy the Café dell' Amicizia, and was married again, to Letizia Galli. She not only was beautiful (and gave him seven children), but was a shrewd businesswoman too and ran the café and liqueur shop that Gaspare subsequently bought in the centre of Milan. The couple enjoyed a real commercial success here, so that they were able to buy another café, in the fashionable Galleria Vittorio Emmanuele, the great covered walk-way, when their first premises were pulled down. He prospered here, his visitors' book showing the signatures of many celebrities, including the Italian King Umberto I and Edward VII of England. Gaspare, even though he wouldn't have known the word, was well aware of the commercial need for a gimmick: at the entrance to his bar there was a statue of a cherub, on the cherub's head there was a basket, in which people took to leaving messages – it was *l'angiolino del Campari* who enabled the admirers of the strictly chaperoned girls of the time to deposit *billets-doux*, which the young ladies could discreetly collect later.

On the birth of Gaspare's son Davide, he evolved the famous bitter Campari, a completely original drink that he hoped would be a profit-making line for him and his·family. It was launched as Bitter all'uso d'Hollandia; in fact, although he was associating the drink with Dutch bitters – already widely known – the recipe was truly his own and owed nothing to Holland. It was this drink, which no one has succeeded in imitating in any way, that did indeed found the family fortunes. To this day the formula is a secret, known only to the chairman, who supervises the preparation of the base of the drink. (A copy of the recipe is under lock and key, to be handed over to his successor, should the head of the firm meet with an accident.) When the Campari is to be made up, the manager who has been given the list of ingredients is in one room, while the herbs are put on to a scale in another; the manager can control and adjust the proportions but no one else can touch this stage of the preparation. In former times the liquid was fined or clarified with egg white, the workers being allowed to use up the thousands of egg yolks plus the vermouth that the Campari company then produced to make a type of zabaglione.

Letizia Campari carried on the business when Gaspare died in 1882, until her sons could take over the running of the café and the making and promoting of Bitter Campari. In 1902 the business was moved to Sesto San Giovanni, on the outskirts of Milan; this is still the headquarters, although there is now another establishment in Rome.

Davide Campari, one of Gaspare's sons, evolved Campari-Soda, the ready-mixed, single-portioned drink, in 1932. It was he who, by commissioning distinguished artists to design posters and publicity material, made the product even more widely known – these posters were veritable works of art and are collectors' pieces today. Davide died in 1936, but Campari is still very much a family concern, the present chairman being Angiola Maria Migliavacca, the wife of Davide's nephew.

Davide Campari also evolved Cordial Campari (also a secret formula, incorporating Cognac and a raspberry distillate), but it did not achieve the same success. However, it is worth mentioning that travellers in Italy who are accustomed to getting an alcoholic beverage when they order 'a Campari soda' should be quite definite about specifying 'Bitter Campari' and seeing that the drink is made with the brilliant pink alcoholic bitters from the large bottle; a ready-mixed pink drink, produced by San Pellegrino, which is non-alcoholic, is what you may get otherwise – although a pleasant, lightly refreshing beverage, it is not at all the same thing!

Although the formula for Campari still defies those who have tried to work out the secret, it is admitted that it is a combination of herbs, among which are the peel of bitter oranges, Chinese rhubarb and, as might have been expected in this type of drink, quinine bark; these are steeped in spirit and then rest in oak casks, eventually being combined with sugar syrup and water. The brilliant colour is given by cochineal.

How to serve Campari. Campari may be drunk neat, but it is so high in strength that it is generally diluted. It must always be stirred, even when, for a Campari soda, the siphon has been used to squirt in the additives quite fiercely; if bottled soda water is used, then the mixture is even less satisfactory, because the Campari will simply settle at the bottom of the glass. So, if the barman doesn't stir the drink, make sure you do!

The Americano is perhaps the most famous drink in which Campari is essential. The Campari company's own recipe is 2 ounces sweet vermouth to 1 ounce Campari, a dash of soda, the mixture being poured over ice and garnished with a slice of orange – the use of orange rather than lemon makes a considerable difference, as I have proved. But the way in which people make their Americanos varies enormously, and the drink can be made long or short to taste. The other drink in which Campari is important is the Negroni: 2 ounces dry gin, 1 ounce sweet vermouth, 1 ounce Campari, with a dash of soda.

The 'cryptically bitter' quality of Campari, a phrase made famous by the advertising campaign conducted in the U.K. in the 1960s, is an apt description for in fact the drink, although in no way cloying, is not really as bitter as all that – hence, no doubt, its popularity among northern peoples, who have a traditional preference for something that is not wholly dry or raspingly bitter. Campari is a marvellous drink to perk up a jaded appetite and extremely refreshing on a stuffy day – the climates of Milan, Turin and London can be similar in this respect and it is therefore no wonder that the drink has become enormously popular.

OTHER ITALIAN BITTERS

The best known of these is Fernet Branca, made first by Fratelli Branca of Milan in 1845. The first part of its name comes from that of a concoction made by hermits who prepared extracts from the herbs and roots of the Alps; this liquid was known as '*fernet*'. Fernet Branca is possibly most famous in the U.K. as a hangover remedy but in fact it can be taken as a digestive after meals or a stimulator of the appetite beforehand; many Italians believe it to have aphrodisiac properties, like the other bitters, Ferro China and Elixir Martini. Ferro China was evolved by Felice Bisleri in 1881. The 'Ferro' part of the name refers to the iron content, the 'China' to the tonic properties of the quinine in the recipe. These bitters soared to commercial success in the United States at the time of Prohibition, when the power of the Mafia was extended in controlling so much of the liquor supply. All these bitters contain various herbs, flowers and spices, and are made up according to individual formulae. A slightly sweeter Italian bitters is Unicum, and there is another called Cynar, which is based on artichokes. It is very popular in northern Italy and also in parts of Switzerland inhabited by migrant Italian workers. All these bitters may be drunk neat or made long or short with the addition of soda.

FRENCH BITTERS

Amer Picon

This was first made in 1835, by a man serving in the French army in Algiers. It is one of those that includes quinine, but is also flavoured with orange. It can be drunk as an aperitive, with or without soda and ice. (See also page 246.)

Selestat

This is a herby bitters, usually made up in two strengths, one being about twice as strong as the other.

Toni-Kola

Based on the kola nut, this was first made by a man called Gaboriau, of Conakry, in Guinea, where the nut is said to be at its best. M. Gaboriau gave his formula to a M. Sécrestat Aîné, who commercialized the drink, which is slightly sweeter than most other bitters, albeit fresh.

Arquebuse

This was once recommended to me as the French answer to Fernet Branca – just as effective but more palatable. It is made by several firms and is colourless. It is indeed an effective digestive, and I used to make frivolous comments about it to the effect that it marched into the stomach like an arquebusier, with his weapon at the ready. However, I find a fascinating reference in Lady Rosalind Northcote's *The Book of Herb Lore* (first published in 1912 as *The Book of Herbs*), where, under the entry relating to angelica, she says that this herb is part of a remedy for a wound from an arquebuse, the first type of firearm, and was in fact called 'un arquebusade', and was first mentioned by Philip de Comines at the Battle of Morat, 1476. Lady Rosalind also says that 'the fruit is used to flavour Chartreuse and other "cordials"'. An informant tells me that makers usually claim that thirty-three herbs are used in most recipes.

Suze

This 'screaming lime' coloured drink is the best known of a number of wine-based drinks, flavoured with gentian and made usually in mountainous regions. I have included it here, rather than in the wine-based aperitive section, because it and its 'colleagues' are indeed very bitter and, when taken as aperitives, are marvellous restorers of the appetite, useful to know about when one feels that to eat anything is quite impossible – and yet, for reasons of courtesy, it is essential to partake of a meal.

Gentian (*Gentiana campestris*) is named for the Greek king and herbalist, Gentius. Although the blue-flowered type of gentian is what will probably come first to mind, there is also a gentian with yellow flowers. The bitter extraction of the root has long been known as a tonic beverage, a remedy for liver troubles, a neutralizer of poisons, and it will ease vomiting. So gentian drinks seem to have their place among those categorized as revivers.

The American Indians actually worshipped gentian for its numerous medicinal properties and, in the seventeenth century, the great herbalist Parkinson commented that 'the wholesomeness of Gentian cannot be easily knowne to us, by reason our daintie tastes refused to take thereof, for the bitterness sake, but otherwise it would undoubtedly worke admirable cures'. (Another instance of the nursery maxim 'If it tastes nasty, it must be doing you good.')

In one of the Maigret detective stories, Georgest Simenon refers to Suze as a popular drink with commercial travellers and the sort of itinerant businessmen who constantly have to stand a round of drinks, because it is only just above table-wine strength.

A gentian aperitive of the Auvergne is Arvèze, which I find even better than Suze (there is a little sweetening in the latter), and many other regions will have a real 'bitter' for the traveller who can make the local barman understand that they do truly want a refreshingly bitter drink.

GERMAN BITTERS

The great name for bitters in Germany, where a variety are made, is Underberg, which has been produced for over a hundred years from a recipe which includes infused herbs. It is made at the town of Rheinberg, a word that one would expect to mean 'Rhein mountain', but here, the second syllable of the name refers to a '*berka*', a Celtic word for a settlement by a river, and not to a mountain (*Berg*) at all – in fact the surrounding countryside is flat. Rheinberg was a city as far back as 1232; in 1846, Hubert Underberg founded his business there, having taken a long time to study and travel in order to perfect the drink that bears his name and that he believed might have a great commercial future. The firm is still a family business. The selling of the digestive in tiny bottles, each containing only two-thirds of a fluid ounce, was started in 1949. Even nowadays, only the family know the secret formula. The words '*semper idem*' on each minibottle stress the continuity of the recipe.

Although the firm likes to recommend that the dark bitter drink is taken either as an aperitive or a digestive in the small triangular glasses (rather like aquavit glasses) on a very tall spiralled stem, these bitters are often the easiest to take as a swift pick-me-up. One Christmas, the U.K. representative of Underberg sent out Christmas presents of a number of the tiny bottles, with best wishes – 'and no after effects'; I distributed many of them among my friends and they were perhaps one of the best 'stocking fillers' for adults that could have been chosen.

11. Vermouth

Some explanation must be given for the inclusion of vermouth in a book dealing with spirits. For vermouth is a wine – 'aromatized wine' is the best short definition of it; its base is wine, and it is only very slightly stronger, alcoholically, than table wine. But it does not come into the category of fortified wines, such as sherry and port, and is essentially totally different from them. In the period between the wars, the great wine merchant Charles Walter Berry held a series of dinners at which one wine only was drunk, and in this were included meals at which only sherry and port were served. But even if he had thought of it, I doubt whether Mr Berry would have given a vermouth dinner. This is not to say that vermouth cannot be served with certain foods, but the purpose of vermouth is not primarily that of a drink to accompany food.

Vermouth is perhaps the best known 'occasional' drink in the world and this attribute partly justifies its presence in this book. It is used in conjunction with many spirits, is an ingredient in many mixed drinks, and, like brandy, can be made wherever wine is made and wherever a stronger form of drink than table wine is required.

But, considered historically and socially, vermouth is the ancestor of many aperitives and liqueurs. If it had never been made, the way in which we use alcoholic beverages today would be totally different, as would our social drinking patterns, so I do not think that vermouth can be excluded from this study.

The great vermouth manufacturers claim that their product is 'the oldest wine in the world'. If we were able to travel in time we should probably find the only 'wine' with which we could make contact with the ancients would be aromatized wine, for the addition of herbs, spices, peels and barks to wine appears to have been a practice since the earliest times. There is a tablet from the Sumerian city of Nippur, dating from about 2000 B.C., which has been transcribed as the notes of a doctor who made use of powders infused with a type of wine.

In Book IV of *The Odyssey*, Helen put into the bowl in which the wine was mixed, 'a drug that had the power of robbing grief and anger of their sting and banishing all painful memories ... This powerful anodyne ... had been given by an Egyptian lady. For the fertile soil of Egypt is most rich in herbs.' Indeed, the ancient Egyptians used wine or, more frequently, beer (hops were widely grown), plus juniper, frankincense, celery, lotus leaves and honey in many of their remedies. 'Green Horus eye' seems to have been a type of this Egyptian spiced wine ('White Horus eye' was milk). The name of the god Horus may be a form of an early use of a brand of superior type.

Hippocrates of Cos made use of cinnamon in wine sweetened with honey. This was known as 'hippocras' even up to the seventeenth and eighteenth centuries; 'Hippocras' sleeve' was a type of filter used in making it. Chaucer refers to hippocras and, in 1662, Dr Christopher Merret gave a recipe for it to the Royal Society, which included sherry, Jamaica pepper, white wine, nutmeg, cloves and sugar candy.

Sweetening agents and other additives were used throughout history to make palatable wines that might otherwise have been more than half way to vinegar or that were undrinkable in various other revolting ways. Possibly because of these additives, many people seem to have thought of hippocras as a weak or even non-alcoholic drink; Samuel Pepys noted that 'wine was offered and they drunk, I only drinking some hypocras, which do not break my vowe, it being, to the best of my present judgment, only a mixed compound drink and not any wine. If I am mistaken, God forgive me!' Some of the compound drinks with a wine base sound very nasty indeed.

Aristotle recommended wine mulled with spices as a hangover cure, as he thought the additives made the drink less intoxicating; Pliny the Elder (A.D. 23–79) recommended using a wide range of both herbs and spices in wine, including oil of black myrtle, which he thought prevented the drink from being intoxicating and Cato also advised boiling myrtle branches in the 'must' of white wine for certain stomach complaints. The reputation of Greek physicians in ancient Rome was high and they seem to have been responsible for introducing the practice of prescribing many spiced and infused drinks: pepper, pennyroyal, nard, mastic, fennel, hyssop, thyme, violets and elder being among the ingredients. The last was used to make a drink called nectarite, which is rather an interesting example of how there is nothing new, for in the early nineteenth century the elder was used to 'improve' port.

The most significant item in the lists of the physicians of this time, however, was *Artimisia absinthum*, or wormwood. Wormwood, a perennial herb, belongs to the *Compositae*, the daisy family. It grows widely in the temperate regions of Europe and as far north as Siberia and Lapland, so that it is almost surprising that even more use of it has not been made. Dioscorides, Nero's Greek physician, described wormwood wine (also referred to by Pliny) and, in *De Universa Medicina* (A.D. 78) he listed it among aphrodisiacs and anaphrodisiacs. Galen (A.D. 131–201), another Greek, used wine with herbs as a poultice, and recommended an infusion of the heads of absinthia to induce vomiting.

The volatile oil of the wormwood plant, which is derived from its leaves, contains a narcotic, thujone; it was the effects of this that, during the nineteenth century, made absinthe drinking such a health hazard in France that its use was eventually banned in 1915, and subsequently banned in both Switzerland and the United States (see page 202). It cannot be established from written evidence that the early physicians made use of wormwood in this way, but certainly they included wormwood flowers in many of the compounded drinks they prepared, and it is from the German form of the name, *Wermut*, that the name vermouth derives. The 'artimisia' part of the name is said by Colin Clair to come from the goddess Artemis, who gave her name to a plant capable of conferring many benefits, and the Latin word itself comes from a pair of Greek words, meaning 'devoid of delight' because of the bitter flavour and rank odour associated with wormwood. From this time on, wormwood was included in many recipes for drinks that were preventative, curative and digestive, or simply refreshing and inclined to provoke appetite.

It is perhaps difficult for anyone today, living in a community sure of ample supplies of safe water and able to buy all kinds of disinfectants, from those intended for domestic purposes to sprays, ointments, lotions and tablets for internal use, to begin to understand the importance of wine as a disinfectant and medicament in former times. It could make doubtful water safe to drink, it acted as a wash for wounds (as in the parable of the Good Samaritan, where the man 'left for dead' had his wounds washed with wine and dressed with oil, as a salve), it provided what was then a unique form of stimulant; used in the kitchen it was efficacious against rot developing in foods – and, when the food was already rotten, it helped the digestion of the diners; in solutions, it made it possible for people to be given certain drugs in their primitive form.

For sacramental purposes, the great religious houses had to have wine and made their own; many of them acted as hostels and hotels, and also schools; and the still-room was of enormous importance. The estates of the laity, too, were often centres of primitive medical resources: the lady of the establishment would supervise the making of alcoholic beverages, often herself specializing in developing remedial drinks and medicaments. Many recipes for drinks of either a social or medical type have their origin in religious foundations that were either isolated, in proximity to mountains where rather rare herbs and plants might be sought and used in the dispensary, or situated along the great trade routes, by which merchants coming from the east brought new spices and ingredients, which they might use to pay for their lodging in a religious house along the way or simply to present to colleagues. The fashion for pilgrimages increased the knowledge of rather homely remedies among travellers just as, in resorts today, people will exchange advice and medicaments for digestive troubles or sunburn. But pilgrims and travellers of this period had more than 'gippy tummy' to contend with, for it is fairly certain that the majority suffered from lack of vitamins A and C, so that almost everyone would have had stomach and digestive troubles, as well as skin complaints. A moment's consideration of what this might mean to those who were in close proximity to people so afflicted but were not suffering themselves, makes one realize how a drink of fresh, even bitter character, with the power to relieve certain internal uneasiness, would have been prized.

In the tenth-century *Leech Book of Bald* it is recommended that a type of skin infection is to be treated by 'seeds of raddish and of colewort' rubbed into oil or wine. At the renowned Medical School of Salerno, in the eleventh century, the most famous woman doctor, Trotula, recommends, 'tops of myrtle . . . grated and cooked in wine until reduced to one half' for halitosis during pregnancy. Arnaud de Villanova, the Catalan physician, recommended raisin wine with cinnamon, and wine strained through cherries (to this day, a French herb tea uses an infusion of cherry stalks '*pour faire pipi*') and Arnaud's prescription cured a cardinal who 'had not passed any urine for three days and was swollen and bloated'.

Wormwood is said to have been introduced to England about the sixteenth century, when there is a reference to it in *My Lordes Garden at Syon* in 1551, and Sir Hugh Platt's *Delights for Ladies*, 1609, includes a recipe 'How to make wormwood wine'. But the English army surgeon John of Ardern, (1307–77), in the Hundred Years War, had already recommended, 'let absinthe be infused in wine and applied.' Wormwood began to be used for cuts and bruises – it still seems to be a country remedy, for when I visited Crete one of the vermouth makers of the island told me that *Origanum dictamnus* (dittany of Crete, sometimes known in England as hop plant), a much sought-after ingredient by vermouth establishments everywhere and exported in quantity, is supposed to be a salve; in the Cretan countryside, vermouth may be used as a dressing and general antiseptic, very much as we might use witch-hazel or T.C.P. In some countries, significantly, wormwood is known as 'the girdle of St John', and is supposed to have power against evil spirits. 'Opens stoppings, helps surfets, cleers the sight, resists poyson, cleanses the blood and secures cloathes fro moth'. In the middle of the sixteenth century, Dr Johannes Dryandes stated that: 'Vermouth wine ... is very good for old age, both for the hot and cold tempers ... It improves the skin and the complexion and is to be drunk before and after eating.' Vermouth was beginning to be recognized as both an excellent aperitive and a sound digestive.

Queen Elizabeth I's remedy against the plague, which she gave to the Lord Mayor of London, included sage, rue, elder leaves, red bramble, ginger and white wine. There was a drink called crespa, so named 'from the fact that a draft of it made the eyebrows pucker'. Another stringent drink, rappis, 'biteth the tongue ... or tastes like wormwood'. In 1576, George Gascoyne wrote in 'A Delicate Diet, for daintie mouthde Droonkords', that, 'wine of it selfe is not sufficient but Sugar Limons & sundry sortes of spices must be drowned therein.' By this time, too, the versatility of wormwood was recognized by doctors: John Peachey, in *The Compleat Herbal of Physical Plants* (1694) says of it that, 'the Juice, distil'd Water, the Syrup, the fixed Salt, and the Oyl of it are used; but the Wine or Beer seems to be the best.'

By the seventeenth century, the great religious establishments had lost much of their power, even in countries that still remained Catholic. The centralization of social life around courts in many of the more important nations meant that many women, even down to the fairly modest landowner's wife, would spend less time in the country; this resulted in the mistresses of households calling in an apothecary or physician for advice on remedies, rather than always compounding their own. Only in the regions where herbs and spices were able to be procured constantly and without too much expense, where the local wine was abundant and cheap, and of a character to be the base of a mixture, did still-rooms and dispensaries continue to flourish. It is difficult, for example, to think of many red wine areas producing a suitable base for an aromatized drink; red wines usually come from differently situated vineyards. Nor would fine white wines, dry or sweet, that could enjoy much local popularity and even a certain demand from markets elsewhere, be economically utilized for compounded beverages. But there were areas where wine production might have increased beyond the requirements of local demand, where, too, herbs were locally abundant, spices available from merchants passing on the great trade routes – and where towns had bars where merchants and businessmen could gather for refreshment. As will be seen in other sections of this book, in some regions wine makers began to distil, inhabitants of fruit-growing areas to make cordials and liqueurs, and northerners to refine on the methods used to make spirits from cereals. In northern Italy the wine, herbs and spices were available – and the social conditions were propitious. (For an account of the pioneering vermouth makers, see page 237). In the eighteenth century, vermouth as we know it today was commercially born, although a form of it had existed for thousands of years, perhaps being taken more for medicinal than social reasons.

WHAT VERMOUTH IS

So vermouth can be made wherever wine is made and therefore it often is. All vermouths are different, some, in remote areas, virtually 'aromatized wines', others, especially the products of the great houses, very definite and individual in their own right. Each establishment makes a style of vermouth according to its own ideas. The constant element, though, is that vermouth is an aperitif drink. Those that are drunk world-wide and appreciated in this context are the vermouths of Italy and France. They set the standards by which other vermouths may be judged.

As the vermouth houses of both Turin and Marseilles make dry and sweet types in their range, and have done so for many years, it seems irrational that the tradition arose that 'French' was dry and 'Italian', sweet. There are still many reference books that give this erroneous information and until quite recently even an experienced drinker might assert the same. As the history of vermouth shows, it was at one time entirely up to the individual customer to specify the type of vermouth that was wanted and this was mixed to order. But in the period between the two World Wars, when mixed drinks advertising was prolific, the great French vermouth concern of

Noilly Prat stressed the properties of their dry vermouth, and many of the Italian firms pushed their sweet vermouths. The error of believing that 'French is dry, Italian sweet' is immediately obvious when it is recalled that a court case of this period established that, in the U.K., the most famous cocktail in the world, the dry martini, is a generic term, not requiring a capital letter – yet the 'Martini' part of the name signified, simply, 'dry Martini vermouth', made in Italy. Whether or not the original dry martini was made with Martini or Noilly Prat, will never really be known (see the chapter on gin, pages 101–2), but vermouths must not be characterized according to nationality. Noilly Prat nowadays make a bianco – in Italy.

What may be definitely stated is that there are certain constant ingredients in the wines used for vermouth production, the additions, and the basic procedures followed in their manufacture. Each vermouth establishment has its own formulae, and every drinker of vermouth or any mixture in which vermouth plays an important part will have to learn from trial and error the brand and type that is most pleasing.

STRENGTH OF VERMOUTH

Because vermouth comes into the category of 'high-strength wine', that is, it is over 14.5° Gay Lussac in alcoholic strength, it pays the duty in the U.K. exacted by H.M. Customs on 'heavy' wine; but, so as to attempt to keep the price of the bottle down, there were often instances of the vermouth being brought in at two strengths – part of the blend paying the high strength duty and the remainder only that of a 'light' or table wine. The two were then blended 'high/low' in Britain. The saving effected was passed on to the consumer.* But producers who are particularly proud of their vermouths often insist on them being bottled in the country of origin, because it is occasionally found that blending by the importer can result in crystals being precipitated in the bottle – these do not affect anything except the appearance of the vermouth, but people who do not know that they merely signify tartrate precipitation can be put off and return the vermouth as 'off'. There used to be a tradition for vermouth being also bottled in litre sizes, but nowadays most vermouths in the U.K. are presented in the standard 73/75 cl bottle.

*In recent years the 'high/low' blending has ceased, since the introduction of different rates of duty on various high-strength wines.

HOW VERMOUTH IS MADE

Vermouth production begins with a wine, made as all wine is made by crushing the grapes and allowing them to ferment until an alcoholic beverage results. In former times the vermouth establishments naturally used the wines of their own locality, many of which would not be of more than mediocre quality for table wine. Nowadays, with huge quantities of wine required for vermouth manufacture – and when wines from regions such as the prolific wine area of the Hérault, in the south of France, are able to be made into small-scale table wines, thanks to improved knowledge of wine-making, to sell under their own regional labels – the vermouth firms have had to buy in wines from other regions. What they mostly need is white wine, fairly high in alcohol already, with at least a moderate fullness and richness; in the past, the Moscato wines from Piedmont were used for the Turin vermouths, but today only a proportion of Moscato can be economically used for vermouth manufacture. Much wine from southern Italy and Sicily goes up to Turin today.

A type of wine called mistelle, made from sweet grapes and having had its fermentation checked by the addition of alcohol before all the natural sugar can be converted into alcohol, may also be used in vermouth production. Or, sometimes, rectified alcohol may be added to the basic wine intended for vermouth. The wine is then to be 'vermouthed' (*vermouté*) which means that it receives the flavouring of such herbs, spices, roots, barks, peels and plant derivatives as may be required by the recipe. In addition to wormwood, coriander, elderflower, lime, camomile, hyssop, marjoram, cinchona bark, cinnamon, cascarilla, mint, the peel of bitter oranges, sage, thyme, orris, cloves, nutmeg, rose leaves, angelica, cardamom and mace are among the ingredients that are frequently used. They are used to impart the flavour to vermouth by three different methods – maceration, infusion, distillation. Sometimes all three methods are involved, or just infusion and distillation, or maceration alone may be used. A certain amount of sugar is naturally used according to the style of vermouth.

In maceration, the herbs are put into a vat and left to steep in the previously prepared blend of matured wine. They are then taken out and pressed, the liquid that runs from them being added to the wine as well.

In infusion, the wine is passed through the herbs, vermouth manufacturers often using the image of the coffee percolator to illustrate this: the wine seeps through the herbs, without being forced and without being heated.

For distillation, the additives are distilled, either separately or together, and the resulting distillate added to the basic wine.

The selection of the different solid additives, which have to be carefully chosen, equally carefully prepared, and some of which have to be rendered into a fine powder, is another stage in the preparation of vermouth making.

Whether vermouth is initially made in vats or casks, the wine is eventually blended to comply with the style of vermouth being made; at each stage in its progress it must be allowed to mature, so that the elements in it marry up and a harmonious whole results. After this, the vermouth may be refrigerated, so as to precipitate any tartar crystals which might spoil its appearance, and it may also be clarified, to eliminate other forms of deposit or impurities, finally being filtered prior to bottling.

MARSEILLES VERMOUTHS

Wine most used for the vermouths made at Marseilles is the white wine from the Picpoul and Bourret grapes, which are high in acidity and very dry, and the Clairette, which is somewhat fuller. Once made, the wine is often subjected to a process of maturation by exposing the casks outside, where the sun, the atmosphere of the sea coast and the drying winter winds give it a particular character, as it becomes 'maderized', a term which, when applied to wine, refers to the change that takes place in it owing to exposure to the atmosphere. The slightly salty flavour and pronounced freshness that may be noticed in many Marseilles vermouths is the result of this open air maturation. Marseilles vermouth is particularly aromatic and although a good French vermouth, whether dry or sweet, should be well-balanced, the Marseilles vermouths possess a marked spiciness and a certain assertive flavour which, incidentally, makes them very valuable for use in cooking.

TURIN VERMOUTHS

Vermouths made in the Turin region are founded on matured wines, although they are not exposed to the atmosphere before being made into vermouth. The most usual method then followed is infusion. Italian vermouths possess a moderate fragrance, a rather full character, and perhaps lack something of the subtlety of the French vermouths, although they may possess more immediate appeal.

The main Italian vermouth is the reddish-tawny type that inclines to sweetness; the dry Italian, generally rather more yellowy-gold in colour than the citrony-gold tone of a dry Marseilles vermouth, is a definite mouthful, with a fullish flavour, even though it is genuinely dry. The colour of such a vermouth may darken after a week or so once the bottle is opened, although this will not affect the flavour seriously.

Bianco, or white vermouth, is very pale in colour but it may surprise many people to know that all bianco is on the sweet side, although the brands of some firms are sweeter than others; it usually possesses a marked fragrance, the scent of one of the added spices often being one of its most delightful attributes.

Pink vermouth, or rosé, is the latest style to be launched on the market at the time this book goes to press. Essentially, it is vermouth based on rosé wines, plus herbs and spices. Martini & Rossi and Cinzano have begun to market their pink vermouths in Europe and Stock have begun to promote theirs in Italy. Naturally, each establishment will follow its own house style, but it is possible to generalize and say that rosé vermouth is full, slightly fruity but with a fresh, almost bitter undertone of flavour.

CHAMBÉRY

In 1821, Joseph Chavasse, described as 'Pharmacien, Herbaliste et Distillateur' began to make this distinctive type of vermouth. Originally the base wine was the light dry white wine of Savoie, high in acidity; but the popularity for this type of vermouth today means that larger quantities of wine than are available locally are required (and anyway the Savoie wines are now marketed in their own right). The Gers, Midi and parts of the Rhône Valley are sources of supply to make the base of Chambéry today.

Chambéry vermouth is individual both in style and in the herbs used to flavour it; the variety of plants of a herbal type to be found in the Chambéry region are peculiar to it, on account of the latitude and altitude. The method of manufacture varies too. Chambéry vermouth is infused, the wine being poured over what my informant describes as 'A sort of bouquet garni of plants and herbs' and only pure sugar is used for any sweetening, instead of the mistelle used in other vermouth establishments.

There is some confusion in people's minds concerning the Chambéry vermouth houses, but there are only two main companies:

Comoz, who make and market their vermouths, which are each quite individual, under the names Boissière and Comoz; and La Grande Distillerie Chambérienne, who make Dolin Chambéry, and also Chambéry Gaudin. This last is very well known in the U.K., where the firm of J. B. Reynier have an exclusivity for it; the famous 'French pub', the York Minster in London's Soho and also the near-by restaurant l'Escargot make a speciality of serving this pale, delicately aromatic dry vermouth, and offering it only as a straight drink. In France, however, this marque is not available, which often causes visitors, who like it, to wonder about its origin. Gaudin also make the only pre-mixed Americano that I find acceptable, using two-thirds of their own sweet vermouth, one-third of bitters, and I think that it is the particular elegance of this vermouth that makes me like the mix, for bottled Americanos I have tried from other firms are always either too sweet, too cloying or somehow lacking in harmony.

Chambéry vermouth is legally protected: it must be actually made in Chambéry, and it received its Appellation Contrôlée as early as 1932. It cannot be made with the addition of extracts or concentrates, unlike other vermouths, although a very attractive version, Chambéryzette, includes the flavouring of Alpine wild strawberries.

SOME MAKERS OF VERMOUTH

Antonio Benedetto Carpano set up in business in a wine shop in the Piazza Castello, in the centre of Turin, in the late eighteenth century. He was an educated man, widely read, and his biographer, Carlo Monelli, relates how he evolved a drink which, he thought, might be more suited to feminine and delicate tastes than the robust table wines of the region. Monelli propounds the interesting theory that, because Carpano greatly enjoyed the works of Goethe, he gave the name of 'vermouth' to his new infusion, using the German word for absinthe, 'Wermut'. His customers sampled it for the first time in 1786, and pictures of the period depicting details of a wine bar and café, and the 'workshop', with a small still and pots, jars and flasks to make the different mixtures, show women as well as men enjoying themselves in this type of refreshment room, while the men behind the bar prepare the individual mixes for each customer.

This first commercial vermouth was in fact called 'Carpano' and basically this was a dry white wine, slightly fortified with alcohol, sweetened with spirit, containing an added infusion of aromatic herbs. The wines, originally from Piedmont and showing the fragrant style of the Moscato grape, are now blended with many of the

Sicilian wines from the Alcamo region, as their vigorous character and highish strength make them eminently suitable for vermouth production. But the herbs used are still largely the product of the mountain valleys of Piedmont itself.

Antonio Benedetto Carpano enjoyed such success with his vermouth that he had to keep his shop open for twenty-four hours a day! The business remained in the hands of the family, Antonio Benedetto being succeeded by his nephew, Guiseppe Bernardino, and it stayed a family concern until Sylvio Turati, a Turin industrialist, took it over in recent times, but the whole style of the products has remained the same, the recipes and the original label still being in use. Many celebrities regularly visited the Carpano bar, including the statesman Cavour, who was such an *habitué* that a memorial plaque was set up to him in the bar, as well as to the composers Verdi and Boito, and many other writers and poets.

Then in 1876 a new Carpano recipe came into being: the drink which nowadays has ousted in popularity all other Carpano vermouths – Punt e Mes.

As has been said, vermouth drinks were mixed for the individual customer, who would order the preferred flavourings, the amount of sweetness or bitterness, and any particular spices or herbs which would be drawn from the bottles or jars behind the bar. A whole language of drinks began to evolve, and people would ask for 'One Mixture', 'Three Jews', 'Four Negroes' and so on. Regular customers, of course, would specify their 'usual' and the barman would know how to mix their drinks. As the Carpano bar was frequented by many of the members of the Borsa, or Turin Stock Exchange, nearby, the terms used in dealing were also frequently employed in the conversation of those who went to Carpano for their aperitives.

One day, certain stocks had fallen by one and a half points towards the end of dealing and, as Carpano's bar filled up, many were discussing why this should have occurred; one businessman, wanting to order the particular type of bitter-sweet vermouth he preferred, said, in Piedmontese dialect, 'Ca'm dag'n Punt e Mes' (Give me a point and a half), thereby signifying that the barman was to add one and a half 'points' of bitterness to the basic vermouth. Everyone around roared with laughter, and asked him whether he really wanted a drink or if he thought he was still dealing. But the blend of 'a point and a half' rapidly became popular and one of those who was actually there in 1870, Maurizio Boeris, who died as recently as 1944, bore witness to the origin of the drink. Customers who wanted to show off gave their order in a sign language – they would hold up one thumb (a point) and then draw their hand horizontally through the air, indicating a half (e mes). Significantly, very few people notice the antique style of the basic label of Punt e Mes today, supposing it to be a twentieth-century recipe, instead of one that is over a hundred years old.

Carpano's 'Classico' vermouth is a rather darkish bianco that is particularly recommended by the firm for making into long drinks.

The last direct descendant of Antonio Benedetto Carpano died in 1917, and in 1943 an air raid destroyed the original Carpano establishment. But the firm is now housed in a palace truly worthy of its proud traditions: the Palazzo Carpano, built in the Via Maria Vittoria in 1648 by Michelangelo Garove, who was a pupil of the famous baroque architect Guarini. The building combines elegantly simple proportions and a plain exterior with an exuberant entrance hall, with twelve pillars like gigantic sticks of barley sugar, an imposing main staircase and wonderfully decorated rooms, all of them used regularly by the firm, and each decorated by famous artists, with elaborate mouldings, paintings, teak furniture, candelabra, and many works of art. Telephones, filing systems, and all the appurtenances of modern office equipment are concealed as much as possible, so that the visitor steps back into the seventeenth century. Even a quick glance through the entrance hall into the courtyard is rewarding for the visitor to Turin.

And: 'No one makes vermouth like Carpano!' This in fact was said to me by the head of one of their competitors. But no one does make vermouth like Carpano – whether you like it or prefer another brand. They were the first to sell vermouth commercially and theirs is unique.

The firm of Martini & Rossi was founded in the 1840s, but had been in business for a long time before that as Martini & Sola, who themselves had taken over the business in Pessione, near Turin, of a firm called Michel Agnel Re and Banding, who had been in the liqueur business and had begun to make vermouth. It may be of interest to know that the Agnel of this establishment was the grandfather of Giovanni Agnelli, the founder of Fiat.

Martini & Rossi is still a family firm. The four original brothers Rossi followed their father, the first of the name, into the firm. They were particularly adventurous in setting up branches of Martini & Rossi in other countries, so that Martini & Rossi vermouth was soon internationally known, as well as the other products being launched by the firm. This internationalism is characteristic of Martini: in

1953 they set up the first of the 'Martini terraces', in Paris, following this with other 'terraces' in Genoa, Barcelona, Brussels, São Paolo and, in 1964, in London. These terraces are on the top of high buildings, and are used for receptions and promotions of Martini & Rossi products. In 1960, the Martini International Club was founded in London; this club arranges for the firm to sponsor many sporting events, and also acts as patron of a number of cultural activities.

The most important achievement in the history of Martini, as far as the drink buying public is concerned, is probably the establishment of their wine museum at Pessione, where the headquarters of the firm and the sparkling wine production plant are today. This is certainly one of the most important wine museums in the world, showing the history of wine making from ancient times, with exhibits of outstanding interest, for their antiquity as well as their beauty. To visit it is a 'must'for anyone who can make the twenty minutes drive from Turin.

In the history of the remarkable firm of Cinzano, the first mention of the Cinzano family cites Carlo Stefano, a spirit merchant, attending the consecration of a church at Pacetto, near Turin, in the seventeenth century. But the family goes back to at least 1568, when they seem to have become established at Pacetto. The Cinzanos were landowners and Pacetto was a particularly fertile region – 'the grape bower of Turin' as some called it. Many other fruits were cultivated, including cherries, and brandy was distilled from the cherry stones. The family had in fact been making cordials and distilling brandy as early as 1707, and the names of Carlo Stefano and Giovanni 'Cuijano' appear in 1757, in records of the Confectioners and Distillers Guilds of Turin, when they became master distillers. A master distiller at this time was obliged to serve a hard apprenticeship, be examined as to his capabilities, obtain a licence after passing examinations before the Turin medical council and, certainly, provide gifts of products in substantial quantities to other members of the Council.

The Cinzanos, although they maintained their headquarters in Pacetto, were frequent visitors to Turin, which, in the mid eighteenth century, was an elegant, art-loving, fashionable and industrial city. The Via Dora Grossa, with many business houses and bars, now included the shop of Francesco Cinzano at number 35; this would have been a particular achievement for the family, because the Via Dora Grossa, the main street of Turin, was directly connected with Pacetto by a four-mile-long road. In the language of the time, an inhabitant of Pacetto who 'walked along the Dora Grossa road' was someone who had gone to seek his fortune in the city. Francesco

Cinzano, son of the Francesco previously mentioned, succeeded as head of the firm in 1859, and bought up business connections in Nice, Savoy, and South America, exhibited at the London Exhibition of 1862, and, finally, took over what had previously been a royal property at Santa Vittoria d'Alba, an establishment that became further known to millions all over the world when the film *The Secret of Santa Vittoria* told the story of how supplies of wine were concealed by the inhabitants from the occupying Germans at the end of the Second World War.

Cinzano is still a family firm, and has extended its holdings even further; among other things, they now own the Florio establishment at Marsala, in Sicily. They produce a range of vermouths, as well as wines, but the most famous is their 'Bianco', which pioneered the fashion for this type of white vermouth on the international market after the Second World War and which is possibly the vermouth that will be offered if, in a bar of international standard, a 'bianco' is ordered, unless another brand is specified.

Other well-known brands of Italian vermouth are Riccadonna, Cora, Bosca and Fratelli. Riccadonna, still a family firm, was founded in 1921 at Canelli, one of the centres for Asti Spumante, by Octavio Riccadonna. The company's expansion is remarkable, being second only to Martini in Italy in the vermouth market. They also sell enormous quantities to Russia.

Louis Noilly, who first made what is certainly the best-known vermouth manufactured in France, started in business in Lyons at the beginning of the nineteenth century. Seeing the great commercial success of the Italian vermouth firms, he decided to make the drink himself, with the aid of his son-in-law, Claudius Prat; they were so successful that in 1843 they moved their headquarters to Marseilles, so as to be more advantageously situated for trading. Louis Noilly's daughter, Joséphine Prat, remained a director of the firm after the death of both her husband and her father, and the concern was then run by her two children – it still remains very much a family business. The Vicomtesse Vigier, Joséphine Prat's granddaughter, entered the firm before 1939 and continued to direct the house until she died in 1970 when she was well over a hundred years of age. (Noilly Prat, in their publicity, have several times asserted that the special formula followed for their vermouth contains ingredients that are both revivifying and restorative of virility.) Noilly Prat today have huge enclosures (one of which commemorates the name of Joséphine Prat) at Marseillan, and an establishment at Sète, on the French Mediterranean coast, as well as their Marseilles headquarters. The Noilly Prat installation originated the unique method of maturing the casks of vermouth outside, exposed to the sun and sea air, and not being topped up. Noilly Prat today also make a bianco in Italy, as well as their dry vermouth, most famous of all, and a sweet variety.

SERVING VERMOUTH

Vermouth was originally a drink to be taken straight, a fashion which has recently been revived. But the rules about serving it apply, whether it is drunk by itself or forms part of a mixture.

Vermouth should always be served chilled and, ideally, this means that the bottle should have been chilled, not that the vermouth should be poured over ice, which naturally weakens the drink. Of course, anyone in a hurry may have to use a few ice cubes, although it is preferable to chill the glass if possible. The addition of a twist of lemon peel, actually twisted over the vermouth, so that the oils in the skin go into the drink, is an enhancement to a straight vermouth and it must be stressed that a slice of lemon, untwisted, is by no means the same. Or course, vermouth can always be diluted with soda water – this makes a particularly useful drink if you do not want to take too much alcohol.

KEEPING VERMOUTH

Something very few people realize is that because vermouth is essentially a wine it should be kept like one – in other words, the contents of the bottle ought to be used up fairly soon once it has been opened. The drier the vermouth, the sooner it will deteriorate once exposed to the air: this decline in the vermouth quality can be slowed by keeping the bottle in the refrigerator, but it will happen none the less, and it will be even more rapid if there is only a little vermouth left in the bottle after opening, because there will be more air inside. Its flavour will have become odd and it will certainly not enhance any mixed drink! A really dry vermouth should ideally be consumed within ten days to a fortnight, even if the bottle is kept in a cool place after it has been opened; the biancos and sweet vermouths can remain drinkable for three or four weeks. When you are using up vermouth in the kitchen, where it is possibly the most useful of all bottles, remember that, although the herbiness will make it an admirable flavouring for any sauce, soup, or certain types of stew, a vermouth that has been long exposed to the air is not really suitable for adding to anything that isn't going to be cooked – such as a salad, fish cocktail, any cold sauce or dressing.

WINE-BASED APERITIVES

Anyone who has read the history of vermouth will realize that a drink of vermouth style is likely to be made in any region that produces wine. This can be varied both by the addition of flavourings and by methods of production, such as have been explained in the previous section. The most obvious type of additive is some sort of sweetening, because, without very skilful blending and long-term maturation, an aperitive simply made as an imitation of vermouth can be harshly disappointing. Economics also enter into this, for, although it is pleasant to have a local speciality, it is no good producing this kind of thing on a large scale unless it can subsequently attract national and even international demand on an open market. A drink that is only drunk locally – whether by natives or tourists – tends to remain a cottage industry. Most regions have their local 'specials', and the casual, between-times drink in regions that do not make spirits in large quantities tends to be a wine-based beverage that is definitely related to vermouth. In the Iberian peninsula the fortified wines fill this role; in northern countries the cold tends to make people drink spirits, if they can afford them, as the between-times or social drinks; and in many hot countries, notably those with religious restrictions on the consumption of alcoholic beverages, the place of the aperitive is filled by quantities of flavoured tea and coffee, or mineral waters.

Italy, as has been seen, is dominated by vermouth itself, and in recent times certain bitter drinks have become very popular, but the pattern of life in France has, for a long while now, included habitual visits to the café, before the man goes home from work, later with his wife and family, or as the place where he meets his friends. French cafés have not been as exclusively masculine places of refreshment as many Italian bars or British pubs, nor has 'strong' drink played a dominant part in their sales. Neither do they sell large quantities of beer, except in the brasseries of the industrial regions, where the fluid replaces the sweat lost in the hard physical work of the day. The variety of drinks that are fairly light alcoholically, and consequently can be consumed in a short time without undue extravagance or risk of spoiling the meal still to come, represents the efforts of French aperitive manufacturers to cater for a variety of tastes and to provide drinks that can be between-time pleasures as well as aperitives.

The following are some of the best known French drinks of this sort, all of which, as will be seen, derive from at least a type of vermouth.

Dubonnet

A Paris wine merchant in the last century, Joseph Dubonnet, made up a 'blended quinine wine', which he offered to his customers in his shop in the rue Ste Anne in 1846. Originally, he called it 'Dubonnet Tonic Apéritif' but the drink became popularly known as Quinquina Dubonnet, although the name was not registered until some time afterwards. The new drink was so successful that Dubonnet was able to give up his wine business to concentrate solely on the aperitive.

It may seem strange to drinkers who prefer sweetish things that quinine should have attracted a large clientèle, but its medicinal properties had been recognized in the seventeenth century, and in 1830 the French campaign in Algeria resulted in the chief medical consultant, Dr Maillot, ordering the distribution of the bark and powder of the quinquina herb to the civilian population and farmers of the country, as well as to the troops. So people were well disposed to believe that quinquina did them good. (The cat on the Dubonnet label, incidentally, was put there at the suggestion of cat-loving Madame Dubonnet.) Joseph Dubonnet's recipe included red and white wines, made from the Grenache, Carignan, Muscat and Malvoisie grapes, plus his own additives.

Quinine is Peruvian bark, with a bitter taste; the Spaniards, when they conquered Peru, brought knowledge of quinquina back to Europe (the word 'quinine' in fact comes from the Spanish '*cin-chona*', itself deriving from the Indian expression for the bark, '*kin-kina*'). The Jesuits are credited with discovering its uses and Montpellier, already a famous centre for medical and scientific research, specialized from early times in producing these aromatized, vermouth-type wines flavoured with spices and barks. It is said that Louis XIV and Louis XV made gifts of quinquina during their various visits in provincial France, and I suppose the royal gift may have been regarded as some kind of elixir; Napoleon I is reported to have copied this royal habit but, more practically, as a remedy against fever. However strange it may sound to anyone who has grown up in the age of antibiotics, the use of quinine as a regular dose of preventive medicine by those serving in the tropics, and especially as a remedy for malaria, was widespread until the Second World War.

Dubonnet today is a blend of red and white wines, plus *mistelle* (a type of wine concentrate to which spirit is added to prevent the completion of the fermentation). Quinquina bark is then steeped in the mixture and the resulting liquid is matured in oak at the Dubonnet winery at Thuir in the south-west of France, where the winery boasts it has the largest cask in France. This is the ordinary type of reddish Dubonnet, but Dry Dubonnet has been recently introduced to export markets, and is described as 'a dry vermouth'; it is drier than the ordinary Dubonnet and is rather an updated version of what, about twenty years ago, was known as Dubonnet Blonde. Dry Dubonnet is made from *mistelle* from the Vallée d'Agly in the Roussillon region of France, and white wines from the Hérault. The freshness of the 'dry' type derives from the ingredients.

Lillet (*Kina Lilet*)

These are two names for the same product. Sometimes in the South of France the second version is seen advertised. Essentially, Lillet is a vermouth, and it is made at Ccnon, on the east bank of the Garonne, opposite Bordeaux. Its base is white Bordeaux wine, to which is added some Armagnac, the mixture then being macerated with herbs and fruit elements, after which it is matured in Yugoslav oak casks before being offered for sale. Because of this ageing in wood, Lillet acquires a slight golden tinge.

St Raphaël

This is another drink supposed to have been derived from the Spanish Jesuits making use of Peruvian quinine and, later, promulgating the beverage in France. In fact, the registered drink dates from 1830, when a Frenchman called Jupet, who was engaged in making up a quinine-based drink, suddenly lost his sight; he prayed to the Archangel Raphaël, patron of the blind, and his sight was restored; in gratitude, Jupet gave the Archangel's name to the perfected mixture. Quinine-based drinks had begun to be very popular, and, in his Egyptian campaign, Napoleon decreed that his troops should have their daily wine ration mixed with quinine, as a health measure.

Jupet had enormous success with his drink and indeed there is still a popular belief that those who drink it will never go blind! In 1897 Jupet sold out and St Raphaël now belongs to the mighty Martini and Rossi. The original drink was white and somewhat sweet but recently two other types have been introduced: an 'Extra Dry', pale and definitely like a dry vermouth, and the 'Rouge' which, like the original 'Blanc', yellowish and somewhat sweet are based on aged *mistelles*.

Byrrh

This is another wine-based type of vermouth from the Roussillon, where the Pyrenean pastures provide ample supplies of herbs. Simon Violet, a shepherd, is said to have evolved the original recipe in 1866, and it too contains some quinine, although it is a rather sweeter type of 'bitter' drink than St Raphaël.

Cap Corse

This darkish red-brown aperitive, somewhat sweetish, comes from Corsica, 'the scented isle', so called because of the many aromatic herbs that grow there. It enjoys wide popularity throughout France.

Ambassadeur

The town of Ornans, in the Jura region of France, is in the centre of an area devoted to the cultivation of many fruits, including plums and cherries, and herbs; the Cusenier family had been making drinks for their own use from these for generations, so it was a natural process for Eugène Cusenier to establish himself in business with a distillery in 1858. His family recipes became enormously popular and other distilleries were built in Mulhouse (then in Germany), Paris and Marseilles, and the family also bought both vineyards and a distillery in Cognac. With these interests, the Cusenier firm were in an advantageous position to make a wide range of liqueurs. Ambassadeur is still a secret recipe, but includes oranges macerated in wine, and various herbs, seeds, roots, barks and peels are subsequently included. Gentian, the bitter herb that grows wild in the Vosges mountains, gives a refreshing, slightly bitter, cleansing final flavour.

Amer Picon

This is also based on spirit and flavoured with gentian, quinine and oranges. It was first produced in 1835 by Gaeton Picon in Algeria and, like other mixtures containing quinine, proved popular among soldiery and civilians alike. The traditional way of drinking it is to serve it iced, topped up with soda water, but in the U.K., where bitter drinks are not always liked, the substitution of fizzy lemon or orange instead of the soda water can give a touch of acceptable sweetness. (See also page 224.)

Other wine-based aperitives

There are many other wine-based aperitives. From France there are Bonal, Bartissol, Nicolet, Pikina (the bitter orange mixture, with the addition of quinine, made by the Amer Picon establishment, as the name suggests). In Spain there is Xérès Quina, a sherry-based aperitive plus quinine, which I admit I have never tasted.

The French Gauloise, from which the well-known cigarette took its name and not the other way round, and which was originally made in three versions, dryish, medium and sweet, is seldom seen today. The yellowish, herby Raspail, considered more as a digestive, is no longer made; it was named for its inventor, François Raspail, the chemist for whom the boulevard is also named.

12. Liqueurs

It is impossible, I find, to provide an exact definition of 'liqueur'. Indeed, until there is an international board occupying itself with the wines and spirits of the world, this will probably continue to be so: for example, in the United States what an Englishman might call a liqueur is often referred to as a cordial. Recently, there was a furious argument within the E.E.C. because the French wished to insist that fortified wines, such as port and sherry, should be solely referred to as 'vins de liqueur', a term that would certainly have as different a meaning for an English-speaking person as the term 'fortified' has for a Frenchman. (In literal translation, the expression 'fortified wine' in French implies a wine of which the alcoholic strength has been increased, whereas the term for a wine fortified in the sense that the English-speaking world understands – by the addition of brandy – is 'un vin viné'.)

At what stage does a spirit become a liqueur? How may one differentiate between a spirit-based aperitive and a spirit-based digestive? Is the aperitive *only* for serving before a meal and the digestive for serving after it? Can the same drink play both roles? Should the term 'liqueur' be defined according to the use of the drink or the way that it is made? Is there a stage in alcoholic strength at which a spirit begins to be a liqueur or should a liqueur merely be considered as some type of spirit? It will be seen that such matters might be argued at length.

Until quite recently it might indeed have been possible to achieve a greater precision regarding liqueurs by taking the word to refer solely to drinks served after meals. In addition to the various fruit and herb drinks, there were 'liqueur whisky' and 'liqueur brandy', terms signifying that the spirits were of a quality superior to that used for ordinary purposes, intended to be drunk neat, and mostly as a post-prandial digestive. But I think these terms strike the ear as somewhat old-fashioned today, when conventions control us less rigidly and those who choose to take a drink at times agreeable to themselves are not considered social outcasts by doing so. Indeed, such breaks with tradition may form new conventions, in accordance with the ways of our times: readers of Simenon's Maigret detective stories will remember how Maigret develops a habit of sticking to one particular drink, no matter at what time he goes into a bar or café, with each of his cases. The order for a 'Cointreau on the rocks' is a commonplace today, but would have been an astonishing aperitive in an English-speaking country before the end of the Second World War. The mixtures of drinks, in short or long form, that are routine orders in many bars now would have been a shock in the period between the two wars, and some of the spirits then considered acceptable only in masculine company, together with the type of sweet drinks that had their largest sale in cafés or bars frequented by the *demi-monde*, are all drunk anywhere, anytime today and by anyone who wishes.

Nor is it possible to indicate the exact historical point when liqueurs became social rather than medicinal drinks. The importance of the digestive in former times, however, was very much greater than in our own, not only because food, in spite of the seasonings and sauces that acted as some type of disinfectant, might nevertheless be in a state we should not consider fit for human consumption, but also because, when so few people ever really got enough to eat, those who did invariably tended to over-eat when they could. The main meal was taken after the hardest work of the day, although 'dinner' might be what we should consider early. For the majority of people whose work was regulated by the hours of daylight, the break for food would have been around midday or early in the afternoon in most instances. For all that, those who came to table would often do so tired and, if they then over-ate and drank, some form of equivalent to the indigestion tablet was an obvious attractive addition to the repast.

As might be expected, Italy seems to have been the first major producer of what we can generally refer to as liqueurs. The great trade routes – by sea and land – around the Mediterranean would have encouraged the cooks and still-room directors at the courts and the houses of the nobility, as well as the religious establishments, to experiment in making new beverages. Strong drinks based on fruits and herbs certainly began to form part of the repertoire of any country house, once the basic knowledge of distilling was widespread. When Catherine de Medici went as a bride to marry Henri II of France, Italians will tell you, it was her cook that laid the foundations of the great tradition of French cuisine and the Queen herself is known to have been adept in making up sweetmeats and potions – they need not all have been the poisons with which she is rather unfairly credited. She is also credited with the introduction of liqueurs. It would be logical to assume that the prolific orchards and gardens of the Loire region of France, where the court spent so much time at this period, supplied basic ingredients for distillation and infusion. I also think that it is a short step from the peasant girl going to the wise woman, or even someone suspected of being a witch, to purchase some form of charm for good or ill, to the court lady or gallant visiting an alchemist, or the type of midwife who could provide 'helpful remedies', for the purchase of some potion by way of charm, aphrodisiac, or simply a strong sleeping draft for a boring husband. If such a drink titillated one sense or another, so much the better, whether or not it actually performed the purpose for which it had been bought.

The French made certain types of liqueurs fashionable in the seventeenth century during the reign of Louis XIV, the Sun King. Although I can find no reference to the King ever getting drunk, he certainly possessed a characteristic common to many of the Bourbons for what we should consider excessive indulgence in exercise, sex and eating – perhaps the one led inevitably to the other, in a vicious circle. Louis XIV became enormously fat and subject to digestive ailments late in his life; Dr Fagon, the horrific-sounding court physician, of whom Nancy Mitford remarked that he managed to kill off most of the heirs to the throne, made up a spirit drink for Louis which contained aniseed, fennel, dill, coriander and caraway – all of these associated with indigestion remedies. The mixture was made palatable with camomile and sugar and called Rossoli. It even went on sale publicly in 1676, as did another drink of the same type, essentially being spirits with sweetening elements and flavourings, which was called Populo.

Some of the spirit drinks recorded as being on sale in seventeenth- and eighteenth-century France seem the direct descendants of the honey and spiced wine beverages supposed to encourage sexual prowess in classical times: Huile de Vénus (invented by a M. Cigogne), Belle de Nuit, Eau Nuptiale, and Huile de Cythère, reputedly efficacious '*pour accélérer les accouchements*', which sounds as if it might have been some kind of an abortifacient.

Liqueurs in the general sense do not seem to have been made on a large scale in the British Isles, but it would be rash to assume that this apparent lack of interest was due to the superiority of the Anglo-

Saxon digestion, or to the Briton's ability to cope with sex without additional stimulus. Of course there was plenty of distilling going on in Scotland and Ireland, quantities of spirits were increasingly imported from the Low Countries and France, and, with the religious houses having been dissolved in the early sixteenth century, the still-room of the castle and country house was preoccupied with medicinal drinks pure and simple, in addition to the other activities of wine making and brewing.

But in 1749, Giacomo Justerini arrived in England from Bologna, infatuatedly pursuing an opera singer on tour. He had little money with him but he had brought some recipes copied from the craft book of an uncle of his, a distiller, and it was with the aid of this and the contacts who provided him with some backing, that he and his partner, George Johnson, set up a shop selling drinks in Pall Mall. Justerini possessed a still and concocted a variety of incredible 'strong waters', some of them extremely complicated, others making use of the fruits and berries that were easily available. Piedmont water, fever water, walnut water, treacle water, stag's heart water are only a few of the names from Justerini's records; he also had a recipe for ratafia, using black cherries and gin.

Ratafia is an odd drink. In the Middle Ages, when all legal work was conducted in the Latin then spoken by most educated people, the end of a document concerning an agreement was as follows: '*De quibus est res, ut rata fiat, publicum fecimus instrumentum*', meaning: 'We have executed a public document concerning the matters which the transaction deals with, so that it may be confirmed.' The two parties to the deal had to repeat this phrase in front of a lawyer and, following this, the deal was 'ratified'. The lawyer then made both signatories to the document drink together, and the drink itself took on the name of ratafia. In the eighteenth and nineteenth centuries ratafia sometimes appears to have been a fruit drink, of a non-alcoholic nature, but it was certainly strong liquor before that. In *The Way of the World*, Congreve's great comedy (1700), Mirabell, attempting to lay down the law as to the conditions of marriage with Millamant says: '. . . I banish all Foreign Forces, all Auxiliaries to the Tea-Table, as Orange-Brandy, all Anniseed, Cinamon, Citron and Barbado's-Waters, together with Ratafia and the most noble Spirit of Clary.'

Clary is not, as I have heard some people state, Mirabell's pronunciation of the word 'claret'; he would not have referred to claret as 'noble spirit' however much it might actually have been doctored or slightly strengthened to please the public taste. Clary was made from raisins, plus 'half a peck of the tops of Clary when it be in blossom'. The herb clary was used in salads, omelettes, made into fritters and used in brewing and making perfumes, and there are several recipes for Clary wine. Clary (*sclarea*) originated in the Mediterranean and Middle East but was brought to Britain in 1562. Its leaves were often added to wine to give it the taste of muscatel or raisins and it now grows wild in Pennsylvania, where it was used as a herb for the kitchen, often in place of sage.

Around the middle of the eighteenth century in England, there seem to have been three types of ratafia: the fine, the dry, and the common, and these appear to have been infusions of fruits with brandy. The ripeness of the fruit was important, because with berries and fruits rich in natural sugar (such as strawberries, raspberries, currants and mulberries which are all cited as being used), the greater the natural sugar, the less was required for ultimate sweetness. For white ratafias, nuts, quinces, plums and seeds were utilized.

The glasses used for the different sorts of ratafia were usually on a stem, with a trumpet-shaped bowl, whereas those for cordials had even smaller bowls and the stems were inclined to be taller. Some of the small glasses sometimes sold as 'custard cups' were used for syllabubs – they have one handle. Another type of glass in use at this time resembles a very small vase, having no stem or handle and a bowl that inclines slightly outwards at the rim.

Today, the only ratafia I know is that made in Champagne, where it is made by stopping the fermentation of the freshly pressed grapes by the addition of brandy, preferably Cognac, the procedure being somewhat similar to that whereby Pineau des Charentes (see page 265) is made.

A cordial was a predominantly medicinal drink in England until the seventeenth and eighteenth centuries, its name coming from the Latin '*cor*', meaning 'heart', the drink being particularly associated with illnesses that required a stimulant. It became a social drink with the advent of the heavy drinking sessions of the beginning of the great age of port, in the early eighteenth century. Dinner began to be a very lengthy business even in the routine of the ordinary day, quite apart from celebrations. 'It was "morning" till one dined' and, the meal finished, the ladies would withdraw while the men circulated bottles and decanters on the polished board. An hour or more later, tea would be served in the withdrawing room, and the men, after their potations, would certainly have been in need of a reviving drink, possibly with the properties of a pick-me-up. The cordials of the period were extremely strong (as are the alcoholic pick-me-ups of today, see pages 223, 226), which is why the elegant glasses intended for their use have very small bowls. This type of drink was probably often intended to be knocked back in a gulp. In any event, the cordial glass was, according to reports, seldom filled, and the drink itself might be measured out by the single spoonful.

In the nineteenth century, liqueurs seem to have been drinks mostly taken in bars and cafés, sometimes in restaurants, but seldom, according to contemporary memoirs, being served at private dinners; men about town might offer a drink of this kind to visitors to their chambers, but women of good family did not dine in public restaurants until Edwardian times (a private room would usually be specially reserved, even for the most respectable type of meal), and in the United States the prudishness regarding eating in public seems to have lasted even longer. In France, however, the bourgeoisie as well as young men and the *demi-monde* were frequenters of the big cafés, which, with their lavish décor and attractive, brilliantly coloured drinks, played the same sort of role in the social life of the time as the pub did in Britain.

As in Europe, the American housewife, especially in the country, was accustomed to making her own 'house specialities' of fruits, herbs and spices. Liqueurs and cordials, such as the 'Cordial Excellent' of Dr Salmon, published as early as 1710, and many recipes for shrub, anisette and 'Perfect Love' or 'Another Perfect Love' (using flowers as well as fruits and spices), were included in books of the mid nineteenth century. There were ratafias made from pinks, pomegranates and absinthe, elixirs, including 'Troubadours' Elixir', with musk roses, jasmine or orange blossoms. An unusual type of drink that is mentioned in American books of this period is the Cream – but of course this must have been from the French word '*crème*'; it does not make use of dairy products. There are mint, laurel, jasmine, absinthe, and rose creams among the less usual. The U.S. housewife even made *usquebaugh* – 'a strong compound liquor...', made in the highest perfection at Drogheda in Ireland'; the recipe, however, uses oranges, cloves, cinnamon, raisins, saffron, nutmeg and cardamoms, brown sugar and 'best brandy'! Audarge brandy sounds as if it might have originated in Hendaye, for it uses Spanish brandy, anise, coriander, iris, orange zest and 'alcohol'.

Reconstructions of rooms in houses and taverns of the time, such as are in many U.S. historical museums, show a variety of equipment for making and serving a wide range of drinks. The potter William Leake, of Bennington, Vermont, made spirit flasks in the form of the neat, pointed shoes and ankle boots of the time and these, sometimes only 2 inches high, or even as small as $\frac{7}{8}$ inch, held a concealed 'nip' of spirit in an ornamental and portable form. The Bennington Museum has an extensive display of these and other drinks' accessories.

In many countries, especially those where port, sherry and Madeira had never been widely consumed, it was still common for a liqueur to be offered to visitors at virtually any time, quite outside the context of a meal, and this is perfectly understandable when it is remembered that in those days there were no cocktails. Spirits such as whisky or gin and, to a certain extent, even brandy, were certainly not beverages that would be openly drunk in mixed society by respectable people. And spirit-based drinks were cheap, so that the family on an outing to a café or similar place of refreshment could enjoy a wide choice, at moderate cost.

In the period between the World Wars, liqueurs seem to have been fairly often drunk, although they had become expensive. Novels of the 1930s, such as those by Evelyn Waugh, Michael Arlen and Dornford Yates, dealing with the lives of the wealthy, make numerous mentions of them, but when the taste for cocktails became prevalent the popularity of liqueurs declined. The virtual disappearance of domestic staff in all but the wealthiest of houses resulted in meals and drinks becoming much simpler. The fashion for many American habits was against the liqueur, as indeed was the price of most of them.

After the Second World War many of the major liqueur manufacturers, fearing a decline in consumption that would seriously affect them, began to publicize some liqueurs as essential ingredients in new and often exotic mixes, and also as drinks that could be taken virtually at any time and in place of the cocktail, now itself becoming somewhat old-fashioned except in its simplest form. The increasing availability of ice – even as late as the early 1950s, the proportion of homes owning a refrigerator in the U.K. was still low and the easy availability of ice-cubes was limited to the smarter type of pub and bar – made it henceforth possible for many liqueurs to be served either poured over crushed ice or 'on the rocks'. Cointreau on the rocks became a world success, and the jewel-toned frappés of certain liqueurs poured over crushed ice and drunk through straws made it acceptable and even smart in the 1960s to order drinks that would have been considered both out of date and 'tarty' in the 1930s. Swiftly changing fashions, that made it at one time voguish to evoke the tastes of the Belle Époque and similar past periods when liqueurs were widely consumed, encouraged the revival of interest in them.

The market for drink in 'swinging London' in the 1960s was stimulated by the remarkable progress made in colour advertising of drinks, which were now often featured, both in the advertisements, and, subsequently, the editorial sections of magazines that had previously omitted mention of alcohol in any form in features about entertaining for the average consumer (especially magazines aimed solely at women); many of these had previously refused to accept advertising from drink manufacturers.

In the 1950s there was, to the best of my knowledge, only one up-to-date book on liqueurs in existence (that by Mrs M. I. Fisher; see page 292). At the time of writing there are several, and several more in preparation; directories of drinks include liqueurs as a matter of course and consumer magazines have regular editorial features about them. Through various amalgamations and marketing methods adapted to the times, the great liqueur establishments are still very much in business and expanding; those who suppose that liqueurs are all made by holy men and women, painstakingly pounding, mixing and filling their bottles in medieval style are in for a shock when they go round a modern liqueur establishment. Even when the drink is still made according to an ancient recipe, and in the few instances when its preparation is conducted by members of a religious order, all the skills of the modern laboratory and scientific techniques are also involved – inevitably, because the modern consumer has been conditioned to expect a certain standard of quality in drinks and would probably find the authentically ancient version of even a favourite beverage quite unpalatable.

Although all liqueurs are alcoholic, the alcohol used in the manufacture of some of them may be neutral, without any taste itself. With other liqueurs, the flavour of the base spirit plays an important part in the result. The pulp or mash of fruits, berries, grains and other things may be distilled, and in the instance of what in France are known as *alcools blancs* the result is a true brandy of whatever the original substance is; this kind of spirit, too, may be used as a flavouring or additive to a liqueur.

The main methods whereby liqueurs are made are: distillation, which the reader who has understood pages 26–34 will now be able to take for granted, and maceration, whereby the flavours are extracted from the various herbs, fruits and so on, by using either cold spirit, so that the result is a type of infusion, or warm spirit, when the process is known as digestion. By compounding, types of liqueur resulting from the processes previously mentioned are assembled to result in a harmonious unity.

Approximate range per BRITISH FLUID OUNCE

HERBS

BRITISH: Glen Mist [70] Brontë [60] Can-y-Delyn [70] Glayva [70] [70] Drambuie

EUROPEAN: Cuaranta-y-Tres [55] Parfait Amour Dutch [52] French Trappistine [75] Millefiori [70] Vigevano Strega [70][73] Bénédictine [75] Yellow Chartreuse Green Chartreuse [96] [56] Ponche Soto Yellow [64] Izarra [73] B & B [75] Vieille Cure Aurum [70] Elixir d'Anvers [66] Pernod [79] [70] Cordial Médoc [70] Galliano [85] Green Izarra

FRUIT

SEED: [44] Anisette Greek Ouzo [65][67] Anis del Mono [79] Pernod [70] Danzig [70] Liqueur d'Or Kümmel [68] Goldwasser 'Der Lachs'

MINT: Dutch [52] Crème de Menthe [52] French [50] Royal Mint – Chocolate

CITRUS: Van der Hum [54] Orange [70] Curaçao [52] Royal Orange-Chocolate [68] [70] Cointreau Curaçao Triple Sec [68] Grand Marnier [55-8] Forbidden Fruit

APRICOT / PEACH: [42] Trotosky Apricot Brandy [52] French Apricot Brandy [56] [54] Dutch Apricot Brandy [52] French Peach Brandy Southern [87] Comfort

CHERRY: Grant's Cherry Whisky [43-44] Brandy [50] Scottish Cherry Whisky [52] Royal Cherry-Chocolate [42] Trotosky [42] Dutch Cherry Brandy [47] Maraschino [70] Wiśniówka Kirsch Peureux [70] French Cherry Brandy [43]–[43] Cherry Heering

ARCTIC FRUITS: [39] Suomuurain Mesimarja [39][50] Karpi

MISCELLANEOUS FRUITS: [29] Crème de Cassis (1/6) Blackberry [52][52] Crème de Fraise Pedlar [47] Sloe Gin Crème de Framboise [52][30] Crème de Banane [52] Royal Banana-Chocolate Blackcurrant Rum [42] Pineapple Rum

BEAN & KERNEL

COFFEE: Kahlúa [46][55] Tia Maria [60] Gallweys Scotch Coffee Whisky [50] [52] Crème de Cacao Noyau Rose

CHOCOLATE: [50] Royal Mint – Chocolate Amaretto [49] di Saronno

FRUIT KERNEL: [52] Crème de Cacao

SPIRITS

FRUIT (EAUX DE VIE): Polish Slivovitz [70] Tequila [70] [70] Calvados [70] Kirsch d'Alsace Framboise [78] Quetsch [78] Mirabelle [78] Poire William [75]

Gin / Vodka / Whisky / Whiskey / Brandy:
[65] British Gin [70] British Vodkas Smirnov [65-5] Wolfschmidt [70] Geneva [80] Smirnov [79] Aquavit [100] White Spirit Polish [73] Vodka Russian [70] Vodka Kosher Russian [98] Krepkaya Polish [100] Spirit Polish White Spirit [140]
Scotch Whisky [70] American Whiskey [70] Irish Whiskey [75] De luxe Scotch
Appleton Estate [70][70] [70] Grape Brandy [70] Armagnac [70] Staub Fine Champagne Cognac [70] V.S.O.P. Cognac Liqueur Cognac [70]

RUM DARK / WHITE: Jamaica, Demerara [70][70] Caroni [90] Imperial Diamond [70][70] Daïquiri [70] Ron Bacardi [100] Woods

---

Egg Liqueurs
Advocaat 30° proof Dutch, Guernsey

☐ Approx. proof strength of a liqueur type at various strengths by several distillers

[70]=70° proof in British proof (Sykes)

[70] = 70° US proof

(70 British proof = 80 US proof = 40% alcohol by volume)

LIQUEUROGRAPH Liqueurs, Eaux de Vie and Spirits

Reproduced by kind permission of the House of Hallgarten.

In compiling this chapter, I have to restrict myself, for reasons of space, to those liqueurs which are likely to be widely available because their distribution is considerable among the various export markets, and to those which are so famous in their own country that, even if they are not easily obtainable anywhere else, the visitor may at least have heard of them. With the increase of foreign travel in the medium and lower price ranges of package tours, an inevitable consequence has been that many resorts have attempted to cater for the tourist trade by evolving a specific beverage that can augment the local catering and provide a souvenir. Michelaine of Mont-Saint-Michel is one example, the Arômes de Monserrat another, both of them produced possibly in the first place for the refreshment of pilgrims, but nowadays being a unique memento for the tourist.

It is usually possible to relate even an obscure and apparently purely locally-produced liqueur to something better known in the range of liqueurs: the link that makes it part of the liqueur family may consist in the predominant flavouring, whether this is a fruit, a herb or a spice, or something such as chocolate or coffee (though I suppose these could, strictly, come into the category of fruits and berries), or it may be the spirit which is either the base or the main element in the liqueur. There are probably thousands of liqueurs in existence, just as there are certainly thousands of sauces.

Because this is a book for the lay drinker, who is probably primarily concerned with what liqueurs are like, and when and how they may most enjoyably be drunk, rather than with their chemistry and any legal controls (which are subject to constant change anyway), I have sorted out the different types of liqueurs in the way that I myself would find most helpful. Sometimes it is difficult to know into which category one should put liqueurs that might be claimed by two, but, if there should be any doubt, I have explained why I have made up my mind in favour of one category rather than another. It is also inevitable that some liqueurs with which certain readers are familiar may have been omitted; I have relied primarily on my own experience of as many liqueurs as I have been able to try and on reports by those in whose judgement I have confidence.

Although, as has been said, there are no internationally applicable definitions in use regarding liqueurs in law, the French traditions include the following definitions, which are of general interest and may be useful to the traveller in France. A 'liqueur' is a sweetened spirit which must contain 200 grams of sugar per litre. A *fine* s 49° proof, a *demi-fine* 40° proof and a *surfine* about 52° proof. The *surfine* is the sweetest, the *demi-fine* the least sweet. A liqueur described as '*double*', as in '*double crème de cassis*', in general will contain double quantities of the ingredients that flavour it; sometimes, however, there may only be 50 per cent more of them – the concentration of many of the flavourings in liqueurs is so great that to double the proportion of them might unbalance the whole. The drink might look too dark in colour, or cloudy. Exactly the same sort of thing can happen in cooking – it is not always satisfactory simply to double the ingredients in a recipe if you want to double the quantity; some flavourings can only be used sparingly. It should be noted that it is the flavouring elements that affect the use of the word '*double*', not the alcoholic strength; a double liqueur is generally about as strong as a *surfine*. The term '*crème*' followed by the name of a particular spice, flower or herb, implies that this is the main flavouring. Ratafia today, when the term is used, which is not often in everyday restaurant parlance, implies a liqueur made with fruits or nuts, infused in spirits of wine. This type of liqueur is usually sweetish.

French law requires that more than the content of the bottle and the strength of the liquid should be given on the label. The letter 'A' means that the bottle contains either a wine-based aperitive less than 18° Gay Lussac, or spirits that are flavoured with aniseed below 45° G.L. or bitters below 30° G.L. The letter 'D' on the label means that the contents are liqueurs and spirits of more than 15° G.L., except for aniseeds, bitters, and wine-based aperitives over 18° G.L. This is an attempt at clearing up a complicated subject, but in fact, as the reader will have gathered, it is nowadays impossible to categorize any drink of this kind as indisputably A for aperitive or D for digestive. In addition, E.E.C. and even international regulations may, at any time, alter the situation.

LIQUEURS ASSOCIATED WITH PARTICULAR SPIRITS

It will be appreciated that some of the drinks included in this section could equally have been listed under the fruits that flavour them, but in order to split up what might be an unwieldy category, for the purposes of quick reference and easy understanding, I have chosen to categorize certain drinks by the spirits, which are often part of the name of the drink as well.

Gin-based liqueurs

The best-known liqueur here is sloe gin. The sloe (*Prunus spinosa*), is a wild plum, with a small, purple-black fruit, found in Europe, North Africa, the East and the United States. It is also known as the blackthorn. It can be used to make jam, and as a pickle, but it is not particularly attractive to eat when cooked like other fruit. The leaves of the sloe are supposed to be useful in 'stretching' tea. Wine can be made from the sloe and no doubt also from its relation, the bullace, which looks like a rather large sloe, and the damson, a more oval purplish-black fruit. There are references in Sturtevant (*Edible Plants of the World*, New York, 1919) that juice of the sloe 'is said to enter largely into the manufacture of the cheaper kinds of port wine' – just as the elderberry did in the nineteenth century. But I don't think it features in port today at all!

Sloe gin is very much an English tradition, made when gin could be bought cheaply, either via a friendly smuggler or even through a legal supplier. 'Winterpick wine', the English country name for sloe wine, was also widely made; compendiums of traditional English drinks usually accompany the instructions for making sloe wine by recipes for sloe gin. Sloe gin is essentially made with equal quantities of sugar to sloes; the fruit is put into bottles (I think they must have been more like jars, unless the bottles had moderately wide necks) and topped up with gin. Some recipes add bitter almonds and recommend shaking up the ingredients. The sloe gin is then kept for some time – a year according to one writer who says 'the liquor will then be in perfection'. I think I can personally vouch for this, because, when my grandparents died, my parents took into their household a bottle of my grandmother's sloe gin, made when they had a large country house; this particular bottle certainly dated from before 1914. No attention was paid to it until the middle of the Second World War when an otherwise abstemious household broached it during one of the bombardments of London, when we were all sitting under the dining-room table, the air raid shelter being too cold. The silky warmth and concentrated fruitiness of the drink, of which I was then only allowed to have a small glass, has remained in my mind.

Traditionally, sloe gin was the stirrup cup, or drink served by the household at which hounds met, servants bringing round refreshments on trays, which would be offered to those who did not get down from their horses.

Sloe gin is commercially available today, the most famous in the U.K. being that of Hawkers of Plymouth, who market their version of the drink under the brand Pedlar. They have supplied the Royal Household for three centuries. (See also page 106.)

Blackcurrant gin, blackberry gin and damson gin are drinks that I have found referred to as commercial products but have never sampled. There seems no reason why such fruits should not be utilized in this way to make excellent gin-based drinks. In the Dordogne valley in France, the locals make crème de genièvre, from juniper berries, which is what might be described as a gin liqueur.

Whisky-based liqueurs

There are today a number of these, the most famous certainly being those based on Scotch, though Irish whiskey is used for some. It is a tribute to both Scotch and Irish that those who drink them tend to prefer them in their neat state and, ideally, in luxury form, rather than as an ingredient in a mixture, but some of the whisky-based liqueurs are both pleasant and of historic interest.

Athol Brose. There are many versions of this drink, which is probably of great antiquity. The name is sometimes spelled Atholl or Athole, the various accounts of it indicating that it may have been considered more in the nature of a food, even a type of porridge, than a drink.

There are two picturesque accounts of how it may have originated, from as early as 1475 in the Highlands – those who consider Scotland as all one country should be reminded that, in former times, the differences between the Highlands and Lowlands were considerable, and on many occasions so was the antagonism.

It appears that, in 1475, the Lord of the Isles, the Earl of Ross, was in revolt against the King, who sent the Earls of Crawford and Atholl to put down this rebellion. The Earl of Atholl was informed that the Lord of the Isles would come to drink from a particular well, and promptly therefore topped up this water supply with generous amounts of whisky, honey and oatmeal; the Lord of the Isles, who must have been considerably surprised by the beverage, was tempted to go on drinking, and, after a time, was understandably easily overpowered.

The more romantic, but similarly odd version (for how anyone intending to quench their thirst would not be made suspicious by a well containing a potent alcoholic mixture never seems to have struck the recounters of legend) concerns the heiress of the Duke of Atholl, the Maid of Tullibardine. Her favourite walks in the forest on the banks of the River Tay became hazardous because of the presence of a wild man, Rory Mhor (Big Rory), who attacked and robbed passers-by and even threatened the heiress; in fairy-tale fashion, she promised her hand and her estates to anyone who could rid the countryside of this nuisance – which should not have been a difficult task for a few efficient guards. But then, Big Rory appears to have assumed gigantic proportions and strength. One bright young man dosed the well at which he had discovered the robber used to come to drink, putting in it whisky and honey; after a few copious draughts the wild man fell into a coma and could easily be captured. The event probably was recorded in the armorial bearings of the Dukes of Moray (the Maid married Moray), which show a half-naked savage, and their motto 'Furth and fill the fetters!'.

It seems highly probable that each large household in the Highlands evolved its own recipe for Athol Brose and most of them include oatmeal and honey. The simplest version was probably made just by stirring some oatmeal into the spirit. As there are plenty of wild bees among the heather of the Highlands, it would be natural to add honey and, in Robert Louis Stevenson's novel *Kidnapped*, the drink is made of 'old whisky, strained honey and sweet cream'; in other recipes, an egg is beaten in as well – it can be seen that the concoction is a nourishing one. The family recipe of the Dukes of Atholl omits the cream, and probably this was the version that the Duke of the day gave to the dramatist Sheridan who 'relishing, partook of rather freely'. In 1844, Queen Victoria and Prince Albert, visiting Blair Atholl, also sampled what the Queen referred to as this 'giant's drink'.

According to authorities on Scots drinks, Athol Brose is really crowdie, for 'brose' is supposed to be a hot drink – and the only heating element in Athol Brose is the whisky. Crowdie, a name which may be familiar to eaters of Scots cheese today, was originally a name for 'all food of the porridge kind'; 'crowdie time' is a term used both by Robert Burns and Sir Walter Scott to mean breakfast.

At Hogmanay (New Year), a quaich, the traditional Scots open drinking vessel, filled with Athol Brose, is borne by two subalterns into the sergeants' mess of the Argyll and Sutherland Highlanders, preceded by a piper, and each officer and man must down a quaichful. This is a tradition which is followed in other Highland regiments and at family gatherings at Hogmanay.

The commercial versions of Athol Brose are sometimes used today as the basis for a type of pudding – one might say the Highland answer to syllabub – but it is both strong and rich and, especially if it is additionally enriched with more cream, more honey and more Scotch, then a very little goes a long way.

Drambuie. This word is the anglicized version of the Gaelic phrase '*An dram buidheach*', signifying 'the drink that satisfies'. It is possibly the liqueur that is best known throughout the world for its origin in the British Isles, and I once astounded a party of Frenchmen, earnest, longwinded and humourless as only the French can be when they are determined to make you learn something, who were taking me round every single department of a large Bordeaux supermarket, attempting to impress me that, in this field of merchandize, as certainly in all others, especially to do with drink, they were supreme. Picking up a bottle of Drambuie from a wire rack, I asked them if they knew what this was – and harangued them in return. At that moment, the Hundred Years' War seemed a mere yesterday – but I achieved my object, which, on a very hot day, when I had been on my feet and working hard for over three hours, was to get out, have a drink and relax.

The story of Drambuie is romantic, as are many stories to do with the House of Stuart, who were obviously strong on charm though, to my mind, so short on efficiency (except for Charles II, who made up for the other members of his family by simply sticking on his regained throne regardless) that it is difficult for anyone today who is not able to believe wholeheartedly in the divine right of kings to be tolerant towards them. Most of them, however, possessed glamour in the true sense of the word, and Charles Edward Stuart – the Young Pretender and 'Bonnie Prince Charlie' – certainly possessed the Stuart ability to make a memorable gesture, even at a most unfortunate moment.

The rebellion of the '45' was when the Young Pretender arrived in Scotland from France to rouse the country to the Stuart cause. At first he and his supporters were successful and victorious at Prestonpans and Falkirk. But at Culloden, near Inverness, the last battle fought on British soil resulted in a victory for the Duke of Cumberland – 'Butcher' being his nickname – and Charles Edward, with a price of £30,000 on his head, had to hide and flee. 'The Skye Boat Song' records how Flora Macdonald disguised the Prince as her maid and, in a small boat, got him to Skye. Here, one of the Mackinnons of Strathaird rowed him to a safe hiding place until, in September 1746, a French ship arrived to rescue him.

One of the few things that the Prince could still give his protector and rescuer was the recipe for his personal liqueur, which he bestowed on Mackinnon. The idea of travelling with a digestive or tonic specifically evolved for one's own needs is nothing new – there can be few members of the drinks trade who do not go on a business trip without their particular bottle of 'calming potion', although nowadays this tends to be a variation of the morphia and kaolin mixture, instead of anything spirituous!

The Prince's liqueur remained a treasure within the care of the Mackinnons for nearly 150 years. They made only just enough for their own needs and for the annual Gathering of the Clan. Occasionally privileged visitors or friends got a bottle, but the name wasn't even registered until 1896.

Then, in 1906, 25-year-old Malcolm Mackinnon decided to make it commercially. Malcolm, generally known as Calum, had come from Skye to work in Edinburgh in the establishment of W. Macbeth & Son, who were making whisky. He was shrewdly aware that, after Queen Victoria had made Scotland and Scots products fashionable, there could be a demand for a new drink and he watched the growth of the whisky business. He thought that the time was ripe to launch a Scots liqueur.

Malcolm managed to persuade his relations to let him learn the secret recipe for the Prince's liqueur; this he began to make in a cellar in Union Street, Edinburgh, using quite primitive equipment, such as jelly bags and copper pans. It took a week to make enough Drambuie to fill a dozen bottles.

Malcolm had already established something of a reputation for himself as an authority on whisky and his knowledge was invaluable in the blending of the base of Drambuie, which, it is known, is a blend of fine old Highland malts, up to fifteen years old. But the initial stages were hard going: only twelve cases of Drambuie sold in the first year it was available, even though it cost a mere 7s 6d a bottle! However, Malcolm persevered and was encouraged by the response from Scots abroad, who wrote asking for the liqueur. Drambuie began to be advertised and in the First World War it became popular in messes overseas.

Between the wars, Drambuie continued its export and domestic drives and the successor to Malcolm Mackinnon was his brother-in-law, who took over in 1945 when Malcolm died; Malcolm's son and daughter are also in the business and, until her death in 1973, it was his widow, Mrs Gina Mackinnon, who alone made the base of the drink according to the family formula – four of the vials she would make up in her home outside Edinburgh were sufficient to make up 1200 gallons!

Drambuie is an admirable liqueur, whisky tinged with herbs, spices and elements that make it crisp and clean.

Other whisky-based liqueurs. Glen Mist seems to have been another version of what were no doubt at one time the personal whisky liqueurs of many Highland households. It was first evolved by Hector Macdonald and put on the market in this century; for a time, when Scotch was in short supply for U.K. consumption it was made in Ireland, hence the temporary name 'Irish Mist'. Today Glen Mist, based on Scotch contains various herbs and spices plus honey, and it is once again made and indeed bottled only in Scotland. Its revival – and the re-creation of the recipe – was due to Peter Hallgarten.

Glayva is another fairly recently commercialized whisky-based liqueur, which contains herbs and spices. Lochanora, made by Chivas Regal, is named for a legendary loch. Lindisfarne is based on Scotch and includes honey among its ingredients.

Gallweys Irish Coffee Liqueur, matured in oak, is based on Irish whiskey with a flavouring of honey and herbs and a predominant taste of coffee. It is a recipe originating in the Gallwey family, associated for generations with distilling.

Baileys Irish Cream, an 'Irish Cream Chocolate Liqueur', with a whiskey base, is a curious and delectable drink, which even people who do not usually like sweet liqueurs enjoy enormously. Scientific friends tell me that the way in which the cream is incorporated, without losing its own flavour and without separating, is in itself a technical triumph; the liqueur looks rather like a parfait or liquefied coffee/chocolate ice and in fact it does freeze well. Although of course it can be drunk by itself, it makes something extra special out of the traditional version of Irish Coffee (Irish whiskey topped with strong black coffee with thick cream floated on the top through which the drink is sipped). Baileys is only marred for me by having some coconut in the recipe – as I detest this flavouring, my enjoyment of it is qualified.

Irish Mist is said to have evolved when nineteenth-century distiller Daniel E. Williams attempted to re-create the 'heather wine' of the legendary Irish warriors – this was supposed to have consisted of a type of whiskey and an extract made from wild heather. Williams ran the Tullamore Whiskey Distillery, but neither he, his sons, nor his grandsons ever succeeded in producing a liqueur that satisfied their ideas as to what this heather wine might have been. In 1948, however, an Austrian refugee brought to Daniel E. Williams's great-grandson a family recipe based on heather honey and whiskey, which, he said, was of Irish origin – and this proved to be the type of liqueur for which they had been searching. Nearly all the Irish

Mist made today goes abroad, particularly to the United States.

George M. Tiddy's Canadian Liqueur is based on Canadian whiskey and is reported to have a flavour of oranges. Rock and Rye is a U.S. 'liqueur', based on rye whiskey with sugar. Different makes vary slightly in flavourings, which appear to be mainly fruity.

Brandy-based liqueurs

Pineau des Charentes. This drink, which should not be confused with *pinard*, the daily wine ration of the French Army, or the grape variety, Pinot, comes from the same region of France in which Cognac is produced – hence the 'des Charentes' part of the name.

It is supposed to have been discovered by chance. A peasant proprietor of the region, probably looking round for storage space in an abundant year, tipped some newly made wine into a cask which happened to contain some forgotten brandy. When the new-made wine was tasted, the owner was aghast – so much so, that he simply sealed up the mixture and left it alone. But when some time later he opened it and, before throwing it away, again tried the liquid it contained, he had a pleasant surprise.

This seems a possible explanation for the origin of pineau, although some writers think that it was discovered in about 1580 on an estate near Burie, and others, possibly somewhat chauvinistic as regards the region, claim that it was evolved as early as the latter part of the twelfth century in Angoulême. Personally, I don't think that this kind of drink could have been evolved as early as is claimed.

Pineau did become popular from the time it was made on a reasonably large scale. Henri IV is supposed to have liked it – but then, his appetite for all the good things of life was voracious – and Louis XIII described it as 'a whetter of the appetite and a distiller of bad moods'. Producers of pineau today may tell you that the consumption of pineau by Louis XIII gave him both the inclination to visit his wife after many years of neglect, and endowed him with the necessary ability to beget a son – Louis XIV; history is a little more prosaic, recounting how the King was caught in a thunderstorm and had virtually nowhere else to go except to the Queen's apartment. Louis XIV is certainly said to have taken pineau as an indigestion remedy.

In 1935, Pineau des Charentes was given an *appellation contrôlée*. It must be made from fresh grape juice of the grapes cultivated in the Charentes region only, this then being combined with a Cognac of the previous year, the proportions being one of Cognac to two of the grape juice, although the latter may be that of black or white grapes.

The pineau is then matured in cask: this is not required by law, but is necessary for the production of a quality drink. Cyril Ray points out that the pineau producers tend to be those who make Cognac from outside the more important region plus the smaller producers who give up space and invest in pineau production. He does not like pineau very much: 'a bland drink, which does not smell so nice as it tastes'. I myself think that it is somewhat better than this if you get a reputable brand, and, although it is fruity, it need not be sweet. Whether served straight or with soda (all chilled of course) it can provide a pleasant, slightly stimulating drink before a meal at which wines are to be served, and when it is not ideal to have a strong spirit as a preprandial refreshment.

Other brandy-based liqueurs. Brontë is made in Yorkshire from French brandy, honey, and a blend of herbs and spices, flavoured lightly with orange and presented in a ceramic flagon. It has been commercially produced for twenty-five years, but is certainly much older, and a silver bottle-label bearing its name and dating from possibly the eighteenth century was recently sold at auction.

Honey brandy, a liqueur produced in the U.K., and not, as far as I have been able to trace, related to any similar product made elsewhere, is marketed under the brand name of Casque. It is one of the exclusivities of the Liverpool firm of Lamb & Watt. The taste is exactly as the name implies – a most successful combination of honey and brandy, and delicious, only as sweet as honey is naturally sweet and with the warmth of the brandy behind the initial flavour making it delectable. I am only surprised that it has not enjoyed a greater commercial success than has apparently been the case.

Macvin is a curious drink. It is a speciality of the Jura region of France and its name derives from '*marc-vin*', because the local red wine has its fermentation checked by adding *eau de vie de marc*. It is sweet, pungent and made subtly interesting by the addition of certain spices, notably cinnamon and coriander.

Rum-based liqueurs

There are several very well-known liqueurs with a rum base; this spirit seems to be particularly successful with certain types of fruit and coffee or chocolate.

Tia Maria comes from Jamaica and contains extracts of the Blue Mountain coffee of the island plus spices. It was commercially perfected from a family recipe by Dr Kenneth Evans and for many years was the best-selling liqueur in the U.K., even though the advertising and publicity for it were minimal. It was said that in the days before wine bars and before wine by the glass was available in pubs, the man who would order a pint for himself would automatically order a Tia Maria for his wife! It's a good liqueur.

Kahlúa is made by the Heering establishment of Denmark, and includes Mexican coffee. It is a little more assertive and obviously scented than Tia Maria and is, at the time of writing, the best-selling liqueur in the United States. Its popularity indicates that, as with Tia Maria in Britain, countries that assert their preference for 'dry' drinks, in fact really like sweet ones, especially at the end of a meal.

Solbærrom is Danish blackcurrant rum. This is extremely fruity. In Denmark it is often used with ice cream or to pour over pancakes. The intense blackcurrant flavour cuts the richness admirably.

Swedish Punsch is a curiously named drink, very spicy and based on rum. It can be served cold or hot; the latter being the way it was always served until the nineteenth century. In addition to the commercial brands now on sale, it is very much a traditional home-made drink, and to quote one recipe will give an idea of its power: two bottles arrack, one bottle brandy and one bottle 95 per cent spirit, plus sugar, water and two teaspoonfuls of turpentine. Swedish Punsch is on the sweet side and therein treacherous, because at first the drinker does not realize the alcoholic strength.

Miscellaneous spirit-based liqueurs

There are, as might be expected, many drinks which simply cannot be fitted in to one particular category. Sometimes names vary from one country to another, and there are instances when a local liqueur, sold proudly as unique and special, is really only a variation on a much better-known product. The following are some of the better known.

Arrack, arack, raki: the Arabic word from which this name comes means 'juice' or 'sweat'. It can be made by distilling various things, including grapes; and sugar-cane, milk, rice, and dates are mentioned as being the base for it, although the best arrack is supposed to be distilled from toddy, which is the fermented sap of palm trees. This should not be confused with the type of hot drink which is spirit topped with water and often sweetened, or the cold version which often includes lemon juice and is topped with soda water and therefore best when freshly made; in Singapore the 'toddy parlours' must sell the toddy the day they make it, then throw away that which is not consumed. When served, arrack is topped up with water, when it becomes cloudy and milky in appearance, and ideally it should have ice added to it. It is sipped slowly, always being accompanied by some form of food, such as olives, dates, pieces of cucumber, or similar small-scale refreshments (rather like ouzo, see pages 209–10).

Batavia Arrack, somewhat confusingly, is made from the molasses of the sugar processing establishments in Java, near Batavia. This form of spirit is really a type of rum, which after ageing in Java is shipped to Holland, where it is again aged up to six years before being blended and bottled. Its quality is supposed to derive both from this maturing and from the special red Javanese rice which is made into cakes and put in the molasses undergoing fermentation.

A spirit called arake was made by Tartar horsemen from mares' milk plus grape juice or such sugar as they could get – it sounds an appalling beverage and I have not been able to find anyone who has tasted it.

Ponche is a sweetish Spanish liqueur, which is made from distilled sherry. There are several brands but the silvered bottle of Ponche Soto is probably the best known.

CHOCOLATE-FLAVOURED LIQUEURS

Chocolate, which comes from the cocoa bean (*Theobroma cacao*) was served as a drink at the court of Montezuma, the Aztec Emperor. Cortez, entertained there in the early sixteenth century, was given this *tchocolatl*, which Alexandre Dumas believed was a word from the Aztec '*choco*', meaning a noise and '*atl*' meaning water. The Aztecs would beat it up with a little whisk, not unlike a wooden swizzle stick, and put spices in it. The Spaniards took to drinking chocolate in enormous quantities, and its popularity also spread in the Old World to such an extent that ladies would have cups of chocolate brought to them in church and fashionable young women, wanting to persuade their confessors that taking chocolate did not break their fast before communion, were even reported as passing a cup of chocolate through the grill of the confessional. The expulsion of the Jews from Spain and Portugal in the sixteenth century meant that the knowledge of the use of chocolate spread to France and it became a very smart drink because Anne of Austria, wife of Louis XIII, and Maria Theresa, wife of Louis XIV, both of them Infantas, continued to drink chocolate when they married into France. The Aztecs had mixed their chocolate with maize and peppers, as well as spices, but the Spanish and French preferred sweeter additives, although they did serve chocolate mixed with cloves and cinnamon. It was credited with being vaguely aphrodisiac, and also with having therapeutic properties, being good for the digestion and against fever. Brillat-Savarin recommended drinking a pint of chocolate with ambergris, which he called 'chocolate of the afflicted', for various forms of depression, and for hangovers and weariness. Madame de Sevigné drank it as a remedy and also for pleasure, but records that a friend of hers had such a passion for it during pregnancy that she gave birth to a chocolate-brown baby! It is thus not at all surprising that chocolate has been used in alcoholic drinks from the time of its introduction to Europe. The most famous form of this type of beverage is crème de cacao, a distillate of cocoa-beans, which is sweetened; crème de cacao may be colourless or brownish.

There are a number of chocolate-flavoured liqueurs made throughout the world, including one from Mexico, actually called Chokalu. Grossman says that when the word '*Chouao*' appears on a label, this indicates that the cocoa beans have been harvested in the region of this name in Venezuela, which is supposed to produce the best in the world.

Cheri-Suisse is a Swiss liqueur, flavoured with both chocolate and cherries.

Vandermint is a Dutch chocolate liqueur with a mint flavour, sold in a bottle imitative of blue and white Delft ware.

Sabra, made in Israel, is a combination of bitter orange liqueur and Swiss bitter chocolate – a highly successful drink, handsomely presented in a vaguely eastern-style bottle. The name 'sabra' is that of the fruit of the desert cactus of Israel, but the word is also used for Jews actually born in that country – as native as the cactus.

One of the most important liqueurs based on chocolate, however, was evolved comparatively recently in England. Peter Hallgarten, son of a German lawyer who came to England and went into the wine trade, qualified as a chemist in Zurich and London, and then went into the family firm himself. Liqueurs became one of his hobbies and, as his wife was a creative cook, their kitchen became the centre of lengthy experiments. Because of his qualifications, Peter Hallgarten was able first to think of the type of liqueur he would like to make as a whole and then proceed to analyse the different ingredients and the way in which these should be combined: the order in which one element is added to another is of particular importance in this type of compounded drink. For about two years he made up various versions of a drink involving mint and chocolate and several versions of the recipe were prepared, eventually being put aside for possible use in making up ices and other sweet dishes. But when a week later one of these samples was tasted, the excellence of the drink was surprising – and this was the origin of Royal Mint-Chocolate Liqueur in 1966. It gained an almost immediate success, being publicly praised by the late H. Warner Allen, who admitted that, prior to trying it, he liked the flavour of neither chocolate nor mint – but in the form of this liqueur, the delicacy and freshness was remarkably appealing. Royal Orange-Chocolate Liqueur was produced in 1969, and subsequent liqueurs based on chocolate have been made with ginger, cherry, banana, raspberry and, in 1977, lemon.

COFFEE LIQUEURS

Drinks whose names involve the words *'café'*, *'mokka'*, *'crème de mokka'* or 'coffee' are widely made, and some of the better known will be found under other sections, according to their spirit-base: Tia Maria, Kahlúa and so on.

Bahia is a Brazilian liqueur made with coffee and based on a grain spirit.

Another liqueur, Kamok, is made by the firm of H. Vrignaud Fils, an establishment founded in 1812 at Luçon. The manufacturers stress that it is aged in oak for a considerable time and suggest that it can be served hot; chilled, as a digestive; or made into a long drink with tonic. However it is served it can be garnished with orange or possibly lemon.

Two other coffee liqueurs are made by the establishment of Liqueur Giffard, founded in 1885 at Avrillé, Angers. They make a coffee liqueur called Baska, as well as a crème de cacao.

There is an Italian coffee liqueur called Expresso, which I have not tried but which, from the American publicity (it is being promoted in the U.S.), sounds on the sweet side.

A Danish coffee liqueur, Coffee Bestle, is made by the House of Bestle; it is of very concentrated flavour and not as sweet as some of the other types of drink in this category.

As might be expected, the Turks also have evolved several coffee liqueurs, one name being marketed in the U.K. being Pasha. It comes in a flask-like copper-coloured bottle.

Irish Velvet is reported to have been made first by Joe Sheridan, while he was chef at Foynes village, on the River Shannon, in Ireland. It was here that flying-boats landed – this was in the 1930s before the building of Shannon Airport – and the passengers would be ferried from the flying-boats to the village, arriving tired and very cold. Sheridan said, practically, that these 'poor souls with shivering hands in their pockets' needed a warming drink – so he would serve a tot of Irish whiskey, plus sweet black coffee topped with an inch of thick fresh cream. Sheridan emigrated to San Francisco in 1949 and died there in 1962, but his invention is now available as a ready-mix, based on Jameson's Irish whiskey, with Brazilian coffee.

FRUIT AND HERB LIQUEURS

In many instances, a single establishment will produce a wide range of liqueurs, making use of different spices, herbs, barks and peels, and a variety of spirits as the base, often exploiting recipes that might originally have been a family formula. Such liqueurs tend to be made in regions where a variety of the basic materials are easily to be had, such as any of the fruit-growing regions or the foothills of mountains, where special herbs are plentiful and it is no problem to make a range of products, especially if the essential manufacturing procedures are the same.

In a modern liqueur distillery, visitors may often seen an enormous range of stills, blending vats, maturation casks, vats and glass vessels, through which different liqueurs pass, directed by the controls on a master switchboard. Such firms, too, may be associated in business with or even belong to the same organization as another concern primarily producing a spirit, or they may be linked with a producer or even several producers of wine. Even though they may have started by making only a few liqueurs or, indeed, only one, their range today may be so wide that the visitor may not have even heard of half the lines the establishment now produces. The scope of such a modern concern will extend far beyond the liqueurs of the original locality and, in an organization such as that of the mighty Cointreau group, which also owns the liqueur house of Regnier, as well as Bardinet Rhum, the ramifications are difficult to follow. One day, perhaps, somebody will compile a directory of the major liqueur producers of the world, and be able to comment on each one of the drinks they make. For this book I have restricted myself to the best-known lines of the major establishments with which I am familiar, although it should not be forgotten that, in most instances, firms such as Marie Brizard, Rocher, Schladerer, Cusenier, to name only a few, will make many liqueurs beyond those of which I have personal knowledge and can mention here.

Citrus liqueurs

The most important members of this group are those made with oranges. Other citrus fruits are used but, whether the sweet orange or bitter orange is used, there seems to be a particularly felicitous balance of acidity and fruit that makes the orange ideal for incorporating in recipes that are digestive and enjoyable. And among the orange liqueurs, the Curaçaos are the outstanding ones.

The name 'Curaçao' is sometimes spelt 'Curaçoa', but this is incorrect, for the first type of Curaçao was made from the dried peel of the bitter oranges growing on the island of Curaçao, off the west coast of Venezuela. This island belonged to Holland, which is the reason why so many of the Dutch liqueur establishments make Curaçao, in various forms. Many people, including the compilers of some reference books, think that Curaçao is some kind of brand name, but this is not so.

Only the peel of the bitter orange is used for the liqueur. Orange-flavoured liqueurs of this type are not invariably orange in colour; many are colourless, and Curaçaos of blue and green are also made. This is why many establishments will list their particular product as 'orange Curaçao' so as to distinguish the orange type from the colourless or other varieties. It is interesting to taste a blue or green Curaçao, but I do not know that the colour makes much difference to the flavour, if one tries to be objective; it does, of course, greatly change the appearance of a mixed drink in which Curaçao may be an ingredient. In the mid-1930s, for example, when Princess Marina of Greece married the Duke of Kent and made 'Marina blue' a fashionable colour, a special cocktail was created for the occasion, making use of blue Curaçao.

Triple sec is not a brand name either, although this is another mistake quite commonly made. It is a type of Curaçao and tends to be somewhat sweeter than the ordinary Curaçao which is usually described as *sec* or dry.

Cointreau. This is not merely the biggest name in the world of Curaçao but the most important and powerful liqueur establishment in the world. It was founded by Edouard and Adolph Cointreau at Angers in 1849; the brothers were confectioners and had begun to experiment with making use of the fruit abundant in this region of France, combined with alcohol. They also made use of the bitter orange peel arriving at the port of Nantes from the West Indies; they combined this orange peel with matured spirit, distilled the result and mixed sugar syrup and other secret ingredients into it. By the Second Empire, the growth of communications made it possible for the popular local liqueur to become better known and fifty-eight gold medals in various international exhibitions were won during this period.

In 1871, the first Edouard Cointreau retired, and was succeeded by his son, who began to advertise the product, known as 'Specialité Cointreau', in what was then a novel promotions programme. The first poster showed a pierrot in typical white costume (signifying that Cointreau was a colourless liqueur) using a lorgnette and licking the bottle of the liqueur. The poster served for the introduction of Cointreau to the United States, Russia and several other European countries, but in Britain, because the pierrot was licking the bottle, the poster, which would now certainly be a collector's piece, was not acceptable and there had to be a special one designed showing a sea lion balancing a bottle on its nose with the caption 'the well-balanced liqueur'. In the period between the two World Wars, Cointreau changed the name of their liqueur, which had originally been generally referred to as triple sec, to 'Cointreau', to differentiate it from the product of any other liqueur establishment.

Edouard Cointreau II died in 1923 and one of his heirs, André, continued the business. A big modern factory was built in the centre of Angers in 1935. On André's retirement, two of his sons and a cousin took over the business, all three of them under thirty. Today, the Cointreau establishment has a new, outstandingly modern production line housed on the outskirts of Angers and a head office in Paris and, alert to the modernization and export side of the business, as has been mentioned elsewhere, the organization now controls the gigantic organization of Bardinet and certain great *rhum* concerns in Martinique.

Cointreau really caught on in Britain when an English wine-shipper, George Glendenning, visited Bordeaux in 1902 and had his first taste of Cointreau, which impressed him so much that he went specially to Angers to meet Edouard. As the result of this meeting a firm friendship developed and eventually the Glendenning firm began to import it. But in 1923 George Glendenning informed the Cointreau family that he thought the liqueur, still made exactly according to the original recipe, was somewhat on the sweet side to please British taste (the British have always tended to like dry drinks, and had to insist on this with the majority of Champagne houses, at a time when most of this sparkling wine was definitely sweetish). So Cointreau 'extra dry for England' was produced specially for the

British market and its success resulted in the recipe for the dry version of the liqueur being followed for world sales.

Cointreau produce an enormous range of liqueurs, as they also control the establishment of Regnier. But it is Cointreau itself that is the outstanding success; after the Second World War a publicity campaign encouraged the drinking of it 'on the rocks' as an aperitive or anytime refresher as well as a liqueur, and this habit has caught on and remained. The influence of the Cointreau family is enormous and benevolent; they are remarkable ambassadors for their product and Robert Cointreau, the current head of the firm, is also much concerned with the wines of the region, which he has publicized throughout the world, in addition to the liqueur that bears his name.

The best-known mixed drink made with Cointreau is certainly the White Lady – one-third each of Cointreau, lemon juice and gin. But there are many other drinks, and it is a liqueur which can be incorporated successfully in many recipes, including those with strawberries – the flavour of orange always enhances that of strawberries – and in soufflés and pancakes. The freshness of Cointreau makes it a liqueur of which it is impossible to tire – indeed, during the sampling of many of the obscurer liqueurs involved for the research for this book, I have come to appreciate how classic and admirable a liqueur Cointreau is! (My personal recipe for a Champagne cocktail involves using a little Cointreau with the brandy.)

Other citrus liqueurs. As might be expected, there are plenty of other citrus liqueurs made around any region where citrus fruits are abundant and, as northern countries find the freshness of such drinks highly acceptable, their popularity is virtually world-wide. Many houses making liqueurs make a Curaçao and/or a triple sec, some have unusual and interesting histories.

Van der Hum is an excellent South African liqueur which was first made because the Dutch settlers at the Cape of Good Hope in the seventeenth century were able to make their own wine, but missed the liqueurs they had enjoyed at home. They especially minded being deprived of Curaçao and, as plenty of oranges were grown at the Cape, they soon evolved a satisfactory recipe using the skin of the *naartjie*. This fruit may have developed from a mandarin (so called from its yellow colour, resembling the robes of the Mandarins at the Chinese court) or tangerine (so called on account of its possible origin at Tangiers). *Hilda's Where is It?* by Hilda Gonda Duckitt, the first cookery book to be printed in South Africa (in 1891), includes a formidable recipe for a type of Van der Hum. It requires twelve bottles of brandy, twelve glasses of ship's rum, twelve glasses of orange-flower water, twenty-four tablespoonfuls of *naartjie* peel, twelve dessertspoons of cinnamon, cardamom, nutmegs, and fifty cloves. After the ingredients have infused in the brandy, sugar syrup is added and then the rum. The mixture is then returned to a cask, clarified with egg white, whisked and left standing for three weeks, when it can be bottled. The name of the drink is of uncertain origin: some think that it may have been called Van der Hum after a Dutch sea captain who liked it very much, but it is possible that the old Afrikaans expression 'Van der Hum' signifies 'Mr What's His Name' or 'Thingamajig' – because no one could remember who first made the drink. Various firms make Van der Hum commercially today, but that of Bertrams, which has been produced for over a century, is among the best known. The liqueur has a marked aromatic fragrance and is very fresh in the mouth. It is an excellent digestive.

Pimpeltjens Liqueur is a curiosity. The recipe is the property of the De Kuyper family, and the drink is mentioned as early as 1652, in the menu for a banquet celebrating the landing of the Dutch at the Cape of Good Hope – the settlement now known as Cape Town. When, in 1952, the airline K.L.M. ran a special flight to the Cape for the three hundredth anniversary, the same menu was repeated on board and De Kuyper were requested to supply the liqueur. Pimpeltjens is a secret formula but it has the definite taste of bitter oranges and might roughly be described as a type of Curaçao but with a more assertive, warming flavour. It can be drunk as a post-prandial liqueur or made into a long drink or used in many cocktails.

San Michele is a Danish liqueur made from tangerines and, as has been seen in the section devoted to aquavit, the Danes are very fond of drinks of this kind. The Copenhagen distillery in which San Michele was made for the first time was established by Marius Jensen in 1881 and San Michele was produced first in 1930. A Herr Muenden, who evolved the recipe, was a particular friend of Dr Axel Munthe, author of *The Story of San Michele* and other best-selling books that came out about this time, so San Michele was named in honour of Munthe, which is why there is a picture of his Capri house on the back label.

Grand Marnier is probably the best-known liqueur made by the firm of Marnier-Lapostolle, founded in 1827. It was produced by Monsieur Marnier-Lapostolle for the first time in 1880 and there are two varieties: Cordon Rouge and Cordon Jaune; the yellow one, as with many paired liqueurs of this kind, being slightly lower in alcoholic strength than the Cordon Rouge. The thing that is also different about Grand Marnier Cordon Rouge is that the spirit on which it is based and in which the bitter orange peel is steeped is Cognac, not just brandy. It is therefore like Cognac, with agreeable overtones of orange. The Cordon Jaune is lighter and less definite in style.

Mandarine Napoleon is a mixture of distillate of Andalusian tangerines and old Cognac, the type of tangerine used being a rare one. The skins of the fruit are soaked in grape brandy before being distilled and eventually blended with the Cognac. This liqueur is made by the Fourcroy establishment of Brussels, who took over the original formula from a small Belgian family company; the liqueur gets its name because, it is said, 'Mandarine' was the liqueur served at the end of the intimate suppers given by Napoleon I to the theatrical star of the day, Mlle Mars. The drink began to be referred to as 'Mandarine Napoleon' after Napoleon's death and remains so to this day. It is a pleasant drink, although slightly softer in style than some of the Curaçaos.

Aurum is made at Pescara in Italy, from herbs and oranges grown in the Abruzzi mountains. It is a deepish orange-gold and the name obviously refers to the golden colour, rather than a variety of the lily, which I have known people assume was its base.

Australia makes several orange liqueurs, the best known probably being Marnique, which is based on quinces, but definitely tastes as if oranges were the main ingredient.

Forbidden Fruit is made in the United States from the shaddoc, a variety of grapefruit, with oranges and honey included in the recipe. The Del Monico restaurant in New York first popularized it, describing it as 'nectar of the gods – forbidden to man'.

There are several German and Dutch liqueurs, notably Pomeranzen, originally made in Latvia and the Baltic States, and so called because of the type of orange used, while the fruit is still green. King Edward VII is supposed to have liked it. Nowadays it may be described as a type of Curaçao. Other German and Dutch liqueurs are called respectively Halb und Halb and Half om Half. They are a combination of orange Curaçao and orange bitters.

In Corsica, a type of digestive liqueur known as Cédratine is made from the sweet lemon, and Kitron, a distillate of brandy with lemon leaves, is a Greek citrus liqueur. Mersin, named for a port in the south-east of Turkey, is a type of triple sec. Filfar, a really fine orange liqueur, is a Cyprus recipe, originally made at Famagusta, being distilled from the local oranges. It gets its name from 'Fillipo Fecit', because it is a family recipe that the present Mr Fillipo went to register – and the clerk taking down the words made the mistake. The grandfather of Mr Fillipo used to take the liqueur on fishing trips and the refreshing quality of the drink is marked.

Cherry liqueurs

Liqueurs with a predominant cherry flavour should not be confused with the distillates of cherry which are 'white alcohols' (see page 309). The name used for the former type of drink, however, is usually 'cherry brandy' and most of the main continental houses market a liqueur of this kind. It is surprising, if one is able to taste a variety of these cherry liqueurs, how great the difference can be between them; the late Allan Sichel – who, more than anyone else, taught me about wine – was particularly proud of the way in which, at one of the 'blind' tastings held by his particular tasting group, he was able to identify the brands of thirteen different cherry brandies. Many years later, I made a comparison of some of these for my own interest – and indeed, each one was quite distinctive. The type of cherries used and the exact method by which the liqueur is produced is of course the reason for this.

In Britain, cherry brandy is definitely a traditional drink. Many nineteenth-century memoirs bear this out and guests invited to a shoot at country house parties would put their silver flasks out in the hall the night before a beat, for these to be filled with cherry brandy. The fruity character of the drink, plus its warming qualities made it a natural for such occasions. Cherry brandy also seems to have been popular with officers in the Royal Navy – maybe the circumstance of it being made in quantity along the south coast of England, near many ports, can account for this. Anyhow, on 11 September 1805, Lord Nelson, sailing for the Mediterranean on what was to be his last battle (Trafalgar), issued a last-minute order for more wines and spirits for the officers of the *Victory*, which included five dozen of 'Cherry Brandy'. (The order, which, it must be remembered, would have been additional to the stores already on board, consists of the rather strange assortment of five dozen each of gin and 'plain Brandy', twelve dozen each of 'Vin de Grave' and claret, a mere three dozen of 'Champagne' and fifty dozen each of port and sherry.) The cherry brandy could have been a warming tot on a cold day or night. Even so, and even bearing in mind that the Admiral would have expected to do a fair amount of entertaining of the officers from the other thirty-three ships of the fleet, these quantities alone seem generous allowances for a mess which, at that time, consisted of about sixty-five men, although of course the bottles of the time were smaller than those used now.

Cherry brandy was also much used to make up punch, still a favourite in Victorian England, although it was possibly better known in the early days of the nineteenth century. Of course, cherry brandy can be made in a simple way, as sloe gin is made, by simply steeping cherries in brandy, but more complex and scientific methods are used by firms producing these drinks commercially.

British cherry brandies. The most famous establishment producing cherry brandy in Britain is probably that of Thos. Grant & Sons of Maidstone. The firm was established at Dover in 1774, but moved to Maidstone in 1853, because part of the cliff behind the distillery suffered damage in an unusual way; the autumn of 1852 was particularly wet and the chalk cliff (part of the 'white cliffs of Dover') absorbed a lot of the water. In the following December and January the sharp frosts actually cracked the cliff, parts of which began to fall. A huge chunk of cliff sticking out over the distillery itself began to show signs of a crack and, with both the police and the military having been called in to move families and property to safety, this crack widened and the cliff fell like an avalanche in the early hours of 20 January 1853. No lives were lost and Thomas Grant, who had become the owner of the business in 1847, was fortunate in that, although his garden was destroyed, his house was intact. The distillery itself was destroyed.

It was this Thomas Grant who originated 'Grant's Morella cherry brandy', using the local Kentish Morella cherries for the purpose. This cherry, the firm's publicity asserts, is different from the generally known Morello, and grows only on small trees, thriving particularly on a very narrow strip of land in Kent. The slogan 'Welcome always, keep it handy, Grant's Morella cherry brandy' is an early example of a highly successful advertising jingle. The cherry brandy became enormously popular and was enjoyed by Queen Victoria. When I tasted it, I noted its particular fruitiness without any trace of cloying sweetness. The firm of Grant continued to flourish and in 1960 the Maidstone premises were acquired by Rawlings & Sons Ltd, which were eventually to be taken over by the Luis Gordon group.

Ross of Leith, another family concern, who have been in business for four generations, make their cherry brandy from French brandy and English cherries. This is rather light in colour and the flavour is seriously and interestingly herby.

The firm of James Hawker of Plymouth, first established in 1808, make a cherry brandy that is very bright red in colour and pronouncedly fruity in taste.

Peter Heering's liqueur. The Danish cherry brandy commonly known as Cherry Heering has recently had its name changed by the Copenhagen firm to Peter Heering's Liqueur, because they consider that this very well-known cherry brandy deserves being distinguished by the name of Peter F. Heering, their founder.

Peter Frederick Husfuhm Heering was born at the beginning of the nineteenth century and, leaving home at the age of fourteen, was apprenticed to a grocer. He not only worked well, but seems to have been on friendly terms with his master, because he remained with him for two years after finishing his apprenticeship, and then served a short spell with a merchant on the island of Christianshaven. Danish housewives, like their sisters elsewhere, made maximum use of such local fruits and berries as were available to produce drinks for the home and Peter Heering's first master's wife was able to give him her own recipe for a cherry liqueur. When he set up in business on his own in Copenhagen in 1818, he began to make up her recipe and sell it in his shop, where it became extremely popular with the seafaring men who were among the regular customers. One of these was a naval officer who, finding the drink liked by his guests in the West Indies, set up in business there, acting as Peter Heering's first agent.

But Peter Heering's interests were diverse. In 1833 he built his first ship and eventually owned a fleet of ten. In 1838 he bought a large house on Christianshaven's Canal which was used for trade in all kinds of goods – cheese, ham, butter and a variety of provender, plus, of course, the cherry liqueur – and moved to live there in the same year. The liqueur went on increasing in popularity; it was first exported to London in 1836.

The Heering establishment at Christianshaven's Canal, a beautiful house, with an elegant, gabled façade and finely proportioned courtyard, became not merely the business premises but the home for most members of the Heering family and even some of the employees; both family and premises saw much activity. The first Peter Heering died in 1875 and was succeeded by his son, also a Peter Heering. In 1978 the firm moved their administration from the original Heering mansion to the distillery at Dalby, about forty miles south of Copenhagen. The house with its museum of casks and presses had been a famous place to visit, but had become impractical as business headquarters. Even today the firm is very much a family concern, and the establishment now makes many different liqueurs. They still, however, stress the cherry liqueur for which they are perhaps best known and own cherry orchards at Dalby; it is important to them that the locally grown cherries at the plantation at Dalby are used. The finished drink is matured in gigantic oak casks, some of them beautifully decorated, and extremely old. Peter Heering's Cherry Liqueur is a very dark red in colour, extremely smooth and fruity and the taste is definite and concentrated, with a delightfully fresh, uncloying finish.

Other cherry brandies. Cherry Bestle is made by the House of Bestle from the Stevnsbaerret cherry, grown only in certain chalky soils in Denmark and particularly around the east coast of Sjelland. Both the variety of the cherry and the climate achieve the particular balance of fruit and acidity in the cherry. George Bestle, established in Copenhagen in 1730, have their own plantations and processing plant for cherries. From these they make both the liqueur Cherry Bestle and the 'wine' Cherry Dana. Both are matured in oak for several years before being bottled and offered for sale. Cherry Dana is described as a cherry wine, and is a fortified drink, to be drunk either as an aperitive or a liqueur. Cherry wine is traditional in Denmark and may therefore be described as a country wine; the fermentation of pressed cherries is stopped by the addition of spirit. As the stones of the cherries are crushed together with the fruit, there is a pleasantly almond-like flavour in the resulting drink. The stones are removed from the mash of fruit before fermentation is complete. Therefore, if the generally accepted definition of the word 'wine' as being 'made from the juice of freshly gathered grapes' (in this instance, cherries) is accepted, this is not precisely cherry wine.

In Holland, both Lucas Bols and De Kuyper make cherry brandy, De Kuyper using dry Dalmatian (Yugoslavian) cherries, imported in wooden casks, which are then kept in cold storage in Rotterdam. These cherries, which are used for a number of other European cherry brandies, are dried in the sun.

The House of Marnier-Lapostolle make Cherry Marnier, also from Dalmatian cherries, which are pressed and macerated in specially selected *eau de vie*. The firm of Dolfi make a cherry brandy which is very dark in colour and distinctive in both its aroma and taste. Cusenier's cherry brandy is made from both red cherries and the black type. The red, described as 'English' cherries, come from either Burgundy or the outskirts of Paris and provide a great deal of juice although they are high in acidity. The black cherries come from Alsace, the Massif Central or the Alps, and are fleshy and sweet. They are combined to make two different infusions which are subsequently blended for the ultimate cherry brandy. Guignolet, the French name for a type of cherry, is a speciality of the region around Angers in the Loire. Many liqueur houses produce a guignolet.

Around 1700, Joseph Rocher, living in the Rhône Valley at La Côte St André, began to make up special preparations of the local fruits in brandy. The region was and is famous for its cherries, peaches, apricots and table grapes. The Rocher fruits in brandy were presented to the King and, in 1763, a record in the archives of the City of Grenoble acknowledges – with a substantial payment – 'the annual present of honour', consisting of 100 pots of Liqueur Rocher, which had been sent to the Duc d'Orléans, at that time governor of the province. Rocher liqueurs of various kinds began to be highly successful. One early label is of one called Elixir Végétal d' Esculape. In 1889 the then head of the establishment – still a family concern – became one of the jury judging French and other liqueurs, which meant that those of Rocher had to remain *hors concours*. The range produced today is still a wide one, but possibly the cherry brandy is the most famous.

Maraschino. This is another cherry liqueur, although many people who associate it purely with making the traditional English pudding, trifle, might be surprised to learn this. It is made from a distillate of the type of cherry known as Maraschino, in which the kernels are also crushed. The best-known brand on the U.K. market is Drioli: this firm has been in production for over 200 years and their maraschino has always been put up in a four-sided bottle, partly covered with straw. The cherries used for making this type of liqueur come from Dalmatia where the Amarasca variety has been found particularly suitable; since the eighteenth century, Dalmatian maraschino has been famous, the senate at Venice having established a monopoly for it. The Drioli firm now make the liqueur in Venice. Dolfi makes another good maraschino and so do other firms. Luxardo maraschino was first made by Girolamo Luxardo in 1821 at Zara (the firm moved to Padua after the factory was destroyed in 1943). Girolamo introduced the double distillation process for his maraschino: the bottles are now, as then, green glass with plaited straw covers. Maraschino is a cherry liqueur, not an *alcool blanc* (see page 309), because it does in fact receive added sweetening and agents to enhance its bouquet – sniff it side by side with kirsch and you will see the difference.

In this section may be included Sakura Cherry Blossom liqueur, which, I am told, is made by macerating cherry blossoms in neutral spirit. It is produced by the giant Japanese establishment of Suntory (whose beer dominates the Japanese market) and, on the one occasion when I tasted the prettily pink drink, I found it sweetish and rather indeterminate in flavour.

The U.S. Cherry Karise, made by Leroux, is another cherry spirit, but I have no personal experience of it.

Calvados and applejack

Calvados is apple brandy, which of course can be made wherever apples are extensively cultivated, but Calvados itself is peculiar to Normandy. The name is supposed to derive from one of the Spanish Armada vessels, the *Calvador*; this word, in Spanish, means 'the dis-master', implying that the ship was capable of defeating all its adversaries. Unfortunately, it no more justified its name than the 'invincible' Armada itself and, eventually, was wrecked off the Normandy coast. Cider has been made in Normandy for many centuries and a distillate produced from it, but the word 'Calvados' and the Région de Calvados really only came into use in the nineteenth century after the French Revolution.

Apples were cultivated in Normandy at least from the twelfth century and, in 1553, in the north Cotentin, the Sieur de Gouberville received a visit from a native of Touraine, who aroused his interest by describing the way in which distillates of fruit were made in this area of the Loire. So it was that, at Mesnil-au-Val, the Sieur de Gouberville got the blacksmith to construct a still and began to make brandy from apples.

The Calvados makers are proud of their traditions and, in past times, a seven-year apprenticeship was required for anyone to qualify as a distiller; the trainees were kept strictly under control, being forbidden to swear, to let their nails grow long or to wear short stockings, on pain of various penalties. Since 1946 the production of Calvados has been controlled by the Institut National des Appellations d'Origine and the stamp of the Institut (usually known by its initials as I.N.A.O.) must be acquired before it can be sold; in addition, the Bureau National Interprofessional des Calvados et Eaux de Vie de Cidre et de Poires (B.N.I.C.E.), plays a supervisory role in its production, as well as negotiating both national and international markets.

Calvados is distilled from a mash of apples, fermented with yeast. It must not be confused with Eaux de Vie de Cidre, which is a spirit made by distilling cider; this last is rarely found, unless you are in a rural part of Normandy. For Calvados, both the pulp and the juices of the apples are used for the distillate. Calvados is distilled twice, after which it is matured in oak for between six and ten years. It has to be submitted to a tasting committee who will issue the certificate of quality that allows it to be sold. Calvados of the Vallée d' Auge has its own A.O.C.

Calvados, of which there are many reputable brands on sale, is still very much a product of the farm and the visitor to Normandy may well find a home-made Calvados in some of the farms and private estates. The traditional way of drinking it, apart from using it as a digestive at the end of a meal, is the *trou normand*, the word 'hole' meaning the service of the spirit in the middle of a large meal, very much as the sorbet was used in Britain in former times. Normandy food, particularly rich in cream and butter, makes the need for a digestive of this kind all the more important and this region, strong in traditions, has another one of making celebration meals last for several days; the classic example of this is the wedding feast in Flaubert's novel *Madame Bovary* where the meal on the first day lasted for sixteen hours and the whole affair continued for several days.

The North American region of New England, being good apple country, has also made cider and a distillate of apples since early times. American writers refer to it as both applejack and Apple Jack. It seems to be made in various ways, generally being the product of a double distillation in a pot still, although continuous stills are in use. The distillate is brought down to a lower strength with water, after which it is aged in oak casks for up to five years. Obviously, the product of the pot still will have greater individuality, but the maturation in wood will give the spirit any colour it may ultimately possess. I have heard of a type of applejack, made on farms, where the cider is frozen, the coating of ice removed, the remaining liquid providing the refreshment – a sort of 'ice wine' of cider and a most interesting link with the way in which the Chinese are reported to have extracted alcohol by freezing 'wine' or fermented liquors in ancient times.

Cassis

Cassis has nothing to do with the town of that name in the south of France. The word '*cassis*' signifies the blackcurrant, from which cassis liqueur is made. This fruit, rich in Vitamin C, is cultivated in many regions, especially eastern Europe, where blackcurrant syrups feature in many recipes and doubtless provide a valuable addition to a diet that can be deficient in fresh fruit and vegetables. These days the idea of 'blackcurrant tea' for a sore throat or a cold may seem 'folksy', but it was routine in my nursery, and blackcurrant jelly was made regularly to ensure adequate supplies for this use in the winter.

Although blackcurrant liqueurs are probably made in many countries, it is the cassis of Burgundy that is the most famous. The blackcurrant bush may have been planted by the various religious on account of its healthful properties. The blackcurrant is a sturdy shrub, able to withstand quite low temperatures – indeed, it needs a cold winter so as to give of its best – so it is well suited to the exposed slopes around Dijon. The type of blackcurrant now grown in this area is either the Noir de Bourgogne, or the Royal de Naples.

The obvious and delectable fragrance of the blackcurrant leaves must have been known since the bush was first planted. In the first written record of the name cassis (*Ribes nigrum*) – it is mentioned by Jacques de Fouilloux in 1561 in a treatise on hunting – Fouilloux recommends a solution of six plants and a handful of leaves from 'a little shrub called cassis' for a remedy against viper bites for both hounds and men. In 1712 the Abbé Bailly de Montavand, writing at Bordeaux, praised the liqueur which, at that date, seems to have been made mainly for medicinal purposes, as efficaceous against fevers and plague, and for worming both adults and children.

In the eighteenth century the making of cassis was primarily a home craft but, in the middle of the nineteenth century, several establishments began to produce it commercially and, in 1923, cassis received an *appellation contrôlée*, defining where it may be made, with further legislation determining that only cassis with a minimum strength of 15° and a certain sugar content was entitled to the description 'crème de cassis'. In addition to being a liqueur, it is widely used today to flavour dishes, pour over ices, fill sweets and chocolates.

The best-known names of cassis on export markets are probably those of l'Héritier Guyot, Védrenne Père et Fils, Boudier and Lejay Lagoute, but many firms make the liqueur, including a number whose blackcurrant liqueur will not be 'Cassis de Dijon' and will, therefore, be slightly different in style.

The fully ripe blackcurrants are usually gathered at the beginning of July and then, after being cleaned, macerated in vats – formerly of oak but today more likely to be stainless steel. This takes around two months, during which time the fruit conveys its flavour to the molasses spirits in which it lies. Then the juice is squeezed out and thoroughly mixed with sugar prior to being distilled; the fruity debris left behind must also, by law, be distilled. After the alcohol content, the sugar and the over-all quality are adjudged to be adequate, the cassis is ready to be bottled. Many firms will make several different strengths of cassis, as low as 14° for the more ordinary uses, 15° or over for crème de cassis and 20° for what Védrenne term their 'supercassis' and some firms call 'double crème'; Védrenne also make one as strong as 25° but of course the high spirit duty that cassis has to pay puts a liqueur of this strength at a disadvantage in the U.K. market. The higher strength is obtained by allowing the blackcurrants to steep for a longer time. Interestingly, Trénel, of Charnay-lès-Mâcon, put a vintage date on their cassis because, they state, with time the colour declines and the spirit 'eats' the fruit – although the liqueur may be perfectly drinkable it will not be as enjoyable as when young.

Boudier list the things to look for in an appraisal of cassis: the colour should be red-purple not brownish-red, which signifies that the cassis is old. The cassis should flow thickly, sticking to the side of the glass – the thicker the liquid, the richer in fruit the cassis. Finally, it should be a balanced liqueur, the alcohol and the fruit proportioned to each other. But the term 'Liqueur de cassis' can only refer to a drink resulting from 'sugar or glucose added to blackcurrants macerated in brandy' and it is worth checking a label to make sure that this is what is in the bottle, should something very cheap or a 'bargain' tempt a purchaser.

The drink most associated with cassis is the Burgundy aperitive, *vin blanc cassis*. This essentially is a portion of cassis topped up with Bourgogne Aligoté dry white wine; Burgundians often recommend proportions of one to five or even four, but I think this is too strong for a preprandial refresher – a good teaspoonful in a generous glass is enough to give a peony-pink drink that has just a slight 'kick' (blackcurrant syrup is not an acceptable substitute ever). Cassis can be the base for a drink known in Burgundy as a *'rince cochon'* but which the Dijonnais called *'un Nikita'* on the occasion of Mr Khrushchev's visit: the cassis is topped up with chilled young

Beaujolais and the drink is brilliant red. But cassis can be topped up with dry vermouth, Chambéry vermouth, half and half dry and sweet vermouth, and any fairly robust dry white wine, still or spar- kling – when used with Champagne the result is called a Kir Royale. Indeed, *vin blanc cassis* is now widely known as *un kir* (even when it isn't made with cassis at all as the base, but some other fruit liqueur). The 'Kir' part of the name is that of the late Canon Félix Kir, a tiny little man who was Mayor of Dijon and a hero of the Resistance during the Second World War; he loved all the Burgundian good things of life.

There have been attempts to popularize *vin blanc cassis* in a ready-mixed version, but, as always, I prefer to make my own mixtures. The essentials are: good cassis (not necessarily the strongest), a robust white wine and a fair-sized glass.

Other fruit liqueurs

Vast numbers of different fruit liqueurs are made, some particularly successful ones being flavoured with apricots. The Apry of Marie Brizard and Abricotine of Garnier and the apricot brandy of Cusenier are widely known. Cusenier make theirs from the 'Muscat' apricots that are cultivated in the Roussillon, an infusion of the fruit being mixed with Fine Champagne Cognac. Cusenier also make a peach brandy from peaches from the Rhône Valley, the Alps and the Cévennes – the fruit is a cross between a peach and apricot and this, too, is finally blended with Fine Champagne Cognac. For their Prunellia, plums and other fruits, mainly greengages and sloes from eastern France are used.

Many liqueurs are made from berries, especially in the Scandi-navian countries, where cranberries, rowanberries and others are plentiful. The Finnish Suomuurain, made from cloudberries, is worth trying on the spot. Other liqueur houses make blackberry brandy, and in Corfu there is a liqueur made from the cumquat. I suppose there is no reason why any fruit shouldn't be used to flavour some kind of liqueur, although obviously much depends on the quality of the fruit, the other ingredients and the spirit, plus the methods used. It should be borne in mind that many drinks are delicious when one tries them on holiday, but are not necessarily as impressively enjoyable back home; I have drunk quantities of boukha, the Tunisian fig liqueur, when on the spot, but I don't think that it is a commercial proposition outside its homeland.

Amaretto di Saronno is a comparatively recent arrival in the U.K., but at the time when it was introduced to Britain it was the top-selling liqueur in Italy and number three in the U.S. It is made by I.L.L.V.A., at Saronno, near Lake Como, which is run by the Reina family, its present chairman being Signora Costanza Monte Reina. The Reina family have their coat of arms in a sanctuary to the Madonna dei Miracoli built outside Saronno in the Middle Ages. This small building was erected in 1460 and in 1525 Bernardini Luini was commissioned to decorate it with frescoes. While the painter was producing the work – a fresco which depicts the Madonna showing the Infant Christ to the three kings – he stayed at the local inn, run by a young widow with two children, whose face he used as a model for the Madonna. The young woman was delighted with the compliment paid her and, indeed, the face is that of a beautiful, serene person. As a reward, the model made the painter a special present, a drink made up by herself from almonds and apricots out of her garden, which she had infused with the local 'Acquardenza'. She put the drink in Luini's room on Christmas Eve as a present for the next day. Amaretto di Saronno is a pleasantly fruity drink which can be successfully incorporated in many fruit and sweet recipes.

Southern Comfort is an American drink, described as 'a unique American spirit, 87·7° proof, flavoured with oranges, peaches and other exotic fruits and herbs'. The recipe is said to run for over a hundred pages, but it is guarded by the Fowler family, in whose possession it has remained for three generations. The publicity material describes how, in 'the greatest days of the Old South', a gentleman of New Orleans chose to 'smooth his spirits' with other rare and delicious ingredients, because he found that even the finest whiskeys were then more to his taste. Because Southern Comfort is the subject of negotiations as to how it should be described in both the U.S. and U.K., this is all I can find out about it, but it is enormously popular. In the U.S., sales exceed a million cases a year, and it is marketed in many other countries. When it was introduced into Britain, the sales astounded even the distributors; in many pubs, Southern Comfort began to outsell Scotch or gin. The fruity flavour particularly appealed to young drinkers, and the way in which it can be pleasantly combined with non-alcoholic additives, such as fizzy fruit-flavoured drinks, has added to its attractions. It appealed very much to the critical palates of the British gastronomic press when they first tasted it, and in the U.K. it is a classless and widely enjoyed new drink.

A drink I understand to be a popular cocktail, in addition to the dilution of Southern Comfort with fresh orange juice or white wine, is a Teul: this consists of half and half Southern Comfort and white Tequila, shaken over ice. The combination is certainly agreeable, albeit powerful. (Many otherwise reliable reference books state that Southern Comfort is based on Bourbon whiskey – the distributors assure me that this is incorrect.)

Both pineapple and banana have been used as a basis for liqueurs, but the rather aggressive flavour of the pineapple seems to be a disadvantage. Banana liqueurs, although almost as aggressively flavoured, seem to me to be more successful, but my experience is limited. Bardinet's Banadry seems satisfactory, although one would probably not want to drink it very often.

Anise-flavoured liqueurs

Anise (*Pimpinella anisum*) is a herb bearing small, hard, greyish-brown fruits, which are extremely aromatic. This form of anise belongs to the *umbelliferae*, or hemlock family and is completely different from the star anise (*Illicium verum*), which is a tree belonging to the magnolia family, native to south-west China.

Anise has long been esteemed for flavouring. It was known to the ancient Egyptians, who were using it as early as 1500 B.C., and the Greeks particularly esteemed Cretan anise. Hippocrates prescribed it for coughs. Pliny recommended it for bad breath. He also liked it as a flavouring agent in sauces and recorded its use in seed form sprinkled on bread. Virgil's poem 'The Salad' includes it as 'bundl'd anise' and its use to spice cakes is supposed to be the origin of the modern wedding cake – the type of sweetmeat which was given as a concentrated form of nourishment to bride and groom and distributed among the guests.

Anise had many different uses: St Isidore, Archbishop of Seville, praised its versatility in the seventh century and, in the ninth, the Emperor Charlemagne ordered its cultivation at his farms in Germany. Albertus Magnus and many other medieval writers make mention of it, sometimes using the name 'Roman fennel'; it was so prized in England that in 1305 it became subject to tax at London Bridge where it was imported; but it began to be cultivated in Britain and King Edward IV had all his linen scented with it. It was reputedly efficacious against the evil eye, 'the sword of a magician should be bathed in the blood of a mole and juice of Pimpinella'; horses 'suffering from nightmares' were recommended balls (pills) of aniseed, liquorice and garlic by the seventeenth-century writer Gervaise Markham. The sixteenth-century herbalist recommended it as 'good against belchings and upbraidings of the stomacke'. The first settlers in North America took cuttings of anise with them and it is now cultivated extensively there, although even now some herbalists consider that the aniseed of Alicante is superior to any.

Marie Brizard. Although liqueurs had been made throughout France since early times, the French liqueur business, as a commercial operation, virtually begins with the career of Marie Brizard, one of fifteen children born to Pierre Brizard, a carpenter, in the parish of Sainte-Croix, Bordeaux, in 1714. Marie (she had two other sisters of the same name) was the third child and from an early age felt drawn to charitable work, looking after the poor, sick and indigent; the port of Bordeaux was enjoying a boom period, but infections and epidemics came in as well as trade and Marie was kept busy. One of her patients was a West African native, who, in gratitude, gave her the recipe for a particular drink which he asserted could cure many stomach complaints and also act as a preventive. The basis of this was anise. Marie Brizard followed the recipe and gave it to many of her patients who were extremely appreciative. Soon she received so many orders for the liqueur that she had to engage a book-keeper to look after her accounts and actually founded her firm in 1755. She made the first stocks of her anisette in her own kitchen. In 1762 she had to move to larger premises, and took into partnership Jean-Baptiste Roger, son of a jobbing tailor. The firm was registered as Marie Brizard et Roger and the business association was increased by Roger marrying Marie's niece, Anne Brizard. Marie herself, according to a portrait taken in 1755, was a beautiful and striking woman.

The then Governor of Bordeaux was the Duc de Richelieu. This man, able in many ways, was virtually a satyr and seems to have gone in for quantity rather than quality as regards his conquests of women. Anything that he ate, drank or used was automatically smart (and might even be considered as tonic and aphrodisiac), so that after Marie Brizard had introduced the liqueur to him it became sought after in markets far remote from Bordeaux. The firm's liqueurs were sent to Senegal, West Indies, Canada, all parts of the Americas, India and South Africa and their commercial successes encouraged the evolution of other types of liqueur. Marie Brizard risked ruin in the French Revolution and was saved by a priest to whom she had given refuge; when his pursuers caught up with him in her house, he saved both himself and her by pretending that they were having a heavy drinking session. In 1796, Marie handed over the business to her niece, Anne, now widowed. In 1804, Anne's son, Jean Baptiste Augustin Roger, was in serious trouble with the sinister Fouché and his secret police, who believed that the firm were using their business to cover up dealings with England; although Roger escaped the guillotine, the firm went through a bad period and Roger's brothers, one of them devoted to butterflies, the other to water-colours, were of little help; fortunately their fortunes revived and today the firm is still a family business, the present installation being one of the most modern in Bordeaux, progressive in every way.

The anisette of Marie Brizard remains the firm's most famous product and it is distinctive in character. The firm recommend as a refreshing anytime drink: the juice of half a lemon, one quarter of anisette to three quarters of soda, the whole poured over ice, which they call Sol-y-Sombra.

Other liqueurs flavoured with anise. Many (indeed most) French liqueur houses make an anise liqueur and this flavour is used in liqueurs throughout the world. Two French examples that may be fairly widely seen are Oxygénée, and La Tintaine; La Tintaine has a sprig of fennel in the bottle and its name refers to the quintain, a target against which jousters would practise in medieval times: if their lance did not hit the quintain in the middle, it would swing round and deliver them a blow or even knock them off their horse.

An anise liqueur made in Portugal is called Escarchado, and there are sugar crystals in the bottle. In Spain, the most famous anise-flavoured liqueur is Anise del Mono, made in Barcelona, which is available in both dry and sweet types. There is also the Italian Elixir di China, which is on the sweet side. Anesone is a high-strength anise and liquorice-based liqueur which is made in both Italy and the U.S., and I have found a reference to one called Tres Castillos, which is made in Puerto Rico.

Caraway liqueurs

Caraway (*Carum carvi*) is widely grown, in Europe, Siberia, North Persia and the Himalayas. The so-called 'seeds' are actually the fruits and both they, the oil that they contain, and the leaves of the plant have been in use for thousands of years. The Arabs are supposed to have been the first users of caraway on a large scale, the Arabic name for the seeds being '*karawya*'. There is a mention of it as a remedy for flatulence in an Egyptian papyrus dating from about 1500 B.C., and the Greek doctors in classical times thought it helpful for young women suffering from anaemia. Herbals relate that caraway seeds improve the sight, and they are said to be efficacious in preventing theft, because anything that contains caraway seeds would hold captive the would-be purloiner until the true owner of the object could come and claim it. Caraway seeds were supposed to be efficacious against fickleness in love and also able to prevent pigeons straying – even today, there are reports that some pigeon fanciers keep a caraway loaf in their pigeon loft.

The most famous reference to caraway is possibly that in Shakespeare's *Henry IV*, where Justice Shallow invites Falstaff to share 'a pippin with a dish of caraways'; apples baked and accompanied by caraways were served at Trinity College, Cambridge, and at certain livery dinners in London until the Second World War. In many parts of Europe, and particularly in Jewish communities, caraway is incorporated in bread, or used as a decoration on the crust. In the form of seed-cake it was popular in the nineteenth and early twentieth centuries, although there must be many like myself who could never acquire a taste for it and think of it as 'toe-nail cake' in the language of the schoolroom. Caraway seeds are also often provided for serving with cheese, in salads, and dishes such as goulash and many soups and vegetable recipes from central and eastern Europe, and from Scandinavia.

But the medicinal properties of caraway, since its being recommended by Dioscorides and Galen, are probably even more numerous. The herbalist Parkinson recommends it for 'winde' in 'Tragas ... Dredges that are taken for the cold and winde in the body', a curious use of the more elegant French word '*dragée*'. To this day, caraway, in the form of gripe-water, is still used to 'wind' babies.

I have found an interesting comment by Marghanita Laski that *kümmel*, according to the Oxford English Dictionary, is flavoured with cumin (she spells it 'cummin'), which is *Cuminum cyminum* and not caraway. But although cumin is certainly a plant highly regarded by herbalists and is cultivated by drying the seeds, like caraway, contemporary herbalists and reputable writers on liqueurs indicate that cumin, which is more aggressively flavoured than caraway, is not the usual herb involved with making kümmel.

Commercial kümmels. The first commercial caraway liqueur seems to have been made by Lucas Bols in 1575; the Bols family had a small business, just outside the city walls of Amsterdam (see page 88). Bols made a commercial attraction out of their location: the business, called 'the little shed', or '*t Lootsje* in Dutch, began to be frequented by people walking out from Amsterdam with earthenware jars, which they would have filled up with either the gin or various liqueurs of the Bols concern. The direct line of the Bols family came to an end in 1815, when the firm's name was changed to Ervan Lucas Bols, the first word meaning heirs.

When, in 1696, Peter the Great came to Amsterdam to learn about ships and worked in the yards there, he too visited the Bols Distillery and therefore it is probable that he brought kümmel to Russia when he went back. The Dutch distillers at this time were enjoying the increased supplies of all kinds of herbs, seeds, barks, berries and fruits resulting from their trade with the New World, and their products were much in demand because the importation of table wines and brandy from France was considerably restricted and at times prevented.

Caraway liqueurs were subsequently made in a number of countries, but in the early nineteenth century the Allasch estate, belonging to the family of Blankenhagen, at Labura in Latvia, whose brand name became Mentzendorff, began to make this liqueur with particular success. The Blankenhagens were obliged to leave Latvia at the end of the First World War, but their London agents, Mentzendorff, managed to continue the production of Allasch Kümmel in Germany, and now in Holland, and it still remains an important quality brand.

The Wolfschmidt distillery was established at Riga, also in Latvia, in 1847, and began to make several different varieties of caraway liqueur, one in competition with the Allasch kümmel, and another, Crème de Cumin, of special quality, which was bottled in clear glass, the punt or hollow in the base of the bottle having a point on it inside, so that crystals of sugar would form and 'there appeared to be a little snow mountain in the bottom of the bottle'. This description of the kümmel was written by Mary Fisher, whose father, Maurice Meyer, who had set up in the wine and spirits business in London in 1869, became the British agent for Wolfschmidt.

Maurice Meyer had been the first person to bring vodka and vermouth to Britain on a commercial scale and Mary, who joined the firm in 1909, travelled widely, getting other agencies and developing a sideline that was promotionally valuable as a lecturer and teacher. She began to specialize in liqueurs and, even as an old woman, would undertake schedules of travelling and speaking that sounded exhausting to me; in 1951 she published a book on liqueurs, written with great individuality and authority and, in 1959, she celebrated the ninety years of the firm of Maurice Meyer being in business, her eightieth birthday and her fiftieth year in the wine trade.

Today there are many producers of kümmel, although it remains something of a speciality in Holland, where big distilleries all make a type of their own. As well as Lucas Bols, the Fockink distillery makes a good kümmel. In Denmark, the Danish liqueur C.L.O.C. is flavoured with caraway, but not to quite such a pronounced degree as in the Dutch version. The initials mean *Cumin Liquidum Optimum Castelli*: 'the best caraway in the castles'.

Danziger Goldwasser is flavoured with both aniseed and caraway and the Der Lachs firm has been making it since 1598. 'Lachs' is the word for salmon, hence the picture of the fish on the label. The inclusion of flakes of gold in the ingredients is probably to do with the long-held belief that gold has life-giving properties, something that is certainly associated in medieval times with various magic potions: gold dust or gold leaf used on food made it special, enhancing the supposed properties as well as the eye appeal – hence the gilt being on or off the gingerbread. The gold flecks in Danziger Goldwasser can be seen, as in the old fashioned snow-storm like paperweights, when the bottle is shaken. Today the liqueur is made in West Berlin. The distillery also produces a Silberwasser (silver water) version.

Mint liqueurs

There are various types of mint, the three most important probably being spearmint, peppermint and pennyroyal. It is spearmint that is mostly used in cooking; peppermint is mainly the source of peppermint oil, obtained by distillation, and widely used in sweets and also for indigestion remedies. The name comes from Menthe, a nymph beloved by Pluto who was turned into the herb by his jealous wife, Proserpine. Because of this, Greek brides would wear wreaths composed of mint and verbena, although later the myrtle, dedicated to Venus, superseded the earlier type.

The fresh aroma of mint seems to have appealed since the earliest times: according to Ovid, a table might be scoured with mint as an appetite-provoker; the Greeks used it as a scent specifically for the arms and they were forbidden to eat it in time of war because 'it did so much incite to venery', although Pliny in his *Natural History*, considered that mint might stop generation by preventing the seminal fluid from obtaining the required consistency. Other herbalists, however, prescribe it to treat infertility and lack of desire, as well as the more prosaic digestive complaints. Mint was also rubbed into the joints of those suffering from rheumatism and was much used in the bath. In ancient times sprigs of mint were used to revive people who felt faint.

Because the English climate is particularly favourable for the cultivation of mint, English mint is greatly sought after by foreign liqueur establishments. The mints did not start being cultivated in Britain until the Romans brought them, and this may be how we got our love of mint sauce, a way of serving mint that, to the best of my knowledge, is not followed in any other country; although Pliny says that mint 'stirs up the appetite for meat, which is the reason that it is so general in our acid sauces where we are accustomed to dip our meat'. So mint sauce may have been an ancient Roman speciality.

Several traditional recipes for cups and mixed drinks of a cooling refreshing nature incorporate mint, and most large-scale makers of liqueurs will include a mint liqueur in their range. Sometimes this will be bright green, but it can also be white. One very well-known brand is Cusenier's Freezomint which is green or white, and has been made since the foundation of the firm in 1857 by Eugène Cusenier, at Ornans in the Jura region. Get Frères (pronounced 'jet') make their Pippermint in both green and white varieties, Liqueur Giffard make Menthe Pastille which is described as their 'star liqueur for a hundred years'; it is distilled from the small leaves of *Menta porrita*. Peppermint Pastille is another Giffard Liqueur, which is bright green.

This form of mint liqueur was apparently the traditional tipple in many French 'houses' or brothels, which may account for the tag attached to crème de menthe until recent times of being 'the tart's drink'.

The Liverpool firm of Lamb & Watt, established in 1847, are particularly proud of their reputation as compounders of liqueurs and their crème de menthe is made with Mitcham peppermint, 'considered to be the finest and most expensive peppermint oil distilled in the world'.

In Italy, Mentuccia (the word means 'little piece of mint') was originally compounded by Brother San Sylvestro, from approximately a hundred herbs gathered in the Abruzzi mountains; it is therefore sometimes also known as Centerbe.

Marie Brizard make a white crème de menthe, which is included in the recipe for their Monte Carlo cocktail – half dry gin, one quarter white crème de menthe, one quarter lemon juice, all shaken with ice, poured into a glass and topped with Champagne.

The most famous mint drink is certainly crème de menthe frappé, the liqueur being poured over crushed ice in a moderately sized goblet and drunk through a straw. This drink is associated with the 'Belle Époque' and until comparatively recent times tended to be looked down on, maybe because the frappé, a refreshing drink that can be enjoyed at any time, as well as at the conclusion of a meal, seemed to have become slightly dated. But nowadays anybody who wants such a liqueur has no shyness about ordering it.

Chartreuse

This is one of the best-known liqueurs in the world and possibly the only one in widespread commercial production that can still claim to be the product of a great religious house where it has been made for at least 300 years. Because it bears the name of the Carthusian order, it is important to realize the significance of this. St Bruno, born at Cologne in 1033, founded the Carthusian order in 1084 when the Archbishop of Rheims forbade him to continue teaching theology there – understandably, because he had denounced the Archbishop for simony. Bruno took six companions and went to the Grande Chartreuse, a remote mountainous site near Grenoble, where the brothers built a church and surrounded it with small dwelling huts, so as to establish a mode of religious life that combined communal worship with silent and solitary devotion. Pope Urban II, who had been a pupil of Bruno's, called the saint to Italy and here he founded another Carthusian establishment in Calabria, where he died in 1101.

An establishment such as the Grande Chartreuse at Grenoble would naturally have made use of the plants and herbs of the surrounding mountains to compound remedies and preventatives in the laboratory and still-room. But the original recipe for the liqueur Chartreuse is of unknown origin: a manuscript which contained a recipe described as an 'elixir of long life' came into the hands of François Hannibal d'Estrées, a marshal in the French artillery, in the early seventeenth century. D'Estrées, a companion of that lover of the good things of life, Henri IV, gave it to a Carthusian establishment at Vauverre, outside Paris, in 1605. But the fifty pages of closely written instructions were hard to decipher and no one really studied it seriously until 1735, when it was passed to the original foundation of the Carthusians near Grenoble. Here, Brother Jérôme Maubec carried out detailed work in deciphering the recipe and working out the method of production; it is said that he dictated the final instructions for making it on his death-bed in 1762. In 1765 the recipe, made up in the monastery by the monks, finally reached the outer world, when it gradually became extremely popular, especially so during 1832, when there was a local epidemic of cholera, in which the elixir was reported extremely efficacious. This is why the greenish liqueur is sometimes referred to as '*liqueur de santé*'.

At the end of the eighteenth century the religious houses were closed by the Revolutionists in France and the inmates scattered. It is said that one of the Carthusians, in desperate need, actually gave the recipe for the liqueur in exchange for a loaf of bread to a pharmacist in Grenoble. This man seems to have been benevolent rather than shrewd, because, although Napoleon I decreed that all 'secret remedies' should be revealed to the State, no one seems to have made use of the Chartreuse formula until, in 1817, the Carthusians returned to their monastery and recovered the formula. The manuscript actually got into the hands of the then Minister of Secret Remedies, but he was quite unable to understand it and stamped it 'rejected' with a red seal which is shown today at the monastery, to which he returned it.

In 1838, Brother Bruno Jacquet evolved yellow Chartreuse, slightly sweeter and less strong than the original green version, which had by then become known as '*la reine des liqueurs*'. These liqueurs were made up in the pharmacy of the monastery and Brother Charles is reported to have gone out to sell them in Chambéry and Grenoble bearing samples and supplies on mule-back.

In 1848, 'the year of Revolutions', the rifle brigade of the Chasseurs Alpins was stationed near Grenoble and thirty of the officers were entertained by the monks; the Chartreuse liqueurs were served at the end of what was probably a rather modest meal, but the officers liked the drinks so much that they acted as virtual P.R.O.s for them, with such success that, in 1860, the Carthusians were obliged to build another distillery, about eight miles away from the religious establishment at Fourvoirie.

The fame of Chartreuse spread rapidly in the nineteenth century. Pauline Metternich, 'our princess' according to the Viennese, made it smart in the Austro-Hungarian Empire and introduced it to the French court. Empress Eugénie and Queen Victoria were the only two women ever to have been allowed to enter the Grande Chartreuse. The Queen recorded in her journal: 'I asked for some of their liqueur and by mistake, they gave me some of the strongest. Got home, much satisfied with our expedition, at 8.'

In 1903 all the religious orders were again expelled from France and the Carthusians of Grenoble went to Tarragona, where they set up a distillery. In France, another company, La Compagnie Fermière, began to make 'Chartreuse', but their version of the liqueur was a rather feeble imitation and was not successful – the company eventually went bankrupt. The Carthusians in Spain referred to their liqueur as 'Une Tarragone' and kept up production in Tarragona even when, in 1931, they were once more able to continue producing their liqueurs in Fourvoirie.

In 1935 a landslide destroyed the entire distillery, although the stills and some of the vats (the original ones) were preserved. Subsequently the brothers moved to the distillery of Voiron, where they are still in production. There are now two companies making Chartreuse: La Compagnie Française, which owns the buildings and the stocks of liqueurs, and is responsible for buying the raw materials, while Chartreuse Diffusion deals with the marketing of the product and any related items, such as sweets and chocolates. But the Chartreuse concern still remains very much a religious-backed establishment: for example, the Carthusians are able to approve or veto all the promotional and advertising material, which is why anything of this kind is of a fairly austere nature – and why women are not featured in the illustrations!

Only the brothers of the order are allowed to gather the herbs within the part of the estate belonging to the establishment – this is by a decree of the French State. Although tens of thousands of visitors come to see the Voiron distillery each year, it wasn't until the mid-1960s that they were allowed inside; the stills are viewed through a glass window and it was only after the strongest representations from those in charge of the marketing of Chartreuse that the Father General of the order agreed that visitors might be shown the cellars by hostesses, dressed in green, who were able to give some indication of the skill required in preparing the product. But these are the only concessions. The road to the monastery itself is barred by an electric gate, and the Father Procurator of the monastery, the only one of the brotherhood who travels, oversees new foundations throughout the world and approves the organization of the establishment as well as the architect's plan. There are now twenty-six Carthusian foundations, all of them built because of the success of the liqueur.

The formula for the elixir that is Chartreuse is still a secret, known only to three of the brothers, who each day travel from the monastery to the distillery. They are the only people allowed in the Hall of Herbs above the distillery, where they blend the ingredients which then go down into the vats where the liqueur is distilled. Chartreuse is aged in Limousin oak and the oldest is '*vieillissement exceptionnellement prolongé*' Chartreuse, or V.E.P. The Carthusians admit that

Chartreuse is the only French liqueur made with ingredients that are 100 per cent pure, no colourings or additives of any kind being permitted except those deriving from the components of the formula. It is this, probably more than anything else, which accounts for the price of Chartreuse.

Although about 130 different herbs are used, plus quality brandy and mountain honey, it is certain that among the ingredients is the herb *Myrrhis odorata* (sweet cicely). In former times the leaves and seeds of sweet cicely were much used in salads, and the root was boiled and dressed with oil and vinegar; in Gerard's *Herball* (1579) it is recommended for its 'wholesomeness for the cold and feeble stomacke', as well as for flatulence and digestive troubles. Another ingredient in Chartreuse may well be saffron (*Crocus sativus*). This has been known as a dye and a perfume for thousands of years, being mentioned in the 'Song of Solomon', by the Persians and as one of the cosmetics used by Cleopatra.

No one has ever been able to imitate Chartreuse closely, although there have been numerous attempts. It is an assertive drink, with very subtle undertones; it is a pity that it is often served in small glasses, as the drink should be swirled around to enable the complex fragrance to be enjoyed. Although it is probably best when simply drunk alone, it can be a simple and highly effective enhancement to vanilla ice cream – even a teaspoonful of Chartreuse poured over this makes a memorable sweet.

Another product of the distillery is the greenish Elixir Végétale, which is 140° proof and comes in small bottles about the size of a miniature, which are in wooden containers. This is a very strong drink indeed and the traditional way of taking it is as a digestive by means of a few drops on a lump of sugar.

Bénédictine

This is possibly the most widely known liqueur with a monastic origin. It is certainly very ancient, and its history, quite different from that of Chartreuse, is even more intricate. Bénédictine is made at Fécamp, on the Normandy coast, where the Abbey of the same name was founded in A.D. 988 by Richard I, Duke of Normandy. The great Norman abbeys of the region are famous, both as places of pilgrimage and as the establishments from which many learned men came to exert profound influence upon kings and international affairs. They are all Benedictine, and their scholarship and culture was remarkable.

Fécamp was dedicated to the Holy Trinity, the first church being built there in 665, but its chief claim to fame was that it possessed a remarkable relic: some drops of the blood of Christ which Joseph of Arimathea caught in his gauntlet glove and which he later bequeathed to his nephew Isaac. During a persecution of the Christians, Isaac sealed the sacred gauntlet in a coffer of lead and hid this in a hollowed-out tree trunk, which he consigned to the sea; the wood was carried by the waves to the Normandy coast and here, where it came ashore, it burst into foliage once more. The gauntlet was hidden during many of the Viking pirate raids but seems to have been rediscovered in 1090, when it drew enormous crowds of pilgrims to the abbey. The monks travelled far and wide and, in 1066, it was a monk of Fécamp who was sent by William of Normandy to parley with Harold of England before the Battle of Hastings. In 1164, Henry II of England, also Duke of Normandy at that time, granted the Abbey a charter giving to it rights in perpetuity to a considerable property around the establishment. The charter may still be seen today.

In the sixteenth century, one of the Fécamp Benedictines, Dom Bernardo Vincelli, an enthusiastic botanist, made a study of the plants of the Normandy countryside and coast, and used many of them in preparations he made up for the infirmary of Fécamp Abbey. One very successful recipe was for a cordial, in which he incorporated the juices of twenty-eight different plants which had been specially treated after soaking and were finally combined into a special compound. From about this time (1510), the fame of his elixir began to spread and the golden liquid attracted considerable attention. In 1534, François I of France came to Fécamp to sample it.

When, at the end of the eighteenth century, the French Revolution resulted in the destruction or sequestration of the property of the religious establishments, and the members of the religious orders were expelled from France, the treasures and secret formulae of many orders were entrusted to loyal lay friends. Alexandre le Grand had been associated with the Abbey of Fécamp through his family, some of whom had been business managers for the lay affairs of the monastery; he found in his possession many old books and manuscripts and, in 1863, after years of experimentation, he succeeded in once again making the Bénédictine elixir both to his own satisfaction and to that of those who were able to remember the original. In the latter part of the nineteenth century, as a result of the considerable commercial success of the revived sales of the elixir, M. le Grand built what he considered was a worthy house for the distillery and offices of the liqueur, on the site of the former Abbey.

The Bénédictine establishment today is quite fantastic, and even anyone prepared for its appearance from pictures will at sight of the real thing either be stupefied or roar with laughter. In the most exuberant style of the opulent period of the later nineteenth century, it incorporates Gothic, Baroque, even Romanesque styles of architecture, with anything else that could be added, the result being something that surpasses even the most extravagant creation of what a Hollywood mogul might suppose a 'historic' building to look like! Tours of the distillery are well organized, guided commentaries being given on portable speakers, which even differentiate between 'American' and 'English'. The various processes involved in the preparation and bottling of the liqueur are shown and, in addition, the enormous halls and galleries of the establishment include several museums, in which may be seen various works of art and specialized collections made by M. le Grand, including locks and keys, travelling chests, weapons, food, and other objects associated with the original Fécamp Abbey. There is also a museum of all the various imitations of Bénédictine that have been made at various times.

The Bénédictine liqueur, in its dark green, slightly squat bottle, bears the wax seal of the Abbey of Fécamp and the Benedictine initials D.O.M., signifying 'To God most good, most great'. In fact, the distillery, although modern, does preserve the traditions of the original establishment. Many of the works of art are of great beauty and piety. The plants used in the making of the liqueur are the same as those which Dom Bernardo originally found on the Normandy cliffs, where the pungency of the sea air helped to give an individual flavour. Among the ingredients of Bénédictine are myrrh, saffron (now brought from Spain), vanilla, lemon peel, maidenhair, yarrow, cloves, cardamom, nutmeg, mace, thyme, coriander, hyssop, balm and angelica, the last three still being cultivated in the Fécamp pastures belonging to the distillery. But the tea and the honey used in the recipe must come from far afield, the honey being imported from the United States, as the French type has been found to have too definite a flavour.

The secret formula is still in the hands of the le Grand family. They make up the mixture – or, rather, mixtures, for the liqueur starts with five different ones, which are steeped in alcohol and then distilled. After this, they are matured in oak and finally combined; the brandies – which include Cognac – being added at this stage, plus distilled water to break down the high strength of the liqueur.

In addition to Bénédictine liqueur, Fécamp produces 'B & B', which is a mixture of brandy and Bénédictine, which has proved a success in recent times. It was first produced in 1938 in response to requests from the United States for a ready-mix, as American drinkers were topping up their Bénédictine with brandy.

The Bénédictine establishment acquired the firm of Revel of Toulouse in 1969; it is this concern that produces Pippermint Get, according to a recipe dating from the eighteenth century.

One curious market for Bénédictine is in Lancashire. Sales there seemed, to the U.K. agents, extraordinarily large in relation to other areas of the U.K. It was discovered that in the First World War a Lancashire regiment was stationed at Fécamp and the tommies brought home the taste for Bénédictine, which they tended to like as a 'grog', with hot water. In the Second World War the East Lancs. Regiment was also stationed at Fécamp – as a result there is now a Bénédictine Festival held annually in Blackburn.

Both Bénédictine and B & B can be made into long drinks with the addition of soda water and, used in coffee, with cream in the same way as Irish coffee. Bénédictine can be incorporated in sauces or with grilled grapefruit, melon, fruit salad; and in the flaming of fruits such as bananas. Bénédictine topped up with tonic water and garnished with a slice of lemon makes the long drink St Trop; another mixture is Tropic, which is one third of grapefruit juice, one third of white wine, plus a large spoonful of Bénédictine and a teaspoonful of fresh lemon juice.

Strega

The Italian word '*strega*' means 'witch', and it is said that, in Benevento, just north of Naples, witches would hold a coven on the banks of the River Sabato, which flows through the town, every Saturday night, and dance round a gigantic walnut tree. The witches, who obviously seem to have been benevolent rather than otherwise, made up a magical potion, which would ensure that any two people drinking it together would remain in love.

The Strega Liqueur, as it is known today, was invented by Guiseppe Alberti of Benevento, who was in the wine trade. He evolved the liqueur from more than seventy herbs, subjecting it to long-term maturation in wood. It was first commercially marketed by Guiseppe Alberti's sons and became very popular in the nine-teenth century. The producers are still the Alberti family (the current President of the Company is a grandson of its inventor) and it is today known throughout the world. It can be used in various mixed drinks as well as being made long by the addition of tonic water, soda, fizzy orange, lemon or grapefruit, but it is probably best known as a post-prandial digestive. It is both herby and slightly sweet.

Galliano

This liqueur in its tall, almost triangular bottle and with a brilliant, acid-yellow colour, was first made in Livorno (Leghorn) and the publicity announces proudly and accurately that it is 'the Italian liqueur which has conquered America' (it was the top-selling liqueur in the mid 1970s in the U.S. and is now about fourth); in comparatively recent times it has been available in Britain as well.

Liquori Galliano is made today at Salara, north of Milan, and, as the recipe is secret, the only information available seems to be that it is 'high-quality spirit blended with herbs, roots and flowers ... stored for up to six months in glass tanks to allow proper marriage of the ingredients before being repeatedly filtered and finally piped to the bottling line'. It gets its name from Guiseppe Galliano, a major in the Italian Expeditionary Force in the campaign against Abyssinia in 1895–6. Major Galliano had received orders that at all costs he must hold the fort of Enda Jesus, and – although he had only twenty-one officers, just over 1000 Italian infantry and artillery and even fewer native troops – he managed to do this against 80,000 men from 8 December 1895 until he received orders to abandon the fort on 20 January 1896, a date that he said was 'the saddest day of my life'. His courage and ingenuity inspired his men throughout. The label of the liqueur bears a picture of the fort of Enda Jesus.

Galliano can be drunk as a digestive or made into a long drink with the addition of any of the fizzy waters. It is used in numerous cocktails, but possibly the most remarkable of these is the Harvey Wallbanger. This is made by pouring 6 ounces of fresh orange juice over ice, adding 1 ounce of vodka and stirring the drink, finally floating ½ ounce of Liquori Galliano on the top. This is said to be named for a Californian surf-rider, named Harvey, who on one occasion celebrated a win in a surfing contest with a Screwdriver (orange juice and vodka) adding a measure of Liquori Galliano on the top of it: his eventual reactions were interpreted by his friends as bouncing from wall to wall as he left them – hence the name 'Wallbanger'. This drink was the one that popularized Galliano in the U.S. and it is certainly a very pleasant mixture. Sweetish, it also has a fruity, herby undertaste.

Izarra

The name of this liqueur is the Basque word for 'star'. It is made from herbs and flowers gathered in the Basque region of the Pyrenees, which are blended and mixed with Armagnac, after which they are distilled and slowly rectified in a particular type of still, to produce an essence called 'spirit'. This is the foundation of the liqueur. The spirit is then combined with the honey of the region and more Armagnac, the ingredients remaining together for twenty-four hours. The liqueur is filtered and aged in wood casks, so that its flavour and bouquet may develop and then, after being once more filtered, it goes to the bottling line.

Izarra is the creation of Joseph Grattau, who founded the Distillerie de la Côte Basque and evolved the liqueur in 1835. There are two types, green Izarra being slightly stronger than the yellow variety. The British tend to drink it simply as a digestive, but it is worth noting that the flavour is greatly improved if the liqueur can be chilled or at least poured over ice cubes. A very pleasant drink, called an Episcopal (because of the combining of the clerical colours of yellow and green) is a type of frappé, made by pouring half and half yellow and green Izarra over crushed ice in a large goblet and drinking the result through a straw. This is an anytime drink.

Other herb liqueurs

Vieille Cure is made from at least forty different types of herbs, which are macerated in both Armagnac and Cognac. The result is a dark-coloured drink, made nowadays by the Compagnie de Vieille Cure de Cenon, across the river from Bordeaux. The recipe is supposed to be of considerable antiquity.

Cordial Médoc is a liqueur made by G.A. Jourde, Compagnie Fermière de Liqueurs, also at Cenon. It is based on claret, with certain herbs used to flavour it, and is a deep reddish brown in colour. It is rather sweet, although it can be a pleasant digestive.

Trappistine was much publicized by Madame Simone Prunier at her former St James's restaurant in London, where it was used in pancake and other sweet recipes, although it is definitely herby. Trappistine is greenish yellow and is made with the use of herbs from the Doubs region of France, according to a recipe in the possession of the Abbey of Grâce Dieu. The base is Armagnac.

Verveine du Vélay is a slightly bitter herby liqueur, made up in both green and yellow versions, by the firm of Pagès, in south-western France. Vervain (*Verbena officinalis*) is a herb with a long history; Hippocrates included it in many recipes and it is supposed to have been worshipped in Greece, Italy and in England in the time of the Druids. The Romans used it for purifying their homes and for cleansing the altars of their household gods. Tulley recommended the sprinkling of a room with vervain water to encourage conviviality at dinner, because in the language of flowers vervain means 'enchantment'. It is sometimes referred to as 'holy herb', and in Wales it was used as the herb with which holy water was sprinkled, being referred to as 'devil's bane'. The Druids apparently thought that it could only be gathered when neither sun nor moon were above ground and when the great Dog Star was rising, also insisting that anyone who pulled it up should replace it by putting a honeycomb on the earth. Medically, vervain is associated with many cures for fevers, diseases of the eye, and against plague, but Gerard in his *Herball* is discouraging and thinks that 'the Divell did reveale it as a secret and divine medicine'.

Sénancole is a bright yellow, fresh-smelling liqueur; the name derives from the river that runs through the valley below the Abbey of Sénanque, at Salon in Provence, a Cistercian foundation established in 1148. The monks still have the secret of the formula, but the liqueur is made in a modern distillery, in private ownership since 1930.

Aiguebelle, otherwise known as the '*formule de la liqueur de Frère Jean*', was discovered by a Trappist, Père Hughes, at the beginning of the present century, when he was going through some old papers in the principal Trappist monastery in Normandy. Aiguebelle is said to contain about fifty different herbs. It is based on herbs local to the great monastery of La Grande Trappe and supposedly worked out according to an ancient formula.

Sapindor is a greenish liqueur of the Jura, very definitely piney in smell; it might be frivolously described as a northern answer to retsina! The presentation is usually in bottles resembling a chunk of a tree branch.

Cuarenta-y-Tres is a yellow Spanish liqueur, made, as its name implies, from forty-three different herbs. It is made at Cartagena in Spain, the distillery claiming in its publicity material that the drink has its origin in the liqueurs made at the ancient city of Carthage, in what is now Tunisia. Cuarenta-y-Tres is a rather sweet drink, which can successfully be incorporated in a number of recipes for puddings, fruit salads, ice creams and so on. Enzian Calisay is another sweetish herby Spanish liqueur, a pale golden-brown in colour.

Elixir de Spa was originally made by the Capuchin friars at Spa in 1643, where it proved a commercial success until the monastery was dissolved in 1797. The recipe is now made up by a commercial establishment. Elixir d'Anvers is an Antwerp liqueur, made by the firm of F.X. de Beukelaer, another rather sweet drink, with a brandy base.

Kloster Ettal, near Oberammergau, is a Benedictine establishment where green and yellow herb liqueurs are made, and this, like the Czechoslovak Carlsberg Liqueur, is on the bitter side, as are the German Stonsdorfer and Jägermeister, which is dark red. St Hallvard comes from Norway and is bright yellow, with a spirit base usually made up from potatoes. Tapio comes from Finland and is another herby drink.

Among the most famous Italian herb liqueurs is the colourless Fior d'Alpi, generally presented in tall bottles, in which are placed twigs, with sugar crystals clinging to them. The three best-known makes are Millefiori, supposed to contain extracts of a thousand flowers, Isolabella and Eidelweiss.

ANGELICA LIQUEURS

Angelica (*Angelica archangelica*) is said to flower on 8 May, St Michael's Day, hence its name. It has been credited with remarkable properties: a monk was once told by an angel that angelica should be used in the then prevalent epidemic of plague, and in the Great Plague of London, in 1665, angelica was often referred to as 'root of the Holy Ghost'. In Lapland, poets were crowned with wreaths of angelica to inspire them. Bohemian angelica was esteemed as the best of all and English angelica was considered only slightly inferior. Much dried angelica was imported from Spain.

Angelica oil is made from the seed and used in making scent. The seeds themselves are sometimes a substitute for juniper berries and the leaves are used to make tea and poultices. Angelica oil can be used in gin, vermouth and Chartreuse; and angelica liqueurs are also made. In East Germany there is one called Krambambuli, which also makes use of an extract of violets; and recently I found one at Niort, in western France, called Liqueur d'Angélique, which is based on old Cognac.

NUT LIQUEURS

It is quite easy to make a liqueur from nuts, but nuts are usually more valuable as a form of food, or sweetmeat, so nut liqueurs tend to be made only in regions where nut trees yield abundantly. Few of these enjoy a wide commercial success, but they are a pleasure to sample in a particular locality, all the more so when it is a home-made product. In the region of the River Dordogne in France, the Perigord liqueur is eau de noix – the 'noix' means that it is made from walnuts, which are abundant there. Crème de noix is a sweeter version of the same thing, crème de noisette is made from hazelnuts.

Cacao mit Nüss is a colourless German liqueur, flavoured with hazelnuts and chocolate. De Kuyper's Crème de Noyau (Persico) is a well-known Dutch brand.

There are numbers of these commercial nut liqueurs made from the kernels of soft fruits such as apricots as well as specifically from nuts. Those that I have been able to try have all been rather sweet and without much distinction; they can be useful in trifles and similar sweet dishes or in fruit salads.

GINGER LIQUEURS

Francisco di Mendoza is supposed to have been the first to bring ginger plants from the East Indies at the beginning of the sixteenth century, and ginger (*Zingeeiber officinale*) was the first spice that Europeans used in quantity. But they tended to use it in the kitchen rather than the still-room or pharmacy. However, its stimulating, warming qualities were soon recognized: Queen Elizabeth I much valued a particular 'powder' which was a mixture of ginger, plus cinnamon, aniseed, caraway and fennel. Ginger tea is recommended in several herbals as useful to counteract nausea, and in the exhaustion of childbirth.

King Edward VII's Ginger Liqueur was evolved by the firm of Berry Brothers and Rudd while he was still Prince of Wales. The present head of the firm wrote to me saying that his grandfather had invented it as a warmer for the Prince, 'when he came in from driving in his horseless carriage'. I had heard that it was a drink he liked after shooting. It is made by macerating ginger roots in spirit and it is of a pungent flavour, definitely ginger.

Ginger wine is not strictly a 'wine', but something more. It certainly evolved from home-made beverages of the warming type, such as any housewife might put up in the still-room. The two most famous names making it in the U.K. are Stones and Crabbie's, the latter having been in business for nearly two centuries. Their recipe is a family one, and they use grapes that have almost dried up on the vines. These are then shipped to Leith and steeped so that fermentation can start. Fermentation continues for several months; the 'wine' is then matured in oak vats for up to two and a half years. To this is then added the secret family formula, which includes ginger, flowers, fruits, herbs and spices.

The most famous mixture using ginger wine is undoubtedly the 'Mac' – a spirit being added to the wine. Any spirit can be used, but Whisky Mac is certainly the best-known combination.

MISCELLANEOUS LIQUEURS

Parfait Amour is one of those drinks of the late nineteenth and early twentieth century which are seldom seen, although still made. Cusenier say that Parfait Amour and Crème de Noyau are basically sweetened, flavoured alcohol:

> They represent the lowest form of liqueur and any manufacturer such as Cusenier is not proud of them as he knows they are no better than those of his rivals. The flavour of Crème de Noyau, which smells of almond icing, comes in fact from apricot kernels. Each manufacturer has his own version of Parfait Amour, all of them highly scented and brightly coloured. The principal flavouring here is rosewater.

Such other references as I have been able to find indicate that citrus oil is one of the ingredients, that the liqueur is still made both in France and Holland and, although the most usual brands colour the liqueur violet, it can also be red. On such occasions as I have tasted it, I have thought it remarkably undistinguished.

Recently, Heublein have introduced an unusual-sounding high-strength drink which is called Pink Squirrel; this, according to information, is Crème de Almond (sic) laced with Crème de Caçao and 'other delicious ingredients'. It sounds very sweet.

Tea liqueurs have been made, as well as coffee ones, and a travelled friend informs me of one made from ginseng, which has what is supposed to be a mandrake root in the bottle. The mandrake was supposed to promote fertility and generation; because of its slight resemblance to the lower part of the human form, it was legendarily imagined to shriek as it was pulled from the earth and to drive the hearer mad (they used to have a dog attached to the root for its extraction). It is mentioned in Genesis and crops up in many writings. My informant about this form of liqueur assured me that it was perfectly horrible in flavour.

The huge Suntory concern, who make Japan's biggest-selling whiskey, also produce a 'Green Tea Liqueur', marketed, as are their other liqueurs, under the brand name Hermes. This tea liqueur is stated to be a blend of teas macerated in brandy and neutral spirit and the result is very sweet.

Saké-Gekkeikan, also from Japan, is a pleasant accompaniment to Japanese food. It is made from rice, steeped, and then made into a mash with the introduction of yeast, so that it ferments, after which it is filtered, pressed and filtered again before being pasteurized. It is served warm in the small handleless cups traditional in Japan, and, although it is available all the year round, it is supposed to be best in the autumn, when it is about a year old, because it does not improve with maturation.

13. Fruit Brandies

The French term for these is *alcools blancs* or 'white alcohols', because these spirits are colourless. They are not matured in wood but in glass, and therefore take on no colour at all. They are true *eaux de vie*, and although they are sometimes called fruit brandies, the term tends to be misleading, especially in the English language, because people may think that a liqueur such as cherry brandy is an *alcool blanc* – it is not.

A real fruit brandy or *eau de vie* of this kind may be made either by distilling the mash of the fruit, or by macerating the fruit in alcohol and then distilling the mixture. The kernels of soft fruits are often included. In Germany, the suffix *'wasser'* implies that the liqueur has been made by distilling the fermented fruit mash, whereas, if the name of the liqueur ends in *'geist'*, the liqueur has been made by macerating the fruit in alcohol before the process of distillation. The latter procedure is necessary when the fruit being used is itself low in sugar.

Fruit brandies in this strict sense of the expression really are the distilled essence, in alcoholic terms, of the fruit from which they are made. They usually originated in regions where certain fruits and berries grew in profusion, and attained high quality. This usually means the foothills of mountains, for, as in the world of wine, the best sites are on slopes, the finest wines generally being made in vineyards that are neither at the top, where they will be too exposed, nor at the bottom, where the soil will tend to be too rich and the water will drain down in too great an abundance. The foothills of many of the mountain ranges of Europe have for centuries yielded fine crops, often of berries and fruits that could not, without considerable technical resources and skill, which the local housewife does not possess, be otherwise adapted for human consumption. It must be remembered that sugar, with which jams and similar preserves can now be made, would have been far too expensive for the peasant farmer to use in quantity in former times.

People who expect all after-dinner drinks made from fruit to be sweet will get a surprise when they try an *alcool blanc* – it will not have been sweetened at all and will contain no more sweetness than is in the original fruit. There should be a beautiful fragrance as well as a definite flavour of the fruit and, in order to enjoy this to the best advantage, the tradition in Alsace – possibly the most famous of all regions for producing *alcools blancs* – is to pour a small quantity of this high-strength drink into a glass that has been chilled, either by putting it in the refrigerator, or, as is most usual in a restaurant, by shaking several ice cubes in it and tipping them out just before the *alcool blanc* is poured. Both the amount poured of this type of drink and the glass itself should be of moderate size, so that the alcohol can be swirled round to release even more of its bouquet. It is perhaps worth warning adventurers in the regions where these spirits are home-made that to taste one is an impressive experience; the commercial types may be familiar, but the strength of the home product may be very much higher.

TYPES OF WHITE ALCOHOL MADE FROM FRUITS

Kirsch

It has been necessary to invent the title for this sub-section, because the liqueur known in French as kirsch is an *alcool blanc*, therefore not a 'cherry brandy'; it is a true fruit brandy made from cherries. It is made in many parts of Europe where cherry trees grow abundantly. The cherry is a *Prunus* and is 'a one-seeded drupe', the stones and sometimes the leaves possessing an almondy flavour. The wild cherry, in any of its numerous forms, is much used for distillation; wild cherries are small and high in acidity. For kirsch, the cherry kernels are included in the mash. The distillation takes place twice. Kirsch is a versatile liqueur, an excellent digestive, and is also used a great deal in fruit salad, or poured over various fruits, notably pineapple. It is one of the spirits often used to flame sweet dishes.

Kirsch Peureux. For many years I had never seen this particular form of kirsch and had been content to accept the reports in several otherwise reputable publications that it was a type of sweetened kirsch. Then one day, while lunching with the wine merchants Dolamore, a half bottle of 'Kirsch Pur, Vieux' was produced, bearing the label 'Kirschwasser' and the name of August Peureux, of Fouger-olles in the Haute Saône. It was colourless and somewhat assertive, and gave the impression of being fuller – but not sweeter. Because of my interest, my hosts sent down for a bottle of ordinary kirsch from Alsace, and in the comparison the more definite style of the Alsace spirit was evident; it was also very slightly tinted and, we agreed, was a more aristocratic version of kirsch. The Kirsch Peureux was not a 'sweeter' kirsch, but more obvious, possibly even to be described as coarser, but it was possible to see why anyone unable to make the direct comparison might have gained the impression that it was sweeter.

Plum alcohols

There are several types of white alcohol made from plums, differing in character according to the variety of fruit used. In France the small golden type known as the Mirabelle makes the liqueur of the same name, and the Switzen or Swetschen plum is another variety, hence the German Swetschen, or Quetsch, made with these black plums. Plum brandy in Yugoslavia is called slivovitz and doubtless wherever plums of a type suitable for cooking are found in abundance (the sweeter dessert type of plum can of course be sold immediately for eating), the fruit may be used for distilling.

In the Dordogne Valley in France, the local people make an *eau de vie de prune*, the 'prune' being a particular type of greengage. Sometimes they combine this with one of the local walnut liqueurs (see page 306), and the result is called Mesclou, an odd but by no means disagreeable drink, which I think is peculiar to this beautiful region.

Other fruit brandies

Many other fruits are used to make brandies, including raspberries – *framboise* in French, *Himbeergeist* in German. This spirit, incident-ally, can be used to make a delicious drink by putting a small spoonful in a glass and topping this with Champagne; a version of this is the 'house cocktail' at the Grand Hôtel Clément at Ardres, just outside Calais. Strawberries, or *fraises*, can also be used, the version made by the firm of Dolfi in Alsace being particularly good, as it is based on wild strawberries, and is therefore particularly delicate in flavour. Other fruits used include apricot; Mirabelle plum; *myrtille*, or bil-berry; *sorbe alisier*, a type of rowan berry, better known in Britain as the mountain ash; *coing*, or quince; *mûre*, or blackberry and *prunelle sauvage*, or sloe (the Maigrets, in Simenon's detective novels, sometimes drink prunelle when they are entertaining, as Madame Maigret is of Alsace origin). Tutti-frutti is a mixture of fruit brandies (not, in my experience, a particularly distinguished drink). An odd one called *houx* is made from holly berries, and there are doubtless plenty more.

One definitely curious and excellent fruit brandy is made from the William pear: it is sometimes called *poire Williams*, or simply *poire*, or else Williamine. It is made in Alsace, in Switzerland, in Germany and probably other regions – I have heard of it being made in several of the eastern European countries. It can vary a great deal, and is sometimes a slightly golden colour, if it has been aged in wood instead of just in glass. In some rather 'chi-chi' versions, there is a pear inside the bottle, within the fruit brandy; I don't know that this necessarily adds anything to the spirit, but it can look attractive.

Some people have told me that home-made pear brandy is made by merely allowing the pear to give its flavour to the subsequently added spirit but, although of course this might be done, it would not make the resulting liqueur an *alcool blanc* or true fruit brandy, as will have been understood from the earlier description of this particular type of distillate. If, however, you simply top up the bottle containing the pear with a genuine pear brandy, then the presence of the fruit is virtually a garnish and the original distillate does comply with the description previously given. How does the pear get into the bottle? There may be other ways of achieving this, but I can only describe the pear tree in the garden of the Restaurant de la Pyramide at Vienne, where the bottles are slipped over the branches on which the small pears are beginning to form, so that the fruit grows inside the bottle.

It seems probable, although I have not been able to trace any historical references, that fruit brandies of this type could and probably were made in the British Isles from the various fruits and berries growing wild; but as distilling is illegal for the ordinary household today, the type of 'fruit brandies' and similar drinks based on spirits that may be found, and for which recipes are still published, consist mainly of preparations put up simply by steeping the various fruits in a spirit.

The English do not seem to have ever gone in for distilling at home in the way that the Irish and Scots did, which may be because those who could afford spirits were able without too much trouble to get them, whether smuggled or legally bought, from Europe. In addition farm and country houses made fruit wines, brewed ale and made cider in large quantities – the cider of former times was proudly produced for visitors even by the side of imported wines. So the English do seem always to have had enough to drink without having to use the products of the countryside for distilling, although people probably did so on a small scale. If the legendary 'heather ale' did not enjoy a reputation centuries older than the arrival of distillation in Europe, I would suspect that this might have been some form of distillate, but neither this, from what one has been able to learn about it, nor the Cornish mead are quite the same as the white alcohols. It might seem odd that the Welsh never took to distilling in this way, but I think that perhaps the influence of the chapel, with its ban on alcohol in general, at a time when the Welsh might have otherwise become interested in making strong liquors out of berries and fruits, may account for this.

Appendix 1: Alcoholic Strength

By the term 'strength' is understood the amount of alcohol in a particular liquid. Unfortunately, it is not something that can be explained scientifically in wholly straightforward language so that the layman can easily understand what is meant.

All alcohol is lighter in weight than water. This is why it is given off in the form of vapour when distillation is performed, the water remaining behind. But, because the stronger the alcohol, the lighter it is in weight, there is an affinity between alcohol and water and, therefore, it is simply not possible to attain a stage at which it can definitely be said that the alcohol is 'absolute' – in other words, that it is 100 per cent alcohol and nothing else at all. The strongest level of alcohol is only achieved up to about 95 per cent.

As any reader of this book will know, the liquids termed 'spirits' are not made just by adding various strengths of alcohol to a prepared mixture of flavours. And, whereas it is possible to say that the higher the alcoholic strength of a liquid, the fewer impurities will remain in it, it is precisely those impurities or 'extras' that give the individuality and charm to the great spirits. High-strength alcohol, such as that used for medical purposes, will affect the human who drinks it because the alcohol will affect the system – but the drinker will miss the smell, taste and after-taste, because they are simply not there in the neutral spirit. If you took the finest Cognac, your favourite malt or preferred brand of rum and distilled them so that the strength rose to the top limits possible, you would be quite unable to differentiate between them or say which started out by being grape, grain or sugar-cane.

If there is any sugar in a liquid, this makes it heavier. But, when wine is being made, to increase the sugar content in the 'must' or unfermented grape juice is also to increase the alcoholic strength of the ultimate wine. George Ordish, in *Vineyards in England and*

Wales (Faber, 1977), gives the delightful example of how, in the seventeenth century, Sir Kenelm Digby, writing on wine making, advised that sugar was to be added to the must until 'a fresh egg floats to the depth of twopence'; the more sugar in the must, the higher the egg would float – unless, of course, it was not really fresh, in which case the air in it would cause it to float higher on the surface of the liquid and falsify the conclusion. This is a homely instance of an early form of the hydrometer (see page 46).

Although the use of the hydrometer to estimate the alcoholic strength of liquids has been routine since the beginning of the nineteenth century, the form in which this strength is expressed (or written down) has varied from country to country. It seems extraordinary that there are still so many different ways of giving the alcoholic strength of liquids but, at the time of writing, there is about to be a new hydrometer produced in Britain, calculated at 20 degrees, and, it is to be hoped, a single system of 'strength' will gradually be adopted by all spirit producers and spirit-consuming countries.

Meanwhile, here are the tables which show the correspondence between the various systems. It should be borne in mind that, whereas in the wine trade the terms 'Gay Lussac' and 'percentage of alcohol by volume' are thought of and spoken of as virtually the same thing, they are not. Because, in wine, the discrepancies between the two systems are minimal and of no significant importance, people use the two indiscriminately. But, with spirits, the difference becomes greater and therefore should be marked.

John Doxat, in *The Book of Drinking* (Hamlyn, 1973), explains the term 'proof' admirably:

> 100 represents absolute alcohol [which, bear in mind, does not and cannot exist scientifically] and all strengths are given as percentages of that down to zero (water). The U.S. proof system is quite comprehensible when one realizes that, since absolute alcohol is 200 and proof spirit 100, and is exactly 50/50 alcohol and water, it follows that if a spirit is marked, say, 90 proof U.S., it contains 45 per cent alcohol. You simply halve the given U.S. proof to obtain the alcohol content. Not so with British proof, with absolute alcohol (in practice) 175, and proof spirit represented by the figure 100, giving it no convenient alcohol strength but one of 57·14 per cent (to be pedantic).

He goes on to make the point that:

> It was once customary to use the terms 'over' or 'under' proof, and these are encountered in trade circles, but more usually the

expression '00°' or '00 per cent proof' are employed. If a spirit were over proof (OP) today, it would most likely be marked, say, 115° proof.

If, therefore, you need to know the strength of any spirit, it is necessary to remember the system used by the country where that spirit is made or where it is sold on any export market, before you translate the figure relating to this on the label. Then it should only require interpreting in terms of the tables given here.

CORRESPONDENCE BETWEEN OLD AND MODERN ALCOLHOLIC DEGREES

Gay Lussac 15°/15° 1824	Légal français 15°/15° 1884	Windisch 15°/15°	Reichard 20°/20° 1951	Tralles 15°5/15°5	Richter in g. p. 100 g	Sykes 15·56/15·56 1816	American Proof 15·56/15·56	Tessa 15° 1810	Cartier 15° 1771
0	0	0	0	0	0	100	0		10·03
1	0·96	1·00	1·01	1	0·8	98·3	2		10·23
2	1·97	2·02	2·04	2	1·6	96·3	4		10·43
3	2·94	3·00	3·01	3	2·4	94·6	6		10·62
4	3·95	4·00	4·04	4	3·2	93·0	8		10·80
5	4·90	4·96	5·02	5	4·0	91·3	10		10·97
6	5·89	5·95	6·02	6	4·8	89·5	12		11·16
7	6·89	6·96	7·05	7	5·6	87·8	14		11·33
8	7·85	7·92	8·01	8	6·4	86·0	16		11·49
9	8·92	8·99	9·09	9	7·2	84·3	18		11·66
10	9·85	9·94	10·01	9·9	8·0	82·5	20		11·82
11	10·98	11·01	11·10	10·9	8·8	80·8	22		11·98
12	11·86	11·98	12·05	11·9	9·6	79·0	24		12·14
13	12·85	12·98	13·05	12·9	10·4	77·2	26		12·28
14	13·87	14·03	14·10	13·9	11·2	75·5	28		12·43
15	14·81	15·00	15·09	14·9	12·0	73·8	30		12·57
16	15·76	15·96	16·05	15·9	12·9	72·1	32		12·70
17	16·73	16·98	17·03	16·9	13·7	70·3	34		12·84
18	17·71	17·98	18·03	17·9	14·5	68·6	36		12·97
19	18·59	18·89	18·93	18·9	15·3	66·8	38		13·10
20	19·57	19·88	19·92	19·9	16·2	65·1	40		13·25
21	20·57	20·89	20·91	20·9	17·0	63·3	42		13·38

22	21·67	21·88	21·93	21·9	17·9	61·5	44		13·52
23	22·66	22·97	23·01	22·8	18·6	59·7	46		13·67
24	23·75	24·05	24·06	23·8	19·5	57·6	48		13·83
25	24·74	25·02	25·03	24·8	20·3	56·1	50		13·97
26	25·82	26·10	26·09	25·8	21·1	54·4	52		14·12
27	26·77	26·99	26·96	26·8	22·0	52·7	54		14·26
28	27·80	27·99	27·96	27·8	22·8	51·0	56		14·42
29	28·81	28·98	28·95	28·8	23·7	49·3	58		14·57
30	29·78	29·92	29·89	29·8	24·5	47·6	60		14·72
31	30·81	30·95	30·93	30·8	25·4	45·9	62		14·90
32	31·81	31·95	31·92	31·8	26·2	44·1	64		15·07
33	32·78	32·92	32·89	32·7	27·0	42·3	66		15·24
34	33·80	33·94	33·91	33·7	27·9	40·6	68		15·43
35	34·87	35·0	34·97	34·7	28·7	38·9	70		15·63
36	35·82	35·95	35·92	35·7	29·6	37·2	72		15·83
37	36·82	36·95	36·92	36·7	30·5	35·4	74		16·02
38	37·89	37·92	37·89	37·7	31·4	33·6	76		16·22
39	38·80	38·93	38·90	38·7	32·2	31·8	78		16·43
40	39·78	39·91	39·88	39·7	33·1	30·0	80		16·66
41	40·79	40·93	40·90	40·8	34·1	28·3	82		16·88
42	41·77	41·92	41·89	41·8	35·0	26·5	84	—1	17·12
43	42·79	42·95	42·92	42·8	35·9	24·8	86	—0·75	17·37
44	43·79	43·96	43·93	43·8	36·8	23·0	88	—0·50	17·62
45	44·78	44·96	44·93	44·8	37·7	21·2	90	—0·25	17·88
46	45·79	45·97	45·95	45·8	38·6	19·4	92	0	18·14
47	46·79	46·98	46·95	46·8	39·5	17·6	94	0·25	18·42
48	47·77	47·97	47·95	47·8	40·5	15·9	96	0·50	18·69
49	48·87	48·99	48·97	48·8	41·4	14·1	98	0·75	18·97
50	49·78	50·00	49·98	49·8	42·3	12·3	100	1·00	19·25
51	50·75	50·97	50·95	50·8	43·3	10·6	102	1·25	19·54

Gay Lussac 15°/15° 1824	Légal français 15°/15° 1884	Windisch 15°/15°	Reichard 20°/20° 1951	Tralles 15°5/15°5	Richter in g. p. 100 g	Sykes 15·56/15·56 1816	American Proof 15·56/15·56	Tessa 15° 1810	Cartier 15° 1771
52	51·72	51·97	51·95	51·8	44·2	8·8	104	1·50	19·85
53	52·74	52·96	52·95	52·8	45·2	7·1	106	1·75	20·15
54	53·71	53·93	53·92	53·8	46·1	5·4	108	2·00	20·47
55	54·71	54·92	54·92	54·8	47·1	3·7	110	2·33	20·79
56	55·71	55·92	55·92	55·8	48·1	2·0	112	2·67	21·11
57	56·70	56·91	56·91	56·8	49·0	0·2	114	3·00	21·43
57·1	—	—	—	—	—	Proof	114·2	—	—
58	57·69	57·90	57·90	57·8	50·0	1·6	116	3·33	21·76
59	58·72	58·93	58·94	58·8	51·0	3·3	118	3·67	22·10
60	59·73	59·94	59·95	59·8	52·0	5·0	120	4·00	22·46
61	60·73	60·93	60·94	60·8	53·0	6·7	122	4·33	22·82
62	61·76	61·95	61·95	61·8	54·0	8·5	124	4·67	23·18
63	62·77	62·95	62·95	62·8	55·0	10·3	126	5·00	23·55
64	63·80	63·96	63·96	63·8	56·0	12·0	128	5·33	23·92
65	64·80	64·95	64·95	64·8	57·0	13·8	130	5·67	24·29
66	65·79	65·94	65·93	65·8	58·1	15·6	132	6·00	24·67
67	66·81	66·94	66·93	66·8	59·1	17·3	134	6·33	25·05
68	67·82	67·94	67·92	67·8	60·2	19·0	136	6·67	25·45
69	68·82	68·93	68·91	68·8	61·2	20·8	138	7·00	25·85
70	69·83	69·93	69·91	69·8	62·3	22·5	140	7·33	26·26
71	70·84	70·94	70·92	70·8	63·4	24·2	142	7·67	26·68
72	71·84	71·94	71·92	71·8	64·4	26·0	144	8·00	27·11
73	72·87	72·97	72·95	72·8	65·5	27·8	146	8·33	27·54

74	73·89	73·99	73·96	73·8	66·5	29·6	148	8·67	27·98
75	74·90	75·00	74·97	74·8	67·7	31·3	150	9·00	28·43
76	75·89	75·99	75·96	75·8	68·8	33·0	152	9·33	28·88
77	76·90	77·00	76·97	76·8	69·9	34·8	154	9·67	29·34
78	77·91	78·01	177·98	77·8	71·1	36·5	156	10·0	29·81
79	78·90	79·00	78·97	78·8	72·2	38·3	158	10·5	30·29
80	79·88	79·98	79·95	79·8	73·3	40·1	160	11·0	30·76
81	80·88	80·98	90·95	80·8	74·5	41·8	162	11·5	31·26
82	81·87	81·97	81·94	81·8	75·7	43·6	164	12·0	31·76
83	82·89	82·99	82·96	82·8	76·9	45·4	166	12·5	32·28
84	83·88	83·98	83·95	78·0	78·0	47·1	168	13·0	32·80
85	84·86	84·96	84·93	84·8	79·2	48·9	170	13·5	33·33
86	85·86	85·96	85·93	85·8	80·5	50·6	172	14·0	33·88
87	86·84	86·94	86·91	86·8	81·7	52·3	174	14·5	34·43
88	87·84	87·94	87·91	87·8	82·9	54·0	176	15·0	35·01
89	88·85	88·95	88·92	88·8	84·2	55·8	188	15·5	35·62
90	89·96	89·96	89·93	89·8	85·5	57·6	180	16·0	36·24
91	90·88	90·98	90·95	90·8	86·8	59·5	182	16·5	36·89
92	91·88	91·98	91·95	91·8	88·1	61·3	184	17·0	37·55
93	92·90	93·00	92·97	92·8	89·4	63·0	186	17·6	38·24
94	93·89	93·99	93·96	93·8	90·8	64·7	188	18·3	38·95
95	94·90	95·00	94·97	94·8	92·2	66·4	190	19·0	39·70
96	95·91	96·01	95·98	95·8	93·6	68·1	192	19·8	40·49
97	96·93	97·03	97·00	96·8	95·0	69·8	194	20·6	41·33
98	97·93	98·03	98·00	97·8	96·5	71·6	196	31·4	42·25
99	98·93	99·03	99·00	98·8	98·1	73·3	198	22·2	43·19
100	99·92	100·02	100·00	99·3	100·0	75·08	200	23·0	44·19

Appendix 2: The Major Groups of Companies and What They Own in Scotch

The Distillers' Company Ltd (D.C.L.): Aberfeldy, Aultmore, Balmenach, Banff, Benrinnes, Benromach, Caol Ila, Cardow, Carsebridge, Clynelish, Coleburn, Convalmore, Cragganmore, Craigellachie, Dailuaine, Dallas Dhu, Dalwhinnie, Glen Albyn, Glendullan, Glen Elgin, Glenkinchie, Glenlochy, Glenlossie, Glen Mhor, Glentauchers, Glenury-Royal, Hillside, Imperial, Knochdhu, Lagavulin, Linkwood, Lochnagar, Mannochmore, Millburn, Mortlach, North Port, Oban, Ord, Port Ellen, Rosebank, Royal Brackla, Speyburn, St Magdalene, Talisker, Teanich. *Grain distilleries*: Caledonian, Cambus, Cameronbridge, Port Dundas.

Arthur Bell: Blair Athol, Dufftown-Glenlivet, Inchgower, Pittyvaich-Glenlivet.

Joseph E. Seagram: Alta' Bhainne, Benriach, Caperdonich, Glen Grant-Glenlivet, The Glenlivet, Glen Keith-Glenlivet, Longmorn, Strathisla-Glenlivet, Braes of Glenlivet.

International Distillers & Vintners (I.D.V.): Auchroisk, Glen Spey, Knockando, Strathmill.

Hiram Walker: Balblair, Inverleven, Lomond, Glenburgie-Glenlivet, Glencadam, Glencraig, Miltonduff-Glenlivet, Pulteney, Scapa. *Grain distillery*: Dunbarton.

Highland Distilleries: Bunnahabhain, Glenglassaugh, Glenrothes-Glenlivet, Highland Park, Tamdhu.

Invergordon Distillers: Bruichladdich, Ben Wyvis, Deanston, Tamnavulin, Tullibardine. *Grain distillery*: Invergordon.

Inverhouse Distillers: Bladnoch, Glenflagler. *Grain distillery*: Moffat.

Long John International: Glenugie, Laphroaig, Tormore. *Grain distilleries*: Kinclaith, Strathclyde.

Scottish Universal Investment Trust: Dalmore, Fettercairn, Tomintoul-Glenlivet.

William Grant: Balvenie, Glenfiddich, Ladyburn. *Grain distillery*: Girvan.

Teachers: Glendronach, Ardmore.

Macdonald & Muir: Glenmorangie, Glen Moray.

Bibliography

GENERAL REFERENCE BOOKS

Alexandre Dumas's Dictionary of Cuisine, edited, abridged and translated by Louis Colman (W. H. Allen, 1959)

Alexis Lichine's Encyclopedia of Wines and Spirits, second edition (Cassell, 1974)

Barrel and Book, Walter James (Georgian House, Melbourne, 1949)

The Book of Drinking, John Doxat (Hamlyn, 1973)

The Book of Herb Lore, Lady Rosalind Northcote (Dover Publications, New York, 1971)

A Book of Herbs, Dawn Macleod (Duckworth, 1968)

Booth's Handbook of Cocktails and Mixed Drinks, John Doxat (Pan Books, 1966)

Brandies and Liqueurs of the World, Hunst Hannum and Robert S. Blumberg (Doubleday, New York, 1976)

The Diary of a Country Parson, 1758–1802, James Woodford, selected and edited by John Beresford (World's Classics, 1949)

Drinks and Drinking, John Doxat (Ward Lock, 1971)

Early American Beverages, John Hall Brown (Tuttle, Rutland, Vt, 1966)

Elixirs of Life, Mrs C. F. Leyel (Stuart & Watkins, London, 1970)

The Englishman's Food, J. C. Drummond and Anne Wilbraham, revised edition, Jonathan Cape, 1951)

The English Table in History and Literature, Charles Cooper (Sampson Low, Marston & Co, ?1937)

Every Man His Own Butler, Cyrus Redding (William Tegg, 1852)

The Fine Art of Mixing Drinks, David Embury, second edition (Faber, 1958)

Food and Drink in Britain, C. Anne Wilson (Constable, 1973)

Food in History, Reay Tannahill (Eyre Methuen, 1973)

France : a Food and Wine Guide, Pamela Vandyke Price (Batsford, 1966); second edition published as *Eating and Drinking in France Today* (Tom Stacey, 1972)

The French at Table, Raymond Oliver (International Wine & Food Society, 1967)

A Garden of Herbs, Eleanour Sinclair Rohde (Dover Publications, New York 1969)

The Gentleman's Companion, Charles H. Baker Jnr (Crown, New York, 1946)

Gods, Men and Wine, William Younger (International Wine & Food Society, 1966)

The Golden Age of Herbs and Herbalists, Rosetta E. Clarkson (Dover Publications, New York, 1972)

Grossman's Guide to Wines, Spirits and Beers, Harold J. Grossman, fifth revised edition (Charles Scribner's Sons, New York; Frederick Muller, London, 1974)

Herbal Delights, Mrs C. F. Leyel (Faber, reprinted 1947)

Herbs and Savory Seeds, Rosetta E. Clarkson (Dover Publications, New York, 1972)

Herbs, Flavours and Spices, Elizabeth Hayes (Faber, 1963)

L'Histoire à Table, André Castellot (Plon–Perrin, Paris, 1972)

Histoire de la vigne et du vin en France, Roger Dion (Paris, 1959)

A History of Wine as Therapy, Salvatore P. Lucia (Lippincott, Philadelphia, 1963)

The Illustrated Herbal Handbook, Juliette de Baïracli Levy (Faber, 1974)

Kitchen and Table, Colin Clair (Abelard Schumann, New York, 1964)

Leaves from Gerard's Herball, arranged by Marcus Woodward (Thorsons, London, 1972)

Liqueurs, Peter Hallgarten (Wine & Spirit Publications, 1967)

Liqueurs, M. I. Fisher (Maurice Meyer, 1951)

Le Livre de l'amateur d'alcools (Solar Publications, 1970)

A Modern Herbal, Mrs M. Grieve, edited and with an introduction by Mrs C. F. Leyel (Jonathan Cape, 1931; Peregrine, 1976)

Movable Feasts, Arnold Palmer (Oxford University Press, 1952)

Notes on a Cellarbook, George Saintsbury (Macmillan, 1923)

Off the Shelf, Anthony Hogg, third edition (Gilbey Vintners, Harlow, 1977)

The Oxford Book of Flowerless Plants, F. H. Brightman and B. E. Nicholson (Oxford University Press, 1966)

The Oxford Book of Food Plants, G. B. Masefield, M. Wallis, S. G. Harrison and B. E. Nicholson (Oxford University Press, 1969)

Pilgrimage: an Image of Medieval Religion, Jonathan Sumption (Faber, 1975)

The Pleasure of Your Company, Jean Latham (A. & C. Black, 1972)

The South American Gentleman's Companion, Charles H. Baker Jnr (Crown, New York, 1951)

Sturtevant's Edible Plants of the World, edited by U. P. Hedrick (Dover Publications, New York, 1972)

The Vegetable Book, Yann Lovelock (George Allen & Unwin, 1972)

Wine and Wine Countries, Charles Tovey (Hamilton Adams, 1862)

Wines and Spirits, L. W. Marrison (Penguin, 1957; third edition, 1973)

Wines and Spirits of the World, edited by A. H. Gold (Virtue, London, 1968)
Wine, the Vine and the Cellar, T. G. Shaw (Spottiswoode, 1862)

PUBLICATIONS

Decanter Magazine
The Journal of the International Wine & Food Society, since its first appearing as *Wine & Food* until the present day
Marine & Air Catering (articles by the author)
Number 3 St James's Street (the house magazine of Berry Brothers & Rudd)
Wine & Spirit (Haymarket Publications)

BOOKS ON SPECIFIC SUBJECTS

Whisky

The Bourbon Institute: publications
Illicit Scotch, S. W. Sillett (Impulse Books, Aberdeen, 1970)
Irish Whiskey, E. B. McGuire (Gill & Macmillan, Dublin, 1973)
Glenlivet (The Glenlivet Distillery, 1959)
Guide to the Whiskies of Scotland, Derek Cooper (Pitman, 1978)
The House of Haig, James Laver (John Haig, 1958)
The House of Sanderson, Ross Wilson (Wm. Sanderson, 1963)
Scotch, Sir Robert Bruce Lockhart (Putnam, 1951)
Scotch, Its History and Romance, Ross Wilson (David & Charles, 1973)
Scotch Made Easy, Ross Wilson (Hutchinson, 1959)
Scotch, the Formative Years, Ross Wilson (Constable, 1970)
Scotch Whisky, David Daiches (André Deutsch, 1969)
Scotch Whisky, J. C. Marshall Robb (Chambers, 1950)
Scotch Whisky, Bill Sampson, Hugh MacDiamid, Theodora Fitzgibbon, Jack House, Donald Mackinlay and Anthony Troon (Macmillan, 1974)
Scotch Whisky, Questions & Answers (The Scotch Whisky Association, 1969)
Scotland's Malt Whiskies, John Wilson (Famedram Publishers, Gartocharn, Dumbarton, Scotland, 1973)
The Scots Cellar, F. Marian McNeill (Richard Paterson, Edinburgh, 1956)
The Spirit of White Horse, Jack House (White Horse Distillers)
The Whiskies of Scotland, R. J. S. McDowall (John Murray, 1967)
Whisky, James Ross (Routledge & Kegan Paul, 1970)
The Whisky Barons, Allen Andrews (Jupiter Books, 1977)
The World Book of Whisky, Brian Murphy (Collins, 1978)

Gin

The Georgians at Home, Elizabeth Burton (Longmans Green, 1967)

Housekeeping in the 18th Century, Rosamund Bayne-Powell (John Murray, 1956)
The Kindred Spirit, Lord Kinross (Newman Neame, London, 1959)
Merchants of Wine, Alec Waugh (Cassell, 1957)
Mother's Ruin, John Watney (Peter Owen, 1976)
Stirred – Not Shaken, John Doxat (Hutchinson Benham, 1976)

Brandy

Le Cognac, R. Lafon, J. Lafon and P. Couillaud (J. B. Baillière, 1964)
Cognac, Cyril Ray (Peter Davies, 1973)
Histoire du Cognac, Robert Delamain (Stock, Paris, 1935)
Le Livre de l'amateur de l'Armagnac, Jean and George Samalens (Solar Publications, 1975)
White Wines and Cognac, H. Warner Allen (Constable, 1952)

SOURCES OF OTHER SPECIALIZED REFERENCES

Danish Akvavit, Henning Kirkeby (Høst & Son, Copenhagen, 1975)
A Guide to Tequila, Mezcal and Pulque, Virginia B. De Barrios (Minutiae Mexicanae, 1971)
The Journeys of a German in England in 1782, Carl Philip Moritz, translated and edited by Reginald Nettel (Jonathan Cape, 1965)
Number Three St James's Street, H. Warner Allen (Chatto & Windus, 1950)
The Seven Ages of Justerini's, Dennis Wheatley (Riddle Books, London, ? 1949)
Short History of the Art of Distillation, R. J. Forbes (E. J. Bull, Leiden, 1948)
The Wines of Spain and Portugal, Jan Read (Faber, 1973)
Spirits and Liqueurs, Peter A. Hallgarten (Faber, 1979)
The Complete Book of Spirits and Liqueurs, Cyril Ray (Cassell, 1977)
Brandies and Liqueurs of the World, Hurst Hannum and Robert S. Blumberg (Doubleday, New York, 1976)
The World Guide to Spirits, Tony Lord (Macdonald & Jane's, 1979)

Index